Two Trees

A Memoir

D1502526

Julie Beekman

Credits
Cover Artist: Ingrid Muller
Editor: Sherry Derr-Wille

Printed in the United States of America

Dedication

For Emily

A huge thank you to Allwriters' Workplace and Workshop
and all who believed, even when I didn't.

Prologue

I was twenty years old and sitting at a Waffle House in Phoenix, waiting to meet my mother for the first time. The restaurant was empty when I arrived. I hoped she would be there waiting, but I was half an hour early, so I was the one who had to wait. Wait and watch people pull into the parking lot, wondering if one of them was my mother. Waitresses in bright yellow and brown sat huddled together, making small talk and filling condiments. The place smelled of maple syrup and old coffee.

After a few people came in, I felt more at ease. I'd found myself worrying the servers would hear our conversation. I wanted it to be private, personal. Still, a part of me felt like screaming out, "Hey, everybody, I'm meeting my biological mother for the first time!" I'd been searching for her for so long.

I sat and thought about all the phone calls, the letter writing, and traveling to find her. What it might be like, would she embrace me, would we have things in common, would we look similar, all of it went through my mind. I'd been in Phoenix less than twenty-four hours and it was finally going to happen.

Around five-thirty, an older model white Volare pulled into the Waffle House parking lot. The driver, a woman, parked the car and sat there. I watched from the window and nervously picked at my cuticles. She sat there for quite some time, sat and smoked. She adjusted her rearview mirror and put her fingers through short hair. I watched every move because I knew it was her. My heart pounded. When she finally opened the car door, she got out and flicked her cigarette to the side. As she walked toward the restaurant, she pulled at the hem of her black stretchy dress that nicely hugged her tall, thin frame. Once inside, Shirley stood at the door, motionless. I knew she spotted me.

I scooted toward the edge of the booth and she finally walked toward me. I didn't stand up to hug her, like I imagined I would. Her sunglasses were still on and I sensed no enthusiasm in her stride. She approached the booth and slid in across from me.

Chapter One

I don't remember the baby showers family and neighbors threw for Marge after the Beekmans adopted me, or that I refused to eat anything other than lima beans. I was nine months old when Warren and Marge brought me home. I listened to stories about how it all came to be. "We kept having boys and, after three, I just wanted a girl, so bad." These were the moments when I loved listening to Marge, when she was just being my mom. She was endearing and it reminded me she meant to love me. "I just told the caseworker we wanted a girl with blue or green eyes. I mean, no one in our family has light eyes!" she explained dramatically. The speech was always the same; Marge telling me it took four years for the adoption agency to approve them, that I cost three-hundred and fifty dollars.

"When we went to visit with you for the first time, you were wearing a little pink dress. You held out your arms to Warren and said, Da Da." She raised her arms out and made a face that looked helpless. "We knew then, we just had to have you." She seemed to always refer to him as Warren and not my dad.

"Did Randy, Scot and Dan want a sister?" I asked like it was the first time I heard the story.

"Oh, of course." Marge lit a cigarette, took a short drag, and then held it near her coffee mug. I hated when she just held her cigarettes and didn't smoke them or take the time to tap the ashes into the ashtray, because I couldn't focus on her. I could only stare at the long cylinder of ash, wondering when and where it would fall. "We came home after meeting you and told the boys all about you. We were especially concerned when it came to Danny because he was only five and used to being the youngest." Marge took a sip of black coffee without the slag of her smoke even moving slightly, although I could see the slight orange glow move fast toward her fingers. "I don't want to be the youngest, Mama! I want a sister, is what he told me." Marge pushed her cheeks out to imitate her idea of what Dan looked like when he was a kid and she laughed. "He was so damn cute! All you kids..." She smiled, stamped out her cigarette and looked far away like it had been some other lifetime and now she was let down. It felt the same to me because I didn't remember any of it.

My first memory is my third birthday and that Grandma Beekman made me a cake in the shape of a lamb. The white sugared icing was thick and billowy, like wool. The lamb's eyes stared back at me with chocolate glare. It was also the first year of many that Grandma made me a baby purse. She washed out old dish detergent bottles, cut out the bottom half and punched holes along the edges. Then she crocheted the holes so that she could build a purse with drawstrings from the plastic base. She showed me how to pull the drawstrings and yarn over the plastic sides, to reveal a crib with a tiny doll baby inside. The crib had a pillow and knitted blanket, too. She demonstrated over and over. It seemed she rather liked talking about her own creations and it drove Marge over the edge sometimes. Thankfully, Marge allowed Grandma to stay on my birthday and the cake didn't end up on the floor.

Grandma didn't come over too often. My dad would go to her house every week and sometimes take us kids. I especially liked to go, because Grandma gave us sugary treats and we rarely got sweets. Once, I spent the whole day with Grandma and we made church window cookies. We melted butter and chocolate, stirred in mini colored marshmallows, rolled everything out into a log coated with coconut, and refrigerated it in wax paper. Once the cookies were chilled, we sliced the log to find all the colors like on a stained-glass window. Grandma cut a lot of slices for me to take home.

When Marge picked me up and we headed for the car, she threw the bag of cookies into a snowbank. "How many times do I have to tell you and that woman, no sugar. You're fat enough!"

I huddled against the passenger door on the way home.

Wherever I wandered, there was Blackie. Blackie was adopted about a week after I was. She was the runt from a litter of short-haired mutts. She was a sweet little dog that, right from the start, tried jumping into my crib. She ate everything I didn't want and protected me as best she could. At night, she slept under my covers and growled when anyone entered my room.

~ * ~

Even though I was making friends in the neighborhood and at nursery school, Blackie was my best pal.

Bob Barker was my friend, too. When I first started watching him on Truth Or Consequences, I couldn't pronounce his name and I screamed, "Fuck Farker's on! Fuck Farker's on!" and it made my family laugh.

Bob hosted the show where contestants were asked to answer a silly question and if they couldn't answer it correctly or the buzzer went off because they were taking too long, the contestant would have to pay the consequence. This meant that the player would have to do something embarrassing and I loved it. Bob Barker made me so happy. He was warm and safe. He made me forget the things that worried me. It was his voice I heard over Marge's yelling, not my dad's.

The contestants didn't seem to mind making fools of themselves and they were all so nice on television. I wanted to be in that audience every night.

My favorite part of the show was Barker's Box. He would go into the audience and have someone pick from the drawers in the box that contained money or a surprise. In three of the drawers, there was money. Either a ten, twenty, or fifty-dollar bill, which was huge! The surprise was always a snake that jumped out and usually startled the hopeful player. No matter what, though, the person won prizes from American Tourister Luggage, china from Stonegate or a gift certificate from Spiegel Catalogue.

I felt like I knew Bob Barker since I saw him every day. I often cried when the show ended and Bob saluted. It meant bedtime, for one thing, but it also meant I couldn't tune out or escape. I retreated upstairs to my room where I heard arguing or wondered what got broken. I never heard my dad raise his voice, I only heard mumblings through the floor and figured he was trying to reason with her. She screamed. If only Bob were around always.

I was not as fond of Jack Lalanne, he couldn't compete with Bob, but Marge and I exercised with him every morning. Jack had huge muscles like the kind Danny and Scot were always looking at in the back of their comic books. I didn't see what was so great about muscles.

He wore a short-sleeved jumpsuit with a shiny belt. When Marge had time, she put on a leotard. I just stayed in my pajamas and followed every step. I didn't want to wear a leotard because I was afraid Marge would tell me I was chubby. I was always happy when she commented on my exercise abilities. "Julie, you are so limber!" I sat with my legs stretched out in front of me, buried my face into my knees and peeked through my long hair to see if Marge was looking. "You still could stand to lose a few pounds," Marge moaned into a stretch.

When we finished the exercises, Jack sat, straddling the back of a chair, and gave a talk about what it takes to be happy and lead a good life. He showed menus of a perfectly balanced meal and I hated him for it. Jack Lalanne was the reason we didn't have anything fun to eat in the house and I blamed him for some of my issues with the neighborhood kids. Jack told Marge that it would be best to feed her family whole wheat bread and all natural foods. The kids in my neighborhood equated brown bread with being poor. They teased me as I unpacked my roasted soy nuts that looked like dried cricket torsos, and my banana along with a brown peanut butter sandwich. I told Marge about it and she got really mad, said that Roman Meal cost a lot more than Wonder.

There was one health food store in town and every time we went in there, we seemed to be the only customers. Marge stocked up on brewer's yeast and wheat germ. Every morning, she blended the two with milk, a banana, natural peanut butter, honey, and an egg. She poured the concoction she called Tiger's Milk into tall glasses for us kids to drink. I loved it, but the boys gave her trouble until she practically forced them to swallow it.

~ * ~

The boys were always difficult and I couldn't understand why they wouldn't just follow her rules and keep peace in the house. Once, when she was trying to clean and the boys were running all over the place, she yelled at them, "Stop horsing around or go outside." But, they continued wrestling and running. Finally, she tied them all to chairs and made them sit quietly while she finished vacuuming. They were all lined up like little soldiers and I sat on a chair, quiet, but occasionally sticking my tongue out. She seemed to do these things while my dad was at work. My dad was patient and kind and I know he wouldn't like some of the things she did, even if the boys were sometimes bad.

Scot was the worst, but she seemed to connect with him because he was weird, I guess. She sent him to art classes at a very young age. Randy, the oldest, always said Scot's expensive art classes were the reason we drank Carnation powdered milk and we couldn't afford real milk. Meanwhile, Randy sure enjoyed his Karate classes at the Y and he made money cutting lawns so I figured he could buy real milk if it was such a problem.

The majority of Scot's artwork was based on the solar system and random body parts. He came home with colorful, thickly coated oil canvases that made me feel uncomfortable. There were whirling planets, gooey asteroids, and then, a flying leg or an eyeball. Scot was strange and gross, as far as I was concerned, but I loved him because I was supposed to.

Dan was only a year and a half younger than Scot and always tagged along with him. It never made sense to me that they were so close. They seemed to have very little in common. They shared a big bedroom that was attached to the attic, but the room was separated by a large sheet. Scot's side of the room was filthy, while Dan's side was tidy and fun to visit. When I went to his side, he was usually reading or studying for school, but would stop everything to play games with me. He had blue plastic cabinets on his bookshelf that had tons of little drawers in them. Each drawer held something like a nail, a penny, a stamp, or a Tootsie Roll. Dan asked me a question and if I got the answer right, I was allowed to pick a drawer. It was kind of like Bob Barker's Box, but Dan's questions were always serious.

"What is the capital of Alaska?"

"Juneau!" I leapt for a drawer.

"Wait." Dan held up a finger. "That answer is...correct! Now, pick a drawer!"

"It's a paperclip." I frowned and shut the drawer.

"What's two times six?" Dan smiled and picked at the rubber on his tennis shoe. He knew I hated math.

"I know the answer," I assured him.

"I know you do. I've taught you this over and over." Dan waited.

"I know, but I'm not supposed to know because I'm only four!" I giggled and held my hands behind me to count fingers.

"You forgot. No drawer for you." Dan brushed his hair from his face and grabbed his book, like the game was over.

"It's twelve!" I grabbed his arm. "It's twelve! Don't stop playing."

"Time's up."

"No!" I pleaded. "Please, may I have another question?" Blackie barked in support.

"Well, since you said the word may instead of can, yes, you may." Dan placed his book on his pillow and sat with his legs crossed on the edge of his bed. "Who is my favorite catcher in the Major Leagues?"

"Joe Gargee-lo-eel!" I yelled with pride.

"Gar-oge-ee-o-la," he corrected me. "Pick your drawer!" This time, I got the Tootsie Roll.

Whenever I left their room, I tried not to look at Scot's side. If he called me over to him, I felt obliged to go and he would end up touching me with clammy hands in places where I didn't want him to.

Randy didn't have much time for me since he was ten years older, but occasionally, we played Go Fish. His room smelled of metal from his trombone and coins that he carelessly threw on the floor. He seemed to be an authority on most subjects. Even his looks were somewhat domineering; tall, dark hair, and black rimmed glasses. He was always sweet to me and even bought me a Bobby Sherman record, Julie, do you love me? He played the record and games until he had to leave to meet friends or go to some practice.

I had plenty of ways to stay entertained. I sometimes put on shows in front of the three-way mirror my dad made for me. The mirror was a lot bigger than I was, and he painted it lavender, along with my closet door and set of drawers. Marge made my flowered curtains with traces of lavender and green in floral print.

I stood in front of the mirror and practiced imitating Cher. I stuck my tongue in my cheek and flipped my hair behind my shoulder and Blackie lay on my bed and watched me. I called her Sonny. "Sonny, someday, we're going to leave Grand Haven and be big stars with Bob and Cher."

She wagged.

Chapter Two

Grand Haven, Michigan is home to the world's largest musical fountain and The Coast Guard Festival. The town sits right on Lake Michigan and is flagged by a giant red lighthouse. The musical fountain played every night during the summer since 1962. Colorful water displays dance over a hundred feet in rhythm with whatever music is played. On most nights, I could hear it from my bedroom window. Blackie and I sat on my bed, my ear pressed against the screen. Every night, it started the same way, "Good evening...I am the voice of the musical fountain." The voice was soothing, yet strong, like waves off the lake.

Thousands of people crowded the downtown beach area during summer, to watch the fountain, get ice cream, or a Pronto Pup from the original corn dog stand. The busiest time was the first week of August, Coast Guard Week.

The festival started at least thirty years before the fountain and included a parade, a carnival, fireworks and a pageant to crown Miss Coast Guard. During the late sixties and early seventies, there was also a pageant for Little Miss Coast Guard. Pictures of the four and five-year-old contestants were on display at the community center for a whole week before the pageant, so everyone could catch a glimpse of the young girls.

In my picture, my long curls lay hair-sprayed softly against the pink dress Marge made for the photo shoot at Olson's Photography. She seemed to think it was a big deal. She spent hours sewing while I sat under a portable dryer on the floor in the living room. For the pageant, I wore a light teal cotton dress with white polka dots, patterned tights, and white patent leather shoes. I would have rather worn Dan's old cut-offs, but I didn't seem to have a choice in the matter. I liked the idea of being on stage, but I didn't want to be dressed like a doll.

During the pageant, many girls were eliminated, but five of us remained from the original twenty-some girls. The announcer told us to go back on stage and when were called out, we should answer a question. Marge ran backstage to make sure my curls were in place and there were no wrinkles in my tights. "Just be honest, Julie." She pulled my tights up so that I left the floor a little. "I've always taught you kids to tell the truth."

The lights on the stage were bright, but I could see my dad near the front. He was smiling at me. The announcer talked with some girls while I waved at my dad and some neighbors that I recognized.

"My next question goes to Miss Julie Ann Beekman of Grand Haven." I perked up and moved close to the man, waiting for a chance to talk into the microphone. "Your question, Miss? What would you like to be when you grow up?"

Without hesitation, I stood on my toes, felt the cool metal of the microphone on my lips, and said, "I want to be a witch."

The audience roared with laughter. My dad and Marge sank into their seats. They were looking at each other like they didn't know what to do. My heart raced for fear that I may have done something wrong. I didn't want Marge to yell at me, or worse.

I stood still and waited, and then she started laughing, too. Relieved, I basked in the attention. Not only did I win the pageant, I got to ride on a float in the parade and attend special events, all while wearing a red velvet cape and beautiful crown.

The girls in the neighborhood, Sheila, Susie, and Angie, all wanted to see my crown. Too embarrassed to have them come in for fear of my parents arguing, I brought it outside and showed it off with pride. "My mom says I can only have it off my shelf for a few minutes, so I have to take it back into the house," I said, satisfied that they eyed every rhinestone. Then it was back outside to be a tomboy.

~ * ~

Summer afternoons were the worst because Marge would call me in from playing to rub her varicose veins. "Julie, my legs hurt so bad. I'll pay you a dime." She made it sound like I had a choice. The only good thing about the situation was the dime. Ten cents would buy me candy at John Casmier's grocery store a few blocks away. Marge never asked what I did with the dimes, so I felt I could do as I pleased.

I squirted lotion down the length of her legs and rubbed it in while she told me I needed to become a nurse because I could make people feel better. She also told me she hoped I would never get varicose veins because they were awful. I made faces at her as I pushed the lotion over the ripples. I wondered if they were so awful, why I needed to have anything to do with them. I stayed silent so I could hear her breathing. Once she fell asleep, I could take the dime that was on her nightstand and be on my way. A few times, she said, "Uh-uh, I'm still awake."

A few weeks after the pageant, I earned my dime and took off to get the new candy bar that Angie told me about. It was called Chunky. I felt a little weird buying a Chunky bar since Marge already yelled about having to shop in the husky section for my kindergarten clothes. But I had to have it.

When I approached the store, some kid came up behind me on his bike. He said he was the fire chief's son and that I better get him some gum or he would take my crown or have me arrested.

"I don't have money for gum." I frowned, thinking I might have to give up my Chunky. Besides, he couldn't have been the fire chief's son because my uncle Frank was the fire chief of Grand Haven.

"Well, whatcha doin' here, then?" He moved his bike back and forth as he straddled the bar.

"I just have to get something." I turned to leave him.

"Hey!" he yelled as I approached the automatic door. "Get me the gum, or the crown goes bye-bye." He pointed at the top of his head and pretended to pout. "I'm not kidding, I'll be right here."

My breathing changed and fear took over me. He wasn't kidding. I thought about how my brothers would pummel this kid. Unfortunately, I was already somewhere I wasn't supposed to be, so it's not like I could be rescued. I stared at the boy and tried to memorize his rotten face. "Adam's grape." He motioned to the already opened door. "Now move along."

I took a deep breath and went into the store. I thought about just staying there. Maybe after a while, he would go away. If I was gone from home for too long, I would be in trouble, so I couldn't wait around. Walking around the store and contemplating my fate, I wanted that candy bar and as I approached the checkout lines, there was the display for the new Chunky bar. It was beautiful. It was a large square wrapped in silver, with red lettering. I picked one up, held it and promptly got in line. While waiting, pretending to look at everything, I slipped a pack of Adam's in my pocket and put the Chunky on the conveyor belt. My hands shook as I gave the cashier lady the dime, but I walked slowly and steadily as I exited the store. The boy was waiting at the corner and started to pedal toward me. Then suddenly, he made a quick turn and took off.

"Excuse me, miss?"

I stopped in my tracks and turned to face a man in a short-sleeved dress shirt, tie and name tag. I'd seen him before behind the service counter. I walked to him with my head down, reached into my pocket and handed him the gum.

"You need to come inside so we can call your parents." He grabbed on to my shoulder.

"Please." I started to cry. "Please don't call my mom," I begged. I wish he could call my dad but, he worked at a newspaper and I just couldn't have my name showing up for stealing especially since I was just in the paper for Coast Guard.

"Honey, you did something very wrong and we need to let your mom know that you stole." He led me through the produce section and back to an office. "Now, I need your name and do you know your phone number?"

I recited the number through sobs and apologies.

After making the call, he seemed upset and started walking me to the front of the store. He stopped in an aisle that had paper products on one side and cookies on the other. We both saw Marge storm in at the same time. She pounded down the aisle and hauled off to punch me right there. I landed on the floor with my nose bleeding. The manager fumbled to open a roll of paper towels. "I'm sorry," he whispered.

"Get the fuck up, Julie!" Marge's nose flared and her lips pursed tight. "What in the hell are you doing in this store and what in the fuck are you doing stealing?"

"The fireman's son wanted me to steal him gum." I stood up, held the paper towel over my face and cried.

"So, you just do what everyone tells you to do?" She held her hand up again, but caught the eye of the manager. "What happened to the dime I gave you?"

"I wanted a Chunky bar." I sobbed the words quietly.

"What?"

"I wanted a candy that Angie told me about." I realized that somehow, I lost the candy. I ducked and covered my head, expecting another blow.

The manager grabbed for a package of cookies and tore them open. He shoved them toward me. "I'm so sorry," he repeated.

"Get those away from her!" Marge practically growled. "Julie, get your fat ass in the car!"

Marge followed me to the parking lot and demanded more of an explanation before I opened my door. "Who is this boy?"

"He's a fireman's son and he said he would take my crown."

I think Marge believed me, but she still wanted me to get the lesson about how bad it was to take things without paying for them.

When we got home, my dad was still at work. Marge used one of his belts against my naked bottom. "Are you ever going to steal again?" Whack!

"No!" I reached to cover the next blow.

"Move your hands, Julie! Move your goddamned hands!" Whack!

I could hear Blackie barking outside of my parents' bedroom door. I could hear her over my own cries and Marge's yelling.

Eight times, the belt came down. I knew because Marge counted them. "If you hadn't tried to cover, you wouldn't have gotten so many," she reasoned.

I went to my room and cried while looking at the welts in the mirror. She spanked me before and slapped me, but never anything this bad. I prayed I could go live with Sheila and Susie Wildrom or Angie McCaleb. I didn't even care about the Chunky bar. The boys came home and then my dad came home. Marge explained why my eyes were red and my face was puffy. "Julie did something she wasn't supposed to do." She smiled and glared at me. "Didn't you, Julie?"

"Yes," I turned away and looked at Blackie.

"Well, what happened?" My dad smiled gently.

"A boy said he would take my crown if I didn't get gum for him. I stole and I'm sorry." I slipped a green bean down the edge of my chair where Blackie was waiting.

"Well, that's not good."

Chapter Three

Marge rarely came upstairs. Since she started attending classes at Grand Valley State College, she didn't have as much time to make sure the upstairs was in good order. It was up to us kids to get our dirty clothes down to the basement and keep everything neat. With my dad working six days a week, printing at The Grand Haven Tribune, and Marge pouring coffee third shift at the Donut House on weekend nights, it was tough for them to keep tabs on us.

Every once in a while, though, she came upstairs to have a look. My room was in decent shape because I needed things cleared out for tea parties. I had a little table and four chairs in the center of my bedroom. The places were set for Blackie, a stuffed bear, and my Crissy doll. The boys' rooms usually passed inspection, too. She didn't seem to care that Scot was a pig.

One summer morning, I was up early, dressed and ready to go to college with Marge. I wasn't happy about it. I would have much rather played with Susie and Angie, like I did every summer. Marge didn't think the boys were around enough to keep an eye on me, so I had to go to classes with her. As I was getting ready to leave my room, I heard Marge yelling at Scot across the hall. I quickly retreated to my bed and sat down. I waited and prayed that she would leave me alone.

"What in the hell is all of this?" I heard a loud rumble that sounded like she was moving furniture. No one answered her. "Jesus Christ! Whose are these?" Still, no one responded. Music that was playing, was suddenly shut off. "Both of you, get this pile downstairs into the bathroom, now." I heard the scurrying and then stomping down the stairs. Suddenly, my door opened. I stood quickly. "What are you doing? Get downstairs!" Marge turned away and followed the boys.

She stood at the bathroom door, barking orders. I was curious to see what was going on, but I was afraid she would pull me into the situation. I wanted to eat breakfast, but that might cause more chaos. I looked and she hadn't made Tiger's Milk. I decided to go to the front door and let Blackie out. I couldn't be yelled at for doing something useful. "Scrub, dammit! I want all of that clean!" I heard her snag her keys. I quickly got Blackie back into the house, grabbed a notebook and a few markers, and waited for Marge to reach the doorway. "Let's go," she said.

On the way to college, Marge rambled about how disgusting it was to find dirty underwear with shit stains, how those boys would learn not to do that again by having to scrub them in the toilet with Comet, and how I better never go in my pants or I would have to clean my underwear with toilet water, too. "And to hide them in the attic?" Marge pounded a fist down on the steering wheel. "What were they thinking?"

I felt bad for Danny because I knew he could not have done something like that, but he was taking the blame with Scot and scouring his brother's underwear. It was smart for Dan to appear weak and keep his mouth shut when it came to Marge. That came naturally to him. It was smart for all of us to stay silent.

When kindergarten started, I went to the morning session at a school in downtown Grand Haven, which meant I was late almost every day. Long after the boys went to school, I sat patiently by the door. "Go wait in the car." I heard most mornings. While I waited, Marge screamed at my dad. She threw things. I could hear stuff hitting the walls from all the way outside. She was loud, but I couldn't make out what she was saying. I rarely heard a peep out of my dad. I thought about what the boys would do if they had to be late every day. I figured Randy would tell her to shut the hell up, run out to his truck, and go to the farm where he worked. Scot would have viewed having to wait as an opportunity to miss school. He would have gone to his room, put on his big headphones and listened to Frank Zappa. If Dan were in my situation, he might have asked them politely to please stop arguing, and when she didn't stop he would have walked the three miles to school not to miss anything.

Once, I went back into the house because she was taking so long. I walked in to find Marge on the floor, lying on her back. My dad crouched over her with his hands pinning her wrists to the floor. "Enough!" he pleaded. "You need to stop this!"

I stood watching, horrified, yet amazed. Marge was struggling with him and sobbing until she saw me standing there. "Julie, go wait in the car!"

My dad jumped off of her and walked me back outside to the station wagon. "Your mom's just upset today." He spoke softly and opened my door.

"I know." I sat down in the front seat.

"You have a really good day, okay?" He bent down and kissed my forehead. "Don't worry about anything, honey."

I did worry. I worried all the time. I acted out in school that day and threw a book at my teacher, Miss Lilly. We always read books about kids or animals that had good relationships with their families. Miss Lilly was reading something sweet while everyone sat on their mats nicely. I got fed up with Bedtime For Frances, so I grabbed another book from a nearby shelf and flung it toward the front of the class while yelling, "I hate Frances!" stunning everyone around me. I immediately regretted it. Miss Lilly took me out into the hallway and made me sit alone until school was over. I pretended not to care when I saw my classmates playing and enjoying the morning snack without me.

"How could such a nice young lady get so angry?" Miss Lilly sat next to me after class and tucked her hair behind her ear.

"I'm sorry." I picked at the buttons on my jumper dress. I knew I couldn't tell her why I got so mad. Marge threw things, my dad tried to calm her, my brothers were washing underwear in the toilet, and now I was throwing things. I'm not going to be like her! I wanted to be good like Dan, Randy, and my dad.

During the spring of kindergarten, my parents separated. My dad went to live in a small cabin in Fruitport, which was only fifteen minutes away. Since the cabin wasn't big enough for me to live there with him, I decided it would be best if I went to live with the Partridge Family. They were a good family and they didn't have a father, so I wouldn't be replacing my dad. I could sing backup or twirl a baton. The Brady Bunch would never have worked out; everything was perfect and in place in that house.

I told my dad about the plan and then scribbled a letter to Mrs. Partridge. He helped me mail it. We took a trip to the downtown post office and my dad handed the letter right to the postmaster and winked. It was that important.

I looked out at my front yard often, hoping to see the Partridge Family bus pull into the driveway. After a few days, I packed a bag with some clothes and a peanut butter sandwich for Blackie and me to share. Blackie and I waited at the corner for what seemed an eternity. At some point, we went back to the house where I found Marge crying.

"I won't go, Mom." I kneeled in front of her.

Marge looked up, lifting her head from her hands. "What?" She put her glasses on.

"Tell them not to come, I'll stay here," I said with regret.

"Oh, Julie." Marge stood to walk away. "I don't know what you're talking about, I'm crying because I'm divorcing your father."

I realized she didn't even know I had been out there, waiting for a bus to take me away from her. I went back outside and sat on the front steps.

~ * ~

The Partridge Family never came. The summer before first grade, my parents signed their divorce papers, but we kids still got to spend time with our dad. Sometimes, he took all the boys for a Saturday and then me for a Sunday, or we all went somewhere together. He still taught the boys wood shop in the basement so they could finish some big project. He often dropped by on his way home from work. I missed him, but I always missed him, even when he still lived at home.

When I saw him coming, I either ran to him and held on like he was coming home from a war, or I flung myself onto the sofa and played possum so he would wake me from the 'dead'. He would be the first person I would see when I opened my tightly shut eyes, and all would be good in the world. I loved his wingtip shoes, his pressed white shirts, and the feel of holding onto his hands. I could have sat with him for hours, tugging on his fingers and the ring that he still wore, pointing out his freckles, or placing our palms together. He didn't stay long because the few times when he did, Marge ended up yelling about something.

I'd rather he lived with us, but it was probably better they separated. Marge stopped throwing things, I stopped throwing things, and suddenly, I was considered one of the 'good' kids in the first grade. It was awful not having him around for Halloween and Thanksgiving. "Dad's working all the time," Danny told me when I asked where our dad was. "With this second job, he even worked on his birthday." Dan and I sat on the living room floor and played with Lincoln Logs.

"Why does he work a second job?" I didn't understand why he couldn't just work at the Tribune and come over afterward.

Randy walked in and spoke in his serious voice, "He has to pay for a lot of stuff. I have to work and Scot should have his ass out there, cutting more lawns, to help Ma out." I looked for a reaction from Dan, but he just stared at the floor. Randy stomped swiftly through the room and wanted his presence known. "Next year, you two can start picking blueberries for dough," he called out from the kitchen.

"What?" I whispered to Dan.

"Don't worry about it." Dan suddenly sprung from the floor and left. I heard him pound up the stairs to his room.

~ * ~

Although we got to spend some of the Christmas holiday with my dad, we had to go to Marge's family party without him. Every year, we spent Christmas Eve at Marge's oldest sister's house. Aunt Sue was a wonderful hostess. She not only invited all five of her siblings and their spouses and kids, but a few ex-husbands, too.

"Where's Warren?" Aunt Sue hugged us all as we came in. I watched Scot make a face and squirm away from her endearing arms.

"He's actually in the hospital." Marge's voice was low, but I heard her loud and clear as I made my way around the table, hugging my aunts and uncles.

"What on earth for?" Aunt Babe grabbed her drink from the counter.

"He just isn't feeling well, Babe." Marge had a tone. It was a tone that suggested she was privy to information, like she read a whole book, but Babe was only allowed to know the title. It happened often with her family. Once she spoke that way, they knew not to pry any further, because it might cause a fight.

Dad came over for a few hours on Christmas Day. I asked why he was in the hospital and had to miss the party. "Just getting a check-up, honey."

When he wasn't watching us play with all of the presents he brought, he was sitting at the dining room table, talking with Marge. She appeared overly dramatic, almost animated, when I watched her, but for once, I couldn't hear her. I hoped they were getting back together because she changed, like she realized she loved him more than anything in life. It was only my wish, because for months after their conversation, they still weren't together and she seemed to cry more often.

Chapter Four

I was completely ecstatic when my dad showed up at school during lunch one afternoon. My teacher, Mrs. Walma, seemed to know my dad and talked with him once I finished smothering him with kisses. At recess, he played with me and my friends. He swung on monkey bars and twirled an end of our jump rope. I felt incredibly special, even more so when he started coming to recess all the time. Sometimes he came early and we ate lunch together. No one else had parents coming to play. I was indeed very lucky.

As my dad was visiting school more often, Marge was getting more involved with her college classes and friends that she was meeting there. I didn't even talk to her about my dad visiting at school, for fear that she would somehow take that special time from us, and I didn't tell the boys because I thought they might get jealous.

When summer approached and first grade ended, I was sad because I didn't see my dad as much. I had more freedom running around the neighborhood though, and Marge didn't make me come to her classes. I spent a lot of time at Susie Wildrom's playing grocery store and running through the sprinklers.

Marge was in a better mood since she started smoking a pipe and stopped worrying about what we kids were doing. She even stopped making Tiger's Milk and going to the natural food store. It was only slightly disappointing. She was so involved with her school work she forgot about Jack Lalanne altogether.

"Kids, get in here!" Marge yelled from the living room. Randy was working, but Scot, Dan, and I gathered and watched as she opened a can of beer and emptied the contents of a bag of Doritos into a large wooden bowl. "I've been taking a really great health class and I think it's time that Julie learns about reproductive systems, what do you think?" Marge was so excited to teach this lesson that we realized quickly our opinions weren't going to matter. Scot shrugged and reached for the pipe.

Dan stared off toward a set of encyclopedias and grumbled something.

"I think she wants to play a game." I tried to get Dan interested. "Maybe it's flashcards or a memory game!" I poked his arm. I had no idea what she wanted to tell us, but I wanted him to be happy. Maybe it would be like the Spanish she was trying to teach me.

"Sure, a memory game." Dan huffed and crossed his arms while Scot sucked in smoke from the pipe and handed it back to Marge.

I wanted Dan to get out of his bad mood because he was going to make Marge really mad, but then I realized she had no idea what his mood was. She and Scot were giggling and I thought they might have forgotten about the game. "Are we going to play?" I asked.

"Play?" Marge slowed down her laughter. "No, this is about you learning something, Julie." I looked to Dan and he still acted miserable. I guessed then that the lesson was going to be crummy. "Julie, how do you think your real mommy and daddy made you?"

I thought about it and had an idea, but I didn't want to say it out loud. I knew it was from kissing or mixing pee or something. "I don't know."

"It takes love. Like your daddy and I love each other a whole lot and with that love, we were able to make your brothers." I nodded and glanced at Dan who was still sulking. Scot just sat next to Marge's chair with a permanent grin across his face.

"So boys have different parts than girls and you need both parts to make a baby." Marge looked past me and seemed to finally notice Dan.

"Do you know that technically, you could marry your brothers?" Dan shot a look at Marge and furrowed his brow. "Well, it's true, you aren't related!"

"Still," Dan responded.

"Danny, why don't you draw a picture of a penis?" Marge kept staring at him.

"No!" He quickly stood. "I have stuff to do and I don't want to draw anything!" He walked out of the room, dismissing himself from the big lesson.

Instead of yelling at Dan, Marge laughed and said, "It's not like I'm asking you to whip it out!"

Within a minute, Scot drew a picture his version of a penis. Underneath it, he penciled a vagina.

Marge continued to talk about how the parts functioned, while Scot sketched things I didn't recognize. "They have to really love each other." Marge repeated.

"Or it doesn't work?" I asked.

"I guess you could say that." Marge laughed a little while she held a flame over her pipe.

"I think it's all yucky." I stood, hoping to be excused.

She sucked in and finished with a coughing spree that allowed me to leave and go to my room, where Blackie was already asleep.

The following morning, Scot called to me from his room as I started down the stairs. I immediately turned around and stopped just inside the room, taking notice that Dan was missing. "What?" I held onto the door frame.

"C'mere." Scot smiled.

"Why?" I stepped a few feet closer.

"Just come here." He continued being nice through his voice.

"What?" I inched toward him. I really hoped he wasn't going to do anything.

"Feel." He clasped my wrist and pulled my hand into his underwear.

"It's a penis."

I looked out Scot's window to see Susie Wildrom already in her sandbox. She was probably wondering where I was. Scot held my wrist tight against warm flesh that was changing against my balled-up hand. He pressed against me and reached for the waistband on my shorts. His clammy hands worked their way to my vagina. I continued looking at Susie, across the yard.

I thought maybe Angie and Sheila would get out there and everyone would start playing without me. I wondered if we were going to run through the sprinklers or maybe go to the beach. I should have put on my bathing suit, I thought. I heard Scot make a noise as he tried to pry open my fist.

"This is a secret," he whispered and let go of my arm.

"Susie wants me to come over." I stepped back and quickly left.

~ * ~

My dad decided to take all of us kids to Cedar Point Amusement Park in Ohio, one weekend in July. He bought me new clothes to wear on the trip, as well as his new car to get us there. It was really exciting, especially since we stayed in a Holiday Inn with a swimming pool and went out for breakfast.

The boys went on the big roller coasters, while my dad watched me on the kiddie rides. He stood against the railing and simply smiled. We ate junk Marge would never approve of and I wished we didn't have to go back to her. My family seemed really happy and that made me happy.

When it was my turn to spend the day with him, my dad and I usually went to the beach or to a movie, and always to get ice cream. During the last week of August, he came to get me one afternoon. We drove to the dunes at Hoffmaster State Park. I loved it there. It was like looking at a picture of mountains, made completely from sand. My brothers liked to go there and ride down the dunes with old cardboard, like they were sledding.

As we climbed the log stairs to get to the top, my dad suddenly stopped. "You go ahead." He took heavy breaths.

"I want to wait for you." I grabbed his hand.

"No, I want to watch you fly down those dunes!" He waved his arms like he was soaring and smiled, "Go ahead. I'll watch for you."

The idea of him watching me run down the dunes thrilled me. I climbed fast, careful to look back and wave to him. When I reached the top, I spotted him watching with his hand held up like a visor. He hadn't budged and that made me squeal. I took a deep breath and raised my arms. I took off and ran down taking long strides that cooled my heels and made me feel like I had super powers, laughing all the way. My dad clapped for me and walked down to meet me at the bottom.

"You really were flying!" he laughed.

"I know!" I said while suddenly noticing that other people were on the dunes. "Can we get ice cream now?" I skipped toward the car while my dad walked along slowly.

"I really need a nap, but we can go later." I heard him call out from behind me.

"Okay!" I yelled back, even though I hated naps.

While my dad rested at his cabin, I watched television. I got through several shows and realized it had gotten dark outside.

"Dad?" I knocked softly on his bedroom door and heard no reply. "Daddy?" I stared into darkness. When he still didn't respond after several minutes, I looked through my dad's phone book and called his best friend, my Uncle Lou. Lou would be reasonable and calm and would get there quickly.

"I'll be right there, honey." His gravelly voice sounded shaky, but kind.

My plan to have Uncle Lou wake my dad so we could get on with our night didn't work. He came through the door and went straight to my dad's bedroom, with Marge close behind. He turned on the light. "Warren, Warren!"

"Julie, go to the car," Marge said firmly.

Why do I always have to wait in the car? I thought. This is my night with him.

When Marge came out to the car, she explained that we were going to bring Daddy to our house. "Julie, he's sick. He's going to come stay with us for a little while."

"Why don't we call Dr. Groat? He always makes me feel better," I said.

Chapter Five

Uncle Lou and Marge put my dad in the back of Uncle Lou's car. Marge drove me to the store where we could pick up some things we might need for my dad. I don't remember what we bought because Marge was scurrying around so much and babbling, even crying. I suggested Sucrets and maybe some aspirin like I saw in the commercial. When we got home, Uncle Lou was talking to the boys in the living room. He left soon after Marge and I arrived.

Daddy lay in Marge's bed, his old bed. Dan and I took turns holding orange popsicles over his mouth because Marge told us that he was probably dehydrated and it would help. I couldn't figure out why anyone would want a popsicle while they slept. Plus, he didn't wake up to tell us to change flavors or anything. Randy and Scot came into the room, but never stayed very long. Everyone just walked in with their heads down, sulking. On the second day, Marge took me out front to sit on the steps.

"I don't want you to be frightened," she sat tall and rubbed her palms over her knees, "but an ambulance is going to come and pick up your daddy."

"Why?" I immediately started to sob.

"Julie, please don't cry. Your daddy is on the other side of that screen." She pointed to her bedroom window. "He's in a coma, but I bet that he can still hear, and he wouldn't want to hear his little girl crying." She started talking about everything he was to her and what a good man he'd been. The ambulance pulled into our driveway as she talked. Then, before I could even ask what a coma was, she told me he had cancer and he was going to die.

I ran to the side of our yard and I cried hard. A crowd of neighbors gathered on the sidewalk and I could hear someone calling me. I wiped my face with my arm and came full circle around the house to the front. Ambulance workers lifted my dad's stretcher over the steps and on to the front walkway.

"Julie," Marge spoke calmly with tear-filled eyes, "come kiss your daddy."

I walked slowly to the back of the ambulance and kissed my father's orange-stained mouth before they drove him away.

Most of the neighbors that gathered in our front yard dispersed quickly. Mrs. Wildrom and Sheila came to the front steps where Dan and I sat. "Can we do anything for you kids?" Mrs. Wildrom asked.

I caught sight of Marge who was pacing along the sidewalk. I wanted Mrs. Wildrom to hug me and take me to her house with Sheila. I wanted to find Susie and Angie and play a game of Red Light, Green Light. I wanted happiness and safety. "No," I looked to see if Marge was paying attention. "Maybe I can come to play tomorrow or something."

"You come over anytime." She looked into my eyes like she knew what I was feeling; the deepest sorrow possible. The person whom I loved the most was just taken away in an ambulance and I might not be able to talk with him again. Blackie came running from around the house and jumped up to sit on the steps next to me. Mrs. Wildrom smiled for a moment, looked back at Marge, and then her expression changed. She turned back to me like she knew that Marge was fitful and a tricky one to deal with. I wonder if she knew I was trapped.

As she turned to leave, she patted Dan's knee and then spoke to Marge who was now lighting a cigarette. "Marge, we're here." Mrs. Wildrom must have known to keep it distant, short and sweet. She waved a hand behind her leg as she turned the corner of our house. I tried to imagine Marge showing the same kindness. I doubt she would have ever travelled all the way from our backyard through the alley and past the small field to comfort Mrs. Wildrom's children. Well, maybe if there was a beer waiting for her.

Marge finished pacing and walked to the steps where we still sat. "Julie, get some night clothes together. You're going to have to stay at my friend, Norma's, tonight."

"But I can stay at the Wildrom's." I never even met Norma. "Mrs. Wildrom said…"

"Mrs. Wildrom is nosy and fake!" Marge cut me off. "She does not want you over there."

I bowed my head and wrestled with oncoming tears. "May I bring Blackie?"

"Oh, for God's sake, Julie!" Marge opened the front door and held it open. "Just get your shit, so the boys and I can get to the hospital."

Marge dropped me off at her friend's house. Before she left, she explained I couldn't see my dad because no one was allowed to visit who was under the age of twelve. I was the only one under the age of twelve. She would come to get me in the morning.

Norma seemed nice enough. We talked for a little while after Marge left. She asked about my school and if I was excited to go into the second grade. She asked about my brothers and my friends and if I was scared about my dad. I didn't know her, so I kept my answers short. Even if I was scared, Norma's daughter coming through the back door changed everything.

Irene was in between Randy's and Scot's age. She was probably sixteen and must have babysat before, because she had tons of plans for us.

"Do you want to curl all of those locks?" She pulled at strands of my tangled hair.

"Then I have to sit under the dryer forever." I shook my head.

"You wouldn't have to and we can use my Dippity-Doo!" She jumped up and reached for something from her purse. She pulled out a jar that looked like pool water Jell-O. I imagined one of the Wildroms' Barbie dolls standing on the edge of the jar and diving in. "Okay, you can go upstairs to my bathroom, take a shower and we'll get you all fixed up."

"A shower, yes!" I jumped out of my chair. "I always wash my hair in the kitchen sink and we just have a bathtub."

"Have you ever seen or taken a shower before?" Norma asked.

"At a hotel when I went on a trip with my dad." I turned and stood in the kitchen doorway. I remembered what was happening with my dad so I stared at the hair goop again and this time, Barbie was getting out of the jar and she was all mad because she was coated with slime. I smiled weakly and headed upstairs.

Irene's shower was fantastic. She had shampoos I saw on television like Lemon Up and Gee Your Hair Smells Terrific. I used the Lemon Up because I liked the cap that was shaped like a lemon. I washed my body with all the different flower shaped soaps, and then I washed my hair again with Gee Your Hair Smells Terrific. I didn't want to stop lathering because I felt so clean, on the inside too.

When I finally came downstairs, Irene had me sit in a chair directly in front of a slew of beauty products. She gently combed my hair then scooped the Dippity-Doo with pink-painted fingertips. She coated strands of my hair and then used different sizes of pink and white plastic curlers. Norma smiled and chatted with us in between sips of coffee. When Irene finished, we sat at the table and had some dinner together. My head hurt from the curlers, but I didn't care. I was just happy that I didn't have to sit under the dryer.

Norma showed me a spare room where I would sleep. I did feel so very tired from all that happened during the day and while I desperately wanted to stay up and have more fun, I had to go to bed. It wasn't even difficult to fall asleep with the curlers in.

At some point during the early morning hours, I woke, feeling nauseous. I raced to Irene's beautiful bathroom and threw up repeatedly.

Norma tried to help, but I was too embarrassed to let her in.

When I finally came out of the room, Norma took me by the hand. "Honey, your mom is going to be here soon. She just called. You okay?"

"But it's dark out." I could see street lights outside of Norma's house. I sat and started to pull the curlers out. Norma helped and then asked me to brush my teeth and get my things.

When Marge showed up, there was a twinge of pink in the sky.

"Norma, thank you for watching her." Marge was calm.

"Well, she was sick this morning." Norma squeezed my shoulders. "Marge, I'm so sorry. This is just terrible."

"Thank you," Marge repeated. "C'mon, Julie, I'm going to take you to a special place."

As we drove, Marge barely said anything at first. She only asked a few questions about my stay at Norma's. Then she talked about how Norma was such a good friend, how she couldn't count on any of the Beekmans, that they were trying to take all the time away from her at the hospital, and how they thought that since she divorced him, she didn't deserve to be alone with him.

"They think I'm a bitch, I'll be a bitch," she said. She seemed to calm down once we reached the entrance to Duncan's Woods. I wished I had known that we were going there. We could have picked up Blackie on the way. It was her favorite park; just loaded with squirrels.

Marge parked the car and led me to a picnic table where she told me about my father's death. "He passed away peacefully this morning. He just took a deep breath and let go." She was telling me this like I was some stranger and she needed comforting. "I just kept saying, Warren, you can go now, it's okay, I'll take care of the kids, you can go."

I covered my face and sobbed. The worst thing in world just happened and I didn't know how I was going to live without my dad. None of this was really happening, it couldn't be. I didn't know what to do. I couldn't breathe. The only other time I really cried in front of her was when she hit me.

Now, I was just going to have to die too. That's the only thing that could make anything better. She must have noticed that I was still there.

"Oh, honey, he loved you so much." Marge untangled my stiffened arms and pulled my hands away from my face. She held me to her chest and her words led me to cry harder. Her familiar voice, subtle hint of White Shoulders and cigarette smoke, seemed safe enough that I could let it all go and just wail.

"Why did he have to leave?" I cried. I kept thinking, if someone had to die, it should never have been him, not him.

"Oh, Julie, God needed him." She pulled away from me to look me in the eyes. "Lie down here."

She patted the top of the table. "Daddy did everything he needed to do here and now he's needed in another realm."

I wiped my eyes and looked up at her, standing over me. "What do you mean?"

"You play your dad and I'll play God." She stood over me. "Okay." She cleared her throat and seemed to be taking time to settle into her role, which scared me. "Warren." Marge loudly whispered, "Warren? Julie, answer me."

"But Daddy hasn't said anything in over three days," I responded.

"Yeah, but you see, communication is different with God." Her eyes searched in the direction of our car, like someone might appear who could better explain. "God and the universe is all knowing. So, even though Daddy was in a coma, he could still talk with God."

"I just wanted him to talk with me, with us." I started crying again.

"I know, honey, and trust me I wish I could have a chat with either of them." She sat on her feet and rested her hands on her knees. "Someday, when I figure out all the Edgar Cayce readings, I'll know how to." She looked at the sky and smiled.

I almost believed her.

"Warren, it's time to come back and go on to the next plane." She stood on the picnic table seat and gestured with her hands for me, well, my dad, to follow her or him. "Come, Warren, you're needed."

She talked about this guy, Edgar Cayce, and how he could communicate with the dead and predict things, and how my dad was being born again somewhere else and might have even ended up on the lost continent of Atlantis. This went on for another ten minutes until she was sure that I understood, which I didn't. I figured I must have powers kind of like Edgar Cayce because I got sick at Norma's when my dad died.

Marge told me that on the other side of Duncan's Woods, there was a cemetery, and that was where my dad's body would be buried. I thought I would never look at the park the same way again. The memories of tobogganing, Blackie chasing squirrels, and Easter egg hunts were all going to include the idea of reincarnation and how my dad was called away from me and to another life.

The funeral was on one of the first days of second grade. The night before the funeral, we all went to the Vanzantwyk Funeral Home to view the body, which didn't make sense to me. Everyone was so social that looking at a dead body seemed surreal. It reminded me of my cousin's wedding reception line, only there wasn't going to be any cake.

We stood around, and once people told us how sorry they were, they went to my dad's casket and stared at him. I found myself going to his casket, both that night and the next day at the funeral. Each time, I stood, holding the gold rim on his white casket and I reached out to touch some part of him. I got used to doing it. He smelled like carnations and felt like cold, hard leather. I skimmed lines on his forehead with my fingertips and traced his nose and chin line.

"Julie, don't touch your father! You might smear his make-up." His sister, my Aunt Betty, walked fast to pull my hand out of the coffin.

"Where are his legs?" I pointed into the casket. His grey suit seemed to suddenly end in a tunnel of satin.

"He's all there, don't you worry about that." She smiled and I ran off to find Dan. Dan was standing with Scot in the coffee room.

"Hey, Julie." Scot smiled wide. "You know what you can say to people that are telling you how goddamned sorry they are?" He didn't wait for my response "Why? You didn't do it!" Scot smashed sugar cubes onto the counter. "Get it? They didn't kill him, so why are they so sorry?" Dan laughed quietly, along with Scot.

The sugar on the counter made me yearn for a cookie or piece of cake, but there was only coffee. So, I made myself my first cup of coffee, extra sweet. I took a few sips of the horrible concoction, and returned to my father.

At the funeral, Randy dedicated the song, Lucky Man by Emerson, Lake and Palmer. I figured most people in the room thought my dad wasn't a lucky man at all. I wondered if everyone was judging Marge during the service. I overheard Randy tell Scot and our cousin, Terry, that cancer came from stress. That meant Marge caused the cancer.

~ * ~

Though Marge insisted everyone in town hated her, she remained cordial to all who showed up to pay their respects. I was grateful for the peace in each day and considered she might have smoked her pipe before attending the services, plus, she wasn't concerned where we kids were. I sat next to her during the service and then in the limousine that took us to the cemetery.

At Lake Forest, we got out of the car and Dan took me to our grandfather's headstone. It was in the same row where my dad was going to be. "See, his name was Russell and he was in World War One."

"Why does it have Grandma's name on there?" I asked. "She's alive, right over there." I pointed.

"Well," Dan spoke in a serious tone. "It only has her date of birth on it, not her date of death, but this is where she'll be buried when she dies."

"That's creepy to have your name on a grave marker and you're not even dead," I said.

"Well, it was cheaper if they had most of it printed all at once," Dan explained as we walked back to the opening in the earth that was meant for our dad. "Ma's not getting her name on Dad's stone 'cause they're divorced."

Chapter Six

Marge sold her old brown station wagon and started driving my dad's newer, green Dodge Dart. She said he wanted her to have it and that it would be safer to drive than the old wagon. It took some time getting used to it, though. Sometimes when I saw it making the turn onto our street, I had a second's worth of heart-stopping excitement, thinking it was my dad, followed by a large exhale of reality and disappointment.

We all had our ways of coping with his death. Marge studied, drank beer, smoked her pipe, and cried a lot. I cried mostly when I went to bed and had nothing else to think about. I figured no one but Blackie could hear me. She scooted closer to me every time my face smashed into the pillow.

At school, I pretended my dad was sitting on the edge of my desk, watching me. I could feel him smile as I attempted to perfect the cursive writing lesson taught by the lady on PBS. I started acting out a little too and poor Mrs. Breagle 'the bald eagle' was a saint about it.

Dan seemed quieter, so Marge called Big Brothers and got him a male friend who worked at the Grand Haven Airport. Dan seemed to like him, so he worked at the airport too, just helping his 'Big Brother'. Randy started his first year of college and Scot hung out at his friend's house all the time. We all just kind of did our own thing until the end of the school year.

~ * ~

When Marge graduated from college that June, with a degree in

Psychology, she decided we all needed to see the Rocky Mountains. She and Dan planned the trip, and we left in June. Randy stayed home to work at his farm internship for the summer and to watch Blackie.

Marge and Dan had the front seat of Dad's car, while Scot and I sat in the back. I sat as close to the door as possible and tried to focus on anything but Scot. As cornfield greens danced and cattle muck filled my nose, I envisioned Blackie and me, running the rolling hills. The wide-open world was in my future and in my view, until Marge lit a Benson and Hedges and dragged her arm in the wind as she drove. I could only concentrate on the white from the tan line of her watch and duck the ashes that flew to the backseat.

For the first few days of our trip, the best part was Stuckey's, but only if I didn't have to use the bathroom. The travel stops were everywhere. Marge stopped there to get gasoline and we kids pawed through the souvenirs. Sometimes, we got their famous pecan logs because Marge wasn't so worried about sugar on the trip. I tried to get lost in all the little weird games and knick knacks.

I was mostly hiding until Marge exited the restroom so that I could go in. I learned early on in the trip not to even mention having to go to the bathroom. If I did, Marge walked right into the same stall and stood over me.

"Come on, Julie!"

"I can't go if you're standing here." I stared at her knee caps.

"Why in the hell not?" Her eyes seemed like they were going to pop right out. "I'm your mother! Go, dammit!"

I knew other women were coming in and out of the bathroom and could hear us. I was mortified by her ridiculous anger. I worried for other little girls that came in and out with their moms. They might be scared too, or worse, they might not ever want to come into a public restroom again.

"Go! I want to get back on the road!"

"I can't." I quickly raised my hands to cover my head when she moved slightly.

"Oh, for fuck's sake, what, am I going to hit you?" She raised her hand. "What do you think I am?"

A torture monster, I thought, but I didn't answer at all. I never knew if her hand was coming down or not.

The afternoon that I heard Marge yell out, "Oh my God, oh my God, the Rockies!" I felt total excitement right along with her. I could see snow caps far in the distance because it was such a clear and beautiful day. None of us had ever seen anything like it in real life. We stopped and took pictures every time we got ten or so miles closer. Songs like Dreamweaver, Band On The Run and Wildfire played on every station we picked up. The boys made fun of me because I cried about Wildfire, the horse, the owner, and loss in general.

After spending the night at a motel in Denver, we took the following day to visit the zoo and scout around before heading up to Rocky Mountain National Park. We seemed to travel every road up in those mountains, careful to stop and take pictures whenever we saw mountain goats or elk. We wrote our names in a wall of snow, just because it was summer. Everyone seemed so happy in Colorado, and though I still stayed clear of Scot physically, it was kind of fun to be around him.

My favorite part of the trip was driving the San Juan Skyway. Not only were the towns beautiful, like Telluride and Ouray, but the road had so many switchbacks that were terribly high and scary for Marge to drive. With every turn, she sort of yelped and screeched, followed by a guttural moan which made us kids laugh. There were no guard rails and as we took the turns, we could see each bottomless drop.

For me, it was like an amusement ride and I loved it. But Marge was so busy positioning herself closer to the wheel and gripping tighter that she never commented on our giggles.

It was here that I fell in love with Aspen trees. With the smallest breeze, the leaves shimmer like coins and make a sound that's better than playing cards in bike spokes.

Once we came down from the San Juans, we traveled to Mesa Verde National Park and the Grand Canyon. We toured the ruins and then I got to lie on four states at once. All of these places just made the world's largest musical fountain back home seem so very small.

~ * ~

Marge bought us all moccasins at some point and told us to throw the shoes we were wearing into the trash. I guess she started feeling real Indian-like, since her family was part Iroquois. She bought turquoise jewelry, too.

After two weeks, Marge was getting pretty tired of being on the road. Her patience was wearing thin, and when she wasn't yelling at Dan about directions, she was crabby with me because I never had to go to the bathroom.

At a diner in New Mexico, she just had enough.

"That waitress is awfully rude." Marge sipped at coffee that took her forever to get. "I mean, what is taking so long?"

It was taking a long time and it didn't seem too busy in the place. The waitress got our drinks, but never took our food order. After waiting awhile longer, Marge stood up and took ketchup bottles from the nearby empty tables and handed them to the boys. "Just pour the shit all over the tables." She grabbed my hand and led me outside to the getaway car. A few moments later, the boys came running out, laughing.

"Go!" Scot yelled, and we were quickly back on the highway, looking for another place to eat.

Each night, after we checked into a place, Marge would use the hotel stationary and write a letter to Randy. She had us write notes about highlights and she wrote down what the gas prices were, who we met along the way and anything funny that the rest of us kids said. She made the trip sound like a dream vacation. We stayed in beautiful Des Moines,

Interstate 80 has no orchards, only corn and plowed fields, Lincoln has a gorgeous capitol and the scenery has been fantastic, gas averages at fifty-four cents a gallon. We are driving slowly and carefully, only fifty-five to fifty-eight on highways, the car is doing well-no need to worry.

She was right. Other than the bathroom antics and a few screaming fits, we had the time of our lives and I knew where I would someday escape, those mountains.

The ride home was bittersweet. I wanted to stay out west forever, but I couldn't wait to get back home to see Blackie and Randy. When we finally did pull into the driveway, both greeted us warmly. Marge snapped a picture of Randy's face as he opened the car trunk to find it filled with Coors beer. "A delicacy!" he shouted with surprise.

~ * ~

I spent the rest of my summer in my moccasins, running around and playing kick the can with the Wildroms and the McCalebs. Toward the end of summer, I asked if I could get my hair chopped off. I was sick of pulling it up when I had to use the bathroom and always putting it in ponytails. Marge was hesitant but, finally agreed. She cried in front of the hairdresser and put all of my hair into an old nylons package to save.

Chapter Seven

I'm not sure if it was wanderlust brought on by our trip out west, or if she was just tired of our small town, but Marge informed me that when third grade ended for me, we were going to move away from Grand Haven.

"Where are we going?" I pulled on a loop of the carpeting where I sat.

"I don't know yet." Marge didn't take her eyes off the book she rested on her knees.

"Wherever it is, it'll be far away from Michigan."

"But our family is here, and friends," I cried. "Daddy is buried here."

"Damn it, Julie, I don't care. We're leaving and that's that." She brought the book up to read and quickly put it down again. "Besides, your da-ddy," she stretched the word to mock me, "wouldn't want you kids growing up where people are treating your mother like garbage." She slammed the book down on an end table which meant one of two things. She was about to go on a long rant about anyone who ever even looked at her funny, which included our relatives, my teachers, and any Christian, or she was about to go into the kitchen for a beer. My hopes rested on the appearance of a can.

I didn't contest any further, I knew better, but truly, I felt whatever accusations were being made, or whatever was driving her to run away, was brought on by no one but herself. In most cases, I believe she only imagined people were talking about her, and it made me so angry that decisions were made based on the made-up stuff in her head.

~ * ~

Marge waited about six months after my dad died before she started dating. She went out with many different men, but they didn't stay over. She assumed people talked about that, too. She loved discussing the different experiences she had on dates. One man, who was older, flew her to Chicago for their date and she brought back a bionic woman Barbie doll for me. Another man drove all the way across the state, from Port Huron, many times, just to see her. He was half black and very good looking. He wore tight polyester pants and wide-collared shirts. My dad never would have worn those. It was neat when he came pulling into the driveway because we didn't have any black people in our neighborhood. Exciting as all of it was, none of the men seemed to matter, because when she finished telling me about the dancing and eating fancy food, she always went back to talking about my dad, like they were never divorced.

"Your daddy was such a good man and he really loved me." She stared past me while nodding.

"We had such a good life together." Finally, she looked at me, "We were going to get back together again, you know."

I nodded right back, smiled, and wondered if that was so true, why she threw stuff at him and yelled all the time.

~ * ~

Unfortunately, the distraction of dating and stories had to end when she came home with a blue and white pickup truck with a camper top. I was really hoping that one of the men would make her want to stay in Grand Haven.

"Everything that we're taking is going to have to fit into the back of that." She pointed at the vehicle, seeming proud of the trade-in of my dad's car. "Now we just have to sell the house and have a yard sale."

I looked at the boys and they seemed unaffected by all she was saying. I knew Randy didn't care because he was just going back to college. The only moving he would have to do was to leave his dorm and move into his own apartment. Scot said once he was going to miss his friend, Pat, but other than that, the boys didn't say a word. Maybe they were feeling just like me, heartbroken, but they knew it was pointless to oppose our mother.

When it came time for our moving sale, Marge told us to put absolutely everything on the front lawn. "This is not the time to have attachments to things. If it's not on your back, put it out there."

I put everything of mine out, except some clothes, my dog, Blackie, and the two cats, Ted and Tiny which I acquired from Randy's job at the farm. I decided not to care about losing my material belongings. "I can keep my animals, right?"

"Oh, for Christ's sake, Julie! I'm not telling you to put a price sticker on the dog!"

My bike went first. I loved that bike. It was purple with a glittery banana seat and a basket where I often put one of the cats. The ladies down the street bought it for me shortly after my dad died. They held Bible study at their house on Thursday nights, so I visited them on other days. Sometimes I just stopped to chat or get a piece of candy. They were really nice, but Marge didn't seem to appreciate them.

"What are you doing, hanging around with those queers?" Marge probed.

"What's a queer?" I asked, thinking it might have to do with the bible.

"You know, quee-rce!" she enunciated. "Two women living together."

Still, I didn't get it, so I shrugged.

"Oh, for God's sake, they don't like men, Julie!"

"They do, Mom," I protested. "They both love Jesus and his disciples. They're all men." I thought I was hilarious. "Jan and Elaine are really nice people," I said, once I saw she wasn't laughing.

After my bike sold, everything else went to; either into someone's car or into the trash. My heart hurt. My life was being sold, even my bedroom. The purple three-way mirror Dad built for me and I used for my Cher impressions went to some older lady. My games, pottery wheel, Lincoln Logs, and my Crissy doll all went to the greedy hagglers.

~ * ~

Marge promised to sell the house to Lou's daughter, Debbie, and her new husband. When someone came along and offered a thousand more, she sold it to the new bidder. This didn't sit well with Lou Tripp's entire family. Especially since Debbie's new husband was the manager at Cook's Appliances, where just two weeks before, Scot and Dan snuck out in the middle of the night and smashed all the toilets that were stored in back of the place.

I figured Marge just wanted to make everyone mad and cause drama. Our exit from Grand Haven was dramatic, as well. We never got to say goodbye to anyone, even though Marge promised we would. Instead, we left town late one night. I didn't even get the chance to hug all of my aunts and uncles or say goodbye to my friends.

Again, Dan was in the front cab to help with directions and I was in the back with Scot and the other animals. The front cab of the truck was separated from the back by two panes of glass. It seemed like we weren't even part of the same vehicle. I couldn't hear Marge or Dan, just muffled sounds.

I was trapped in the back and everything was closed in. Marge decided to keep a loveseat, so that was in the back, as well as boxes of files and clothes tied down along the sides of the truck bed. We had plenty of pillows and blankets. There was a litter box near the back door and little bowls for the pets' food and water. The cats cried for the first few hours and I did too. I prayed Marge would just take me back to live with one of the relatives.

~ * ~

Our first stop was the Neil Armstrong Air and Space Museum in Wapokoneta, Ohio. Ted had already gone to the bathroom on one of the blankets because he was so nervous, so I had to throw that out in a museum trash can. Marge had me take all the animals, with one leash and two long ropes, to walk in the grass. The cats were terrified from the noise of cars whizzing by on the nearby highway. It was all so wrong and unnatural. Blackie walked along happily, while the cats took extra giant steps with shaky and extended paws. Tiny had diarrhea and it looked much like what Ted left on the blanket. I could hear Marge screaming about the smell, back at the truck and why didn't they use the fucking litter. Like Teddy did it on purpose, I thought. The more I heard her rant, the more I wanted to just take off and run as far away as possible, but I had my pets. Besides, the boys would catch me and then Marge might kill me and no one would ever know.

Marge went into the museum to find out the price of admission and use the bathroom. She came out with four tickets and a bag of dried bananas. My anxiety over the pets caused me to throw up in the grass just before going in, so I blamed it on the banana chips.

After exploring the wonders of space travel, we got back on the road and the cats started crying again. It happened every time Marge started the engine. The cats cried and panted, and I petted them to bring calm. Blackie wagged every time I looked at her, and Scot slept through most of the drive.

Later that night in Kentucky, while we were trying our first sampling of grits, Marge informed us that we were headed to Tifton,

Georgia to visit a friend.

"What friend?" Dan raised his eyebrows.

"Charlie, a pen pal," Marge answered as she cut into chicken.

"From where?" Dan sounded cranky and he must have been awfully tired and sick of her company. We all stopped what we were doing.

Marge quit chewing and glared at Dan. "A pen pal ad in the back of a magazine, okay?" She resumed chewing and then swallowed. "Is that okay with you?" She spoke loudly.

Dan didn't bother to respond. He just stopped eating and folded his arms. I gave up eating too, because I knew what would happen next. Marge was going to ask for the check immediately, storm out to the truck, and then lecture poor Danny all the way to Georgia. And that was exactly what she did. I could hear her screaming through the double windows. Danny just needed sleep, and so did she.

Finally, we stopped for the night at a motel near the pen pal. The next morning, after cleaning up and getting something to eat, we ventured to meet Charlie.

Marge stopped the truck a few blocks from Charlie's address so that she could brush her hair a little and put on some lipstick.

Charlie's house was a small dark green ranch. There was a side porch between the house and garage. We kids sat in the truck and waited for Marge to investigate. The cats were climbing all over the place since the engine wasn't running, and Blackie was excited because she had to pee. I had to pee.

Charlie came to his front door and gave Marge a big squeeze. I wondered how long this plan was in the works. When I first saw Charlie, I thought about liquor stores. Liquor stores with wood flooring and blinking neon. Charlie waved for us to come out of the truck. "Oh, it's great to meet you kids." His words were long and slow, but he seemed excited.

"Nice to meet you." I was the only one to respond at first.

The boys just stood with their hands in their pockets and managed a quiet, "Hi."

Charlie's belly was wider than I was tall. His hair glowed like leftover pumpkin innards when you haven't quite scraped enough, but you want to light the candle anyway. He invited us in and called loudly for Jake. "Ma son is prolly busy weeth his geetar, but heel be out."

Scot and Dan asked to go explore and took off within minutes of arriving. I kept looking through Charlie's window at our truck. "Thar sum-in you wont?" Charlie was looking at me while nodding his head toward the truck. I wanted to get my dog and let her out.

"May I use your restroom?"

"Right down the hall." He pointed and then stared at Marge like she was a cold beer and a bag of corn nuts.

His bathroom wasn't much different from the truck stop bathrooms we had been using the whole way. I went quick and then returned to my spot in front of the window.

"You can walk your pets, honey." Marge smiled and acted sugary in front of her pen pal.

I smiled back. "Thanks, Mom."

While I was out walking everyone, a boy about my age, ten or eleven, came out the side door of the house. The cats looked terrified. I spoke sweetly to them while Blackie sniffed around.

"Hey, I'm Jake." He reached his hand out to Blackie to let her inspect him.

"Hi, I'm Julie." I blushed.

His lips were full and rosy. "So, your mom drove y'all all the way to meet my dad, huh?" He brushed long blond strands from his face.

"I guess so." I felt kind of sick because I remembered leaving everything. I had to think about the present. This was an adventure and this boy was really cute.

After I got the cats back into the truck, I slid all the windows back to expose screens and fresh air for them. Blackie, Jake and I went into the house so that he could show us around.

Marge and Charlie were in the kitchen, talking over a few cans of beer and a filled ashtray of yellowed squished butts. Marge was beginning to show her true self. She was doing all the talking and getting louder.

Jake showed me a few tiny rooms and then we settled on a small love seat in an alcove that had nothing more than a television and a guitar. Jake picked up the instrument. "Do you play?"

"I don't, but my brother, Randy, does."

Jake started playing and then he began to sing. At first, I was uncomfortable. I didn't know whether to look at him or Blackie, or to pick at my nails. He sang music I never heard before; country. I can't say that I liked it, but I was very intrigued by him. When he finished, we sat and talked about our families and music for probably an hour. I heard Scot and Dan come back, but they didn't bother to find me and it was just as well.

I'm not sure how it happened, but Jake and I kissed. I didn't feel anything except happiness that my first kiss was with such a cute boy.

Jake started to play and sing again and suddenly, I heard Marge's voice over his. She was getting louder. "Uh oh." I waved for Jake to stop.

"I don't want my children around some racist redneck!" she screamed. I heard the front door open and I knew the boys were already going for the truck.

"I'm really sorry." I frowned and got up. "It was nice meeting you and, well, kissing you." I giggled.

"Julie!" Marge yelled. "Let's go, we're getting the fuck out of Georgia!"

Marge was still yelling when Blackie and I got to the truck. It turned out that Charlie referred to a black person as a nigger. I didn't think that was right either, but I had to wonder if she still had feelings for the great dresser from Port Huron. Still, I couldn't figure out why she was so mad at Charlie, since she referred to Elaine and Jan as queers. She was just a name caller, too.

~ * ~

I woke up the next morning in Florida. Marge looked at an apartment, but thought she found bugs, so we left Florida. I was disappointed, because I always heard people in Grand Haven talk about their trips to Florida. They came home, looking happy. I thought maybe if we stayed, we would be happy.

As we headed west, we all kept our places in the truck. I often sat, looking out the camper windows. I kept them open to extinguish Scot's awful smell and breathe in each new climate. I stared at people in cars and made up stories about them. A husband and wife might have just visited the wife's great aunt in a nursing home, and had to get back to Alabama. One family was just driving to the local swim club and would have real Oscar Mayer bologna on Wonder Bread when they took a break from swimming. Their mom would open a bag of fresh crispy chips and serve homemade cookies.

Once, a convertible caught my attention because of the woman driving it. She stayed with us for maybe a hundred miles. Her long brown hair whirled behind her and she was free. She devoured the sky and reveled in her lack of limitations. I imagined her music was loud, but I couldn't hear it. I envisioned a glass bottle of Coca Cola between her legs and a pack of all-American Marlboro cigarettes on the seat next to her.

When I felt Scot's clammy hand between my thighs, I wished I was her.

I had been sleeping on my stomach when I first felt it, "Tell me if you like this." His hand climbed beneath my shorts and underneath the elastic of my underpants. I put my face in my pillow and didn't speak. "I want to know if this is what I should do to my girlfriends."

I vaguely heard the mumblings of Marge and Dan conversing in the front. I hated the stupid truck and the separation of the cab and camper. I kept thinking about the girl in the convertible. I wanted to be her. So, in my mind, I left the back of the truck and that family, and I drove. I wore a very white shirt and blue jeans. My hair blew behind me as I drove fast toward the Rockies. Then, I was in control.

I heard Scot, "Do you like this?" I felt his fingers prying. "What does it feel like?"

I decided to answer, especially since my mind trip vanished, and I really just wanted to disappear or die. "It feels like nothing."

Chapter Eight

Marge rented a nice little house in Texas, just outside of Fort Worth. It would be a few days before we could move in because the place needed to be fumigated. "I guess the whole damn south has a bug problem," Marge said after signing the rental agreement and handing in the deposit.

"Okay, kids, we're going to have to hold tight for a few more days and live out of the truck." She sighed. "First things first. Let's get you all enrolled in school."

Dan and Scot would be going to high school and I would be starting the fourth grade. School already started there, so we missed a few weeks. We took a day to get enrolled, get some school supplies, and then Marge took us to a Goodwill to get some new clothes and a pair of shoes. We were to start the next day.

That night, we spent at a rest stop. In the morning, we drove to the nearby McDonald's for some breakfast and a quick bath using the restroom sink and a washcloth from one of the boxes in the truck. I was so used to getting cleaned up and brushing my teeth at fast food places that I wasn't even phased.

The first thing my new teacher said was, "Class, we have a new student and her name is Julianne." I looked around at all the kids staring. I thought about how easy it would have been to enter the fourth grade at my old school. I would have known almost everyone and no one would have eyed me with suspicion.

"My name is Mrs. Ketchum." Her long fingernails pressed into my shoulder. "Julianne, where did you go to school before?" She asked, as she guided me to my desk.

"In Michigan." I lifted the top of my desk to see if anything was stored inside.

"That's a long way!" She sounded so funny to me, like Charlie. "Where do you live now? Close to the school? Most of the children walk to school and some are bussed. Will you be walking?"

I figured she kept asking all the questions because I appeared clueless, because I was. I decided to tell her what I knew at the moment, plus it would serve her right for being so nosy. "Well," I said, "we live at the rest stop right out on the highway." I smiled and folded my hands on my desk.

Mrs. Ketchum's eyes were wide and her mouth hung open for a moment. "So, ya'll are gypsies." Her penciled brows were raised so high that they almost touched her platinum poofy bangs.

I frowned for a moment and thought about what she said. "I don't know," I replied.

Later in the evening, as we sat in our McDonald's, I asked Marge about the gypsy issue. Marge frowned hard. "No, we're not gypsies! Why would she say a thing like that?"

"I don't know." I shrugged. "I mean, I told her we were traveling."

The next day, while we kids were in school, Marge was unpacking at our new place and a young couple arrived to move in as well. As it turned out, the people who rented the house to us were the sheriff and his wife, and he also promised the house to the couple. When Marge went to ask about the mistake, the sheriff denied ever having met her before. He kept her money.

I was trying hard to focus on a writing assignment when Dan knocked on my classroom door and opened it. "I'm here to get my sister!" he announced. I immediately stood and gathered my things.

"Ya'll leaving?" Mrs. Ketchum peeled reading glasses from her face and had a look of horror.

When I got to the door, Dan said, "Mom said we have to give her the finger."

Orders were orders, I thought, and we both turned around and flipped her off.

We didn't leave Texas right away. Marge drove around half of the state first. We cruised through Waco and then Austin, where Marge bought an intercom system, so we could communicate between the camper and the cab of the truck. We went to San Antonio to see the Riverwalk and the brand new Southwest Craft's Center, and then Marge decided to drive to Galveston Island, where we ate expensive seafood while she ranted about what a crook the Sheriff of Fort Worth was.

~ * ~

When we left Texas, Marge drove east, careful to stay out of Georgia. We only used the intercom to talk about food and bathroom breaks, but it kept Scot away from me. After three weeks on the road, we arrived in Norfolk, Virginia, where we would stay for a while.

Our new apartment was in the Willouby Spit area of Norfolk. We lived on a peninsula where we could view the largest naval base in the world. Dan told me that the Willouby name came from Thomas Willouby, who bought the land in the early 1600's, and that the spit part meant that the land was narrow. We had the Willouby Bay outside of our back door and the Chesapeake Bay just a few blocks from the front of our apartment. It was pretty neat to be near the beach again, but the apartment wasn't very big. We had one bathroom and a small kitchen. Marge had a bedroom and the boys shared a room, while I got the living room and the love seat from the truck for a bed. It wasn't always easy to fall asleep with everyone in my room all the time.

When Marge dropped me off at Ocean View Elementary for my first day, she said, "This is going to be a lot different from Ferry School in Grand Haven."

"I know," I responded. I just thought she meant that I wouldn't know anyone. I figured it would be a lot like the Texas school and the teacher would ask me a ton of questions.

"You kids need some cultural awareness." She gripped the steering wheel tightly. "You're just going to have to trust me."

"I do," I lied.

My teacher, Mrs. Walker, was a large black woman that reminded me of Mabel from the show, "What's Happening?" She was large and in charge and I was a little scared of her, at first. Most of the students in my class were black, and when I took my seat, I realized what Marge meant by 'different' from my old school. It was an interesting first week. Mrs. Walker was holding mock elections and we had to choose between Jimmy Carter and President Gerald Ford. It was tough for me to decide. Ford was from my home state of Michigan and Carter was from Georgia, where the boy who kissed me lived. But I liked the idea of change, and despite my brothers' constant jokes about Billy Carter and his beer, I picked Jimmy. I felt smart when he won a few days later and so did Cynthia, the little girl who sat to my right in class. I was mesmerized by Cynthia and it was obvious. Mostly, it was her hair that had my attention. Sometimes she wore a braid on either side of her head and one large twist across the front, or she would have several large twists. I couldn't twist my hair and make it stick like she did. The colors of her ponytail holders and barrettes changed, too. The bands might match her outfit or she would wear several different colors. She was a small girl with delicate features, except for her mouth. Her lips were pronounced, vast and shiny. She often caught me staring and got annoyed with me, "Take a picture, it lasts longer." Her head moved from side to side and her eyes found me for a second. Her mouth stayed open to reveal a wad of gum and her disgust. Then, she closed her mouth, pouty-like, looked up at the ceiling, folded her arms, and waited for my response.

I'd never seen anything like it and I never felt so white. Her attitude was fascinating. But I took the opportunity to talk about her locks. "May I touch your hair?" I wanted to figure out how the twists stayed in place.

"Uh huh," she responded lazily but, leaned toward me, proudly.

After touching her hair, I thought maybe I understood why her lips were so glossy. I felt the slick on my fingertips. She must touch her lips every time she touches her hair. I wanted the glue that she was using, but I was too afraid to ask her about it for fear that there was no such product and her hair just bonded naturally.

~ * ~

In January, not too long after President Carter took office, Mrs. Walker gave us an assignment to watch Roots. Roots was a television series based on Alex Haley's book about his ancestors and the slave trade. We were to watch all eight nights of the series and discuss it in class the next day.

The series started on a Sunday night. Monday morning, I did not want to go to school. I thought that Cynthia and the other black kids would hate me. I was scared and shameful, even though I knew I hadn't been responsible for slavery. I wondered if Cynthia's ancestors had been treated like that. I thought about telling the kids about Charlie Pen Pal saying the 'N' word and us leaving Georgia because of it. Maybe I would tell them about the Indians in our family and remind them of the Trail of Tears.

I was nervous as I took my seat. A few minutes later, Cynthia came into class, sat down and opened her backpack. She took out an assortment of colored rubber bands and moved close to me. As Mrs. Walker began discussing the atrocities of the slave trade, Cynthia reached for my plain brown strands and began to braid my hair. I left the twenty or so 'plaits' in for two days. I looked ridiculous, but somehow, I wanted to honor my new friend. Dan and Scot made fun of me, but

Marge didn't seem to notice.

In the afternoon, I was elected hall monitor and I received a bright orange vest and a gold badge. I wore it proudly along with my plaits. I was accepted.

While I took seriously my new position, got my first training bra from the Lerner Shop, and kept a constant eye on what the President's daughter, Amy Carter, was up to, Marge had new things going on as well. She became a bigwig at TRIS, which stood for Tidewater Rape Information Services, and she got a new boyfriend. I figured she met him at the Old Bay View Inn or the Thirsty Camel since she was hanging out there all the time. Richard was fifteen years younger and he would pull up to our apartment in an old Chevy pickup truck. If they were going somewhere fancy, he drove his Corvette. He was around a lot and Marge was always dressing up for their dates. While he waited for Marge to get ready, he sat and talked with us kids, especially Scot and Dan. He took an interest with focused blue eyes and a welcoming smile. He was very handsome.

~ * ~

The only nights Richard wasn't around, were the nights Marge was on call for her job. The phone rang at all hours of the night and Marge would have to leave the apartment and go help ladies who had been assaulted. On weekends, she woke me and took me with her. I figured it was more 'cultural awareness', but I hated it. I didn't want to see these women and I'm sure they didn't want me around to see their tears, bruises, dirty motel rooms, and apartments. I hated sitting at the hospital with them while Marge consoled them and took her reports. I wanted my love seat bed and Blackie tucked in with me.

Marge's job also entailed educating the public about rape and molestation. She had me 'volunteer' when she went to talk with Girl Scout troops. My job was to count how many girls there were of every race. The counts were part of some report that had to be handed in each week so Marge made it seem like an important task for me. She went to great lengths to make the girls feel comfortable and then described all the things to look for when someone was out to hurt them. How it's scary to be outside when it's dark, how you should lock your doors every night, and when, God forbid, it's someone in your family, you should always tell, even if you're afraid.

I cringed every time she said it. There is no way in hell that I could have told her about Scot. He was her biological child and I'm pretty sure, her favorite. She would never believe me.

The girls seemed to admire Marge with unwavering attention, while I sat, baffled.

~ * ~

During the spring break, Randy came to visit. It was thrilling to go to the Amtrak Station and watch his train come in. When he stepped off, I ran to him and cried. I held on to him and buried myself against his chest as he laughed. We all missed him terribly and our whole family seemed so happy that day. We drove him around Norfolk and then home. He and I walked the beach with Blackie and then we all went to El Hombre's for dinner with Richard that night. Randy talked about Grand Haven and how the new owners painted our old house. He told us about his girlfriend, Kelly, and then he mentioned Grandma Beekman.

"I check in on her just about every week," he said.

"Will you give her my address?" I perked up. "And will you tell her I miss her?"

"Of course." Randy messed the top of my hair.

Marge quickly changed the subject. "Oh, I don't want to hear about those people," she said. "How's school, Randy?"

Randy told us all about his classes and mentioned he was interested in possibly transferring to a school in Philadelphia.

"Oh?" Marge's eyes widened and she halted cutting into her burrito. "That isn't too far from here. Dan, how far is Philadelphia?"

Dan quietly answered, "About eight hours."

"Wonderful!" she said excitedly and returned to her dinner.

I was excited too. I would get to see Randy more often and I could see the Liberty Bell.

After the elation of that first night with Randy, things seemed like old times. During the day, Marge had to work and we kids had off from school, so the three boys hung out together, and I spent most of my time with the kids in the neighborhood. At night, we all ate dinner together and then quickly separated again. One night, Marge went out with Richard on a date and Randy walked down to the Thirsty Camel. He came home late and woke me by sitting on the edge of the loveseat. Blackie was under my blanket, growling softly while Randy talked about things that didn't make any sense. He babbled through fermented stench and suddenly, his lips were pressed against mine. He wiggled his tongue and stopped for a moment to ask how it was that I already had breasts. I raised my arms up to cover them and he tried to kiss me again. Blackie growled louder and Randy jerked suddenly and shook his head like he didn't know where he was. He slid back, away from me. "Oh my god, Julie. I am so sorry!" He started to cry. "I'm so sorry."

"Why did you do that?" I whimpered.

"I don't know, I'm so very sorry." He got up and left the living room, my wide-open bedroom.

He must have been sleep-walking.

We said nothing more about the incident for the rest of his stay. I wasn't exactly warm and friendly to him, but I pretended it never happened. I was now uncomfortable around two of my three brothers.

~ * ~

When fourth grade finished in June, Marge and I moved in with

Richard. Scot graduated and he and Dan went on a two-month road trip in a clunker Scot bought with some of his trust fund from our dad. They travelled all over and then met Randy in Philly, and helped him move into his place so he could attend Temple University. Scot ended up moving there with him and basically bummed around for a year, occasionally applying for jobs. Dan came to live at Richard's, but it wouldn't be for long since he was due to graduate early, just for being smart.

Richard lived in the Ballantine section of Norfolk. It seemed that Richard and another family were the only white people until Marge and I moved in. The homes on his street were modest bungalows with small yards, but nice porches. Crepe Myrtles lined the streets and children played everywhere. I loved his little home with hardwood floors and rounded entranceways. I looked forward to starting in a new school, though I would miss my friend, Cynthia.

I found out rather quickly that I needed to keep my dog close and not let her wander. The first week we were there, I went out to the porch and called for her. "Here, Blackie! Here, Blackie!" I felt many eyes gaze upon me and the voices from the porch next door fell silent. I turned to my right, shivered and felt my tongue go dry as I saw what must have been the entire black family next door. Blackie trotted up the front steps and I quickly picked her up and held her. "Good girl, good Blackie." I let out a deep breath.

My fifth-grade teacher, Mrs. Roberts, was a thin black woman with a look of distaste for children. She rarely smiled, but I could tell when she found something amusing. It was all in her eyes; some sense of humor, even when her nostrils flared and her lips closed tightly, her crow's feet couldn't lie.

I got into trouble with Mrs. Roberts that year and so did Marge. It all started in the lunch room cafeteria. I was experiencing my usual confusion about why my classmates, Marcus and Tyrone, were always touching my butt in the lunch line. It made me want to eat more and hide behind fat until one of them whispered, "Yeah, fat butt," as his hand grazed my bottom. I pushed my tray forward on the conveyor and before I reached the cashier, I snagged an ice cream cup. I was still going to stuff everything down.

As I sat at the table, I contemplated having a huge ass. I really didn't want that. I wanted attention in other ways, so I lifted the little wooden stick with the wad of ice cream still attached, bent it back like a sling shot and flung it across the room. The glob pelted Mrs. Sanchez, the lunch lady, right on the side of her head. The kids at my table laughed uncontrollably. My mouth opened, my body tensed and I quickly dropped the stick. I suddenly wished I had eaten the ice cream; better yet, never taken it at all.

A few moments later, Mrs. Roberts was standing at our table. She had been called out of the teacher's lounge and she was clearly unhappy about it. Mrs. Sanchez stood by her, with a wet rag she kept running through her hair. "Who did this?" Mrs. Roberts had the tightest lips I ever saw on her. "Who. Did. This?" she demanded.

I slowly raised my hand. "I did. I'm really sorry, Mrs. Sanchez, I didn't mean for it to hit you." I blinked back tears.

"I expect more from you." Mrs. Sanchez balled up her rag. "You are supposed to be the leader of this lunch table." She walked away, shaking her head.

"Upstairs!" Mrs. Roberts pointed a long twisty finger. "Upstairs, all of you!"

When we got back to the classroom, Mrs. Roberts asked me and the others from my lunch table to stand in the middle of the floor. "That was not funny," she paced in front of her desk, "but I'll tell you what is. Get down on the floor and give me eighty push-ups," she barked.

What an odd request, I thought. "Mrs. Roberts?" I spoke softly, "They didn't do anything." I looked at the boys that were already on the floor.

"They were laughing at your silliness!" She picked up a yard stick.

"Eighty push-ups, now!"

I got down on the floor and attempted the task. After five or six, I could barely get my chubby body off the floor. Tears welled from my embarrassment. WHACK! The yard stick slapped against my hand. I could see Mrs. Roberts' big feet in front of me. Her ankles were so skinny the hose she was wearing creased and gathered around the bone. "Keep moving, girl!" Her voice sounded happy and militant at the same time.

I struggled. Marcus and Tyrone finished and were already back in their seats. Kevin was just finishing his. "Seventy-six, seventy-seven." He puffed.

I may have been at fifteen when the next thwack of the ruler came. I collapsed.

"Now get up outta here, go sit down!" Mrs. Roberts signaled.

I was still on the floor when the other kids came back from lunch. I slowly stood and found my seat. I glanced around the room while I wiped my eyes. Everyone stared, but no one laughed.

Chetaqua, the portly girl that sat next to me, whispered, "Dang."

Later that night, Marge asked me about school. I mistakenly told her about the ice cream, the push-ups and the yard stick. The next morning, class was barely underway when Marge came barreling in. "No one hits my daughter but me!" She walked toward Mrs. Roberts, hauled off and slugged her on the chin.

"Dang!" Chetaqua yelled.

I covered my face with my hands and prayed that when I removed them, I would be sitting in my class back in Grand Haven.

Marge spent the afternoon in jail. I just kept quiet all day and never looked Mrs. Roberts in the eyes. It wasn't until the next day when kids started harassing me. "My daddy says no white woman should be walking in here hitting no black woman!" Tyrone's twin sister, Portia, pushed me as I entered the school. "I'm calling you out!" She pushed again. Some kids around her cheered. I continued walking into the building. "After school, white girl!"

My heart beat heavily all day. Just a few days before, the girls at school were teaching me to dance to the song, One Nation Under A Groove. We all laughed as I tried to emulate moves that maybe only adults should be making. Now, I was going to get beat up and I couldn't stop thinking about how much it was going to hurt.

I decided to just go out the school doors I normally used and take my beating. The fight was quick because I just stood there. Portia was hopping all over the place and Tyrone stood off to the side, expressionless. Just two days ago, he asked me to be his girlfriend and I agreed.

He asked me out, and his sister called me out. Life was grand.

She only pushed me around and not much came of it but, after that day, Dan walked me home until things got back to normal.

~ * ~

By the time I entered sixth grade, Dan moved to Philadelphia to live with Randy and go to Drexel University for accounting. Scot got a job with an electronics company and moved back to Virginia. Marge started fighting with Richard all the time, so we moved to a duplex in the next neighborhood over, Coleman Place. Even though I could have switched to Coleman Elementary, which was primarily white but, Marge insisted I stay at Ballantine and walk for the exercise. I didn't mind, I rather liked the walks to and from school. Besides, I was making a lot of money at Ballantine.

Every morning, I stopped at the 7-eleven and bought Now and Later candy. I paid twenty-five cents for a pack of ten pieces and then I sold the individual taffy for twenty-five cents. I also made fingernails for all the girls. At the end of class every day, I cleared out my desk and drew Elmer's glue into oval shapes in sets of ten. By morning, the glue dried and I pried up each oval and glued them to the girls' fingertips. A set of nails cost ten cents and it seemed they would rather pay me, than make the nails, themselves.

Business was conducted before class and right after lunch. Chetaqua was my best customer. Sometimes, she bought so much candy that she held up the line and I would get caught talking. Mrs. Jorges was not sympathetic to my being a social butterfly or shopkeeper. She often punished me with writing assignments, which ultimately led to another visit from Marge. This time, it was to instruct Mrs. Jorges on how to teach.

"My daughter does not need to write that she is stupid or cannot listen, one hundred times!" Marge lectured from Mrs. Jorges' chalk board. "I made her write the preamble from the United States Constitution, one hundred times." Marge walked to my desk and grabbed my textbook while I kept my head down and stared at my shoes. "This," she shook the book in the air, "is what my daughter needs to learn!"

Chapter Nine

While we lived in the duplex on Arkansas Avenue, Marge left her rape counseling position and got a new job that involved rehabilitating ex-convicts.

"Julie, this is a very important position." She placed a floral scarf around her neck. "Your momma's not screwing around." She admired herself in the department store mirror. "Virginia Department of Corrections, and I'll be making more than Richard." She smiled.

"I don't get it." I stood behind her. "First you help the victims and now you're going to help the criminals?"

"Julie!" She swung around and placed her hands on her hips. "They are not all rapists. Some of these men just need to get back on their feet!" She turned back to the mirror to try a different scarf. "I can help these men, counsel them."

I felt proud of her and I thought it was admirable for her to help so many people, until she started counseling them in our apartment over a six-pack.

It was all so confusing, because sometimes Marge still dated Richard and everything was happy and calm. When she wasn't with Richard, she walked around sullen and blasted songs like, Sometimes When We Touch, and it kind of made me sick. When she brought one ex-offender to our house, he stayed for a few days. Rudy, the black man from New York, ultimately ended our days with Richard. I felt so bad because Richard just brought me a new, pink fiberglass skateboard and I thought maybe I should return it, since we weren't going to see him again. I just loved the skateboard far too much.

~ * ~

The summer after sixth grade, I managed to talk Marge into buying me an old working lawnmower at a yard sale. I pushed the lawnmower while I rode my skateboard and gathered customers quickly. No matter what size the lawn, my price was three dollars. This money got me issues of Tiger Beat magazine and Friday night roller skating at Olympic Skateway. I only saved enough money for one pair of Levi's cords and I picked baby blue. Everyone wore Levi's with a big comb in the back pocket. I made sure my cords were clean every Friday night, even if it meant washing them in the bathtub. The same kids showed up at skating every week. I had my sights on a blond boy, who always wore different colors of cords. He never seemed to notice me, even when I lost some weight.

I stared as he skated with other girls, one arm across each other's back. Watching his thin, but sporty and tanned frame, was better than any Leif Garrett or Shaun Cassidy poster. But, I wasn't sure if I really liked him or wanted to be like him.

One night, when 'couples skating' was called out over the speakers, I went to my usual spot at the rail where I could watch him. I wondered which girl he would skate with, but I couldn't find him.

"You wanna skate?" I heard a boy's voice from behind me. Then I felt a tug on my shirt sleeve. I turned. "You wanna skate?" It was him! He was asking me! Oh my God! My stomach churned and I smiled with incredible gratitude for finally having been chosen.

"Yes!" I said with enthusiasm and shyness all at once.

Then I noticed all of his usual friends hanging around us. Something wasn't right. Why weren't they skating?

"Okay, let me try to find someone who will actually skate with you," he said.

Laughter. All I heard was laughter. I turned and focused on the couples that were skating. I did not like him or want to be like him, I just wanted to die.

Within a few minutes, he was out there with some girl. Every time he or his friends swooshed past me, they would laugh. I had nowhere to go until Marge came to get me and I didn't know anyone there. I thought about it all the next week and I supposed it was kind of weird that I always went skating alone.

The following Friday, I asked my neighborhood friend, Bonnie, to go with me. Marge took us there and Bonnie's dad drove us home. We had a great time and the blond boy and his friends left me alone. It was like nothing ever happened. When I got back to the apartment on Arkansas Avenue, I walked in to find Marge sobbing.

"What's wrong?" I went to the sofa and sat next to her.

"Oh, Julie, I'm so sorry." She cried harder.

"What, what is it?"

"Blackie's dead."

She was lying. Blackie was not dead. She couldn't be.

"While you were skating, Blackie died."

I pushed away from the sofa and ran to my room. Blackie was curled up in my blanket and not breathing. I tried to move her, but she was kind of stiff. I crawled over her and held her. I never cried so hard. I got up and shut my door. I didn't want to share any emotions with Marge or Scot. He was probably just listening to Frank Zappa anyway and didn't care. I hated them both. I just wanted my Blackie. We were twelve. Twelve years together, my whole life. I told that dog everything.

I assumed that when we drove to the bay that night to bury Blackie, she died from old age. She had little bumps on her stomach, so maybe it was cancer. My dad had a lump under his arm when they found his cancer. I made a beautiful box for her with a blanket, her collar, and some red silk flowers. She rode in the back seat with me all the way to the water front. Marge and Scot stopped at 7-Eleven to get beer and to call Randy and Dan in Philadelphia. Marge made me tell them about Blackie, even though I could barely speak. They were both very sad and understanding. Scot was there with me, and hadn't said a word.

I dug in the sand gently as I whimpered. Scot dug like a maniac who just wanted to get it over with. We dug far enough from the water so that Blackie wouldn't get washed away. Marge stood off to the side and smoked her pipe. Occasionally, I heard her say something to God. I finished digging and Scot went to the car to get a beer. I placed Blackie's makeshift casket in the dirt and said goodbye, privately, silently. I covered her so that nothing could get to her. I made sure that all the sand on top was hard, by patting down on it. I then drew a heart with my fingertip. I sat next to her grave and looked out at lights from the naval ships. She would be protected.

It was two days after burying Blackie when Scot told me what really happened to my sweet dog. I was just getting ready to go skateboarding and hang out with my friends. Marge was in Roanoke and would be there working with some legislator for a few days. Since she didn't want me staying at Bonnie's the whole time, afraid that I would be a burden to Bonnie's family, I had to stay at the apartment with my weird brother.

Scot came strutting into my bedroom, wearing nothing more than a T-shirt. White gunk was all over his exposed penis. He growled almost, between clenched teeth. He spoke words that didn't make sense. Words about toothpaste and masturbating. "Touch it," he barked. He moved closer to me, causing me to feel trapped.

"No." I backed up and thought about opening a window to escape.

He held himself there and moved it around like a Water Wiggler. He told me about how he killed Blackie. "I kicked her against my mirrored wall, but I didn't mean it."

I burst into tears. "I hate your guts!" I screamed. "Just get out of my room!" Angry and horrified, I felt knotted from the inside out. I lunged forward and pushed the door against him and locked him out. He didn't resist. I left my room through my bedroom window and ran. I ended up walking through the woods near the house, just crying my eyes out. When I did come home, I could hear strange whispers coming from his room. Sometimes, he slammed things around or turned music up loud.

I started to wonder if he did something to my cats. Ted had gone missing when we lived out at Willoughby, and Tiny had been missing for about a month now. Now my Blackie was gone. He killed her and I would never forgive him.

~ * ~

I often wondered what the neighbors thought about our family. Did the neighbors in the duplex next door know how crazy everything was? From their apartment, occasionally, I heard what sounded like a chair being pushed under a table. I wondered what they heard from us.

I did find out what Mark's mom from across the street thought. Mark was a little younger than I, but we would talk or skateboard. His mom always came out to sit on their porch. I figured she just wanted to know what the two of us were always talking about. She came to the edge of their fence to say something one evening. I thought she wanted to talk with Mark, but her question was for me. She subtly smirked through purple-tinted lips and swirled the red wine she was drinking.

"So, do you think you'll end up a whore, like your mother?" She giggled and twirled the stem of the wine glass between her fingers. "Ya'll shouldn't bring that to this street. Especially the blacks."

I should have ignored her, but I was already feeling pissed off about a lot of things.

"No," I replied. "But I may end up being a bitch, like you." I instantly regretted saying it. For one thing, it was disrespectful. Second, Marge seemed to admire the term, 'bitch'. I picked up my skateboard, jumped on it and rode back across the street. I remembered all the lectures from Marge about being a woman, not a lady. A woman is a bitch. All the Gloria Steinem meetings with NOW and the ERA really affected Marge and she always took it to the extreme. I think she thought that acting like a bitch meant power and that she wasn't going to bow to any man. "That's MS. Beekman," she often said.

As for the whore comment, I wasn't so sure what to think. I knew Marge was with several different men, I could hear them and I hated it. The first time I heard it, I woke up thinking someone stabbed her and she was dying slowly. I wondered if I was a whore because of the things Scot did.

I never told Marge about what Mark's mom said. I thought she would go across the street and beat her up. Although that would ease it up for me if her angry feelings were taken out on someone else.

Lately, she just seemed so mad at me all the time. I spent too many nights staying out late, playing with the neighborhood kids, even Mark, and she didn't like it. In Michigan, I stayed out past dark all the time and all the kids in the neighborhood played for hours, but in Norfolk, it simply wasn't allowed. I often ran into our apartment to find her pacing and peeved.

"Julie, get your ass in here!" Her lips tightened and her stance seemed ready for combat. "Put your hands on the bar." She announced how many times she was going to hit me and how.

The bar was just a countertop that jutted out from was a place for mail or magazines.

"I was worried the main kitchen cabinets. She called it the bar, but usually it

about you! Do you know what that feels like?" She stood behind me, edging closer.

"No, I'm sorry I'm late," I said. I was going to cry, just knowing what was going to happen.

"I'm going to hit you the amount of times that I called for you and I'm going to use a belt." She walked to her closet as I stood with my hands on the bar. "Do you know how many times I called for you?" she asked like I would really know the answer.

"I'm sorry, I don't know." I gripped my fingers tighter on the Formica.

"I don't know." She mocked my voice. "Eight fucking times, Julianne! Eight fucking times. Now stay turned around and keep your hands on the bar."

The belt went across my butt and I tried to block the sting with my hands.

"Move your hands and keep them on the goddamn bar!" She knew I would try to block her again.

A few times, the sting of leather hit the backs of my thighs.

"Are you going to come when I call?"

"Yes," I cried

"Are you going to disobey me again?"

"No." Tears streamed down my face and the humiliation angered me so much I could only swallow it and keep it down.

When she stopped, she said, "Stop feeling sorry for yourself!"

She always said that and it made me dislike her even more.

Scot came sauntering out of his room, wearing only a pair of cut-offs, but more than I had seen in a while. "I'm moving out." He went into the kitchen and opened the refrigerator door.

Marge looked perplexed. "You know as well as I do that Julie needs to get punished for not listening."

"No, it's because I got a job in South Carolina with an electronics company."

My tears suddenly stopped.

"Scot, that's wonderful!" Marge smiled and walked over to hug him. "But what about our trip to see your brothers?"

"I can start the job once we get back." He had already handled that part.

Why can't he leave now? I thought.

Chapter Ten

The drive to Philadelphia from Norfolk was a neat trip. Instead of taking Interstate 95 from Richmond, Virginia all the way to Philadelphia, we cut out ninety-five miles by going on Route 13, which was more scenic and rural. From Norfolk, we took the Chesapeake Bay Bridge Tunnel, which is a twenty-mile toll road that crosses over the waters where the bay meets the Atlantic Ocean. The road includes various bridges and two one-mile-long tunnels.

I read every sign we passed and I loved the names of exits for towns along the Atlantic Seaboard. We travelled near Chincoteague and Assateague where the wild ponies were. As we drove, I gave up on trying to view ponies through the trees. It was a misty morning and I resolved to writing poems and songs in the back seat while Marge and Scot rode up front. Everyone was oddly quiet, even Marge. I was happy just to be going to see Danny and Randy.

Everything that morning changed when Scot started screaming. "Holy shit! Holy shit!" He pointed across the highway.

I looked up in time to see a car tumbling front over back several times before landing upright. Marge steered our car over the grass median to the south side of the highway and parked next to the field. She opened the door, got out, and yelled for Scot to drive to the nearest phone. "Right up the road, go!" she yelled.

I watched out the back window as we drove away from the scene. Marge ran toward the car that now had smoke coming from it. I turned and looked for dimes in Marge's purse. When we got to the gas station, it was closed. "Where is everyone?" I panicked. The phone booth was out at the street. Scot took the dimes and jumped out to phone the police. I watched him dial with trembling hands. I looked back a few times to see if I could see smoke from the accident, but everything was just too foggy.

When we got back to the scene, Scot got out and ran toward Marge. I stayed back a little, to witness the most amazing sight. Marge was pulling a very large man through the trunk of the wrecked vehicle. Fire enveloped the insides and the man was screaming. I was in awe of her strength as she pulled him through and then dragged him away from his car.

"Ma brotha!" The man winced. "Where ma brotha?"

We looked everywhere and it was as if we all saw him at the same time. He looked like a dark muddy heap in the distance. Scot stayed with the first man while I ran behind Marge to get to his brother. He was just as heavy, lying face down, and covered with mud. Marge gently brought his face toward her and cleared the debris from his mouth. "He's breathing!" she yelled.

His breathing was really hard like he had just been running, and I could hear a low moaning sound.

"Help is coming." Marge was crying now. "Just hang in there." She stayed, knelt beside him, while I stood motionless and shocked. His breathing became more labored as she continued to talk to him. "It's okay, sir, help is on the way." She looked back at the road. "Your brother is fine and you need to hang in there, okay?" She wiped more dirt away. "Where is the goddamn ambulance?" Marge cried out.

The man sounded like he had the hiccups. His breathing was slower now and blood flowed from his lips. I was terrified and prayed that the ambulance would come soon. There were more hiccup sounds and just as Marge kneeled closer to hold him, he stopping moving.

Marge was completely frenzied and tried to turn the man over. I tried to help, but I couldn't even move his leg. "The car is still burning!" I could barely see Scot and the other man because of all the smoke.

"Julie, get back to the road!" Marge screamed. "That car could blow up, get back to the road!"

I ran to the highway and saw the policeman who just arrived. "An ambulance is on the way!" he shouted to Scot and the injured man. He then darted toward Marge and the deceased. He couldn't move the man, either.

The paramedics finally arrived, along with a slew of firetrucks. A stretcher was brought out and placed next to the injured victim who was now leaning on an elbow. He rambled about what happened while the paramedics checked him out. "We was just go'n fish'n and the tire popped," he cried.

"Where were you coming from?" The officer asked.

"D.C." He sobbed. "We come down fish'n ever year." He looked at the smoke-filled field. "What about my brotha?"

The police answered with a question. "Sir, is there someone I can call?"

~ * ~

Scot and I sat silently as Marge drove. "Both of that man's legs are broken," she told us. "They think his brother may have gone through the windshield and the car probably didn't blow because there wasn't enough gas in it."

I imagined his large body flying through the air and thought it would have been better if he just died while flying.

Marge spoke incessantly about the crash, and although I was secretly proud of her for trying to save two lives, I wanted her to stop talking about it.

Marge talked the entire way. We got to Dan's and Randy's by early evening. I was so happy to be outside of the car and heading into their little row house on Taney Street. I couldn't wait to go with Dan to the little corner stores that were scattered throughout the neighborhood, and walk down to the Philadelphia Museum of Art.

Marge wanted to go out to dinner and she was still going on about the accident, so Dan grabbed me for a quick jaunt to the corner store before we had to leave. "Can we get those Tastycake cupcakes?" I asked. "Do you think someone will say the word, yo?"

"Sure and yes." Dan smiled and pushed his fingers through his thick brown hair. He looked a little cleaner than the Norfolk days. His pimples were gone and although he was still wearing torn jeans, he wasn't wearing T-shirts that had Nixon sitting on the toilet, smoking a cigarette, or his all-time favorite tee, that simply read, Bullshit.

We walked a few blocks away from Taney and straight into Terry's Hoagies. Five people were waiting in front of the counter. "Yeah, oil and mayo," I heard a man say.

Dan and I stood at the stand of Tastycakes. I laughed about the funny little names on the wax paper packaging. Krimpets and Tastyklair's both looked appetizing, but I was stuck on getting the cupcakes with buttercream and chocolate. I grabbed the snack and went to the store front. "Yo!" someone called out, "Customa at the regista!" I saw Dan smirk.

When we got outside, Dan opened the cupcakes and we both ate one on the way back to the house. We ate them fast so that Marge wouldn't get mad about us snacking before going out to eat.

We had dinner in a section of Philadelphia called Old City. The Liberty Bell, Dolly Madison's house, Ben Franklin's little post office, and Independence Hall are all located in Old City. The streets are all cobblestone so it feels like colonial times. I imagined Ben Franklin and George Washington walking the streets as horse-drawn carriages hustled by.

We sat at a large round table. Waitresses wore little white caps and funny dresses like pilgrims. Calico prints coated the tables and curtains.

Marge re-told the story of the accident and Randy talked about school. Dan was modest about his straight A status at Drexel. Marge practically had to pull the information out of him. Scot ate quickly and stared out the window. Occasionally, he mumbled something, but no one seemed to care. As the rest of us continued eating, Marge continued talking, but suddenly stopped and stared at her fork. She turned it over and inspected it. I slouched in my seat, certain that she was going to find something wrong and there would be a scene.

She leaned toward the center of the table. "Kids, this is real silver," she whispered. "Pocket it!"

I slouched further and bent forward. Oh no! I thought. We're going to be in so much trouble!

Scot thought the plan was really funny and Randy chuckled nervously as if to say, you can't be serious. But, she was.

Hesitantly, I took the spoon from my place setting and put it into my pants pocket. I looked around the room to see if anyone caught what I did. Only Marge was looking at me, with a pleased grin.

Scot took all of his silverware and, little by little, hid every piece. A fork went into his sock, a knife was tucked inside a jacket pocket. Randy continued to protest quietly with a sigh or a snort and folded arms. Dan just laughed. He laughed hard when Marge opened her purse and dumped in all of her silver, then added a small bread plate just to add to the fun. She took the salt and pepper shakers and the small sugar bowl from the center of the table and placed those in her bag as well. She looked to Dan for attention and laughed right along with him. It was rare to see him like that. He was usually so quiet and serious.

"Jesus," Randy said softly as the waitress came over to clear our table.

"I trust that you enjoyed your dinner?" the server stated as she gathered our dishes.

"Yes, thank you," I said.

Dan could not stop laughing. The waitress paused when she reached for Scot's plate and my heart started beating very fast. She knows, I thought.

When a male server approached the table and asked if we would care for coffee, Marge told him she did and that she would also like sugar. She doesn't take sugar! The waiter looked down at the table for the missing sugar bowl and looked slightly confused. "Yes, ma'am, I will have that right out for you."

After Marge finished her coffee, we managed to leave the restaurant without anyone knowing what we'd done. Scot's pocket clanked as we went out the door and I was somewhat surprised that no one reported us for stealing. I waited until we got down the block to present Marge with my spoon.

"That's it?" She stopped and glared at me. "A spoon?"

"Uh huh," I looked down at the cobblestone and studied the shapes.

"Jesus Christ, Julie! I can understand Randy and Dan not taking anything, they have to live here!" She strutted and ranted. "Whose kid are you anyway? Why are you such a little goody-two-shoes?"

I'm sure as heck not your kid, I thought. My biological parents would never do something like that, I was sure of it.

This was one of those moments with Marge where I felt like I was flying down a twisty hill on my skateboard. I had to stay fast, flexible, and prepared for objects to appear. She could start laughing and let it go or she could turn around and slap me.

Randy tried to stop the whole process. "Why are you being so hard on her?" He said it, careful that his tone was lighthearted. "If she doesn't want to steal, she shouldn't have to steal."

Marge stopped quickly and turned around.

Dan and I moved to the side and stared at anything but her. Scot just walked ahead, oblivious.

"Are you telling me how to raise my daughter?" Her lips tightened and her eyes bulged.

"No, I'm not," Randy said forcefully. "I just don't think it's appropriate to teach her to steal."

I loved that Randy was trying to help and protect me, but we all knew that he was making things worse.

"Well, who in the fuck asked you?" Marge looked him up and down.

"Geez," was all Randy could say.

With a big swing of her arm, Marge grabbed my wrist and started walking fast. "C'mon, Julie, your holier than thou brother can find his own way back!"

"I'm staying with Randy," Scot called out.

"Same." Dan followed.

"Fine. Then fuck you both, too!" She pulled me in the direction of the car.

"That's okay, we'll just walk!" Randy shouted.

I turned around to look at the boys. Randy shook his head and Dan waved to me.

When we got to the car, Marge decided it would be best if we found a hotel for the night. I believed she came to her senses a little, because normally, she would have been more dramatic and driven all the way back to Virginia. She always had a habit of driving off mad and coming back days later. She took off on us many times when we were little and we never knew if she was going to come back. "You kids are driving me nuts! If you don't knock it off, I'm going to leave!" and out the door she went.

Sometimes she returned days later with toys or games for us. No one ever said a word about where she was or why she actually left. A few times, I was dumb enough to say, "We aren't trying to drive you nuts, I swear."

"Yes, you are!" she responded. "You are trying to drive me crazy or you wouldn't do the things that make me so mad." She banged things around and spoke with a nasal mockery. "I ask you kids not to tease each other so much, and you do it. I ask you not to crunch on vegetables so loud, and you do it! Just take your fucking cereal and carrots outside, is that too much to ask?"

"No," I answered even though I thought she was unreasonable. "I'm sorry."

I just let my cereal soak in the milk to get soggy and cringed every time I heard the boys crunch on something.

Marge drove us into New Jersey that night. It's just over the bridge from downtown Philadelphia. I figured she was getting some strange satisfaction by simply being in another state than Randy. We hung out at a twenty-four-hour donut shop for a few hours instead of going to a hotel. We sat on stools and I listened as Marge went on and on about Randy and the boys and how disrespectful they were. "Not my Danny, though." She held her coffee gingerly. "Not my Danny. He's always been a good boy."

I quietly agreed.

Then Marge went on to discuss Richard and my dad. As I listened, I started to feel queasy. I leaned forward to grab the sides of my head and felt a small bump behind my ear.

"Something's wrong," I said as I felt the little lump.

Marge reached behind my ear. "Your lymph node is swollen, look at me." She grabbed my chin so that I faced her. "Oh shit, you're getting the chicken pox."

I quickly got up and ran to the bathroom to see if I looked like a chicken. I stared at my face and saw a few red dots on my forehead. Oh, God, I'm going to be fat and polka dotted. I threw up my donut and when I returned, Marge took me out to the car and set up a little bed for me in the back seat. She then went back to her stool in the donut shop and talked to anyone else who would listen. I watched her and hoped she would take us to a hotel soon.

I woke up the next morning still in the car, but in front of Randy's house. I sat up and looked for Marge, but she wasn't there. I looked in the rearview mirror and saw that my face was now completely covered with dots. I panicked and ran to Randy's door.

"Wow," Randy said as he opened the door. "Someone has chicken pox."

"I know, where's Mom?" I ran in to find her. She was sitting at Randy's little kitchen table. She looked tired. "I'm ugly and I itch all over!"

"Don't scratch them," Marge said. "You're going to have to wear my sunglasses today or you'll just get sicker." She asked me to sit down and she began pouring Calamine onto a cotton ball. "This will help."

I wore her large sunglasses to see all the historic sites and did my best to stand up straight, act like I felt fine, and not scratch. There I stood at the Liberty Bell, feeling like an Albino version of Stevie Wonder with cakey pink splotches all over my exposed skin. I'm sure people thought I was some freak.

I loved visiting Philadelphia, but I couldn't wait to get back to Virginia. I wanted to get back to my skateboard and my own bed, but mostly, I wanted to watch Scot move out. I didn't tell Randy or Dan that Scot killed Blackie. I didn't tell Marge either, and I wasn't so sure she didn't already know. I was afraid that Scot would lie about it or that somehow, I would get into trouble.

It was no different from being molested, really. The boys were Marge's biological blood and no one was going to believe me. Plus, I was feeling guilty. I now knew if I screamed at Scot or ran away, I could make him stop. If I had known, maybe I could have stopped him from touching me, years before.

We continued with the sight-seeing and I kept trying to figure out where there was space enough for Ben Franklin to fly a kite. My favorite parts of Philly were Old City and the Parkway. I liked looking at the Art Museum and the men walking around selling giant pretzels in paper bags. Marge managed to stay pleasant for the rest of the trip and that made conditions much better.

~ * ~

When we got back to Norfolk, Scot moved and I didn't help him or say a word to him. I didn't even say goodbye or good riddance. I was just so happy he would be so far away in South Carolina.

Marge continued to take her business trips to Roanoke and life went on, I just stayed home alone and I loved it. During the summer, Dan came to visit for a few weeks. We laughed a lot and went to the movies. The funniest part of the visit was one night while watching Saturday Night Live.

Like many white women in the late seventies, Marge went and got herself an afro-perm. Barbara Streisand, Janis Ian, and Grace Slick all had the perm. I thought it looked rather clownish. I kept expecting Marge to pull out a big red rubber nose.

While we watched SNL, Marge fell asleep, as she often did. I glanced at her a few times to make sure that she was truly asleep. I then went to my room and came out with a baggy full of the little colored rubber bands that Cynthia gave me. I then began to make little pigtails all through her afro. She stirred occasionally and swatted. Dan looked at me with both fear and admiration. I giggled uncontrollably and the pigmy-style outcome was so hilarious that it was worth whatever the outcome. By the time I was finished, Marge had over forty little fuzzy pigtails. I never laughed so hard at her expense. Just like when I screamed at Scot, I had a little control and maybe, for once, I was trying to drive her nuts.

Marge woke at some point to brush her teeth and get ready for bed. "What's so funny?" She asked on the way to the bathroom.

"Gilda Radner," I answered.

The shriek we heard was followed by laughter. She looked so ridiculous that even she couldn't get mad.

I learned then, that humor could get me everywhere.

Two Trees

~ * ~

It was no surprise when we left Norfolk in the middle of the night and in the middle of my seventh-grade school year. Marge packed what she could in the car, woke me up and informed me we were moving to Philadelphia. Again, we were leaving without saying goodbye to anyone.

"What about your job?" I asked.

"I'll get another job," she said, hurrying to the car.

"What about my school and my friends?" I wanted to cry.

"Julie, you always make friends wherever we go. Now hurry up." What was the rush? I gathered my clothes. What was going on?

Marge talked almost the entire way to Philadelphia and any time she started to get angry, I became a character from the Carol Burnett show. This way, she forgot why she was pissed.

I acted like the bag lady or the character Eunice. Sometimes I would make something up. It worked. Marge would just stop her chatter and laugh. It only worked in the car or when it was just the two of us. If someone else was around, she would say something like, "Knock it off, Julie," or "Now is not the time."

I wish I could have gone into character when we got to Randy's and Dan's. It only took an hour after arriving for her to get into a fight with Randy.

"Well, Julie, I guess we'll be living in the car until we find a place," she said loudly enough to make the boys feel bad.

"Don't drag Julie into this." Randy raised his arms. "At least let her stay."

"She stays with her mother!" Marge turned toward the door. "Let's go, Julie!"

I followed her out. I wondered what the next big plan was and if it involved a donut shop. We ended up driving around with Marge thinking out loud.

That night, Marge parked the car directly in front of Randy's and Dan's row house and that's where we slept. Although the car was a huge Plymouth, there wasn't much room because all of our belongings were in the back, mostly boxes of her paperwork. We both slept sitting upright in the front seat. Incredibly uncomfortable. Plus, I had a habit of twitching and kicking in my sleep, which aggravated Marge to no end.

"Lie still! Lie still, for Chrissake!"

I was miserable. I started thinking about running away.

I could walk back to Grand Haven or Virginia. Living on the streets would be better than sleeping in a car next to Marge. I hate my life. I hate her.

When did I start hating?

In the morning, I was allowed to take a shower inside the house. The boys' bathroom was filthy, but I was grateful, even if I had to smell like a mildewed towel. I sat in Dan's room for awhile and looked at his boring accounting books while Marge went to enroll me in school and take care of some other business. When she returned, I had to get back into the car with her. We drove through the neighborhood, past Terry's Hoagies where Dan and I got the Tastycakes, past Angelino's Pizza, and McNulty's Hardware. We stopped at Henneberry Pharmacy for Marge's Benson and Hedges and I waited outside the car on the sidewalk. I noticed kids playing a game with broomsticks and half a rubber ball. I figured they couldn't afford to replace their broken ball and they were just making the most of things.

We got back in the car and as Marge drove along, I noticed that almost every corner row house had been turned into some kind of business, a little grocery place, a dry cleaner, a lot of bars.

Marge stopped on Brown Street. "Okay, this is where you'll get the 48 bus to school." Marge pulled in front of a little cafe. "All along this street, you can catch the 48. The school gives you a few tokens for the week, but the other days, you'll have to walk." She turned onto the street again.

I was completely confused. "The 48 is a city bus?" I read the signs that included other numbers for buses. "Is my school downtown?"

"Yes, your school is in Center City." Marge made a right-hand turn and I could see the gold from the beautiful art museum in front of us. "Now to walk, you just head from the art museum down the parkway." She pointed ahead. "I recommend you walk your fat ass every day and get healthy." She started down the parkway toward City Hall. "I mean, really, Julie, with all the skateboarding and skating, there's no reason you should look like that." Marge pointed and waved her hand as if tracing the rolls on my belly.

I suddenly remembered my skateboard. I left it in the back shed in Norfolk, along with my lawnmower. No need for lawnmowers here. I sighed. *But* my beautiful skateboard.

"You're going to end up being one of those girls everyone feels sorry for." She clenched the steering wheel. "What a shame, 'she'd be pretty if she wasn't so fat'."

I tried to pull in my belly. I wanted to hide. But, I wanted to eat too. I was getting hungry.

"Now, your mom is a looker. Men find me very attractive." She admired herself in the side mirror. "I may be a bitch, but I can still get a man."

"It's good that your afro is growing out, too," I spurted. She shot me a look.

I thought about how she dressed up for work or went out on a date, she always looked nice and sometimes I was really proud of her. Once, she was on a radio show and I bragged about it.

At this moment, she was not attractive, she was just pissed off at someone or something. I wondered what happened in Norfolk that made her leave. I'd have thought by now, she would have told me with all the talking she was doing.

"Now, Julie, I worked very hard to get you into this school." She pulled the car into a small lot next to a high rise. "I didn't want any more trouble in the black schools, so I fought to get you in here."

I looked around as we exited the car and couldn't see any school.

"It's up there, on the top three floors of this building." She pointed. "It's called A.M.Y School." Marge spoke slowly like I wouldn't understand. "Alternative Middle Years. These kids are getting ready for careers in the Performing Arts."

I thought she might be lying, only because the idea of a performance school would make me so happy. I smiled, blocked the sun with my hand and looked all the way up the grey building.

Finally, something to be excited about.

"Okay, so now you know how to get here, you'll start tomorrow."

Immediately, I worried about what I would wear. If these were all show biz type kids, they would probably have trendy clothes.

I jumped into the back seat and started opening boxes to find a sweater or a decent shirt while Marge drove to the grocery store. By the time we pulled into the store parking lot, I picked out a maroon colored T-shirt to wear with my Levi cords, which were now worn so thin that I was ready to duct tape certain areas of the pants.

"Julie, why don't you go in and buy a few containers of yogurt and some fruit for us." She handed me a booklet of papers that read, Department of Agriculture Food Coupon.

"What about money?" I flipped through the booklet, some kind of anger stirring inside of me. "I buy everything with these?"

"Yes, they're food stamps." She raised her hands off the steering wheel. "Is there a problem?"

"No." I got out of the car and went in to buy the groceries. Why isn't she in here with the food stamps?

I grabbed a few containers of yogurt, a banana and an apple. I wanted a Tastycake, but she would never approve. I got in line and grabbed a pack of Benson and Hedges for Marge, she would be happy that I thought of her. I was embarrassed as I ripped the paper food coupons from the booklet and scurried out of the store hoping they wouldn't remember me.

~ * ~

A.M.Y. School was different from any school I ever attended. There were only about two-hundred kids and we called our teachers by their first names. Almost everyone left the high rise to go out to lunch every day. I walked around and sometimes some of the rich girls would offer to pay for my lunch if I came with them. They were funny girls and very self-assured, especially Sara, who was a dancer and very thin. "I kid you not, guys, this morning, I weighed myself before I pooped and then after." Everyone at the table laughed. "I took a three-pound shit! Like, who does that?" I never heard anything like some of the stuff they talked about. They talked about trips they took, getting into Julliard, what they did in Manhattan over the weekend. They seemed so mature and experienced.

I had classes like dance, where I felt completely out of place, Classical Greek, where everyone else felt out of place, and then regular classes, like English and Math. I didn't get into acting classes or singing or anything like that, because I enrolled too late in the school year. I did join the running club, even though I hated running. My English instructor, Tony, who was also the running coach, strongly suggested that I join.

At first, I ran in the clothing that I wore to school and I was always the last person in from our afternoon miles. Once it got warmer, I felt comfortable wearing shorts. Tony always waited patiently back at the school, with a smile and a high-five. Out of breath, I would reach to clasp his hand, grab my knapsack and walk home.

I loved taking longer routes home so I could explore downtown and see all the shops.

I sometimes walked past Wanamaker's department store, but never had the guts to go inside. Not until the day that I saw a large poster that read, Phil Donahue book signing today. I quickly entered the building through the heavy brass laden doors and took a deep breath. The scents of perfume and new things filled the air. I followed the shiny path of floor to the escalators where there was another poster about Mr. Donahue. Phil Donahue is here, in this very building! I had never seen a celebrity before, except at concerts. I took the escalators to the third floor where a line formed. Ladies with pretty dresses stood chattering away with copies of his book. I walked around the line and stood directly to the side of him. Phil Donahue was talking to each woman and signing every copy. I had no money for the book.

I watched from the side and I was in awe. There was a glow around him and I wondered if all famous people had a glow. The more he shone, the more self-conscious I became. I felt like dirt. I lived in a car. My pants were torn and I was wearing one of Dan's T-shirts that was far too big. I didn't belong there, but he smiled at me a few times anyway and I felt special.

I didn't tell anyone about seeing Phil or the time that I saw Elizabeth Taylor arrive at the Westin Hotel. There were a hundred photographers around her, so I could only catch a glimpse of her brightness and beauty. I wasn't supposed to be seeing these things and the fact I was starting to know Philadelphia like the back of my hand could cause me to get the back of Marge's hand. I walked back to the boys' house where the car was parked.

Sleeping in the car and buying groceries with food stamps became our lives for four months.

Sometimes, Marge parked the car right in front of the school building and other times, she parked on Randy's Street, as close to his front door as possible. Randy often came to the car to ask if I could at least come and stay in the warm house. The answer was always, "No. She stays with her mother!"

I could sometimes take my showers there, but I couldn't sleep there. It never made sense. Luckily, the school had a few showers.

Kids were beginning to talk at school and the police were familiar with the car. They would knock on the window with a baton and tell us to "Move on."

When Marge parked at the boys' Taney Street address, I walked to school and always took the parkway so I could visit St Paul's Cathedral and say a prayer. We weren't Catholic, but I knew it didn't matter. Marge took us to all types of churches. It was part of her cultural awareness idea. She always told us to decide for ourselves. I hadn't decided yet, but I knew St. Paul wouldn't mind me being there to pray.

Please God, get me out of this situation. Please give me normal in my life. Oh, and please make me skinny. Thank you, Amen.

There were homeless people all around the park benches at the church. Every time I left, I tried not to make eye contact, but there was one old man in particular that kind of stood out, he always stared at me, but luckily, he didn't try to converse.

One morning, I didn't feel like walking all the way downtown. There were only a few days left until summer break and I had gotten to know some of the neighbor kids that attended A.M.Y., so I headed to the bus stop where I knew they would be.

"Hey, do you have a match?" one boy asked.

"Maybe." I answered as I started looking through my bag. There were always matches around. Every time I bought Marge's cigarettes, the cashier would hand me a book of matches, sometimes, two.

"I do," I said. "I do have matches." I handed them to the excited eighth grader.

On the corner where we stood, there was a large blue USPS mailbox. The box had some bullet holes and scratches on it. The boy placed a firecracker onto one of the edges of a hole and lit it.

We all waited with anticipation. When the firecracker burned down to the wick, it didn't go off, but fell into the mailbox. I backed up, thinking the mailbox might explode.

Soon smoke started coming out of every crack and hole. All the kids were laughing nervously. One of the kids unzipped his pants and peed into a hole to stop the fire.

Where was the bus?

I glanced around and saw a lady looking out from her row home window. She didn't look happy and I wondered if she mailed something that morning. I imagined burnt envelopes with pee stains. Then, the bus finally arrived.

I was called into the principal's office later that morning. All the kids from the bus stop were there and, according to them, the mailbox incident was all my doing. After all, I had the match.

"But I didn't light it!" I protested.

"You live in a car with your mom!" One of them laughed.

"I didn't light it and I didn't pee in the hole of a mailbox." I looked at them in disbelief.

The principal asked us all to sit outside of his office while he made a few calls. I shook at the idea of such betrayal and what might come of the incident. I tuned out the teasing from the other kids. After waiting for what seemed like an hour, the principal called me in first. "You are suspended for three days." He looked at me sternly. "Do you realize this is a federal offense?"

I stood there in shock. I was getting the rap for the whole thing and those little twits were going to stick together with their story. I bet nothing would happen to them.

"There are only four days left of school," I said.

"That is true." The principal looked down and tapped on his desk calendar. "You can come to the last day. Until then, you need to think about what you've done. I called your father."

"My brother," I corrected him.

"Okay, your brother, someone is on their way and you will need to stop by the police department on your way home.

I took a deep breath as I was excused. Oh my God, I am in so much trouble.

After the boys from the bus got whatever sentencing they received, Marge walked in and simply thanked the principal. She didn't even seem mad.

Why isn't she mad?

"I gave them the match, but that's all." I followed her out.

"Well, Julie, you've got yourself a few days off, just look at it that way." She walked fast.

"We have to go to the police." I cringed.

"I know," she said. "They called, too."

"Where is the car?" I looked around.

"We're walking," she answered.

We hastily made our way to the police department where we were directed to a window. Marge signed a slip of paper and was given a copy. I guessed it was a warning or a ticket. I followed her out of the station and dreaded having to spend the day with her on her job hunts or whatever she did while I was at school. I wondered if she was scarily calm because she was going to take me somewhere to beat me or if I would get lectured all day. It all went through my mind as I tried to keep her pace.

Marge crossed the street and started toward Taney Street. She surprised me when she stepped into a corner bar. "We'll have two beers and a pizza," she called out to the bartender. Huh? She ordered me a beer?

I sipped the beer and hated it. Marge let me order a soda and she finished my beer. She discussed her job search and we never even talked about the incident again.

I attended the last day of school and explained myself to anyone who asked about my absence. The other kids that had been at the bus stop weren't there.

Chapter Eleven

Somehow, right in the beginning of that summer of 1980, Marge made up with Randy and we moved back into his house. She swore we would only be there for a few weeks, but it was more like two months. I was just happy we weren't in the stifling car anymore.

Summertime in Randy's and Dan's neighborhood was unlike anything I ever experienced. Men rode bikes with carts, selling Italian water ice that they would freshly scoop. "Yo, wudda ice!" they called out from the street corners. People sat on their stoops and talked all night. The sun beat down and stayed trapped all night with no sign of relief. There were no breezes as row homes blocked it out and left only the scents of hot brick, men's cologne and hoagie rolls.

Randy and I walked down a few blocks and put my name and registration fee in at the local youth recreation center so that I could try out for softball. I never played before, but I was glad he thought of the idea. I got picked for the team, The Bombers.

"I picked ya cause I like your name." My coach was a solid Italian woman, younger than Marge.

"You're gonna make a great catcher."

"Okay!" I had no idea of what that meant.

"Ya have a glove, doncha?"

"I will," I said

When we got back to the house, I said that I needed a glove loud enough for Marge to hear. We might have been using food stamps, but I saw Marge with cash, plenty of times. Randy shouldn't have to pay for a glove. I thought.

"Well," Randy said, "I want to take you to a Phillies game this week to get you excited about softball. Would you want to do that?"

"I'd really like that." I smiled and performed a small jump. "Do you think they'll be giving away gloves?"

My question came from a story that Marge told me about Bat Day at Tiger's Stadium. My dad took the boys to Detroit for a game when they were giving away bats. Apparently, they had gotten off to a late start and by the time they got to the stadium, they were out of bats. She said the boys sulked the entire time and, on the way home, my dad pulled the car over and spanked them for being so bratty about the bats. I figured she was lying because my dad would never do such a thing.

"No, I don't think so, but I'm sure we can shop for a glove in the next few days." Randy scrapped the top of my head.

I loved the baseball game. We were very high up and I couldn't believe how huge the stadium was and how bright the lights were, like a giant stage.

I decided almost immediately that Pete Rose was my favorite player. Randy told me he could play any position, not just first base.

A few days later, when both Randy and Marge took me shopping for a glove, I picked a Pete Rose glove. It fit snugly on my left hand. I was ready for The Bombers.

As it turned out, I really was ready. I loved getting dressed at each inning with all of my equipment. I wore shin guards, a chest guard, a helmet with a cage, and my Pete Rose glove. I was ready for other teams and I could throw. Just like riding my skateboard or slowly jogging behind Tony's running club, I felt good about myself.

Only once did I see Marge at my softball games. She was sitting in the stands that were meant for the other team and she wasn't even paying attention. She was talking to some man and they were drinking beer. I had to look a few times before I realized that she was talking to and drinking with the homeless man that always stared at me at St. Paul's.

Other than that, no one from my family came to my games, not even Randy. They didn't see my team win in the playoffs and there was no one I recognized in the stands, except the neighbor lady, Susan.

I first noticed Susan during musical rehearsals. The neighbor girls, Rachel, Amy and I, had been rehearsing a musical that we were going to perform in the street. Since everyone sat outside every night, we figured we could try to entertain the crowds. Plus, the girls were younger than I and thought I was a professional since I attended A.M.Y. They went to private schools where they must not have been allowed to express their creative sides.

Rehearsals began every morning when women came out to wash their sidewalks with large soapy push brooms and hoses.

Susan wasn't scrubbing her sidewalk that morning, she was sewing. Sewing and smiling. Her skin and eyes were dark, but her hair was so blonde that it was almost white. She wore a sundress that was bright and bold with color.

"Who is that lady?" I asked Amy who lived directly across from her.

"I think her name is Susan." Amy was wiggling and anxious to start her dance. "I know she's from Greece."

Right then, everything in my world came to a halt. I gasped. My whole body went to mush and I turned to look again at Susan, who was still smiling and now looking back at me. I saw a halo of sunshine yellow over her and music played.

"She's from Greece?" I turned again to my cast mates.

"Yeah." Amy twirled and then looked up at me. "Can we go rehearse Annie at Rachel's?"

"I need to meet Susan." I looked back to where Susan had been sewing, and she was gone.

"Why?" Amy wrinkled her face.

"Because my adoption papers say that I'm Greek. My mom always talks about how my real dad is from Greece and my real mother is Belgian mixed with something."

"So, you're just like Annie!" Amy walked toward Rachel's.

"I wouldn't say that, no." I sighed. "Wow, I've never met anyone from Greece. I've seen pictures of Mykonos and stuff, like white churches against blue sky and even bluer water." I had to meet her and ask her a billion questions.

Amy, Rachel, and I learned every line from the Annie album. We each took turns singing and while looking out the large back window of Amy's house, I saw an old woman dressed in black, slowly walking along the edge of the garden. I was in awe of her long garments and the fact that she was wearing a sweater in the summer and a shawl on her head.

"That's my grandmother from the Ukraine." Rachel turned the record over as she spotted me staring. "I guarantee she's headed out to take a piss."

"What do you mean?" I laughed.

"Every day, she's gotta go out back and pee in the garden. It drives my mom nuts!"

Sure enough, as we all watched the woman stop, she lifted all of her black skirting, spread her legs and created a puddle in the dirt.

~ * ~

Philadelphia was amazing.

The next day, I begged Amy and Rachel to rehearse near Susan's. It wasn't because I didn't want to see the old woman pee, but I wanted to be outside in the sun and hopefully meet Susan.

She came out in the afternoon to sew. "Allo," she said.

"Hi." I blushed.

"Waz your name?" She gestured with her finger for me to come to her. "I not see you before."

I swallowed hard and found my voice. "It's Julie and I'm Greek," I answered.

"You are?" She seemed very happy to hear it. "Waz your name?"

"It's Julie," I repeated.

"No, no. Your last name." She smiled.

"Oh, my last name isn't Greek." I struggled for a minute. "I was adopted and raised by a Dutch and an Indian."

Susan looked confused.

"My father came from Greece, but he didn't raise me," I said as I watched her sparkly brown eyes. Then Susan's phone rang and she sprang to her feet.

"You come see me again, okay?" She tugged at my chin as if I had a beard.

"Okay," I said softly. I was disappointed because I didn't want to leave her steps so soon. I had so many questions and I wondered if she meant what she said. You come see me again, okay?

I backed away from Susan's house and looked at the beautiful detail of white lace curtains behind red brick. Hers was the only row house on Taney Street to have large awnings and full flower pots hanging from each window.

The morning after meeting Susan, I made sure to look my best. I neatly combed and pulled my long brown hair into a ponytail. I wore my best T-shirt, shorts, and tennis shoes. I wanted to talk with her again and I felt I had a better chance if I didn't look like some dingy tomboy.

I saw Susan when I walked out the front door and looked up the street. I went quickly to her.

"Allo, Julie." She smiled big and patted the step next to her.

"Hello." I sat down. "You're sewing again."

"This is what I do." She tore material and looked at me with twinkly eyes. "I make clothes and I sew clothes for people."

Susan's hands were thick and strong. They were working hands, like they could wring ten towels dry with one twist. Yet, they were feminine and soft with painted nails and tanned skin.

"So what you know about Greece?" Susan asked, "You been?"

"No, I haven't." That was laughable. "I've been all over this country, but not to Greece. Not yet."

"You like Greek food?" She searched my eyes like it was the most important question of all.

"I don't know," I answered. "I don't think I've had Greek food."

"I make for you." Susan gathered the cloth and spool of thread that she had on her lap. She placed the needle between her teeth. "You come for lunch later, huh?" She managed to keep the needle wedged between her lips as she lifted herself and the cloth.

I stood and promised I would be back for lunch.

"Okay, one o'clock." She waved and went back inside her house.

I skipped away with intense happiness and interrupted the rehearsal many times to ask about the time.

When I returned at one, I knocked at Susan's door and she yelled from somewhere within. "Come in, Julie!"

I opened the door to a palace of white furniture covered in plastic, like pillow sausages. The color gold accented large mirrors and glass tables. There were fresh yellow flowers and a clear mat that led to the kitchen.

"You come sit down, huh?" she called out.

I entered her kitchen and sat at a round glass table with pale yellow placemats and sunflower napkins. There was a plate of olives and crusty bread. Susan stood near the sink, draining what appeared to be a block of wet chalk. She put the block on a small plate, broke it into many pieces and placed it next to the bread and olives.

"You like feta?" She waited like she knew she would have to explain.

"I'm not sure." I laughed nervously.

"Okay, you try." She pushed an empty plate and spoon toward me. She then broke off a hunk of bread and put it on my plate with the feta and a few olives. I gingerly tore the bread then stabbed at an olive with my fork. I tried smearing the feta, but it stayed crumbly.

I loved all new tastes. The bread was slightly sweet and relieved what could have been a salt mine in my mouth. At first, the feta was salty and hard. The bread made the cheese creamy and smooth.

Susan never sat down with me, but she talked with me the whole time. She told me about her ex-husband and her son. They were both named Tommy Fisher.

"My ex-husband? He a pain in the ass. My son?" She paused. "He a pain in the ass, too." She laughed.

When she reached for my plate, I could smell citrus and summer. "What perfume do you wear?" I wanted to someday smell like her.

"I just splash after shower." She started to leave the room. "I show you."

When she returned, she showed me a large bottle of Jean Nate and placed it on the table. I opened it and smelled beauty. I watched as she worked in her kitchen, which was warm with wood cabinets, cutting boards, and rich people's gadgets.

Susan opened the oven door and I could smell the heaven that I might devour. She pulled out a large glass pan that was topped with crispy brown paper-like sheets. "I make you spanikopita."

At first, I was a little scared to try the green insides.

"Spinach pie," she said. "You like?" She finally sat down and then cupped her chin in her hand.

"This is amazing," I said, "wow!" I couldn't believe how good spinach could taste. And there was that feta again, crumbled throughout. I savored every bite.

I offered to clean up, but Susan insisted that I didn't. It was getting late in the afternoon anyway, and Marge would be home soon from her job search. Plus, I had softball at six.

I left Susan's, believing that safety and home meant Jean Nate, feta and olives, and maybe even plastic covered furniture.

When I got back to Randy's, Marge was sitting on the front steps. "Where were you?" She was not happy.

"I was at Susan's house." I tried not to look scared which probably meant that I looked scared.

"Well, who in the fuck is Susan?" Marge stood and glared at me.

"She's a Greek lady up the street." I really didn't think it was a problem, but I was already answering like I was in trouble, slow and deliberate. "She's really nice and she gave me Greek food."

"We have food here, Julie." Marge pointed at Randy's door.

"I know." Tuna or peanut butter, I thought.

Randy and a pretty girl walked up to us just in time to halt the escalation, but Marge still managed a look of anger and a clenched fist.

"Hi!" I grinned.

"Hello." Randy looked in love. "This is Regina. Regina, this is my mother, Marge, and my sister, Julie."

"Well, hello, Regina!" Marge was someone else suddenly. She was the caretaker, homemaker, the lovely woman who truly loves life and embraces all who exists. Yuck, it's Betty Crocker gone bad. "It's so nice to meet you, Regina."

I just stood there like a dope with my hands in my back shorts pockets. I was thinking about Susan and my softball game.

"Hallo." Regina spoke with a thick accent.

"Regina's from Brazil," Randy announced proudly.

"Wonderful!" Marge exclaimed. "Let's go inside, shall we?"

I was embarrassed by the house. I wouldn't have invited anyone in. It's one thing to have a messy place when two boys share a house, but when their sister and mother live there too, there is no excuse.

Randy brought a glass of water to Regina in a Flinstone's jelly jar. All of their dishes were containers from a food product. It was like a prize. If they bought cottage cheese, they won a new cereal bowl; a jar of mayonnaise meant a new beer mug.

Regina seemed perfectly happy with her jelly jar and we all got to know each other in a fake sort of way.

Chapter Twelve

I continued to sneak to Susan's during that summer. She introduced me to many of her friends. The Greeks who lived in the neighborhood were all very close and they often ate together. I loved when the dry cleaner, John, and his wife had picnics in the back yard of their row house. They usually hosted gatherings on Sundays when their store was closed. John and Elani decorated a large outside table with flowers and colorful things to eat. Elani took pride in telling me about the food. "Dolmades are made with beef, rice, lemon, and mint." She presented a plate. "Then, all is wrapped in grape leaves." She explained that tzatziki is a yogurt sauce that could be eaten with souflaki, which are skewers of pork or lamb. I never tried the meat because Marge told us that pork had worms in it. Besides, I thought that any animal with such pretty eyelashes should never be eaten.

Instead of the meats, I dripped tzatziki on cucumbers and tomatoes. I tried the moussaka which was like eggplant lasagna. The pastitio was another lasagna type dish that had layers of big ziti noodles, ground lamb, cinnamon, and a white sauce. There were mini spanikopita in the form of triangles that were heaped on plates, as well as mini tyropita which were cheese pies. The desserts were another thing. Many were made with honey, walnuts, and phyllo, like baklava. But, then I was introduced to perhaps the best thing on earth, galaktoboureko, a custard dessert with a slight hint of lemon that was layered in crispy phyllo. Pure heaven.

For the most part, these gatherings might have been boring to other kids my age. I was so happy to listen to all the laughter and watch everyone. It was just a Sunday, but it was a celebration of life, family, and friends. I pretended that I was part of the family. It was safe and wonderful. The strangest part was that we were all having such a great time on the same block as Randy's house. It was just far enough away that we could not see Randy's back porch. Marge would never know.

I was learning so much from these hospitable people and they really seemed to enjoy teaching me. The best part of all, though, was when Susan's sister, Georgia Gianakkis, came to visit from Greece.

Georgia looked very much like Susan. Her skin was dark and her brown eyes sparkled, but her hair was red and wavy and much shorter than Susan's. Susan just stood out more and her hair reminded me of Loni Anderson's from the show, WKRP in Cincinnati.

The three of us often sat at the large round table in Susan's kitchen and ate lunch. Georgia cooked just as well as Susan and Eleni. I still played with the kids on the street because I needed for Marge to see it, Susan couldn't spend all her time with me, and I liked Rachel and Amy.

"Thees Avgolemono." Georgia smiled brightly, exposing two gold caps that lit up the sides of her mouth. I had no idea of what she said, but I tried to smile just as big. "You try." Georgia placed a bowl and spoon in front of me. I looked down at the soup and slowly sipped from the spoon.

"You no worry." Susan patted my head. "Es not lamb, es checken, lemon, and rize."

"She no like lamb?" Georgia looked disappointed and baffled.

Susan raised her hands to the side of her pale hair and shrugged, "She only half Greek."

In that kitchen, I wanted to be fully Greek. I wished one of them was my mother and the other, my aunt. I wanted to understand them when they spoke Greek in front of me and took turns looking at me and shaking their heads. I wondered if they felt sorry for me or something.

When we finished our soup, Georgia took a small pot with a narrow spout and placed it on the stove. She noticed me watching her. "Thees bree-kee," she said.

"The little pot es a briki." Susan helped me understand. "She make Greek coffee."

I watched as Georgia placed three little cups and saucers on the table. "They're so cute," I said.

Georgia took the briki off of the stove and slowly poured thick muddy coffee into three dainty cups. I thought about the only time I ever tasted coffee, at my dad's funeral; how the taste took away from the smell of cold carnations that filled the funeral home. A smell I couldn't shake.

This coffee looked very different from funeral coffee. Susan and Georgia watched as I sipped from the tiny chalice. It was strong and bitter, but I pretended to love it. We sat around the table while they talked and I tried to drink more of the mud. The longer I took to drink it, the thicker the coffee became.

Georgia held out her hand and asked for my cup. I was hoping she wasn't planning to give me more. The cup and saucer clanked as I extended my arm toward her. She didn't get up to refill the cup, but instead, she turned the cup upside down and placed it on the saucer in front of her. Georgia rested her elbows on the table and stared at the cup. "She gonna read your coffee," Susan explained.

"There's a message in my coffee?" I sat wide-eyed.

Georgia lifted the cup and placed it upright. She stared into the bottom and shared her findings with Susan. "Look," Georgia said as she tilted it toward Susan.

Susan stared into what now looked like dried clay. "Ees good," Susan shrugged as she tried to assure me.

"What does the cup say?" I wanted to hear the news. I leaned toward Georgia with a worried expression.

"You see the line?" Georgia pointed to a long thin line that traversed the muck of grounds and showed the white ceramic. "That ees travel." She waved her hand. "Go anywhere in life."

"Like Greece." I sat upright and smiled.

"Yes," Georgia grinned. "Thees?" She pointed at light brown waves on the sides of the cup. "You sad go away." She was very serious now.

"All you sadness go in time." Susan quickly picked up all the cups and placed them near the sink.

There was nothing I could say. I really was deeply sad, but I knew that it would go away as soon as I was old enough to escape.

I thanked them and hugged them both. I needed to walk and I would have to figure out where Marge might be. Susan mentioned she saw Marge a few times near St. Paul's over the past week. It didn't surprise me. I knew she was hanging out with the homeless guy and for all I knew, she was down there at that moment, preaching to everyone, or worse, she might be looking for me.

Marge was not only looking for me, she was standing a few doors down from Susan's, talking with a neighbor. She looked up just in time to see me walk out of the house.

"There you are! Get your ass down to Randy's!" She marched toward me while pointing back at my brother's place. I walked slowly across the street and cringed as she stomped up to Susan's door. "Uh, hello!" she called into the screen door and looked back at me.

I decided I wasn't budging. I was going to stand where I was and protect Susan if I had to.

"I thought I told you to stay away from my daughter!" she yelled into what appeared to be an empty house, since neither Susan nor Georgia appeared. "She's my daughter, do you understand?" Marge waited a minute and then crossed the street, where I stood.

"Why did you tell her that?" I protested. "Why did you do that?"

Her wrist and forearm slammed against my left ear. I prayed Susan was still in the back kitchen and hadn't witnessed that. "Why do you disobey me?" She grabbed my arm and pulled me down the street. "I'll tell you what, little girl, we're moving out of here and you will never see that woman again."

When we reached the foyer of Randy's home, Marge shoved me into the second door. I reached for the handle and twisted the door free. As I stumbled into the living room, Marge reached for my hair and pulled me to the floor in front of her. I started crying hard, which made her even angrier. I did everything to hide my tears from her every time this kind of thing happened, but it always failed. I wanted her to think I was strong and she couldn't hurt me, but it didn't work. I felt like worthless dirt.

"You will never see her again, do you understand me?" She looked down at me.

"Yes," I muttered. "I understand you." I got up cautiously and moved to Randy's sofa. I wondered where everyone was as I rested my tear-soaked face in my hands.

"You think she shits vanilla ice cream, don't you?" Marge started babbling. "You think she shits vanilla ice cream, but guess what, Julie. She shits like everyone else." She started pacing. "I don't know what to do with you. If I get this job, we're moving to Montgomery County."

"Where is that?" I thought I might cry harder. I rubbed my hair and sniffled, thinking my life was ending.

"It's about an hour north of here. A good school for eighth grade, out of this city and away from her!" Marge pointed in the direction of Susan's. "For now, you don't leave this house unless one of us is with you. If you even think about going to her, I will lock you upstairs, I kid you not!" She continued to pace and go on about how Susan was probably brainwashing me, how I was her daughter and people should just stop interfering with our relationship and how she was raising me.

The next afternoon, Marge came out of the kitchen after having been on the phone. "It's time to celebrate I got the job!" She slapped her hand against her thigh. "Not exactly the pay I was looking for, but we're getting out of here"

I was heartbroken. "When are we going?" My mouth hung open. "Do we have a place to stay?"

"We're looking at an apartment this afternoon." She started shifting papers in her powder blue briefcase. "If all goes well, we move in August first."

"That's next week!" I couldn't believe it.

As we drove to see the apartment, I memorized the route, so that if I got a bicycle, I could come see Susan. We drove through North Philly and into the suburbs. There were shopping centers and pretty houses that weren't attached to each other.

The apartment was in a complex with about forty other units. Ours was a two bedroom and it was on the second level with a full view of the backyard of Wetzel and White Funeral Home.

"You can go ahead and move in tomorrow if you'd like." The rental lady spoke softly and smiled.

"Wonderful!" Marge grinned. "Isn't it, Julie?"

"Mmm-hmm." I looked away from her.

As we drove back to Randy's to get our things together for the move, Marge told me about a volunteer position I would be taking for the month of August. "Do you remember how you helped me with the rape crises center?" Marge looked around as she drove. "Well, I met a woman who runs the Associated Services for the Blind in Center City, and she has work for you while I get settled into my job up here."

"Are you working with the blind?" I asked.

"No, I'll be working with mentally handicapped adults in a group setting," she said. "Sometimes, we'll be staying there."

"We'll be staying where?" I stared at her. "You work where they live?" I immediately thought of One Flew Over The Cuckoo's Nest and I shivered. Then I laughed inside, thinking about Marge as Nurse Ratchet.

"There are three mentally disabled women and they live in an apartment," she continued. "We will need to stay there about three or four nights a week."

I wanted to say, why are we getting an apartment then? Why can't we stay at Randy's on the off nights? Instead, I risked asking, "Do we really have to live there?"

"Look, Julie, this is the job I got and you should be damn grateful that you'll be in such a nice school! I don't want to hear another word about it." Marge pointed, "Look at all of these gorgeous buildings."

As we drove the rest of the way in silence, I decided to make the most of the situation and whenever I was to volunteer, I would try to see Susan. I thought about the performing arts school and how I wouldn't get to see those kids again or be in the running club. I was so used to changing schools, that I supposed it didn't matter.

~ * ~

I took the train in to Center City a few days a week to collate braille magazines. I felt free and grown up, riding a train all the way from Willow Grove into Philadelphia. I rushed like all the business people on the sidewalks and made my way to Walnut Street.

A huge wooden turnstile held a gazillion slots with many levels of thick Braille paper. On the first day, I was given orange thumb and forefinger rubbers to help me grasp the paper as it slid past. There were many of us seated around the turnstile and it seemed that everyone else had been there for years. They quickly sorted each sheet, while it took me several tries to grab even one piece of paper. "At this rate, I'll have a whole magazine put together by the end of the week!" I tried to make conversation, but no one was humored. Everyone was much older and they barely talked. I may as well be working for a deaf agency, I thought.

I told Marge I would work until five at the Blind Center, but I worked until three and then hurried down the parkway to see Susan. I made sure to come around the opposite block so that Dan or Randy wouldn't see me.

"Julie!" Susan hugged me when she opened the door. She glanced up and down the street as she let me in. "Oh my God!" She grabbed my shoulders, "What did that beech do to you?"

"Susan, I'm fine." I took a deep breath. "I'm used to it." I walked with her into the kitchen. "I don't know how often I can see you, because we've moved so far away."

"Es okay." She caressed my hair. "I tell Georgia you try to see her before she go back to Greece."

"If I don't see her, tell her thank you for everything and I love her." I stared at Susan, hoping she knew I loved her, too.

"I wish you could live with me." Susan looked sad. "I don't have rights."

"I wish that, too." I quickly hugged her. "I have to go catch the train, but I'm glad I got to see you for a minute and I'll come again as soon as I can."

I cried as I ran back to Center City and the train station. I knew it would probably be a long time before we were together again, since school would start soon. I couldn't risk leaving my job early all the time and I didn't want to bother Susan with trying to meet me.

As I rode the train, I wavered between sadness and pure anger. None of what was happening made sense. Susan and her friends made me happy. Learning about my culture made me happy. I remembered how often Marge would say, "When you turn eighteen, you and I will go to Greece together and find your family." I always smiled politely, but knew that she was the last person I would take with me to Greece.

As the train approached the Willow Grove station, I saw Marge's car parked in the lot. I was surprised, because she said I would need to walk home every day. I quickly changed my thoughts and turned on a better attitude. "Thanks for the ride." I sat close to the door as we pulled out of the parking area.

"How was your volunteer job?" Marge asked.

"It was fine."

"Good. So, today you meet the residents I'll be working with."

Great, I thought. Can't wait.

"Betty, Grace and Kathie are excited to meet you." Marge lit a cigarette and rolled down her window.

"That's good." I stared ahead at the old stonework on the train station's exterior. It's not that I didn't want to meet the ladies. I had no problem with disabled or challenged people. I just didn't want to spend so much time there and sleep over and stuff.

We arrived at a two-story duplex and parked in the driveway, alongside another slightly beat-up vehicle. A short little woman was glaring at us from inside the door.

She opened the door slightly. "You're late!" She looked at us with her head cocked sideways. She rubbed her hands together briskly and talked loudly, but slowly. "Come in!" It was obvious she felt she was in charge.

As we walked in, a soft-spoken lady was standing with one of the other residents, helping her with a plate. "Now, Grace, that's no way to greet someone at the door." She spoke calmly as she tucked a napkin into the woman's shirt. Grace followed us in and stomped to her seat at the table.

Another woman yelled out, "I'm Betty!" Her tongue thrusted forward with a mouth full of what looked like potatoes or smashed banana.

"Hi," I waved.

"Carol, thanks for taking care of them while I went to pick up Julie." Marge placed her purse on a counter.

"Not a problem, Marge." Carol smiled and looked at me. "I'm going to get going, you ladies have a good night."

"Bye, Carol!" the women yelled in guttural unison.

Once Carol left, I felt a little more comfortable with the residents. "So, you're Kathie?" I asked a thin woman sitting at the table.

"Yaaaa-yeah." She snorted and watched me through dirty eyewear.

Her back was hunched and it looked like it hurt.

"Continue eating, ladies." Marge said, while handing me a plate of what looked like a school lunch. I looked long and hard at the plate. "It's what we have right now, Julie. Betty likes fish sticks and tater tots."

"It's fine." I quickly sat down next to Grace. I couldn't eat with the three women watching me. Betty sat at the end of the table and continuously mashed her food against the roof of her mouth and pushed her tongue forward for all to view.

Marge could see my curiosity. "Betty has Down Syndrome."

"Yaaaa-yeah." Kathie grunted.

"I don't," Grace moaned, "and I have my own room and my own TV, Betty don't." Grace rocked back and forth and then grabbed my hand to hold it. I liked it and I gave her hand a quick squeeze.

Marge's work shift was from four p.m. to eight a.m. and we stayed there three, sometimes four nights a week. We referred to the women as, 'the residents', 'the folks on Milton Avenue', or just 'the ladies'. Never did we use the terms disabled or retarded.

~ * ~

Every time Marge worked, it was the same routine. I met her at our apartment after volunteering and then we drove to Milton Avenue to spend the night with Betty, Kathie, and Grace.

I walked into the house, greeted everyone, and turned on the oven. The freezer was full of generic white boxes labeled with black lettering that read, FISH STICKS and TATER TOTS. I lined a sheet pan with foil and placed three fish sticks and a small serving of tater tots evenly on the pan. Same thing, every night for Betty. For Grace and Kathie, I popped in a pre-made pan of lasagna.

"Hey, Betty, what do you want for dinner tonight?" I found great humor in discussing options with her. "Do you want fish and taters?" I yelled down the hall.

I could hear Betty breathing through her nose as she got closer to the kitchen. "Um hav'n fid ticks!" she stammered.

"Oh, so you want sticks and tots?" I smiled at her.

"Fid ticks!" She laughed.

"So, you want tates and sticks?" I was relentless.

"Oh, for Christ's sake, Julie!" Marge interrupted my game. "Put the fucking food in the oven!"

I made faces at Marge from behind the kitchen wall and Betty snorted a laugh. "Fid ticks!" she yelled. We both giggled.

Even though Betty only liked those two items, I tried getting some fruits and veggies in there occasionally. I had the most success with anything bland in appearance and easy to smash. Bananas worked best, but even then, there were a few problems. Betty had two front teeth missing, so the thrusting caused bits of banana to fly all over the table. The other bad thing about bananas was that Kathie often stole them.

Kathie stole a lot of things. She took all the fruit in the house. She stole bread, small juice containers, soap, anything that would fit into her bottom dresser drawer. I never understood why she stashed the stuff in the same place every time.

"Kathie, did you take the shampoo from the bathroom?" Marge asked.

"Naaa." Kathie's voice shook as she adjusted her glasses with her long bony fingers.

Marge opened the bottom dresser drawer and there, under a few shirts, was the shampoo, along with some apples and a muffin.

"Well, Kathie, if you didn't take the shampoo, how did it get into your dresser?" Marge asked.

Kathie's arms flew into the air, "I dunno."

Betty sat on the edge of her twin bed on the opposite side of the room. She was dressed and ready to go to work at the factory. Her hair was combed neatly. "She a meth." Her chin came down with a big nod.

"Yes, Betty, she's a mess," Marge said. "Kathie, you need to get ready for work. Look at Betty, she's ready, Grace is ready, and Julie's ready for her first day of school."

"You need to get ready!" Grace shouted while standing next to me in the doorway. Grace loved to yell at Kathie and compete with Betty. "This is why I have a TV and Betty don't." Grace's brow furrowed.

"C'mon, Betty, what do you want for breakfast?"

Betty quickly stood to follow me. "Fid ticks." Betty grunted.

"How about eggs?" I laughed.

I started eighth grade at Upper Moreland Middle School with a great deal of anxiety at first. We were in the suburbs now. Not an all-black school, not a creative school, but the suburbs, which would include a lot of wealthy kids with nice clothing and even nicer parents.

I had to work with a wardrobe of one pair of off-white painter's pants, a few T-shirts, and a dirty old pair of Stan Smith tennis shoes. I just had to stay positive, bring out my humor, and remember we were now in a safe apartment, not living out of the car. I had my own room and Marge allowed me to buy Vidal Sassoon shampoo so my hair smelled like maraschino cherries.

~ * ~

I decided almost immediately to join the marching band at school. I played the clarinet for a few months in sixth grade, so I figured I could pick up where I left off. I knew that joining something would keep me after school which meant more time away from Marge. Joining would also mean that I would need to buy the uniform, which meant I would have another pair of pants.

"The instructions say that I'll need a white shirt, black pants, and black shoes," I pleaded my case with Marge.

"Julie, you don't even have an instrument!" Marge replied.

"For fifteen dollars, they'll rent me a clarinet for the season." I begged.

"Okay, I guess we better get to K-Mart before it closes." Marge got up from her chair.

"But everyone else is getting their uniforms at Santerian's." I panicked.

"Well, we can't afford the sanitarium." Marge grabbed her keys.

"No, San-tar-ian's. It's just a small department store and it even says here on the sheet that we should get our pants there." I pointed to the instruction page.

"We're going to K-Mart and that's that." Marge opened our apartment door to leave. I pouted when she wasn't looking and followed her out.

The next day, I showed up to practice with ill-fitting polyester pants. Mr. Holt, our band director, handed out white gloves and cummerbunds. I was so grateful for the cummerbund because it would cover my hideous elastic waistband. As we stood in formation, I could hear other kids talking. "Yeah, my mom took me to Santerian's last night to get my shirt and while we were there, we picked up some sweet Izod shirts and like five pair of jeans."

I wish, I thought. I wish I was skinny and had Izods and jeans and braces to close the huge gap in my teeth.

"Julie, C major scale? Are you paying attention?" Mr. Holt stood in front of me.

"Yes," I lied. "C Major." I wet my reed and started playing what I could remember while Mr. Holt moved to the next kid in line.

I laughed inside. Not only had my pants idea completely backfired, but I realized I had no clue of how to play the clarinet, and no idea of how I was going to keep faking my abilities to stay in the band.

My entire introduction to this school district felt like I was pulling a fast one. Every day, I tried to conceal my misery, but I started to act out at school. Usually, I was trying to make people laugh, but mostly I was just disruptive and obnoxious. I sometimes got sent to the guidance department so I could explain why I was out of line. It was usually about me talking during math class or clowning around in the hallways. It was never bad enough that the school would call Marge, I knew my limits.

~ * ~

At home, I never knew what Marge was going to be like and she had been acting even worse since we took a trip up to Harlem just before school started. She wanted to see Rudy, one of the ex-convicts that she helped 'rehabilitate' when we lived in Norfolk. I guess he was originally from New York, but somehow ended up in a Virginia prison.

Marge was excited to take me to Manhattan and she was happy to see Rudy again, even though I was quite sure that she was still hanging out with the homeless guy on her days off.

We took a Greyhound Bus to New York and walked around Times Square. It was wildly exciting. I loved all the lights and as we walked, I pretended I was being filmed for the opening credits for Saturday Night Live. We then took the subway to Harlem. Marge seemed to know exactly where we were going and I wondered if maybe she had been here before. We walked up to a tall brick building and Marge pressed on a buzzer. It was very humid out, so windows were open and I could hear conversations, music, and the noise from televisions. We heard a click and Marge pulled the door open. The inside was dimly lit and smelled faintly like the subway we just left, dirt and old pee. I followed her up wooden stairs a few floors and then down a long hallway that was far brighter. Marge knocked on a door and within a moment, Rudy appeared. He smiled wide as I stared at the large comb stuck in his afro. I wondered if he forgot it was there.

"Hey, girl! Let's talk. Maybe your daughter can hang out across the hall with some friends." Rudy came out into the hall, closing his door behind him. "They harmless, trust me." He laughed.

My heart was beating hard. I can't believe she's going to put me with total strangers while they 'talk'.

"Rudy, who are they?"

"Shhh." He put his finger to his lips. "They fags." He knocked at the door directly across from his.

The door suddenly flung open and a very large black woman or was it a black man? stood there in a colorful African looking robe. Rudy asked if they could babysit for a bit. "Of course! Hi, honey" She or he smiled at me. "C'mon in, girl."

I wanted to go in because this person was so interesting and friendly, but I didn't know what was going on. I turned to look at Marge. "Go ahead, Julie. I need to speak with Rudy about some things for a little while."

I looked into the apartment and saw another person, definitely a man, sitting in a rocking chair. "Come on in! We's just watching the tube."

"Okay."

I walked slowly into the room and heard Marge say, "I'll be right across the hall."

The female-looking person asked me to sit and immediately passed me the biggest bowl of M&M's I ever saw and just as colorful as his dress. "Want some?"

"Sure." I grabbed a few and passed the bowl back.

"Just call me Queen."

"Okay." I couldn't help but notice that his eyelashes were longer and thicker than mine. I couldn't stop staring. His nails were painted pink on fingers that were meant for hard work, thick and rugged. His friend just seemed like a regular guy and he was very interested in the show on TV.

I sat back and tried to take an interest in the program and watched for a while. Queen asked me some questions about Philly and I decided to tell her that I saw Phil Donahue once and Liz Taylor, too and how I really wanted to meet Barbra Streisand. "She a Queen, too!" Queen laughed.

I was thoroughly happy, talking with Queen, until I heard a loud thud. The two roommates looked at me and then each other as we heard muffled screams and more banging. I got up to go to the door. I couldn't tell if it was Marge, but if it was, I needed to get to her.

"Stay here for right now." Queen stood up. "Dwayne, go see what's happening' fore this girl have a stroke!" she snapped.

"Is that coming from Rudy's?" I glanced back at Queen, hoping she could tell me. "I'm scared, are you?"

"Girrrrl, I be hearin' all kind a shit up in here. Dwayne gonna see." We heard more yelling and then Dwayne pounding on Rudy's door across the hall. When he got no response, he ran back in.

"Somebody betta call the PO-leece!"

Queen hurried into her kitchen and dialed. I started to breathe heavily. "Where's my mom?"

"Don't worry, police on the way!" Queen stopped and looked into a mirror and fixed her hair, like any good woman before company arrives.

Marge burst through the door with blood on the front of her. "Julie" she cried. "Quick, let's get out of here!"

We rushed out of the building and walked quickly. I noticed that her clothes were torn. We didn't speak until we were a few blocks away. People stared at us as we passed.

"He raped me!" she screamed. "The fucker raped me!"

At that moment, I felt cold and realized I might have to put on my best acting role ever, because I didn't feel sorry for her. Blood was on her lip, neck and chest, her shirt was torn, and I could not muster sympathy. I was angry. I was angry that she put us in situations like she did. We had no business being in Harlem and she just left me in an apartment with two total strangers who, thankfully, were nice people. I said nothing but, "Let's find a bathroom so you can get cleaned up."

As we rode the train back to Philly, she blabbed about all the situations she had been in where men took advantage of her. I wanted to forget about all the drama and Harlem. I wanted her to deal with it without me.

I sat in silence, looking out the window. I could see warm lighting coming from homes as we whizzed by.

Chapter Thirteen

Marge started spending time at the Willow Inn, which was a restaurant with a bar, not far from our apartment. She went there sometimes on her nights off. I imagined her sitting at the bar, talking to men about all the jerks she dated.

On some of the nights that she worked at the residents', she would get the ear and sympathy of a coworker, which always worked out for me because then I didn't have to hear it. However, it did mean I had to babysit and entertain six mentally disabled people at once. The duplex where the ladies lived was also a home for three men that lived upstairs. Michael, Gerald, and Ernie were also cared for by a counselor from Marge's company. I don't know where they went, but I found it odd that two people could collaborate on such a poor decision.

"Julie, you know how I had recommendation letters written for you from the places that you volunteered?" Marge acted sweet in front of her coworker. "Well, I promise I'll get you a letter from here too." She was leaving. "It will all look great on your resume!" she called back as she pulled the screen door shut.

"Can't wait," I muttered as I locked the door. Great, I thought. Now what? I had six pair of eyes staring at me. I exhaled the fly-aways off my face. "So, does everyone wanna have a dance party?" I half smiled.

"Yeah!" Everyone yelled and clapped. Kathie jumped up and started dancing without my having put any music on and Grace grumbled as she walked to her room. "I'm gunna watch TV, Betty don't got no TV."

Michael Jackson just released probably the best album I ever heard for dancing, Off The Wall. It was better than Saturday Night Fever that came out a few years before. I found this gem of a record at the residence and figured it was left there by another worker. I put the album on the record player and started to sing along, "Cause we're the party people night and day." Gerald and Kathie bounced up and down while Michael sat at the end of the sofa and picked his forehead. "Living crazy that's the only way." I sang louder. "Life ain't so bad at all...if you live it off the wall." Betty clapped and kissed Ernie every so often and Ernie laughed, maybe nervously. He also had Down Syndrome and was beyond sweet.

After all the dancing, I made sure that Betty and Kathie got their showers and went to bed. The men were easily entertained by the living room television and I didn't know what else to do with them. Grace knew all the rules and was already sleeping by the time I got done with helping the other two. By the time I got Kathie into bed, Marge and her other coworker were back. As the men went upstairs, I kept a close eye on Kathie to try to figure out when she would start stealing. I never did catch her. She did give me quite the surprise when morning came. I heard Marge yell, "Oh God! What in the hell?"

I came running into Kathie's and Betty's room. Grace followed me and started yelling at Kathie. "Kaffie bedda clean that up! Kaffie bedda clean that up!"

I could not believe what I saw. Kathie was coated in excrement. She had it on her arms, her legs, the wall, but thankfully, not on Betty.

"Julie, go get a bath started for her." Marge's face showed disgust as she stood in disbelief.

I prayed I wouldn't have to carry her in there.

I did have to help her a little and Grace yelled at me. "You bedda clean ha up!" She pointed a finger at me.

"Yeah, I know, Grace. I'll clean her up."

On mornings like these, I was late for school and I hated that. I had Mr. Petrash for social studies first period and he always took roll call. I tried not to be late on Mondays because we started the class with 'Current Events'. This meant that each student clipped an article from the newspaper and gave a short summary of what they read. The hope was that all of us would understand what was going on in the world and it was interesting to see what each student thought was important.

Luckily, I could always find remnants of the Sunday paper either at the residence or in the laundry room of our apartment building. "Mr. Petrash?" I raised my hand high. "I have something about Graterford Prison from this weekend."

Mr. Petrash leaned on the edge of his desk and folded his arms. "Okay, let's hear it."

"Okay, so the head of corrections just asked for a ten percent hike over their budget because, just to house the average inmate, it costs about ninety-three dollars a night." I squirmed in my seat a little and thought for a second that they should have kept Rudy in prison, no matter what the cost.

"Wow, ninety-three dollars a night. Does that include food and clothing?" He pulled at the corner of his mustache while quizzing me.

"Uh-huh." I looked down at the article. "And that's about the same price as a really nice hotel room."

Jerry, the cute boy that sat next to me, raised his hand next. Mr. Petrash reached for his assignment sheet to mark off our names.

"Yeah, so I want to talk about the game last night against the Cubs." Jerry was very serious with his sports.

Mr. Petrash wasn't looking at Jerry. He was looking toward the door. He put his hand up in a gentle manner to signal Jerry that he should wait.

We all turned to see a tall black man and a young blonde woman entering the room.

"Okay, everyone." Mr. Petrash moved away from his desk. "These folks are here from...well, they'll tell you."

"Hello, everyone." The woman smiled. "My name is Emily and this is Vernon." She gestured to the man as they both approached the front of the class. "We're here from Aldersgate Youth Service Bureau and we just wanted to introduce ourselves." She looked around the room. "Vernon and I are going to be here at your school every week."

Vernon stepped forward. "Basically, if you have stuff going on here at school or you have some problems at home and you want to talk about it, you can come and talk to us." Vernon pressed his fingers together as he spoke. He was missing a basketball. "I'll be hanging out in the office in the library on Tuesdays."

"Yes, and I'll be in the library on Fridays." Emily spoke up. "Anything you need to talk about will be kept confidential. Just consider that office a safe haven."

Emily had such a gentle manner about her. She was kind and she was pretty, with big fluttery eyelashes. I knew then that I would find that library office on Friday so that somehow I could meet with her. I kept it to myself and continued thinking about it when they left the class even though everyone else seemed to blow it off. I had to talk with someone, but I couldn't exactly tell this lady that I cleaned shit off of someone's arms that morning or that Marge was crazy or that my entire life was a bizarre embarrassment.

~ * ~

I was really nervous when I entered the library that first day. I got an excuse note from Mrs. Roth, the math teacher. I knew she would understand, especially since I told her I needed to see the counselor to find out why I was doing so poorly in math. I hesitantly entered the library. I worried that if people knew I was going to see Emily, they would think I was mentally ill. There was already speculation. A few of the boys at school called me 'spaz' and 'tard'.

After a few minutes of surveying the check-out area, I went directly to the librarian. I approached the desk and spoke quietly. "Hi. Do you know where I would go to see Emily?" I looked around.

"Oh, you mean the counselor from Aldersgate?" She didn't make eye contact. Instead she stared at my forehead like she was trying to figure out my diagnoses. Maybe I had a zit. "Well, she's in the office to the right," she pointed behind me, "but you're going to have to sign in on the clipboard." She pointed down and tapped.

"My entire name?"

"No, you can just put down your first name," she said.

I looked down and there weren't any names on the clipboard. All the slots were empty. I figured it must mean no one in the suburbs had any problems. I picked up the pen slowly. As I did, the librarian quietly called out, "Excuse me, Miss Emily?" I turned to see Emily walking toward her office with a mug in her hand.

"Yes?" Emily headed toward us.

"This student would like to meet with you." The librarian now seemed to be focusing on Emily's forehead.

"Sure." Emily smiled warmly. "Follow me. What's your name?" She held the door for me as we walked into her office.

"It's Julie." I looked back. "You don't need your clipboard?"

"No." She grinned "I don't need the clipboard. So far, you're it." Her room didn't look at all like the library. The lights were dim and it seemed comfortable with two big, soft chairs. "It's my first day here, so no appointment times are really needed." She pointed to a chair that faced away from the door. "Have a seat. Is it okay if I shut the door?"

"Yes, it's fine." I sat on my hands and swung my feet out to stare at them. I noticed how dirty my sneakers were and quickly tucked them back under the chair.

"So, Julie, what brings you here?" Emily sat across from me and placed her mug on a small side table. "What do you want to talk about?"

"Well," I hesitated. "I'm having trouble in math."

"Oh," She chuckled. "I'm horrible at math."

"There's other stuff." I felt silly and awkward because she was so pretty and patient. I had no idea where to begin. "Your office is nice," I said.

"Thank you. I think it will be better when we get some pictures in here." She picked up her mug and looked at the walls. "So, do you think you might need a math tutor?" Emily asked.

"Maybe." I looked up and half smiled at her.

"Julie?" Emily moved toward me, putting her elbows on her knees. She held her drink there and waited. "What's going on?"

"Well, just the usual. Sometimes I have a hard time with the kids here." I started looking for split ends on my ponytail.

"What happens with the kids?"

"Well, some of them make fun of me. I mean, I have friends and everything. I don't know."

"What else?" She sipped from her cup. "Just math and some teasing?"

"Pretty much."

"I bet you can handle those things," she said softly.

"I am trying." I scooted back in my chair and cleared my throat.

"You're sometimes formal when you speak." Emily put her cup back down. "Where are you from?"

I perked up. "Michigan, originally. And then all over. We were in Virginia for a while." I chewed on my bottom lip.

"This is why you have an accent!" She laughed. "You have an all-over-the-place accent!"

"I guess," I shrugged.

"How do you pronounce the fruit that has the same color as its name?"

"Or-inge" I looked for her approval.

"That's probably the right way." She smiled. "Around Philly, we say, Aw-range, and ta-may-tas, and win-das."

"No, it's toe-may-toes and win-doe-s." We laughed for a moment and then there was uncomfortable silence.

"Is your dad in the military?" Emily was a little more serious now.

"No, he passed away a long time ago."

"Oh, I'm so sorry." Emily frowned. "How did he die? If you don't mind my asking?"

"Leukemia," I said. "Well, non-Hodgkin's lymphoma, which is like leukemia."

"Oh." She continued to look at me. "How old were you?"

"Seven." I looked around for a clock. "Do you know what time it is?"

Emily looked down at her watch. "It's almost one-fifteen."

"Oh, I have to go." I quickly stood.

"Wait," Emily said. "Do you want to find a time for next week?" she asked without pushing. "Do you feel comfortable enough to talk some more?"

"Sure," I said. "I mean, yes." I didn't know what to do with my body as we stood there. I felt uneasy. I reached for the door handle and opened the door wide. "Should I put myself down on the clipboard?"

"Sure," Emily said as I walked away.

I got to the check-out area and scheduled myself for the same time for the next Friday. "Another day out of math class," I whispered. Now what was I going to do? I had fifteen minutes before next class. I should have just stayed with Emily and answered more questions.

I didn't tell Marge about Emily. I didn't tell anyone about Emily except for the guidance counselor, who gave me more excuse notes to get out of math.

~ * ~

The following Sunday, Marge and the upstairs coworker, Kenny, went out for an afternoon beer. I turned on the television and asked everyone to sit down and watch Hero at Large for the tenth time. The residence had cable, which had just become available. The problem was that the cable channels played the same movies over and over. Everyone seemed bored. Grace rocked back and forth while mumbling and Kathie stared at me. Betty sat with Ernie and talked about whatever those two usually talked about. Gerald continuously tapped his thumbs on all his fingers, making sure he hit each digit precisely. Michael was the only one who seemed remotely interested in the movie.

"Look, everyone!" I hoped they would focus. "This is the part where John Ritter gets the bad bank robber!"

"Yeah-ya!" Kathie yelled, still staring at me.

"Okay, Kathie, look at the television, not me." I pointed.

I could hear Betty and Ernie saying the same things again and again. "I like you." Betty held Ernie's hand.

"I lie you do!" Ernie shouted and then hugged her.

"Keep it down over there, you two. Stay in control," I teased.

"Yeah-ya," Kathie followed.

"I day in controw." Grace huffed. "Betty don't!"

I decided to watch Gerald for a while. I had to wonder if his thumbs were smooth from all the movement. As I looked around and really thought about it, I couldn't believe I was there. I wondered why I was stuck inside on a beautiful fall day with six people who had no idea of what was going on. I daydreamed about being outside somewhere with friends or hanging out on Taney Street with Susan. If she could see me now, I thought. It made my heart hurt. I was quickly brought back to the room when Michael yelled, "I want a snack!"

"Yeah-ya!" Kathie bellowed while Grace rocked faster and complained about Betty.

"Okay." I stood up. "How about popcorn?"

They cheered like I was a Rockstar as I headed to the kitchen. I found the jar of popcorn and proceeded to make some while the residents continued with the movie. I could hear them making various noises and grunts, but nothing out of the ordinary. So, it was strange to come back in and find Michael missing. "Where is Michael?" I set down the bowls of popcorn.

"He leff!" Ernie snorted.

"Yeah-ya, he leff." Kathie grabbed a whole bowl for herself.

"Left to go where?" Everyone looked at me blankly. "Did he go upstairs to use the bathroom?" No one answered me. I didn't know what to do. I couldn't leave everyone to go look for him.

"Everybody, we need to go upstairs for a minute."

"I ain't goin'!" said Grace.

I knew Grace would stay put. She hated leaving the house. "Okay, Grace, then you stay here. Everyone else, follow me, we're going on a field trip." I walked toward the door and everyone followed me, even Gerald who hadn't spoken a word all afternoon. "March!" I bellowed, and we all went upstairs through the men's apartment door. I called out and looked around. Michael wasn't there. "Everyone, we are going to march back downstairs!" Betty saluted. I laughed and saluted her even though my heart was beating a mile a minute and my worry increased. We didn't get to leave the men's apartment until Gerald finished some ritual of running down the hall to his room, running back, doing a somersault and turning in circles a few times. When we got back downstairs and outside, I yelled for Michael, Kathie whispered a yell for Michael, and Betty chimed in too. No Michael. I'm in deep shit.

When Marge and Kenny got back and came through the door, I slinked toward them. "Michael took off."

"What?" Marge had that look, like she was just going to lay me out flat.

"It's happened before." Kenny spoke calmly. "He'll come back."

"Why, Julie?" Marge stomped into the apartment further. "Why did he leave?"

"I don't know." I held back tears. "I went to make everyone a snack and when I came back, he was gone."

"You didn't hear the front door?" She had her hands on her hips.

"No, I didn't."

"I just don't understand, Julianne!" Her voice got louder. "I mean, goddamn, we weren't gone that long!"

Kenny backed up toward the door and I was happy about that. I wanted him to. Being in trouble in front of people was almost worse than getting hit. "Uh, Marge, I'm going to go upstairs and listen for the phone. Come on, gentlemen." Ernie and Gerald quickly followed. I guessed Kenny didn't want the guys seeing Marge overreact.

"Okay." Marge looked up quickly like she forgot that Kenny was there.

Marge now stood in front of me, her eyes narrowed. "How in the fuck could you let this happen?"

"I didn't hear him leave," I repeated. I stood motionless, though I felt panic.

"So, what, the residents' are supposed to watch him?"

"I'm sorry," was all I could muster.

"Sorry?" Marge raised her fist. "Poor Julie is so sorry. You're always sorry!" I immediately ducked behind my raised forearms to block her punch, and just as quickly regretted it. "What did you think, I was going to hit you?" she screamed louder and her fist opened and slammed against my cheek. "Now!" She backed up. "Now, I bet you're sorry!"

The side of my face felt like it was on fire. I looked to see if the women residents were still in the room. Kathie was watching me, what was new? Betty sat with her hands in her lap and bits of popcorn stuck on her chin. Grace started back to her room. "Jewey don't get no TV!"

"That's right, Grace," Marge responded while staring me down. "Julie is very bad."

"Yeah-ya." Kathie laughed nervously.

Just as I shot Kathie the evil eye, the phone rang. I was embarrassed, getting hit in front of the ladies but I also hoped they wouldn't fear it could happen to them.

Kenny called to let Marge know that Michael was safe. He walked to the Naval base and tried to cash a phone bill.

Marge laughed as she cracked open a beer. "Somehow, the stupid ass thought it was a check."

I stood there, not sure of what to do next. I thought about how great it was that it was Sunday. School tomorrow and only five days left until I see Emily. I touched my cheek, still warm from the slap, and quickly moved my hand through my hair in case Marge was watching me. A dining room chair seemed the only place I could take refuge, so I awkwardly rested my arms on the back of it.

Marge rifled through her purse and I was relieved when she found a Benson and Hedges and headed for the outdoors. Finally, I could move. I went to the bathroom and checked my face. It was slightly swollen and pink.

Betty came into the bathroom and quickly turned around when she saw me.

"Betty, I'm not staying, you can come in."

"Oday." She sidled up beside me at the mirror.

"Betty, I'm really sorry about my mom getting so angry. She wasn't mad at any of you, just me, okay?"

"Oday." Betty hugged me.

I grabbed my school books from the small bedroom that was meant for the counselor on duty. The room was plain with a twin bed, nightstand, and alarm clock. Sometimes, I slept in there, sometimes on the sofa, but always with my own pillow and a sheet on top. The rule was that the last person working would launder the sheets for the next counselor on duty. It was easier for me to just stay off the sheets. Plus, I thought it was creepy to share the bed and never felt sure that anything had been changed, like in a crappy motel room.

Marge was opening her second beer when I got to the dining room table. I pulled out a chair and opened my notebook. I searched for notes on what my homework assignments were. I couldn't concentrate. I looked into the living room and Kathie was sleeping while sitting up. The television was still on and Marge was opening some files at the other end of the table.

"Julie, aren't you going to make dinner for the ladies?" She didn't look up.

"Yes." I closed my books and didn't bother to ask Betty about her fish sticks. School tomorrow, school tomorrow. I counted on my fingers. Fourteen hours until I get away from her. Four and a half days until I see Emily.

~ * ~

I loved school. Most of the kids were nice and never said anything about my lack of clothing selection. I thought they had to notice because, every day, I noticed everything about them. Like, Janet Parks always wore her blonde hair neatly pinned in a ribbon barrette. Leslie Besecke carried a bright green Bermuda bag with a pink whale on it, and wore sweaters that looked warm with Fair-isle scoops that may have been imported from some Nordic place. Beth Kindt, by far the prettiest girl in school, had braces and applied Bonnie Bell lip gloss between each class. She had a Bermuda bag, too, and wore L.L. Bean Blucher moccasins that I saw in the catalogue or sometimes duck shoes with Jordache jeans. I admired her. Karen Bean always talked to me in class and she was one of those kids that didn't judge me. She was tall and thin and had great clothes. We must have looked like an odd couple when we hung out between classes. I think she liked my sense of humor and I felt I could confide in her someday.

I focused mainly on the social aspect of eighth grade and did my homework whenever I could slip it in. I mostly thought about Friday and Fridays took forever to come.

I got to the library and checked the clipboard to make sure that my name was still there. I waited near Emily's office where the door was closed. I pretended to be looking through the card catalogue when Emily opened the door and said goodbye to Jodi Foust. Great, I thought. Jodi is seeing Emily. Just great. Jodi wore coke bottle glasses, and constantly played air guitar. Her locker was near mine and she often walked over to me to 'play' a song. It was always a female artist she was trying to emulate, but she was tone deaf and lyrically challenged.

"Hey, have you heard the new Pat Benatar song?" She beelined for me when she saw me standing near Emily's door.

I backed up. "Nope," I lied. I tried to ignore her so I could get to Emily.

She looked at me, incredulous. "Well, it goes like this." She placed her left hand on the invisible neck of her guitar and strummed with the other hand. "Git me with your best shot!"

"It's 'hit me with your best shot,' not 'get or git'." I felt mean. Emily watched the whole interaction with a slight smirk on her face. I walked away from Jodi and into Emily's office. I didn't care that Jodi saw me. She probably wouldn't remember anyway.

"How are you, Julie?" Emily's smile warmed me.

"I'm fine." I nervously rubbed my palms on my thighs.

"Good." She exhaled loud through her nose like she was laughing inside and couldn't hold it any longer.

I smiled at her and glanced at her perfectly manicured nails and feminine hands. I then looked at my hands. My fingers looked like small sausages. I couldn't see my bones, only the remnants of fat dimpled starfish hands like those of a toddler. I tucked them under my legs.

"Julie?"

"Yes." I focused on Emily.

"Do you like to draw?" Emily brought a large tablet of paper forward from the side of her chair.

"Sure." I watched as she pulled out markers, crayons, and pens from rubber bands, and placed them in a basket.

"Here, take this tablet and then pick out whatever colors you like." She handed me the paper and placed the woven container of pens on the table between us.

"What should I use?"

"Whatever you want. It's your drawing." She sat forward with her fingers tucked under her chin.

"Well, what's it for?"

"Well, sometimes it's easy to find things to talk about just by having people draw."

I supposed it would help, so I carefully selected a few pencils. I had no idea of what to draw. I looked around the room and noticed that she placed some artwork on the walls, but nothing sparked me. I thought for a few minutes. A tree! I drew a long trunk and then separated it into branches. I drew all the branches thinner and darker at their edges and then I put the pencil down. I stared at my tree.

"No leaves?" Emily looked intently at my work.

"No."

"Where is this?" She pointed at my simplistic picture.

"It's along a roadway." I looked at the paper and then up at her. My tree was far to the right on the paper so there was plenty of room for a road and I drew it, along with a car and a little bunny near some grass. A fence, too. When I was finished, I glanced at Emily who was still paying close attention.

"That's a nice drawing. Where is this place?"

"Well, it's out west. It's a farm where I will live and there is lots of land." I quickly added a few mountain peaks in the background. "Colorado, near New Mexico. Sometimes in my mind, I just go to Four Corners and just stand there so I'm in four places at once."

Emily breathed out through her nose again and smiled. "What's happening with this little guy?" She pointed to the rabbit.

"It's bad." I frowned. "He got hit by the car." I suddenly felt like I was going to cry.

Emily looked like I felt. She took a deep breath. "That's horrible."

"I know," I said. "It's not fair."

"What's not fair?"

"He didn't do anything to anybody, he's just trying to live and be happy."

"He was just an innocent, loveable bunny, right?"

"Exactly."

"Tell me more about this place, where you're going to live." Emily looked at me now, not the picture.

"Oh, it's wonderful," I said. "There are trees everywhere that surround a huge valley and every morning, I hike with my dog. We go way up into the mountains." My fingers directed her to the points that I just drew.

"Does anyone else go with you?" Emily leaned back in her chair.

"No." I tilted my pencil to shade the mountains.

"What else do you do?"

"Well, I have book signings that I attend and I play tennis." I starting biting on my pinky nail, thinking about what I would make up next.

Emily grinned. "Are you the person doing the signing? Your books?"

Sometimes, but I like the works of others as well." I looked for a clock.

Emily took the cue and looked down at her watch. "We still have a few minutes. Julie, does your dad ever visit you at this place?"

"No. Remember? He passed away." I looked at her like she was crazy. I didn't speak for a few moments. "Sometimes I feel him though." My bottom lip started to quiver. My stomach was heavy and my cheeks felt an intense pressure. I was afraid that my eyes would burst with welled-up sadness. I couldn't talk.

"You miss him."

"Yeah, he was a good guy." I desperately tried to be stoic.

"What about your mom?" Emily watched me.

"I don't know." I shrugged and looked around the room. "I was adopted."

"Oh." Emily looked baffled. "When were you adopted?" She looked very serious.

"When I was a baby and then my adoptive parents were divorced when I was five, Dad died when I was seven." I rattled it off like it was old news. "The mom is still around."

Emily didn't say anything for a few minutes. As I put the pencils away, I noticed that Emily looked worried. "I'm fine. Thanks for letting me draw."

"Julie, will you come next Friday?"

I left Emily's office, wondering if she thought I was a little crazy. Even if she did, I wanted to see her again. Maybe I thought I was crazy and she could prove me wrong. Either way, I couldn't tell her too much about Marge and the boys. I just needed to have some sort of outlet for me and maybe later I could tell her more.

I went to the cafeteria and waited for Jimmy Delaurentis. I usually didn't eat. I was embarrassed about being overweight and I didn't want people to see me eat. Plus, I was saving the lunch money that Marge gave me every day for a new pair of designer jeans. Jimmy went through the lunch line and bought his usual soft pretzel. I liked sitting with him at lunch because he usually laughed at everything I said and he was super good-looking. His clothes and wavy black hair were always perfect and he chatted with me like a best girlfriend would. He was going out with Laura Fanelli, but he never sat with her. She sat with many of the girls that were popular. I imagined that Jimmy and Laura went to movies together and made out. I was a little jealous because I liked his attention. I would have loved to have been his girlfriend, but I knew that would never happen. I was just going to be the pudgy, funny girl, always.

After lunch period, in Chorus, I auditioned for one of the solos for the winter concert. I don't know what came over me, but I wasn't scared. I just thought about Marching Band ending and having to go straight home to Marge. If I got a solo, maybe I could get a part in a play or anything that would keep me after school. Basketball wasn't going to happen. I was too short and no one wanted to see a fat girl running down the court, trying to catch her breath. So, I sang with all of my heart.

I left school that day, feeling like a champ. I got a solo and so did Beth Kindt. The prettiest girl in school with the Bonnie Bell lip gloss would be singing with me at the winter concert.

I got off the bus and walked slowly to our apartment. I daydreamed all the way home as I explored the neighborhood. As I approached the complex, I wondered what Marge's mood would be. I walked up the steps to the second floor, Apt. 4C. I took a deep breath and opened the door.

"Hi." I took my book bag to my room and heard no reply. I put my books down and headed to the kitchen to make a peanut butter sandwich. Marge was at our little kitchen table, smoking from her pipe.

"Don't you have the fucking decency to ask me how I am?" She exhaled and coughed. "How my day was?"

I stopped in front of her. "I'm sorry. How are you?" I tilted my head slightly. "How was your day?" I mocked without realizing.

"Julie, I don't know what's going on, but you're becoming awfully bratty." She looked me in the eyes, testing me.

"I don't think I am." I continued toward the bread. My hands shook as I unraveled the twisty tie.

"I work hard, Julie." She tapped her pipe on the ashtray.

"I know you do and I thank you for that." I sounded robotic.

"You know what you need?" She opened her little film canister that held her pot. "You need some gratitude and a little spirituality. Sit down here." She patted the chair next to her.

"May I make a sandwich?" I was holding the jar of peanut butter.

"No. I said, sit! You can get it afterward" She grabbed a legal pad and a pen from the shelf behind her. "People fast when they are taking in religion, sometimes for days. When one is trying to achieve enlightenment, do you think they can do that with a fat stomach? No!" She answered her own question. What about the Buddha's stomach or taking communion? I wanted to ask.

"Write this down." She shoved the paper and pen toward me. "Our Father who art in heaven." She stood up and moved behind me.

"Art?" I turned around for her response.

"Yes! Art. Who art in heaven, hallowed be thy name. Thy kingdom come." She continued to recite and pace. "Now say it back to me." I read the words to her. "Again!" She watched her feet and pointed up as though she was a musician looking for the right chord. "Again! Memorize it!"

I memorized quickly and repeated it.

"This Sunday, I want you to go to a new church. The Christian Science Church." She stopped pacing to look at me. "There will be no more drugs in this house! No aspirin! No cough medicine!" she lectured. "You can heal yourself, Julie! I can heal you!"

"So...no more pot?" I knew I was taking a risk, but I blurted it out.

"This!" She quickly grabbed her pipe. "Is natural! We just don't talk about it." She stood over me. "You see, Carter and his cronies don't like this. Fat ass Billy can make his beer, but little Marge over here can't have this!" She waved the pipe in front of me. "Get your damn sandwich."

"I thought you liked Jimmy Carter."

"A hell of a lot more than Reagan, but we don't have a choice come January 20th, now do we?"

I scooted my chair out and retreated a few feet into the kitchen while she continued to pace. I searched for a knife. We only had two. A long sharp knife and a small butter knife that we had stolen at some point. We didn't have utensils or matching dishes anymore. We only had a few plates, some plastic forks, and the trusty mayo jars for glassware. I could never invite anyone over, even if Marge was normal.

I stared long and hard at the sharp knife. I felt overwhelming guilt as I imagined spinning around and putting it through Marge's chest. The headlines, I thought. Young fat girl striving for enlightenment stabs mean mother; should have fasted. I felt horrible for thinking such evil thoughts. I could never tell Emily that I often wished my mom was dead. I wrote in my journal when we lived out of the car and Marge found it. She accused me of wanting Susan for my mother instead. She was right and I paid.

I ate my sandwich, then recited The Lord's Prayer several more times until Marge was satisfied. She continued to lecture and tell me all about Mary Baker Eddy, the founder of Christian Science. How she could heal people, how the mother church was in Boston and we would have to see it at some point, how it's so amazing that a woman could start a church in the nineteenth century and how God made us in his likeness and image.

After about an hour of preaching, she released me so I could do some homework and maybe listen to my Barbra Streisand album.

Chapter Fourteen

The next session with Emily included another drawing. She explained that she was getting her Master's degree in Art Therapy.

I drew my future home again, but from a different angle. This time, I included a barn. "See, this is where a lot of the animals hang out." I pointed to the fenced yard outside of the barn. "This is where they get treats, hugs, anything they want."

"What kinds of animals?" Emily grinned as she leaned forward and studied my artwork.

"Every animal." I looked at her seriously. "They're allowed in the house, just not in the kitchen."

"You love these animals, don't you?"

"Yes." I smiled

"And they love you, don't they?" Emily waited patiently.

"They don't need to. I need to love them and take care of them," I said.

"What do you mean when you say, 'they don't need to'?" Emily tilted her head and looked at me quizzically.

"I'm just not expecting it." I shrugged. "They're innocent and need my help."

"Julie, do you have pets?" Emily was talking about my real life now.

"I did." I looked down.

"What kind?" Emily sat, smiling so sweetly that I thought if I told

135

her I once had a rhino in our apartment, it wouldn't faze her.

"My dog, Blackie," I said quietly.

"What happened to Blackie?"

"I had some cats, too." I perked up. "Teddy and Tiny, but they're gone too. Teddy ran away and Tiny disappeared." I slouched in my chair.

"What about Blackie?" Emily frowned.

"She died," I said. "She was my best friend."

"Oh, Jul, I'm so sorry." Emily reached out like she was going to touch my fat hand.

I pulled my hands back slowly and hid them under my arms. "It's okay," I said. "I'll just always miss her."

"Tell me more about your family." She spoke softly.

"Um." I sighed and stared at the wall behind Emily. "I have three brothers."

"Really? What are their names? Are they younger or older?"

"All older. They don't live at home anymore."

"Were they adopted, too?"

"Nope." I found myself sighing again and my brain was shutting down. I didn't want to talk about Scot and it was about to come up in this conversation. "I think I'm done for today." I glanced at her for a minute.

"Okay." Emily laughed a little. "You okay, kid?"

"Oh, I'm fine." I moved forward in my chair. I felt a little sick, but I didn't want her to know. I wanted to stay and leave at the same time. I didn't want to talk about Blackie or the boys. "Do you have pets?" I asked as I stood to leave.

Emily looked surprised that I asked. "I do. I have a cat." She got up from her chair.

"What's its name?"

"We'll save that for next time." She pushed blonde strands of hair behind her ear and crossed her arms like she was chilled.

"Someday, I'll tell you something." I opened the door. I realized how cryptic that sounded. "It's not a big deal or anything." I didn't know where that came from or why I said it, but I didn't regret it.

"See you next week?"

"Yes." I waved and walked away awkwardly.

The following week, I couldn't wait to see Emily. I stood near her closed door in the library and waited. Soon, the door opened and Jodi Foust came out, strumming her air guitar and telling Emily about an upcoming concert. Emily smiled at Jodi and then at me. "Thanks for telling me." she waved to Jodi. "I'll be sure to write that down."

"Hi, Emily." I walked right into her office.

"How are you, Julie?" Emily closed the door behind us, grabbed her mug from the table, and sat down.

"I'm good."

"What would you like to talk about today?" Emily sat back.

"I'm not sure." I suddenly felt out of place. "I really didn't think about that."

"How about drawing again?" Emily reached for the tablet. "Would that be okay?"

"Sure." I reached for the basket. "I'm just going to use a plain old pencil again, not the crayons."

"That's fine." She grinned. "Whatever you would like."

I drew a tree again. This time, it took up most of the page. "Do you have something against leaves?" Emily laughed.

"No." I laughed with her. "It's a winter tree. It's winter, now."

"It looks lonely." Emily frowned and traced the trunk with her forefinger. "Is it lonely?"

"Sometimes it is, but this tree isn't sad," I assured her.

"Julie, why did your family move around so much after you left Michigan?" "Cultural awareness." I added more branches and attempted a small bird's nest.

"What do you mean?"

"My mom said that we kids came from a backward small town where everyone talked about her. So, we needed to leave and live around black people, museums, churches, and stuff." I scratched my ear lobe and tugged on it.

"Oh." Emily crossed her legs and laughed. "Are you getting this awareness in Willow Grove?"

"Yeah, I guess." I thought for a minute. "I now go to a Christian Science church and I help take care of mentally handicapped people." Emily stared at me like she didn't know what to say. "Do you go to church?"

"Sure. Sometimes I go to synagogue," she answered.

"You're Jewish?" I sat wide-eyed.

"Yes. Is that okay?" She looked baffled.

"It's great! It's just that until my English teacher, Mrs. Shechtman, I never met anyone Jewish before." I was thoroughly excited. "Barbra Streisand is Jewish!"

Emily laughed. "Do you like Barbra Streisand?"

"I really do! I love singing along with her albums and I loved A Star is Born." I then remembered Jodi and her air guitar and decided not to go on about it anymore. "Are you married?" I asked.

"No." Emily hesitated. "We're here to talk about you."

"Well, if you were, what would your dream husband look like?" I ignored her comment. "Because I kind of see you with a Kenny Loggins or Michael McDonald type."

"Oh, you do, huh?" She grinned. "Julie, let's get back to you. You and this tree."

"Okay." I sighed.

"This tree is still so lonely." Emily frowned. "Do you miss your brothers?"

"Not really." Then, I thought for a moment. "Well, I miss Dan and Randy, but we visit occasionally."

"Where are your brothers?"

"Randy and Dan live in Center City Philadelphia, and Scot is somewhere south. I don't really care." I folded my arms. "My tree isn't lonely." Emily looked like she wanted to ask another question, but didn't. "But it isn't always happy. The branches get stuck."

"What do you mean?" Emily looked down at my paper.

"The wind blows, but the branches can't feel it. Like they're glued or something. And when the sun is shining, the tree can't feel the warmth, so it doesn't think it's growing." I was talking about stuff that I didn't understand, but it didn't feel made-up either.

"That's very sad." Emily kind of talked to me like I was little. Maybe I was acting like a child. "What's the purpose of this tree?"

"It protects." I pointed to an imaginary barn. "The animals that live over here get shade from the tree. The tree talks to them and keeps them calm and happy." I traced my fingers all over the paper.

Emily looked at me for a while. "But you keep the animals calm and happy, too."

"Exactly." I nodded.

"The tree is sturdy. I mean, it's not going anywhere." Emily smiled. "Do you have someone that is sturdy and strong in your life? Someone you can count on, who isn't going anywhere?"

"Besides the tree?" I thought for a moment. "Well, you're here every Friday."

Emily laughed. "That's true, but there are some Fridays coming up when I won't be here."

"Why?" I asked. "Why won't you be here?"

"Well, Thanksgiving is coming up and then Christmas break." She leaned forward and placed her elbows on her knees.

"Right." I was worried and disappointed. "What will you do for Thanksgiving?"

"Well, I'll spend it with family. What do you usually do?"

"When I was little and my dad was still around, we had a big Thanksgiving dinner with his side of the family. Now, I don't know. I don't think we've done much of anything in years." I laughed nervously.

"What about Christmas? Do you celebrate Christmas?" Emily's fingertips rested on her cheekbones.

"Your eyelashes are so long!" I smiled at her. "You're very pretty."

"Well, thank you, Julie, so are you." She looked politely flattered. "What will you do for Christmas?"

"My mom says that Christmas is communist." I put my pencil back in the basket and Emily shifted in her chair. "And we don't celebrate that anymore, either." I started to wonder if I would be spending the holidays with the residents or if they go off with their families somewhere. I would never tell them that Christmas was communist, I thought.

"I've never heard Christmas referred to as communist before." She smiled slightly. "Tell me about Christmas with your dad."

I smiled big. "Well, when my dad lived at home, we were kind of normal. I mean, we put out cinnamon toast for Santa and we all went to my mom's relatives on Christmas Eve. We opened presents on Christmas morning. I don't know." I looked around the room, searching for some exciting memory that I could share. "I know he found out about his cancer on Christmas Eve."

"Your parents were separated at some point?"

"Yes, they couldn't get it together. They even argued every morning." I thought for a minute. "Well, she couldn't get it together. She was mean to him and threw stuff at him. My dad couldn't control her." I stopped and realized what that must have sounded like. "I don't mean that he couldn't control her, but I mean she was out of control, make sense?"

"Did she throw things at you?"

"Not intentionally, but do you see this scar?" I lifted my hair into a part and tilted my head to the right. "That is from a plate that she threw in the kitchen. We had a long narrow kitchen and she was at one end and my dad and I were at the other. She meant to hit him."

Emily sat still. She didn't say anything and I was kind of happy about that.

"What's your favorite candy bar?" I tried to divert her attention from the kitchen scene.

Emily shook her head and looked suspiciously at me. "Hershey's with Almonds. Why are you asking me that?"

"I was just wondering, just curious." I thought I could take some of my designer jeans money and buy her a candy bar for Hanukkah or something.

"I'm still thinking about what you just told me." Emily sat back. "Julie?"

"Yeah." I laughed nervously.

"I have to ask you this."

"Okay." I held my arms up and stretched.

"Is anyone hurting you now?"

I brought my thumbnail to my teeth and bit down hard. I thought about how much trouble I could be in, depending on my answer. How Emily might not believe me, how Marge could hurt me and even how wasn't that bad.

"You're safe." Emily looked into my eyes and I believed her, but she wouldn't understand.

I rubbed my eyes and put my hands through my hair. I looked directly into her eyes and I lied.

"No."

"No, what? No, you aren't safe? No, no one is hurting you?" She waited. "No, you won't answer?" Emily continued to inspect me like she was searching for any indication that I was lying, and it made me feel horrible.

"Nothing is going on," I fibbed again, as I clenched my teeth and concentrated on making my jaw muscles pop in and out. I placed my fingers on my temples to feel the movement there. I thought about Emily's mascara and Beth's lip gloss and wished I had those items.

"Julie?" Emily startled me. "Are you sure?"

"Yep." I forced a weak smile.

"We have to end now and it's horrible timing." Emily looked worried.

"Oh." I quickly placed the pad of paper back near Emily's chair. "Have a nice weekend, Emily."

"You too." Emily opened the door for me. I wanted to hug her, but I couldn't. I never wanted to leave. My heart hurt because I had nothing planned until I would see her next. Even if I couldn't tell her things about Marge and Scot, those sessions were what I looked forward to most. If I did tell her everything, I might lose her forever. If Marge knew I was talking to someone, she would pull me right out of that school, but not without first causing an embarrassing scene or two.

~ * ~

I got closer with some of the kids in my classes, but rarely saw anyone outside of school hours. Sometimes I got to go bowling on Saturdays with Jennifer Rankin. Luckily for me, her mom always drove us, so I didn't have to endure any embarrassment.

I loved my English teacher, Mrs. Shechtman. She was always funny and engaging. I enjoyed her homework and assigned readings; Casey at the Bat, The Diary of Anne Frank, and The Catcher in the Rye. I also felt secretly close to Mrs. Shechtman because when she assigned journal writing, I wrote about things that really mattered to me and she never judged me. If I wrote something personal in my journal entries, she never asked me to share it in class. She knew which boys I liked and which kids annoyed me. She knew that I went to see Emily every Friday and how much that meant to me. It wasn't until close to the holidays that I started writing a little about my home life, my dad, and a whole lot of made-up stories to detract from real life.

When the Christmas concert came about, I lied to Marge about staying late at school. I didn't tell her it was a concert put on for all the families, I told her it was a movie night for eighth graders. I sang my part of Feast of Lights and then Beth sang hers. The audience seemed to like it and our teacher praised us. The practices during Choir class really paid off. The next day, we were to perform in front of the entire school. I was so excited that Feast of Lights was a Hanukkah song, that I even invited Emily to come see the concert. But, when I woke up, I had the beginnings of a terrible cold and I completely botched my part in front of the entire school, including Mrs. Shechtman and Emily. Now I absolutely had to get a part in a musical or the spring concert so I could prove I could sing. Funny that I should even want to sing since Marge forced it on me all the time. It was always, Born Free, like fifty-thousand times. It usually came out of nowhere, "Come on, Julie, sing it!"

"I don't want to right now." I shied away.

"Sing it, damn it!" She would say, and she was just at the edge of turning the corner at Angry Street, so I obliged. "Beautiful, Julianne! You have a beautiful voice." I followed up with a joke so we could get away from the compliment.

~ * ~

For our Christmas break, Marge planned to take me to Michigan so that I could understand that Grand Haven wasn't as great as I remembered.

I cried in Emily's office the last Friday before break. "I don't know if I'll be back."

"Why do you think that?"

"I just do. I never know what's going to happen." I sank into my chair and covered my eyes. "I can't not see you again." I bawled.

"Julie." Emily leaned forward and placed her hand on my knee. "You'll be back or I'll start calling all over Michigan, okay?"

"Mmm hmm." I kept my head down with my hands over my face. I hadn't cried so hard in a very long time.

"What do you mean when you say that you never know what's going to happen?"

"I don't know." I lifted my head and wiped my eyes with my forearms. "Everywhere we go, we just leave. We leave in the middle of the night and we don't come back. Sometimes my mom gets so angry that she drives like a maniac." It was the first time I mentioned Marge and the word, 'angry' in the same sentence. It was long overdue.

"Julie, why does she get angry?" Emily's eyes narrowed.

"Who knows?" I wiped my eyes again. "She just goes off on rants and lectures. She..." I took a deep breath and exhaled unsteadily. "Never mind, I don't know how to explain it."

"Take your time." Emily sat forward and waited.

"There isn't anything else to say." I was afraid to go any further. I tried to catch my breath from my sobbing.

"When your mom rants, as you said, what does she rant about?"

"It could be anything from government to religion to men and how everyone mistreats her. She even thinks that I mistreat her and I don't even know what she's talking about." I made a disgusted face and folded my arms. "She's really smart, so none of this makes sense." I leaned forward. "I mean, if you asked her why there's a knocking sound in your car when you turn a corner, she knows it's a CV joint. If you ask her about the constitution, she can recite every word."

"Would you ever want her to join us? The three of us meet together?"

"No!" I sat up straight.

"Okay, we won't." Emily put her hand up like a crossing guard. "I was just wondering how you would feel about that."

"I feel that would be a very bad idea and I don't want her to do anything to you or say something mean."

"Julie, I can protect myself." She looked into my eyes. "So why are you trying to protect me? What do you think she would do?"

I thought about how hard Marge was on Susan and how she had bullied teachers around. "We really shouldn't talk about it," I said. "I mean, it's not that bad. I'm just afraid she wouldn't want me seeing a counselor, she might take it personally."

"So she has no idea you see me?" Emily looked stumped.

"Oh, God, no." I shook my head. I started thinking about Michigan and the bittersweet idea of going back. I desperately wanted to see my family and even go to my father's gravesite for a few minutes, but I couldn't bear being so far from Emily. "I'll run away if she decides not to come back."

Emily squinted slightly. "Julie, I think you'll be back, so don't get ahead of yourself. I am so curious about why it would be so bad if your mom knew you were talking to me."

"She would take it personally," I repeated. "She has a degree in Psychology and I just call her Marge."

Emily looked dumbstruck and amazed. "Does Marge practice?"

"Uh, no." I laughed. "She's a nut case!" I sat back in my chair grinning, but Emily wasn't amused by my quip, she just stared at me. "She's smart and she's had really good jobs, but she does things and says things that just aren't normal," I exhaled, "whatever normal is."

Emily sat quietly for a while and looked confused. "Well, this was interesting today, and you didn't even draw!" It was a closing line. Our session needed to end.

I remembered that I wouldn't see her for a few weeks and my bottom lip started to quiver and I couldn't control it. I hugged Emily before I left, but I made it quick. I was afraid I would sink into her and start bawling again. "I'll see you very soon." I walked away and cried. I prayed that it was true.

~ * ~

The ride to Michigan was fairly uneventful until we got to Lansing.

We were only a few hours from Grand Haven and Marge started getting nervous and wouldn't stop talking. "Now you don't need to go telling people all of our business. They don't need to know." Marge sat forward as she drove a little faster.

"Where are we staying?" I looked out the window and watched tall pines whiz in and out of focus.

"You're staying with Grandma Beekman and I'll be with my sister, Dot."

"Do I get to see Aunt Dottie?" I loved Aunt Dottie and all of Marge's family, for that matter.

"Does everyone know that we're coming?" I looked at Marge who was lighting another cigarette.

"How the fuck should I know, Julie?" She banged her fist on the steering wheel. Ashes fell on her leg and I hoped for a hole in her pants. "I told Dot and I'm sure she's told everyone else and I don't really give a fuck! I'm doing this for you!" She pointed her cigarette at me and I slumped into the seat. "Do you think I want to come back here? Well, I don't! But ever since we left, you have hated me and blamed me for your father's death."

I shot her a look of disbelief. "I don't blame you, I don't hate you and..."

"You sure as hell do hate me!" she interrupted. "I saw it in your journal and I can see it in your eyes!"

"Your whole family is here." I spoke quietly, hoping she would calm down.

"Honestly, Julianne, do you think they care about me?" I didn't answer. It would have been pointless. "They don't give a fuck!" She started looking at me more than at the road. "Where were they when your dad died, huh? Where were they for a single widow trying to raise four kids, huh? Instead of maybe offering some help, they made up lies about me.

"Do you know that they accused me of sleeping with Sherry's

husband?" I tried to remember who Sherry was. "My own family! Your Aunt Sue who you love so dearly, my sister, spread rumors about me to the whole family! I don't need this shit, I'm doing it for you! And your father's side of the family? Same shit! They couldn't give a rat's ass about me, that's for sure!"

For the next hour and a half, she continued. She yelled about how horrible everyone was and how no one ever cared about her and then she dropped me off at my Grandma Beekman's house with a grocery bag of some clothes and a toothbrush. I stood on the sidewalk as I watched her pull away so fast that her tires screeched for half a block. I wondered if my grandma knew I was coming.

"Julie!" She was very surprised to see me and looked past me for signs of my mother.

"She's gone and I have no idea of when she's coming back. I hope that's okay." I cringed.

"Well, you get in here!" Grandma's black wig was slightly tilted and clearly didn't match all the gray hairs sticking out around her ears. It was the first time I realized she had most likely worn a wig my whole life. She probably never really even had black hair.

"Hi, Grandma!" I finally put my paper bag down and hugged her. I looked around and found nothing had changed and it made me so happy. I walked along the rubber mat and looked up for the old cuckoo clock. Everything was in place, even the hologram of Jesus that would follow my every move. "Is it okay if I stay with you tonight?"

"Of course! Sit down." She sat down in her rocking chair near the front window. "Hey, did you get your birthday card this year?"

"No." I was confused. I hadn't received a birthday card from Grandma since we left Michigan. Why would I get one this year? "My birthday was two weeks ago. Did you send a card?"

"I have always sent you cards, but your mother always sends them back." She got up from her chair and went into the guest room. She continued talking as she opened a drawer. "Marge always tells me she doesn't want her daughter influenced by your dad's side of the family. I usually get a nasty note or letter from her." My grandma brought a bundle of cards that were banded together and handed them to me.

"I can't believe this." I looked for the beginning by date and began opening the cards. There were birthday cards, Christmas cards, Easter cards, and just small notes to tell me she missed me. There was nothing negative in the notes and certainly nothing about Marge. The best part was that almost every card held a five-dollar bill. "Thank you, Grandma!" I was beaming.

"Are you here tomorrow?" She headed for the kitchen.

"I'm not sure." I watched as she put her craggy index finger in the holes of her phone and dialed.

"Julie is here." I figured she was talking to my aunt Betty who lived next door. "I know, can you believe it?" My grandma smiled at me and I felt special. "Oh, I think the whole neighborhood heard it." She soon hung up the phone and came back to her chair. "Your aunt Betty commented on that little tire squealing tantrum." She laughed. "She'll be right over." Grandma walked to her favorite chair, sat down and looked at me. "Would you like to go Christmas shopping tomorrow?"

I looked down at the pile of fives on my lap. "I would." I looked up at her and smiled big.

"What would you like to get?" She rocked back and forth.

"I would like to get a pair of jeans."

A phone was ringing in my dream. Maybe it was real. It took me a few minutes to acclimate and realize where I was. Still, I couldn't seem to pry my eyes open. Grandma answered the phone, but wasn't saying much. I heard her approach the guest room where I was staying. "Julie," she whispered.

"Yes." I tried again to open my eyes. I could faintly make out a balding head and strands of white hair sticking up. It scared the heck out of me and I woke fully with a jump and a quick scream.

"Oh, I don't have my wig on!" Grandma laughed and patted her head as if to make sure. "The phone is for you."

I laughed for politness' sake and then got my breathing under control so I could get to the phone. "Hello?"

"You have until five o' clock to visit. Be out front waiting with your things and then you can visit with my family, the saner ones." Marge hung up before I could respond.

Grandma came out of her room with her wig on, though slightly tilted again. "How much time we got?"

"She's coming to get me at five." I looked up at the cuckoo clock. It was eight.

My grandma bounced a little and then snapped her fingers. "Well, let's get going then, we don't have a lot of time."

Grandma drove an extra-large, green Mercury. The long front seat was encased with a cotton seat cover with a pillow thrown on the driver's side. It looked like a sofa. We drove down Beacon Boulevard and I reminisced. "Could we go to my dad's grave?" I looked at Grandma. She sat forward and hunched over the wheel.

"Of course!" She tapped my knee with her hand and looked at me. "I was wondering if you might want to do that." The car swerved to the right and then Grandma brought it back between the lines on the road. "We can do that after Russ'." Russ' was a small restaurant chain that started in Holland, Michigan where Grandma was born. She loved going there.

Grandma pulled into two parking spaces and parked a little crooked, like her wig. A hostess sat us at a booth and Grandma pored over the menu even though she always got the same thing. I checked out the cartoon Dutch boy on the front of the menu. He had a page haircut with a little cap, wore overalls and wooden shoes. He hadn't changed a bit and it felt comforting. The waitress came quickly to the table, before I could look at the menu items. "I'll have a hamburger, coleslaw, and a hot coffee," Grandma said.

"And for you, miss?"

"Uh, grilled cheese and orange juice." It was easy and I didn't have to think, plus, if Grandma wasn't getting breakfast, I wasn't either.

I watched Grandma as she rifled through her purse. She pulled out tissues that looked balled up and used. As I watched her, I thought about something my brothers talked about when we were little. A little known fact that made them laugh every time and would ultimately lead to a host of ideal last names for our grandmother. "Grandma, your name is Fannie, right?"

"That's right. Fannie Breuker before I married your Grampa Beekman." She finally found the perfect tissue.

"Do you have brothers and sisters?" I played dumb.

"Oh, yes! I have four younger brothers." She blew gently on her Kleenex and dabbed at her nostrils.

I waited to see what she would do with the tissue which was now balled up like the others. "What are their names?" I felt horrible for using her to get a laugh, but I also had to make sure that the boys hadn't lied to me.

My grandma looked so thrilled to tell me. "Okay, I was born, then Henry, then John, Hiney, and..." There is was, Hiney! Fannie and Hiney! I giggled as Grandma told me the other brother's name and the stories she was telling about chores they had.

I could barely pay attention to her. I kept hearing the bantering of Scot and Dan in my head. "Their last name was Wipe!" "Nah ha, their last name was Hole, no wait, Crack!"

After lunch, we drove to the cemetery. Grandma chatted about how my cousin, Linda, always made sure that my dad's headstone had flowers on it. That made me feel good although I wished it could have been me placing those flowers. "She always loved your dad." Grandma turned a corner wide and went into the opposite lane for a moment.

"Should we get flowers for him, Grandma? I mean, I could use some of the money you gave me."

"No. Julie, that's for you. He'll know that you were here, that's what matters." She smiled at me. "Hey, do you remember your dad taking you kids tobogganing here?" She pointed to the entrance of Duncan's Woods.

"Yes." I smiled and glanced at the stone entrance way to the park. I also remembered Marge taking me there to tell me about how my dad died and I remembered Blackie having a blast, chasing all the squirrels. Grandma drove slowly along Lake Drive toward the beach and the entrance to Lake Forest Cemetery. I winced as she made a left turn to drive past the gates. "Grandma, are you okay with the whole driving thing?"

"Oh yah, sometimes it's a little fuzzy, but don't go telling anybody. I'm not giving it up just yet." She grinned and looked over at me instead of the narrow road which was lined with headstones that was now turning left and uphill. "Oops!" She pulled the wheel and straightened out. As we approached the top of the hill, I could see the massive yard of headstones where my dad was buried. I remembered his funeral and what a gorgeous day it was as we approached blue tarp and a hole in the ground. We drove in a big limousine that day and followed a hearse, just like pictures I had seen of Jacqueline Kennedy and her kids following their dad's hearse, only we didn't walk.

"Grandma, watch out!" The green Mercury boat glided effortlessly over several grave sites and headstones that thankfully weren't too tall or thick. I looked out the back window to make sure that no one saw and that everything was still intact. She straightened the car out and got back on track. We didn't say a word.

My dad's headstone was in front near the road. It was sweet and small, compared to others. There were daisies and hearts etched along the sides. We stood there for a while, despite the cold air blowing off Lake Michigan.

"Look! That's where I'm going to go!" Grandma pointed to a large red headstone a few grave sites back from my dad's. It already had her name and birthdate written on it as well as her husband's name, lifespan, and something about the military. "He fought in World War One, and was disabled after that." She caught me staring. I never met him and I couldn't even remember seeing any pictures of him.

"Your headstone is nice, Grandma." I felt so creepy saying it, but I was sure it was the response she was looking for. I glanced back down at my dad's flowers, faded, much like my memories of him. I knew the empty area of grass next to his was Marge's plot. I had visions of bird droppings on her marker.

Grandma walked a little closer to her future resting place and I went back to wait at the car. I wanted to stop thinking about my dad and the cemetery. What if he really could roll over in his grave if he knew what happened to his family? I tried instead to think about the new jeans I would get.

When Grandma got back to the car, she reached for my hands and held them out in front of me. I let her have them and went limp like a Raggedy Ann. "You okay?" She held my gaze and I nodded. I was afraid to talk because I didn't want to cry. We both missed my dad and she knew how Marge was, I didn't want her to worry.

"May I drive?" I looked at Grandma, just knowing she would laugh out loud and say no.

"Of course you can." She giggled. "Here ya go." She put the keys in my hand. As I walked to the driver's side, I kept looking at her, waiting for her to tell me she was kidding, but she opened the passenger side and got right in. I got into the driver's side, placed the pillow firmly behind me so I could reach the pedal, and started the car. I've watched Marge drive a million times, I can do this. I drove very slowly out of the cemetery and the three or so miles to downtown by way of Harbor Drive and the beach. It was beautiful. "Don't tell your mother about this." Grandma peered at me.

"Oh, don't you worry, Grandma, I won't."

"Good, that woman might kill me yet."

Steketees wasn't as big as I remembered, but they definitely had jeans. They had Gloria Vanderbilt, Jordache, Levi's, and Bon Jour jeans. The smell of all the new clothes was intoxicating. I took a pair of each of the designer jeans into the dressing room while Grandma milled about in the sweater section. I could hear her telling one of the sales ladies that she could just as easily make the sweaters they were selling for a lot less money. As I put my right leg into the Jordache jeans, I knew instantly that they weren't going to fit, not the way I wanted them to. I didn't want to walk around like some girls, all squeezed into their jeans like sausages. Was I going to need Size 12? Really? I quickly took them off and folded them neatly. Next, I went for the Gloria Vanderbilt's. They too, were a little snug and when I lifted my shirt, it looked like I needed a second bra just to contain the roll above my waist. I couldn't go through this again, so I opted out of trying on the third pair of size ten and went back into the jeans area. I quickly grabbed a size twelve pair of Bon Jour and ran back into the dressing room. They fit perfectly. They weren't too tight anywhere and they even made me look a little slimmer. These were going to be mine. I couldn't wait to wear them to school.

I joined Grandma in the sweater area and saw a rich brown velour V-neck. It was only sixteen dollars. The jeans were thirty and I had a total of fifty-five dollars. I bought them and thanked Grandma profusely as she drove home.

~ * ~

That afternoon, my dad's best friend, Lou, and his wife, Dolores, came to Grandma's to visit. I always called them Aunt and Uncle because my dad said they were like my God parents even though I wasn't baptized. They were nice, like my dad.

"Julie, do you remember when we took you Easter shopping for a dress?" Aunt Dolores sat next to me. "You didn't want a dress, but we convinced you to pick out a pink frilly one." She laughed and Uncle Lou snickered while he rocked in Grandma's chair.

"I kind of remember." I squinted as though trying to recall and smiled. I could hear Grandma banging around in her kitchen, getting coffee ready.

"Well, we agreed on the dress and then we wanted to buy you new shoes." Aunt Dolores had such a heavy Michigan accent, that shoes sounded like shows. "So we went to the show department at Meier's and you picked out a little pair of boy's brown shoes to go with your pretty Easter dress." She and Lou laughed, while I tried to remember. "You insisted, you didn't want the white patent leather, so we took you to church in a gorgeous little dress with crummy brown shoes!" We all laughed, but I felt bad. I was sure that Aunt Dolores didn't want to drag me to church like that.

"Sorry about that." I smiled, embarrassed.

"Oh no." She patted my knee. "You were cute."

Grandma brought out coffee for the adults and then scurried back to the kitchen for church window cookies. The cookies were my favorite. Grandma would make a large chocolate log rolled in coconut. Inside the log were tons of colored mini marshmallows. After cooling in the refrigerator, she would slice through it and the colored marshmallows were supposed to look like stained glass.

"How is your mom?" Aunt Dolores took a sip of her coffee while Uncle Lou visibly shuddered.

"Oh, she's good." I glanced at the hologram of Jesus who had been staring at us the whole time, and then at the cuckoo clock. It was four-thirty. I took a bite of a cookie. "She'll be here in a half hour." Uncle Lou quickly shimmied to the front of the chair and Aunt Dolores put her coffee cup down.

"We should get going." Uncle Lou got up and came over to hug me. "We love ya, kid."

"You don't have to leave." I stood to embrace him.

Aunt Dolores hugged me next. "Somehow we made your mother

angry before you left Michigan. To this day, we don't know what we did, but it's probably best if we just go." She held my arms. "It was good to see you."

"You take care of yourself," Uncle Lou muttered as he got to the front door.

"I will. Thanks for the dress and crummy brown shoes!" Everyone laughed and I stood there, dumbfounded by how quickly Marge could clear a room. I looked at Grandma. "I guess everyone is afraid of her."

"I know I am." She grinned. "Now, go get ready before we get in trouble."

~ * ~

I took the quickest shower and changed into my new clothes. I was a bit leery in doing so because I didn't want Marge to mad.

I came out to the living room and asked Grandma about all the cards she sent. "What did my mom say to you in her letters?"

"Oh, I'll show you." Grandma went into the room where I had been staying and opened a dresser drawer. "They all say basically the same thing. I tried to ruin her life, I never respected her, and she didn't want you to be influenced by me."

"I love you, Grandma. I know that you just care about us kids. I know how she is." A horn sounded and we both stared at the front door with looks of disdain. I sighed.

Marge pulled up in front of Grandma's a few minutes early. She just stayed in the car.

"Don't you want to say hello to her?" I asked as I opened the car door.

"Don't you want to say hello to me?" Marge responded.

"I'm sorry." I looked down. "Hi." I got in and waved to my grandma who was standing in her doorway.

"We're going to see my sisters." Marge pulled away and never even looked at Grandma. I continued to wave until I couldn't see her. "Was it fun? Did you see all your cousins? Did they feel sorry for you?" I couldn't even answer. She looked at my new clothes and that sent her further into rant. She went on about how mean they were to her and they must have bought me new clothes to prove what a poor mother she was, how they wanted to pick out my dad's head stone and take control of everything. It was draining. I stared out the window and imagined her falling out of the car or speeding and then I imagined a cop pulling her over and strangling her because she wouldn't shut up. I wondered if I would ever see Grandma again. I wondered if Marge would take my new clothes and throw them out.

When we finally arrived at Aunt Dottie's, I was grateful because Marge had a new audience. Dottie, who was a shorter and nicer version of her sister, listened patiently as Marge sounded off some more. Occasionally, Aunt Dot would look over at me and wink.

Jim and Dot had a huge family with kids of all ages. They lived in Alabama for many years, so they all had thick southern accents and I found them very entertaining. Beverly was my age and we instantly connected any time we saw each other. While Marge and Dot had coffee in the kitchen, Bev and I sat in the adjacent dining room with her dad.

Uncle Jim had a Chihuahua on each knee and he was whispering to them. The dogs responded with shakes and growls. "Don't pay no mind to him." Beverly folded her arms and shook her head. "He's got them all riled up about the dog across the street."

"What do you mean?" I laughed.

Jim hummed low notes with a deep scratchy voice that matched the wrinkles and whiskers on his face. "She's over there talk'n bout you. That old Tonya's itchin for a fight." He now held onto the dogs with one hand, fingers woven through the fronts of their tiny legs.

Bev continued to shake her head and grin at her father. I found him fascinating. He took a big drag of his cigarette and, as the smoke billowed from his nostrils, he continued teasing the dogs. "Look at her over there," he growled. I got up to see a medium sized dog just standing in a fenced back yard. "She's gonna take you down!" The chihuahuas shook as they stared out at her. One of them stood on Uncle Jim's knee, barely able to contain himself. "Now you sit down or she's gonna see you." His voice remained raspy and low. The dog instantly followed the command.

I was amazed and I laughed.

Uncle Jim smiled at me and took another drag. The remnants building up in his ashtray reminded me of the colors in his hair. With his faded red plaid shirt and thin body, he was somewhere between handsome and old farmer.

Aunt Dot called us for dinner. Bev and I stood awkwardly near the table while Dot fixed us heaping plates of her southern cooking. "Now Julie, you have to try my butter beans." She handed me a plate of fried wonderment.

Marge lit a cigarette and ignored the food. "She's fat enough, Dottie! Don't give her that shit!" I stood, not knowing what to do. I was embarrassed.

Dottie turned quickly and stared at Marge. "She's not fat and my cook'n ain't shit!" Dottie winked at me. "She's always called me fat, too!"

"That's because you are fat." Marge took a sip of coffee.

"You girls go on ahead and eat your dinner in the other room." Dottie waved us away.

Bev and I sat down in the living room where the dogs were now asleep, exhausted by Uncle Jim's teasing. "It's hard to believe our moms grew up in the same household." I poked at the butter beans. "Your mom is always so nice."

"My momma said that Aunt Marge tried to make her drink pee when they was little." Beverly grinned. "That's just wrong!" She took a bite of a biscuit.

"Oh, no." I sighed.

"They had it hard. Once they was adopted, they had to live in a chicken coop sometimes and some man that lived with them did things to our mommas."

"What?" I sat with my jaw hanging open. "Do you think it really happened?" I whispered.

Bev shrugged. "Who knows?"

"But they lived in a chicken coop?" I placed my plate on the coffee table.

"It was a very big chicken coop. They lived all over with the Stone family, then their brothers and sisters would find out where they was and come say hey. Like they was looking out for 'em." Beverly tore a piece of chicken off the bone.

"Well, that's good." I picked up my plate and listened for Marge's prattle. "I'll tell you what I've always been told and you tell me if I'm wrong."

Beverly looked toward the dining room. "They cain't hear us, go 'head."

"Okay, I heard their biological mom died when Marge was three and your mom was a baby." I looked for a response.

"That's right." Bev nodded.

"Then their dad couldn't take care of the little ones, just the older kids, so he gave our moms away."

"Yep, but the Stones was real nice people. I met them." Bev got quieter. "You know how their real daddy died, right?"

"No, how?" I leaned closer to Bev.

"He was burned up. Murdered."

"What? I never heard this."

"Yeah, he was drinking all day with some lady and her husband. They went back to some paper shack they was living in and our granddaddy was making moves, if you know what I mean."

"No. What do you mean?"

"He was gonna sleep with the lady and the husband clocked him one, threw him into a stove, and the place started on fire." Bev took a drink of soda and continued. "The husband ran down the street and left his wife and our granddaddy to die."

"Oh my God! I never heard about this." I started feeling sick to my stomach.

"Momma said it was in the newspapers and everything."

It was a lot to take in. I knew Marge had a lot happen to her, but some of it was just bizarre.

~ * ~

We spent the night at Aunt Dot's. The next day, Marge's other sisters, Babe and Sue, came over to visit with us. I sat at the kitchen table with them and relished the banter of the four women while Bev went shopping with her older sister, Pam. It had been so long since I'd seen them, I couldn't believe how much they all looked alike.

Sue and Babe were the oldest, and like their two brothers, they had been spared from adoption. I couldn't help but think about what Bev told me the night before. It was all so sad and weird. Their father, Flint, lost his wife to pneumonia shortly after she gave birth to Dottie. Marge claimed that the Stones wanted Dottie and she came as sort of a consolation. Dottie said the complete opposite.

"Oh, Marge, they wanted you!" Dottie poured coffee for everyone.

"Dottie, they didn't! They wanted a baby and the old man made us a package deal!" Marge got up and opened the freezer. "They couldn't have you unless they took me." She cracked a few ice cubes out of a tray and put them in her cup. "I'm older, I know, so shut up about it." Everyone laughed nervously.

Aunt Babe reached behind her chair for her purse and took out a package of Eve cigarettes. The pack was long and slender with what looked like a mermaid with flowing hair in a field of flowers in the design. Marge's Benson and Hedges were two shades of brown. Brown and angry.

"You know we always knew where you two were and that you were safe." Babe lit the end of thin white stick.

"Blah, blah, blah," Marge hammered. "You don't know what was going on, you don't know what was happening to me!"

"Well, if we did, Marge, we would have helped you," Sue piped in. "Hank and Fran would have done anything for you two. They just never suspected anything strange."

Aunt Babe looked at me and shrugged. "We didn't know your mom was in any trouble." She kept her voice low as if the conversation were just between us. She assumed I knew what she was talking about. "You know, your uncles found them, even all those times they moved."

Marge was staring at us. I didn't say anything.

"Sue, what was I supposed to do? Blurt it out? A.I. is a creep and he won't stop molesting me?" Marge tapped furiously on her cigarette.

Dottie moved quickly about the kitchen. Sue and Babe both shot glances at one another, then at me.

"Who's A.I.?" I asked.

"I don't know," Babe answered. "What was he, a boarder with the Stone family?"

"Yes, he was." Dottie finally sat down. "He was a little off, but his disability checks helped out."

"Oh, I don't care!" Marge slapped her palm on the table.

"Well, you brought it up!" Sue gazed at Marge with wide eyes.

"What should we talk about, Sue? Huh?" Marge glared at her sister. "Should we maybe talk you about all the men in your life?"

"Yes, let's do that!" Dottie giggled and patted my head.

Marge continued, "Should we talk about how you wanted my husband for yourself?"

"Well, we all wanted Warren." Dottie grabbed a danish from the center of the table.

Marge took out a cigarette and tapped it on the table. "Oh, and I did not sleep with Bill!"

Everyone fell silent because Bill was Aunt Sue's son-in-law. I put my head down and prepared for a possible explosion.

"No one said that you did." Sue took a deep breath, folded her arms and looked at Babe.

"Who wants more coffee?" Aunt Dot jumped up from the table.

"Someone sure as hell said that I did!" Marge lit another cigarette. "I damn well heard it before we left town!"

I'm not sure if it was because my aunts were all sitting there and I felt safe or if I had just had enough, but I spoke. "Could you just stop?" Marge's lips tightened as she shot me a look that warned of a beating. My heart pounded. "We're here to visit your family."

"I know where we are, Julie!" She ended her statement with closed teeth.

I looked down and felt stupid. Marge got up from the table and took her cigarette outside. I hoped that I would hear the car start and that she was never coming back.

Aunt Babe put her arm around me and pulled me in close.

"Your mom has always been a tough one to crack." Aunt Sue shook her head.

"I don't get it," I said.

Babe let go of me and cut a small slice of her danish. "None of us do. I'm sorry you have to deal with it." She popped the danish in her mouth. "We worry about you kids all the time."

"She's the smartest one, but nuttier than a fruitcake." Sue laughed. "I don't know where she comes up with half of this stuff."

I looked at Aunt Dottie, hoping she would answer, but she just continued to flit about the kitchen, wiping up imaginary spills. My aunts asked me all kinds of questions about where we lived, how the boys were, and what we had been up to for the last four and a half years. I answered in short spurts because I knew Marge would come back in at any time. I wanted to tell them everything, but I couldn't bring myself to do it. They wouldn't be able to do anything, anyway. So, even through tears, I kept my answers to a minimum.

"What's wrong, sugar?" Aunt Dottie came over and hugged me.

"I just miss everyone." I quickly wiped my eyes as I heard Marge come back in and head to the bathroom. She brought with her an energy that sucked the life out of the house.

Sue and Babe started to gather their things. "I hate to say this," Babe placed her hand on my head, "but take care of your mom." She walked away and put her coffee mug near the sink. "And take care of yourself. Get her to bring you back more often."

"Better yet, have her send you alone," Aunt Sue chimed in as she hugged me. I welled up again. "It's okay. Before you know it, you'll be off on your own and you can do whatever you want."

I nodded and managed a smile. The thought of growing up and being on my own was better than anything I could imagine. Someday, I'd be out west or anywhere she wasn't.

"Marge, we're leaving!" Aunt Sue called out. I heard the bathroom door open. "Stop over before you leave town." We all knew that Sue didn't mean it.

Marge looked dumbfounded as she approached the kitchen. Her audience was leaving. Babe went to hug Marge while Sue stood at the door. The hug was slight. Aunt Dottie and I shared smiles while I traced the stitching of the words, Bon Jour, on my right back pocket.

I wondered if Marge realized she didn't ask any of her sisters what was happening in their lives. She'd taken up the entire morning with all of her sob stories.

I spent the rest of the afternoon with Beverly and my other cousins. Any time that I went through the living room, Jim was there, talking to his Chihuahuas. "He's doin' that to show off. He don't normally do it all the time." Bev pursed her lips and pushed them to one side.

Instead of leaving the next morning as planned, Marge decided to leave right before Dottie was putting out dinner. "Julie, we have to get going!" I heard her call out. I ran quickly to Bev's room and got my paper bag of clothes, which was now torn down the side, and then retrieved my toothbrush from the upstairs bathroom. I placed everything near the door and listened as Dottie protested our quick departure. I thanked Bev and ran into the living room to say goodbye to Uncle Jim and his dogs. Jim looked at me with surprise.

"Bye, Uncle Jim. When she says we have to go, we have to go."

"What's the hurry?" Jim grunted.

"She's kind of like that dog, Tonya, across the street and I'm just a Chihuahua." I spoke softly as I pet the dogs' heads.

Jim grinned. "Mmm. Dottie just made y'all dinner."

"I know. I'm sorry, Uncle Jim." I gingerly hugged him, careful not to squish the dogs.

Once we were on the highway, Marge took a deep breath and said, "Well, Julie, I hope you feel better now that we've seen your little hometown and family. Not missing much, huh?"

"I miss everything and we didn't see your brothers or their families." I shifted in my seat and hoped that I didn't sound whiny.

"I have to get back to work! You have to get back to school, and I really wish you would stop resenting me so much for leaving this small-minded shit hole. Someday, you'll realize I just wanted a better life for you."

"I don't resent you, I appreciate all you do for me." I had to lay it on thick. "I just meant that I'm sure they would have wanted to see you." I stared at the road ahead.

"If they wanted to see me, they knew where I was staying. I shouldn't have to run all over town."

I left it alone.

~ * ~

As we drove, I felt tired, but Marge expected me to stay awake. She opened the windows and chain-smoked. I kept nodding off.

"Damn it, help me! I need you to talk and tell me a story, anything."

"I don't know any stories," I replied. I wanted desperately to sleep. The drive felt like torture and we were only near Lansing with a good ten hours to go.

"Talk to me! Tell me something, for Christ's sake, Julie! I brought you to Michigan, now you need to help me stay awake."

"Why don't we get a room?" I was getting really cranky and took risks. "You didn't have to leave Aunt Dot's at dinner time, right as it's getting dark."

"What is with your attitude?" Marge reverted to banging her hand on the steering wheel. "When we get home, you're going to have to see someone before this problem gets out of control." I could just feel her waiting for me to protest. "I will not tolerate your smart ass remarks."

"I already see a counselor," I blurted.

"What?" Marge kept looking at me and sometimes the road. "Who? And more importantly, why?"

"For my attitude."

"Who, Julie? Who are you talking to?" she stammered.

"It's just some lady from a counseling center that comes to my school." I regretted saying anything.

"Well, when we get back, I need to meet with her."

"No, it's not that big of a deal," I insisted.

"Oh, but it is!" Marge started winding up and suddenly, she was no longer tired. "Remember, I'm the one with the degree in psychology, not you, little girl! I want to know what this woman is telling my daughter!"

"She's not telling me anything!"

"Then, what are you telling her?"

"I just draw and talk about math and stuff." I leaned against the window, wishing I could escape.

"So, she's a tutor and a counselor."

"Yep." Why, why, why did I open my big fat mouth?

"What's her name?" Marge drove a little faster when I didn't respond. "What is her name?"

"It doesn't matter." I chewed on my pinky nail and wanted to rip it right off for having been so stupid.

"Why are you protecting her?" Marge screamed. "What is her name? Tell me, goddamn it!"

"It's Emily and I'm not protecting her." I thought about how I needed to tell Emily more about Marge before Marge could get to her.

"You sure as hell are! What in the hell is so private?" Marge was staring at me and I could feel it.

"When we get back, I'm going to make an appointment so I can see her, too. Maybe we can see her together, huh?" She made a fake smile. "Tell her how great of a mother and daughter we are. Well, we could be, if you would just mind me. Do you tell her that you don't mind me?"

"We talk about school." I looked at Marge and kind of shrugged to make it seem like nothing she said bothered me. Then, maybe she would lay off.

"You tell her that I'm horrible, don't you?" Marge whined like a toddler. "Everything is so awful for poor Julie. Does she feel sorry for you?"

"No." I was careful with the inflection of my voice, though I wanted to scream for Marge to stop.

"No?" The back of Marge's hand came across my mouth fast. I quickly covered the sting with my hand and held back tears. "Tell her about that, why don't you?" The car swerved and Marge's fist came down on my forehead. It hurt so much that I thought I saw patches of white."

I cried as quietly as I could and prayed she would calm down. My hair covered my face and strands stuck to my tears. I always felt stupid when she hit me, stupid and ugly and vulnerable. It felt like I must be in hell. I should have just agreed to go see someone about my attitude and left it at that.

We drove for another hour or so and she lectured. Marge finally pulled off at an exit somewhere near the Ohio State line and got a room at a Red Roof Inn. Then, she left, which made me feel relieved and confused. I just hoped she didn't wake me when she returned.

She was sitting up, fully dressed and ready to go when I woke the next morning. "I'm sorry that I hit your head a little hard. I didn't mean for it to be that hard."

"I'm okay." I glanced at her for a moment.

"You just frustrate me so and I don't want someone brainwashing my kid. There are a lot of sick people out there, Julie, and you're just too nice to realize it."

~ * ~

When I returned to school on Monday, I didn't even have space in my brain to think about how I was wearing new clothes. I was worried about Emily. I asked the guidance counselor if there was any way that I could get in touch with Emily. I wanted to talk with her before Marge got a hold of her.

"I'm sorry, but you would have to call her after school or have your parents take you to Aldersgate." Mr. Mauer shuffled student files and acted too busy.

I stopped at the front office and asked the ladies behind the big counter, "Has anyone called for Emily Chernicoff's number?"

They answered, "No." and looked at me like they had never even heard of her. I was going crazy just thinking of Marge calling around trying to find out about Emily that my actions weren't making any sense.

On Friday, I told Emily how worried I had been. "She can be a handful, so if she calls you or comes to your office, you need to be prepared and I'm so sorry."

"Julie, I am not in the least worried about a visit from your mom. And, what you and I discuss remains private."

~ * ~

It wasn't until the next week that I knew I had to be concerned.

As usual, I took my time walking home from the bus stop. When I came up the driveway of our apartment complex, I saw Marge out on the balcony, smoking a cigarette. I knew from her stance that it wasn't going to be an easy night. I dragged my feet up the stairs and exhaled big before I opened the door.

Marge met me before I could put anything down or go to my room. "I met your friend, Emily."

"She's not my friend." I placed my book bag near the sofa and scooted past her to the kitchen.

"Sure she is." Marge followed me and snickered. "She cares so much about you." She was using a voice that sounded like it came from a Sunday morning cartoon. She paced out onto the balcony and back into the apartment.

"Everyone knows that Sunday cartoons suck," I whispered as she headed outside.

"I know where she lives, too." Marge came back and stood in the doorway of the kitchen, watching for my response.

My heart pounded and my hand shook as I poured a glass of water. She's lying, I thought.

"That's right, Emily Cher-ni-coff." She glared at me. "You won't be seeing her anymore. You'll see who I want you to see, got it?"

I took a drink of water, pretending not to care. "Got it."

I went to my room and closed the door. I wished I could escape out the back window and run to wherever Emily was to make sure she was okay. I wrote in my school journal and cried. I wrote about how much I hated Marge and couldn't wait to get away from her. I wondered if Emily ever wanted to see me again, now that she met Marge. I wrote until my fingers hurt and knew that Mrs. Shechtman would see it all, the next time she read our journals. I didn't care anymore. As long as I left out the physical abuse, of course.

~ * ~

By Thursday, Mrs. Shechtman kept me after class. "Are you okay?"

"I'm better." I stood, looking at her desk and traced the edge of wood with my finger.

"If you need to talk, I'm here."

"I see Emily, the counselor, in the library on Fridays," I said.

"I'm glad t you do. I'm an Emily too, and I'm here every day."

"So, you're telling me that you're an Emily 'cause your name is Emily and you're an Emily because I can talk to you?"

"Exactly." She smiled warmly.

~ * ~

That night, Marge decided to pick a fight. Since confronting me about Emily, I really hadn't said much to her. We had the residents to take care of earlier in the week and, thankfully, that took my mind off the subject. But Marge must have known Fridays were my days to see Emily, because she warned me again not to see her. She yelled for a short while and then left it alone. I read and then went to sleep.

The lights flicked on at some point in the middle of the night. "Julie! Julie, get the fuck up!" I moved quickly to the edge of my bed and tried to pry my eyes open against bright lights. "Get up, I said."

"What did I do?" I stood with the backs of my legs against my mattress, steadying myself.

Marge rambled and I didn't understand what she was talking about. She was saying something about all the grief I caused her and that I caused my dad's death. She kept yelling and spitting on me. I backed myself against a nearby wall and put my hands over my face.

"You're killing me, too!" she screamed.

Without thinking, I called out, "Good!"

Marge turned suddenly and with one good tug, pulled down a metal rod from my closet. "Bend over, onto the bed, damn it!"

I stood, frozen and shocked.

"Do it now, Julianne, don't make this worse!" Her eyes were crazy. I slowly moved back to my bed, buried my face in the sheets and covered my butt with my hands. "Move your hands! Move your fucking hands!" The piece of metal came down on my butt and I thought I would pass out. I waited for a moment and then quickly got up from the bed and moved away from her and toward the door. I fell down and covered my head with my arms. I felt the blow come down on my hand and I cried out.

Marge threw the rod across the bed and left the room. I quietly shut the door and went to my bed. I cried into my pillow for my dad. I cried for Emily.

~ * ~

The next morning, I went straight to the library and waited for Emily. I wondered how she would react to me. I didn't want her to tell me that she couldn't see me.

When she came through a side door the teachers use, she smiled big. "We need to talk," she said.

"I know." I raised my eyebrows with worry. "Are you going to leave?"

"What?" She looked confused as she opened her office. "You mean because of your mom? I'm sure we can figure something out and get her to come around."

"Emily?" I started to cry as I shut the door behind me.

"What is it?"

I raised my swollen bruised hand to show her. "I have to tell you something."

Emily studied my hand. She read my eyes and sensed my fear. She took a deep breath and settled forward with her forearms resting on her knees like she was ready for a long story. "Julie, I need you to know I am obligated to report abuse." She looked at my hand again. "I don't want you to be afraid and I know it's hard, but you can't live in a situation where you're being abused." Emily kept her elbows on her knees and held out her hands. "Do you think anything is broken?" She frowned in sympathy. "Are you hurt anywhere else?"

"I don't know if it's broken and I'm just hurting, period." Then, I abruptly pulled back and folded my arms. "I thought we were confidential."

"Julie," she spoke calmly and deliberately, "part of my job is to make sure clients are safe, and I take your safety very seriously."

"Who do you tell?" I brought my hand that was now folded into a fist, toward my mouth and tapped it on my lips.

"Well, first, I need to talk with the director at Aldersgate."

"What is Aldersgate, anyway?" I barely let her finish.

"Aldersgate is a youth services bureau," she said softly. "It's where my office is and it's a place that helps teens, and we work under C.Y.S. which is Children and Youth Services."

"This is bad. I am going to be in so much trouble." I talked through my fist and stared at parts of the floor. I made animal shapes from patterns of wear on the carpet.

"I know you're really scared, but this can't keep happening." Emily stopped herself. "How long has this been happening?

"She's always been like this. But she can be nice, too." I wiggled in the chair. "I don't think you need to say anything to the director or whatever." I was doubting myself and wondering if it could be considered abuse. Maybe I was a bratty kid and Marge just couldn't take it anymore. Maybe things weren't that bad. "Can we just forget about all of this for now?"

"Julie, how did your hand get like that?" Emily forced me to remember the hellish night I'd had. I looked around the room at everything but her. I tried to focus, but I couldn't breathe. "I don't even know how to explain any of this because it doesn't make sense to me, so how can I explain it to you?"

"Take your time." Emily was patient and kind.

I suddenly remembered that Emily met her. "Was she mean to you? What did she say to you?"

"I wouldn't say she was mean, it was more like concerned." Emily sat upright. "But, we're not talking about me, we're talking about what happened to your hand."

"Right." I took a deep breath. "This is from my closet." I pointed to the lump on my hand. "I mean, it's from the clothing rod that hangs in the closet." Emily seemed to twitch slightly. "It's not that bad. It looks worse than it feels."

Emily positioned herself to face me directly. "Do you understand that you don't deserve that? That it's not okay to hit someone?"

I suddenly remembered hitting Helen Melbaum because someone put me up to it and shoving Gary Smythe for always calling me 'crazy'. "I've done it, and no, it's not okay and I feel bad about it."

"Do you think your mom feels bad about it?" Emily found my eyes.

"She says it's out of love sometimes. She wants to teach me." I stopped talking for a minute because nothing was going to come out the way I wanted it to. I needed to think all of it through.

"Look, I know that it's wrong. I know that most kids don't have to deal with this, but she can't help it and..." I stopped and rubbed my eyebrows with my fingertips. "Ugh." I wanted to cover my face or start over. As I sat there, I started feeling huge, like a big blob, complaining about stuff, and I had no right to be there. I had nowhere to run and everything to run from. "Nothing fits!" I pressed on my temples and stared at the floor. "I don't know what I'm doing here."

"I just don't feel like I fit in anywhere and I don't know what's going to happen."

"You do fit in everywhere you go, but you need to be safe. Love doesn't come in the form of abuse. I'm not saying that she doesn't love you, she just doesn't know how." Emily paused. "Would you be able to tell me what happened with the closet rod?"

"Not really." I thought I would cry from frustration. "She hit me with it, so what?" I realized I sounded mean and I sighed. "I just wonder what's going to happen after CYS gets involved and all that."

"Well, a caseworker will probably come to your home and investigate."

"No!" I interrupted. "That can't happen. She's gonna kill me." I bent down in my seat and hugged my knees. "Oh my God. I shouldn't have ever said anything."

"Tell me what's going on, Julie. What do you mean, she's going to kill you?"

"Not kill me, kill me, but she's going to think this is all so stupid and I'm bratty and manipulative. She's either going to go crazy on the caseworker, or she's going to convince them nothing is wrong. Either way, I'm going to pay for this." I felt like I couldn't breathe.

Emily remained calm. "How are you going to pay for this?"

"She's going to hit me!" I pulled the neckline of my shirt up over my nose and buried my face. I took deep breaths and then popped back out. "Look, I am going to endure a lecture from hell, that just never ends and we'll probably move away." I closed my eyes for a minute and tried to imagine where we would go. "When is the caseworker going to come, I mean, how soon would you tell the director?"

"I have to call today." Emily looked worried for me. "I don't want you to get hurt anymore and that's why I have to do this, do you understand?"

"Yep." I was short with her.

"When did this happen?" Emily was looking at my arms and searching for my hurt hand which was safely tucked away. "Has your mom hit you with objects before?"

"It was in the middle of the night." I suddenly felt the throb in my hand. "The closet rod is a new thing, she's used a belt a few times."

Emily blinked hard. "The middle of the night? Did she just wake you or were you already up?"

"She came in, flicked on the lights, and started calling me to get up. We needed to discuss..." I started to cry as my thoughts shifted back to the night before, in my room. I was backed against my bedroom wall, with the bed on one side of me, and a dresser on the other. I felt blocked and stifled.

"What did you need to discuss?"

"Who knows?" I shrugged as tears streamed.

"What else did she say to you, I mean, after she called you to get up?"

"She started talking about my dad and how I caused his death. She told me to wipe the look off my face and stop feeling sorry for myself." I tucked my head into my arms and leaned onto my knees. I cried hard. "I just don't get it!"

Emily touched my elbow and handed me a tissue. She looked sad. "You don't get what, Julie?"

"I don't get how you can hit someone in the face and then yell at them for crying or even showing pain!" I threw my fist out to mock Marge." Stop feeling sorry for yourself!" I punched the air again. "Wipe that look off your face!" I didn't think I could stop crying. I just sat, sobbing for a while.

"Julie, do you need me to get you out of your next class?"

"It's lunch." I laughed through tears. "I'll be fine." I blew my nose and got up to throw a wad of tissues out.

"I'm worried about you. What are you going to do this weekend?" Emily said as she stood to meet my gaze.

"It depends on when that caseworker is coming."

"Are you sure you'll be okay?" Emily frowned and held my chin.

"We have the residents this weekend, I'll be fine."

Chapter Fifteen

I worried all weekend about the caseworker and when they were going to show up. I was happy we were staying with the residents instead of our apartment. Marge kept to herself for most of the weekend. She was working on some business and had files strewn all over the dining room table. I had to give Betty her fish sticks in the living room and although Betty didn't seem to mind, I thought Grace was going to blow a gasket. She kept reminding me how we don't eat dinner in the living room, we eat at the table. "I know, Grace," I repeated. "Sometimes change is good, Grace."

I kept the ladies busy by taking them for walks all over their neighborhood. While Grace bickered with Kathie and complained, I held Betty's hand and fantasized about what was going to happen with C.Y.S. I wanted them to come in and just take Marge away in handcuffs, but I knew better.

Monday came and went with no caseworker. Tuesday, again no caseworker. When I got home from school on Wednesday, Marge was at the kitchen table. Papers were all over the place, like she just transferred them from the residence and plopped them on our table.

"Hi." I walked back to my bedroom and put my bag down. I was shaking and prayed that no caseworker came and that she was in a good mood. I came back to the kitchen with a textbook as a prop to stay out of trouble.

"I want to know what you've been up to, little girl." Marge stood from the table.

"What do you mean?" I gripped the text book tight.

"Really, Julie, you think you're being abused? Do you really think I would hurt my own daughter?" She walked toward me. "Why in the fuck would I have to sit here all afternoon, talking to some woman who doesn't know me, does not know this family, because you are being abused?" Marge raised her hand. I ducked and put my palm up to cover my face. "I ought to beat your ass!"

That made sense, I thought.

She backed up and moved to the other side of the table. "I have all these files to take care of and I had to sit here and reason with some woman from the state. I had to take time to explain our situation and I shouldn't have to explain shit to anyone!" She grabbed her cigarettes and then shook her hips. "Poor little Julie!" she whined. "You just get everyone to feel sorry for you, don't you?"

"No."

"While I did nothing!" she screamed. "Those people don't know me! How would she like raising three sons and a bratty daughter on her own? Huh?" Marge wiped her mouth with the back of her hand that held a cigarette. "How would Emily like it, huh? I should go to the fucking Aldersgate and just drop your ass off with her." She paced. "But you would like that too much, wouldn't you?" She stood directly in front of me. "Wouldn't you?"

I stood, dumbfounded and wishing she would do just that.

"Answer me!"

"No." I stared at the gold trim that separated the linoleum in the kitchen from the crappy neutral rug that covered the rest of the apartment. I wondered if all the apartments had the same carpeting.

"You know what we're going to do? We're going to get the fuck out of Willow Grove and Montgomery County!" she continued.

And there it was, the suggestion of moving. I knew it. Ignore it, I thought.

I was curious how long until the rugs would get replaced in an entire apartment complex. I figured five years for our complex. It wasn't exactly the best place in Willow Grove.

I slowly took a spot at the kitchen table while Marge rambled on about Montgomery County and Emily. She lectured until she seemed exhausted. We didn't eat that night and I barely said a word. Marge got up from the table occasionally to get a glass of water, turn on a light, or empty her ashtray. I tried to concentrate on school work. The last thing I remembered hearing was, "Get the fuck to bed!"

I lay awake and wondered what would happen next.

She didn't hit me that night. She didn't even come into my room.

~ * ~

"Well, it seems that Marge Beekman is a very convincing woman." Emily seemed business-like for the first few minutes. "The caseworker found her to be intelligent, talkative, witty...I guess a lot has happened over the years, huh?"

"Yeah." I looked down, grateful to be sitting in front of Em. "Does the caseworker lady want to talk to me?" I was disappointed that Marge pulled it off, yet somehow, relieved.

"I'm sure it will get to that point." Emily took a deep breath. "You need to let some others in and expose what's happening at home."

"What do you mean? Don't you believe me? Does your director believe me?"

"Of course, we believe you! That's why I'm telling you to let others know. I don't care if you tell teachers or go straight to the police." Emily looked very serious. "I did what I could, but there are boundaries and now it's in the hands of C.Y.S. and unfortunately, your mom is extraordinary"

"She's not my mom." I interrupted. "She's not a mom. Moms don't do this."

"Okay." Emily spoke softly. "Marge," she hesitated, "has convinced them that nothing has happened."

"She's blaming this on me and saying that I'm manipulative." I tapped the front of my teeth with my fingernails while my eyes darted around the room.

"Yes, basically, that you're trying to get attention." Emily exhaled and stayed quiet for a few minutes. "You could show your hand to someone else and tell them."

I looked down at my hand which now just had a purple mark on it. "I could have just hit it on my locker for all anyone knows."

I spent the rest of the hour talking about the lecture and how Marge threatened to leave town.

For the next few weeks, I thought about telling a teacher or my friend, Karen Bean, but I just couldn't come out with it. I dropped hints in my journal, but Mrs. Shechtman was probably confused because I wrote about wanting to feel safe and wondering if I was going crazy. I figured that tons of teenagers wrote that kind of stuff. I continued to use humor at school to cover my feelings.

~ * ~

Over the course of months that I had been seeing Emily, kids found out about it. Jody, the air guitarist, always tried talking to me in the hall about how cool Emily was and my classmates realized I was missing from math class every Friday. I finally just told them about Emily.

One Friday, after a session where I gave more background on my crazy family, I had lunch period with Jimmy DeLaurentis and then headed off to science class. We were working on a collage project and I was goofing off and leaning on the back two legs of my chair. I had a big piece of poster board lying on my desk, a magazine in one hand, and a large pair of scissors in the other. My chair suddenly slipped out from under me and I hit my head on a row of cabinets. I was embarrassed, but

I rubbed my head, laughed it off and got up. My friend, Nancy, had been laughing with me, but then she looked horrified and pointed at my leg. "Oh my God, look at your knee!" I looked down to see my scissors stuck in my leg and blood coming through the side of my painter's paints. Instinctively, I pulled the scissors out and just stood there, not knowing what to do next. Marge would be so angry with me for fooling around in class and sitting on my chair without all four of the legs down. My pants were all bloody and I was not going to be able to hide it.

"Somebody get the counselor in the library!" I heard someone say. I started for the front of the room.

"Mr. Kelly, I need to go to the nurse's office." I was still holding the bloody scissors.

"Julie?" Emily appeared in the doorway and looked confused. "Your classmate said you're hurt?"

"I am. I was acting stupid and fell back in my chair." I walked out into the hall with Emily following me. "I'm okay." I was crying a little, but I wasn't sure if it was pain, embarrassment, or feeling love from Emily. "I think it just hit an area of fat that easily absorbs this sort of thing," I joked as we walked. "Wait, you weren't in with someone, were you?"

The school nurse quickly put on gloves and took the scissors from me. I hoped she didn't think I would hurt anyone. "Oh dear, I'm going to have to call your parents so you can get some stitches." The nurse stared at the gaping hole of bloody tissue.

"I don't need stitches." I grabbed my pant leg and pulled it down.

"Jul, it really looks like you do." Emily cringed.

"What's your number, honey?" The nurse picked up the phone. I hesitated. It wasn't a resident day so Marge could very well be home. I gave the nurse the number and prayed that she was out. Emily and I stayed quiet while the nurse dialed. "Hello, Mrs. Beekman?" Damn. I chatted nervously with Emily while the nurse talked. My leg was starting to throb and I held on to the spot with another part of my pant leg that was slowly getting bloody.

"Okay!" The nurse hung up the phone. "Your mom is on the way. She says you don't have a family doctor?" She looked at me as if I might tell her something different.

"Right." I watched her as she looked for a number on the wall next to her phone. The nurse put her index finger up toward me after she dialed another number. Her finger stayed steady and indicated that I needed to wait, be quiet, or both. She spoke with someone for a few minutes and hung up.

"I have an address that I'm going to have you give to your mom. It's for Dr. Pezzi and she works with the school district. You'll see her at her home office and she'll give you those stitches. I'm just going to wrap that leg with some gauze, is that okay?" The nurse reached for my foot and started rolling up my pant leg.

"That's fine. Was my mom mad?" I watched as she twirled gauze around my leg.

"No. I think just surprised." She tore off a piece of white tape.

I looked at Emily and smiled at her. I thought about how pretty she was and how I wished she was taking me. Instead, Marge was coming to get me and would probably be there momentarily. "You better go, Emily."

"I know." She smiled back at me. "Are you going to be okay?"

"Yes." I wanted to tell her I would miss her and I couldn't wait to see her again. That I felt comforted by her and I trusted her. "Can I come home with you?" I flashed her a goofy grin.

Emily exhaled a little laugh. "I'll see you next week."

"Okay." I suddenly felt horrible and nauseated.

"Hey, Jul?" Emily popped back from behind the door. "Aldersgate is right in downtown Willow Grove and they know how to reach me."

As Marge pulled up in front of the school, I went through my routine of searching out her mood. Her expression seemed more curious than angry.

"Hi." I opened the passenger door. "I'm really sorry." I handed her the directions for Dr. Pezzi's home office.

"Sorry for what?" She took the paper and studied it. "Sorry for being stupid and falling off a chair?"

"Well, that and disturbing you." I stared at the school as we pulled away. I thought about Emily and wondered what she was doing. I imagined Jody playing air guitar in her office or maybe some other kid was telling her about their problems.

"Where is this injury?" Marge pulled up to the stop sign and looked down at my leg.

"It's just a cut near my knee." Dried blood was all over the side of my pant leg. "It looks bad, but it's not."

"Well, it must be, if we have to get stitches!" Marge had her lecture face on. "Christ, Julie, who is going to pay for this?"

"Maybe the school?" I was making hopeful guesses. I wanted to change the subject. "I auditioned for the school musical, The Wizard of Oz." I waited for a response, but got nothing. I sighed and quietly laughed to myself. "I have a pretty good chance at getting a lead part."

"Julie, I want to know why a caseworker came to my house and who has started this witch hunt?"

I nervously tugged on the hole in my pants to keep the material from sticking and I wondered if she was referring to the Wizard of Oz.

"Emily, right?" Marge glared at me.

At any minute, I was going to have to lie and tell her I wasn't seeing Emily. "I think you have to turn up here." I pointed to a long driveway.

"You and whatever little friends you've made, this is bullshit, Julianne!" Marge pulled the car in front of the garage of the doctor's home that looked like a giant treehouse. She grabbed for the car keys, but just held her hand there, gripping the keys. "What are you going to tell this doctor, huh?" She stared at me coldly. "Are you going to try and manipulate her, too?"

I reached for my door handle and pulled. "I need stitches." I put one foot out the door. Marge didn't budge. she wasn't getting the hint. "Can we go?" I asked softly.

"I don't need this bullshit, understand?" Marge's breathing increased as she stared at the steering wheel. "Mother fucker!" Marge slammed both hands down on the dashboard and I jumped. "Fuck the mother over!"

I took a deep breath. "I'm going into the doctor's, okay? I mean, they're probably wondering why we're just sitting here." I looked for an entrance and saw there was a separate door for the office. I was happy we weren't just going into someone's house. It would help Marge too, to keep the experience less personal.

"I don't give a fuck! I'll sit here all day if I have to." Marge removed the keys from the ignition, but still didn't move toward opening her door. "You need to understand I am not going to be bullied by bureaucratic assholes who want to rake me over the coals."

"I understand and I'm sorry." My knee was now really throbbing.

Marge finally opened her door. "You goddamned better be sorry."

Dr. Pezzi was great. I never felt much pain and she didn't make me take my pants off to get the stitches. I was glad that the accident tore my painters pants and not my BonJour jeans.

"Okay, Mrs. Beekman?" Dr. Pezzi talked as she wrote. "She'll need to have the stitches out in ten days." She handed Marge a slip of paper. "Just call me if you have any questions and you can call the same number to schedule the suture removal."

"Right." Marge took the slip of paper.

"Thank you," I said.

Dr. Pezzi placed her hands in her white doctor's coat pockets. "You're very welcome." She smiled. "Stay on all fours from now on."

"I will." I smiled.

As Marge and I walked back to the car, I thought about what it would be like to run back and show Dr. Pezzi my hand, maybe ask if anything was broken. She could lock Marge out and call the police.

Marge would pound on all the doors and the police would come, but they would just end up believing her side of the story anyway.

~ * ~

The results from the musical auditions were posted outside of Mrs. Shechtman's room at two twenty. I waited all day to find out if I was going to get a part and hour by hour, convinced myself I would get a job as a stagehand or something. When our last class ended, I walked quickly to where the results were posted. The role of Dorothy went to someone I didn't know and I didn't see my name posted. I was disappointed and headed to my locker. I didn't care so much about not getting a lead, I cared I wouldn't have anywhere to go each day after school. I would have to go to the art department and ask about when I could start helping with design and set-up.

"Julie!" someone shouted through the sea of kids in the hallway. "Julie !" I turned to see Karen Kroll jumping and waving her arms.

"What's wrong?" I placed a few of my books on the top shelf of my locker.

"We both got leads and I'm the scarecrow!" She grabbed my wrists and continued jumping. "This is going to be so much fun! This is so great!" I stood motionless and watched her enthusiasm.

The part of scarecrow was perfect for Karen. She was tall and slender with thick auburn hair and freckles.

"I'm so happy for you, Karen, but what are you talking about?" I felt a little irritated that she didn't read the whole list. "I didn't get a lead."

"But, you did! You're Glinda!" She danced around me.

"Who's Glinda?" I crinkled my nose.

"The good witch. You have a solo and the solo makes you a lead!"

I thought about the movie for a minute. I then remembered the good witch and I smiled. "You get to sing too, Karen!" I couldn't believe that I got a part. "I thought that the other leads would be cast with all boys.

Thanks for telling me." I grinned. "I would have never known."

Karen smiled. "See you in rehearsals tomorrow!" She took off down the hall and I raced to my bus.

All the way home on the bus, I tried to remember the good witch. I thought she might have hung out with a group of midgets and I laughed just thinking about it, but I couldn't remember her singing anything. I was excited though and I desperately wanted to tell Emily.

Marge was at her usual spot at the kitchen table. "Hi, Mom." I slid into a chair at the other end.

"Hi." She barely answered and didn't bother to look up.

I sat quietly and tried to figure out how I could get out of the house without causing drama.

Marge was very involved in whatever she was doing. I didn't want to bother her, but I didn't want to sit there, either. Maybe I could actually get away with going to see Emily.

"Do you need me to go to the store or anything?" I offered.

Marge looked at me like she was confused, like I just woke her and she didn't know where she was. "What?"

I rubbed my arm and looked out the window. "I just wondered if you needed me to get anything from the store or..."

"I just want you to leave me alone." I felt her stare. "I'm trying to figure out the taxes."

"Well, can I go for a walk?"

"I don't care! I said, leave me alone!" She pressed hard on a calculator.

I made my way to the apartment door and turned the knob. She wasn't asking questions. I took a deep breath and slowly closed the door behind me. I walked quietly down the steps anticipating that she might go out to our porch and ask where I was going. Once I got outside, I looked up and she wasn't there, so I started to walk fast, then run. I ran behind our apartment complex and into the back woods of St. David's Catholic School. I was going to do it, I was going to Aldersgate to see

Emily.

I had to ask a few people before I found it, but Aldersgate was in a building we had driven past several times. I walked up a ramp and went inside. A woman was sitting near the front door, writing. She didn't acknowledge me until after I stood there for a few minutes, "May I help you?"

"Um, is Emily here?" I looked around the large open space that was flanked by several offices.

"Oh, I thought you were here for one of the groups downstairs. Let me see." She looked down at a schedule. "Do you have an appointment?"

"No, I just thought I could talk with her for a few minutes." I silently prayed that she wouldn't reject me.

"Well, she's with someone right now, but maybe she can see you for a minute when she's done."

"Okay." I smiled and looked around for a place to wait. "May I sit over there?" I pointed to a puffy sofa.

The woman nodded as she picked up her phone to make a call. A few teenagers, reeking of smoke, quickly walked past and headed to a stairwell.

I admired celebrities in the magazines in the waiting area. The movie Xanadu was just out and I stared at Olivia Newton John and then at a picture of Suzanne Somers and thought Emily most resembled Suzanne. I looked at all the pictures from a photo shoot on the set of Dallas. I wanted to play a part on some show where I would get to use an accent and wear outrageous clothes. I might have to stop eating for a few months, but I wasn't any worse looking than some of the characters. Maybe I could go into acting and be someone else. I fantasized about moving to Hollywood, 'pounding the pavement', as they say, and auditioning. How could I get to a point where I wouldn't be self-conscious, I wondered.

"Julie?" I quickly looked up to see a beaming Emily standing in front of me.

"Hi." I stood, put the magazines down and transferred my hands to my pockets. "Is it okay that I'm here?"

"Of course, come on in." Emily signaled with a wave and a grin. "Are you okay?"

"I'm fine and well, I found you." I followed her into her office.

"I see that!" Emily laughed and motioned for me to sit.

"I have passed this place so many times and never knew what it was."

"Well, I'm glad you know where it is now."

"Yeah." I sat and stretched my arms between my legs and past my knees. I forgot why I was there. I couldn't think of what to say. "Do you live near here?"

"I do. I live in a tiny cottage behind a deli."

"Messina's on Davisville? Is that where?" From the concerned look on her face, I instantly regretted asking, but I only knew of two delis in Willow Grove and the one near me didn't have any little house behind it.

"Julie, why do you want to know?"

"Oh, I won't go to your house, I was just curious." I looked around her room and noticed two desks. "You share your office?"

"Yes." Emily nodded.

"Is it that Vern guy from school?"

"No, that desk belongs to Betsy. She's a coworker and another counselor here." Emily sat back in her chair. She studied me curiously and I felt stupid. I liked our place in the library at school. This didn't feel as right.

"I have to get back home." I stood.

Emily looked surprised. "Oh, okay."

I suddenly remembered the main reason I came to see her. "I got the part of the good witch in the school musical," I said proudly. "Maybe you can come see it."

"I would like that." Emily grinned. "Congratulations!"

"Okay, I'll see you Friday." I held on to the handle of her office door and leaned in. "Thanks for seeing me."

I ran home as fast as I could. When I got to the top of the hill at St. Davids, I looked out toward Messina's Deli and tried to spot Emily's little house. It was blocked by a huge construction crane that sat just beyond some railroad tracks. "Goodnight, Emily." I waved to the crane.

Marge never asked me a thing when I returned. -She did seem happy for me when I told her about the musical. "That's great, Julie! I've always told you that you have a nice voice."

"I have rehearsals every day after school, so I won't get home until after five."

"Do what you have to do," she responded. "As long as you aren't near that Emily and no caseworkers come to my house, I don't care what you do."

~ * ~

A few days later, I was called into the nurse's office.

"I just need you for a minute." The nurse looked down at my legs like she couldn't remember which leg got hurt. "I just got a call from Dr. Pezzi's office and she's concerned because your mom never called to get the sutures out." She held out her hand for me to move closer. "How in the world did you get all of that blood out of your pants?"

"Lots of bleach." I started to pull up the pant leg with the big hole in it.

She viewed my knee. "These don't look so great. You could get an infection if you don't get them out soon."

"Can you take them out?" The idea made me cringe. I felt nauseous any time I even thought about the wound, because it was mostly numb and kind of gross.

"I'm not authorized to take them out," she explained. "You really need to have your mom call, okay?"

"Okay." I walked back to class, thinking about laws and how stupid they were. The nurse wasn't authorized to pull my stitches, but Emily was required to report abuse. None of it worked out for me. Now I had to go home and bring up the whole incident.

Later, when I brought the stitches thing up to Marge, she took matters into her own hands. She took a long drag of her cigarette, placed it in an ashtray and held a pair of tweezers in the flame of her lighter. "Stop moving, goddamn it!" I tried to hold still. I tapped my fingers on the table, took deep breaths and looked away. Within a few minutes, my stitches were out, it didn't even hurt.

~ * ~

Rehearsals started and so did getting fit for costumes. I dreaded it trying something on and hoped I could get privacy. My Glinda costume was an old wedding dress that belonged to one of the home economics teachers. I was embarrassed because the dress was too small. "It's not a problem." Mrs. Pennypacker assured me. "I'm divorced now and we can do whatever we want to this dress." She laughed. "We'll just add a little material." I was mortified. "Really," she said. "It's no big deal."

The dress was amazing. It was long and flowing with little pearl beads and shimmering sequins. Mrs. Pennypacker was able to insert elastic stretch panels just underneath the arms where no one could see. I wore it with confidence, both in rehearsal and the first big night.

I went to rehearsals every day, even when I wasn't scheduled to be there. There was always a late bus, so I often sat in the theatre and did homework or talked with other kids that were in the show. I made some new friends, too. I loved when it was my turn to practice my song, because it was all so bizarre to me.

The chorus teacher gave me specifics on how I should sing the word, 'news'. "When you sing, she brings you good news or haven't you heard, pronounce 'news' like the Italian dish, Gnocchi, or like you smell something bad, eww." She opened her mouth and showed me the underside of her tongue against the roof of her mouth. "Neeuze" she repeated. I wondered why that was so important, but followed her instructions. I also practiced "Meer-ee-acle" for the word, 'miracle'. When she fell out of Kansas, a meer-ee-acle occurred.

~ * ~

On opening night, I waited behind the curtain. I was nervous, but once I entered the stage and took my place, everything felt more than right. I loved the lights and I could see the ends of my glamorous eyelashes and feel the sparkle from my lip gloss.

I sang my song and enjoyed every minute of it. Then, my character just kind of stood in the background while Munchkins made the stage colorful.

When the show was over, we all took our bows at the front of the stage. I was entranced by all the applause and camera lights flashing. I pretended that the applause was just for me. I curtsied again and felt a tap on my white shoe. I looked down at the edge of the stage and there was Betty. I squinted in her direction. Was this real? I tried to ignore her for a few minutes. I started to talk with the kids next to me. Finally, when I couldn't take ignoring her anymore, I looked down again and there stood Betty, Grace, Kathie, and Marge. Betty held three red roses. "Here, Julay!" she yelled and her tongue thrust forward. I hesitated for a moment and then bent down to take the flowers. Kathie wouldn't stop clapping, even though everyone else had. Grace was yelling at Betty and Marge looked pissed at me.

I heard giggling behind me. "Is that your family?" I turned to see some of the Lollipop Guild laughing at me. "Well, is it?"

I looked back at the residents and then at Marge, who stood, glaring with disapproval. I knew what was the right thing to say. I knew I should just turn around and proudly state that indeed they were, but I couldn't. "Mom? I have to go backstage. Can we meet at the car?" I held back tears and walked away quickly. I never expected Marge to come, let alone bring the residents.

Once backstage, I quickly changed my clothes and hung my dress for the next show. I tried to get out to the car and ran into one of the music teachers on the way out.

"Julie, you did a wonderful job!"

"Oh, thank you." I managed a smile. "I really appreciate all of your hard work so that we could do a good job."

"Oh my, it was my pleasure." She took the roses from my hand. "These are just beautiful, thank you!"

I stood awkwardly silent for a moment. "You deserve them." How could this be happening? Marge was going to be doubly ticked. "I have to go."

I got into the front seat and for a moment, I felt good again. Marge wasn't even looking at me, so maybe she calmed down. I turned around and looked at the three ladies. "Did you like the show?"

Kathy yelled, "Yeah-ya!" Grace rocked back and forth and Betty might have winked at me.

"Julie, who in the fuck do you think you are?" Marge pulled out from the school parking lot.

"How dare you treat these ladies like you don't know them!"

"No T.V!" Grace pronounced.

I once again, sat close to the passenger door. I wanted to tell Marge to go to hell and then jump out and run. "I'm sorry, I just didn't realize they were coming and it took me by surprise, that's all," I lied.

"Bullshit!" She sat up straighter. "You were embarrassed as shit!" She moved toward me and found my mouth to whack.

I immediately covered the area with my hand. "Can you please not do that in front of them?"

"Why, Julie? You don't think they can handle it?" She tightened her lips. "What they can't handle is your rejection!" Marge lit a cigarette. "They were excited to see you in the musical and you just treat them like dirt."

"Yeah -ya, dirt," Kathie muttered.

Marge blew out a cloud of smoke. "That hurt your feelings, didn't it?" She looked in the rearview mirror. The backseat produced a slew of grunts and nervous giggles.

I turned to look at them. "I'm very sorry and thank you for the beautiful flowers." Shoot!

Marge looked down at the seat and then at the floor near my feet. "Where are the flowers?"

"I put them in water and I'll be able to have them for tomorrow night, too," I responded.

"You better have them!" She stayed quiet the rest of the night.

~ * ~

The following day, we had a performance during the day for the school and then the final show at night. It was Friday and Emily was there. I had a nice chat with her in the morning and she promised to come and watch the show in the afternoon. I peeked out from behind the curtain and saw Emily standing with Mrs. Shechtman. I was very excited that they both were there and I sang my heart out.

Since Emily told me to start talking to other people about what was going on at home, I was writing more details in my journal that Mrs. Shechtman read, but not too much. A few times, she kept me after class and she asked, "What are you going to do?"

I reminded her I was talking to Emily about it and I had to figure it out.

Once, after school, she held nothing back. "I would call the police, if my mother was doing something like that." Mrs. Shechtman spoke seriously, but always made me feel comfortable when I didn't know how

190

to respond. "Do you know that you and my husband share the same birthday?"

"Really?" I lit up. "He must be a great guy. Wait, how do you know...?"

"I looked at your files. I documented a few things," she raised her small hand that held a huge diamond, "without sharing your personal information."

"Okay." I shook my head. "Documented?"

"Yep. So when you are ready to turn her in, you'll have some backup." She walked behind her desk and grabbed her handbag and a stack of journals.

"It's just too scary," I responded. "A caseworker has already been to our house and nothing happened."

"Next time, something probably will happen, but you have to be brave." Mrs. Shechtman walked to her classroom door and turned off the lights. "Totally against policy, but want a ride home?"

"Yes!" I said. "I get to ride in your bug?"

"Zot will be glad to have you." She walked fast out the side door of the school.

"Zot?" I followed her, smiling.

"Yes, see the license plate?" She pointed with a thin finger and perfectly manicured nails. "It came like that. 657-ZOT, so I've always called the car Zot."

Emily Shechtman drove me about two blocks from my house, where I pointed to a good place.

"Thanks for the ride, I liked listening to The Doobie Brothers, too."

"You're welcome. You're a good kid."

"Thanks." I straightened my neck and smirked. "I hope you didn't go too far out of your way."

"No, I usually take Davisville Road, but this isn't far at all."

"That's Emily's street." I beamed and shut the car door. I practically skipped home.

~ * ~

Marge came home a little later than me that day. She came in and announced that I should get ready to go so we wouldn't be late for my counseling session. It caught me off guard, because I thought for a minute that she meant Emily. I wondered if she was playing some game because she found out that I had snuck off to Aldersgate a month or so before.

I followed Marge to her car. "Where are we going?"

"I told you." Marge jingled the keys. "We're taking you to your counselor."

"Who?" I was afraid to say the name, Emily.

"Alice." Marge stared at me as she opened her car door. "I found someone that I like, not someone who's going to go along with your little manipulations and feel sorry for you."

I wondered if Alice was some devil lady that Marge met in an offshoot of a N.O.W. meeting or if she was a hypnotist, or worse, a witch doctor who might make me drink some concoction to make me 'better'. She may have been from the Christian Science Church that Marge was having me attend and that wouldn't be bad. Those people were all super nice, even if they did think they could cure everything themselves.

Oddly enough, Alice's office was on the same street as Aldersgate, only it was about five miles further down the road. Alice was an older woman and very pleasant. "You must be Julie."

"I am." I stood after waiting in a small living area.

"Well, come on in." Alice held the door to her office open and waited for me to enter. Marge tagged close behind and Alice seemed confused. "You wanted me to meet with Julie, correct?"

"Oh, I want to hear everything she has to say." Marge helped herself to a chair in Alice's office. She sat abruptly and seemed incredibly defensive before anyone said a word. Her arms were folded high on her chest, lips tightened and eyes wide.

"So, Marge, you want this to be more like family counseling?" Alice sat at her desk and crossed her ankles. The sight of her blue polyester pants and matching floral blouse made me feel itchy.

"No, I want you to be Julie's therapist!"

"Julie, are you comfortable with that?" Alice closed her lips tight and quickly blinked.

I hesitated and sighed. "I guess." I thought I would cry. "It's just that…"

"Just what?" Marge sat forward.

"I already had someone to see and…"

"And you won't see her again!" Marge barked. She looked at Alice. "She's the one I told you about. The one who was brainwashing my daughter."

I rubbed my forehead and spoke softly. "She wasn't brainwashing me."

"See? See what a brat she is?" Marge pointed at me and looked at Alice like she would agree at any moment.

Alice never took charge during that session. I didn't blame her. She let Marge rant on like everyone else did. The only time anyone ever took charge was the time my dad just pinned her down to stop her from throwing anything more. I was hoping that Alice would just forget the niceties and just tell Marge to shut up! I played different scenarios in my head and humored myself during the hour. I had it where Alice would get up from her desk chair and slap Marge across the face, throw a chair through a window because Marge was driving her mad.

I was never asked another question the entire session. It was just the Marge show and I seemed to be eternally stuck in the audience.

~ * ~

I started taking a different route to the bus stop every morning. Instead of walking through the neighborhood, I went through the woods behind St. Davids, so that I could see Emily's crane. I often prayed or just sent good thoughts. Other times I felt pain through my entire body, like all my limbs and organs were terribly sad. If I stood still too long, I got a lump in my throat and pressure in my jaw or I just cried because I wanted so desperately to be somewhere else. Though I wanted change, my moments on that hill helped keep my prayers nice rather than turning to wishes for Marge's quick and untimely death.

~ * ~

One flowery May morning, I went to the hill, looked out across the railroad tracks and stared at the crane. I wondered how long I would get to view the sight. Marge was talking more often about moving once the school year was over and I was so attached to my friend Karen Bean, Mrs. Shechtman, and Emily, I didn't think I could bear another move. It was one of those mornings that made me hurt all over. But, just as I was about to move on so that I wouldn't cry, I spotted Mrs. Shechtman's little VW, Zot, cruising along Davisville Road. That's the way she takes to school!

When I saw her later, I asked if she would ever give a student a ride to school if she just happened to see her standing on the side of the road. She grinned. "Only if she's in danger of being late to school and only if she is standing on the sidewalk, where it's safe." I smiled and turned away, feeling very happy.

The next morning, I got up early. I walked a good extra mile past my bus stop just so I could wait for Mrs. Shechtman and get a ride in Zot. We chatted about my journals and how things weren't getting any better and she talked about her dog, Alfie, and how the older he got, the more he smelled like wet carpeting. I thought she was funny and I felt privileged to know a little about her life. I watched her thin arms and hands maneuver the stick shift. Her shimmering jewelry and petite outfits made me feel very self-conscious, but it was all worth it. I knew she liked who I was and could see past my clothes and chubbiness. I'm clean, I thought, as I raised my long hair to smell the maraschino cherry scent. I rode in with her a few more times and took the bus home. Marge never knew. Most things that made me happy were things she didn't know.

~ * ~

Friday was still my favorite day. I could finally go in and tell Emily things without hiding so much. I couldn't tell her about Scot though and what he did. For some reason, it just seemed way too personal and scary to talk about. I figured it wasn't important anyway, because it wasn't happening then, since he lived far away.

I told her about the therapist that Marge set up for me.

"How was that?" Emily rested an elbow on the arm of her chair and clasped her hands.

"Dumb!" I nodded once.

"How was it dumb?" Emily grinned.

"I think I said maybe three words during the whole thing." I folded my arms. "Seriously, it was just Marge talking about herself."

"Wow." Emily looked confused. "Did the therapist try to interject? Maybe bring her back into focus on why you were there to begin with?"

"That would be very difficult to do."

Emily looked off like she was searching in the distance. "That's very true, she's a tough one to reel in." Emily smiled warm, like sunshine. "So, what's the game plan with the therapist? Alice, is it?"

"Yeah, Alice." I raised my eyebrows. "I doubt she wants us back. Either that, or she didn't cure me, so Marge won't go back." I shrugged. "I haven't heard anything."

Emily laughed and then glanced at me awhile. "So, what's your plan?"

"To grow up super-fast and get the heck out of her house."

"No, I mean, what's your plan when she hits you again?" Emily's eyes narrowed as she waited for my response.

"I don't know. I mean, no one is going to do anything about her anyway."

"I don't know about that. I think if you want safety and you let the police or someone at CYS know what's going on in that apartment, you'll have safety. You have more support now, Julie."

"Yes, I do." A million thoughts raced through my mind.

It was a lot to think about. I didn't want to cause a huge ordeal if it was something I could put up with. And I had.

~ * ~

Scot was in South Carolina, so he wasn't doing anything to me. Randy was busy with his fiancée, Regina, and Dan was studying at Drexel and working an internship. I barely even saw them. It was just Marge, me, and the residents.

If I tried to leave, the boys wouldn't understand. They had our dad to buffer things and Marge didn't try to control or compete with her sons. She wasn't hitting them anymore. She did fight with them, but still, they might not understand. They just didn't know anything else, but somehow, I did.

Another thing was, I didn't want Randy and Dan to feel like I was leaving them. I didn't want Danny to hate me. Besides, the last time she hit me was after the Wizard Of Oz show, and that was only a little smack on the mouth. I could put up with her.

I thought about all the different scenarios for many days, right up until the caseworker called Marge one afternoon to find out how everything was going.

"Are you seeing that Emily when I forbade you?" Marge asked as she hung up the wall phone in the kitchen.

"What?" I stared at the phone. The hanging curly wire intrigued me.

"Julie! I asked you a question!" She walked to my chair and stood over me. "Are you seeing Emily?"

"Sometimes." I stared at the floor to hide my face. My hands were already getting into position. I raised them slightly, knowing what was coming next. Seriously, what in the hell was I thinking? Why didn't I just lie? "I mean, I see her in the halls and stuff."

I didn't see stars when her hand came down on my head. I don't think anyone sees stars. Stars would be too shimmery and beautiful. I saw blotches of white and black whenever she hit me. It's not like I could go somewhere like I did back when Scot did things to me. I couldn't just float away and pretend I was somewhere hiking or tending imaginary horses. Hitting involved defending myself. It was just natural and I had to be present for that.

The problem was, the more I defended myself, the harder she fought to get to my very core and take me down.

Later, when Marge took the aluminum softball bat from my closet, she was out to strip me of my soul and create in me whatever monsters she held so tight, whatever plagued her. That had to have been her goal. "I'm going to show you what it would be like if I were an abusive mother."

I stood in my room, not sure of what to do next. Why couldn't I run?

"Get over there and lie down on the bed!" Marge pointed with the bat. I would have rather stood naked on the stage at school with a full audience commenting on my rolls of fat than to bow down to her. "I said get on the bed and don't you dare cover your ass!" I moved to the bed and slowly positioned myself, face down. I whimpered before the strike even occurred. "I'll show you what abusive is."

I thought about how many times I whacked at softballs with that bat, the sound it made. There wasn't going to be a sound like that, but I was scared out of my mind. My hands flew back to protect myself.

"Move your fucking hands!"

I moved them momentarily. The bat came down and all in the world was evil.

I jolted to my side and clutched at my butt cheeks. The bat slung at the backs of my thighs and I screamed out.

"That is what an abusive mother would do, so how dare you!" Marge flung the bat back into the closet and left my room.

I didn't come out of my room except once when I went in to use the bathroom. I lay in bed, planning my escape. I decided t if the police didn't believe me, then I would just run away forever, even if it meant giving up Emily. My plan was to take off after school and just not come home.

All the next day, I worried about where I was going to go and what I would do. My legs and my butt felt bruised. I couldn't go to Karen Bean's house, because Marge heard me speak of her and she'd find me. I couldn't go to Aldersgate, because it would probably be the first place Marge would look. If I went straight to the police, they would probably send me home. Plus, she only hit me twice this time and maybe that wasn't enough for them to do anything. They would need to meet an irate Marge before my story could unfold and she would make that happen just by calling about my disappearance.

Nancy Nelligan, a girl from some of my classes that made me laugh all the time, often invited me to her house, but I always declined. On this day, I asked if I could come over. She would take my mind off things and help start the hours of my disappearance. I took her bus home with her while Marge expected me at my usual time. Nancy and I watched soap operas. The hours flew by and just before Nancy's family was going to sit down for dinner, I told her I was calling my mom to come get me, but if I wasn't at school the next day, she should call the police.

Nancy looked very worried. "What in the heck is going on?"

"I'm not sure," I said as I dialed the apartment number. I had to run away and I wasn't clear on what to do until Marge answered. When I explained that I was at a friend's house, she responded, "Get home now, I'm going to beat your ass for worrying me!" Nancy's mother looked up from chopping lettuce and Nancy stood dumbstruck. They heard her. "Do you hear me, little girl? Get home!"

My hand shook while clasping the phone and I felt my nostrils flare. I took a deep breath and clearly responded, "No." I hung up the phone as Marge yelled something else. "Thanks, Nancy," I said as I walked to her front door.

"Where you going?" She looked frightened.

"I have a place to go," I lied. "Just remember, call the police if I'm not at school tomorrow."

It was still light out and would be for some time. I started walking south and stayed off the main roads. I knew that Mrs. Shechtman lived in some place called Roxboro. It was within Philadelphia City limits, but still close to the suburbs. She talked about some huge radio towers near her house, one time when we were in her car. I figured if I kept walking, at some point, I would see the towers and find Roxboro.

I walked for what seemed like forever, but only ended up being about eight miles. A few times, when I approached the top of a hill, I could see the radio towers with blinking red lights. It was dark and the closer I got to the city limits of Philly, the less frequent the street lights. And, suddenly, the huge stone homes with sprawling yards turned to tightly clustered row houses with old sofas on the porches, boarded up windows, and cement gardens. A few people walked fast between houses and into alleyways. I was getting scared, but I walked with purpose and didn't look at anyone. I had been in every kind of neighborhood. If I could walk through Harlem leading a blood-covered Marge, I could surely walk these streets.

Focusing on my purpose and keeping tough, I never noticed the cop car slowly trailing me. Finally, he pulled up quickly in front of me and caused my body to startle. He rolled down his window.

"Hey, where you headed?" he called through the passenger side.

"To my friend's house," I responded. I stood motionless, not sure of what to say or do next.

The cop stared straight ahead through his windshield. "You probably shouldn't be out here. Where does your friend live?"

"Roxboro," I said calmly.

"Roxboro is quite a ways away."

"Yes," I replied for a lack of a better response.

"Do your parents know you're going to this friend's?"

"Not exactly." I cringed.

"Why don't you get in the car." The officer pulled the car closer to me and signaled that I should sit in the back. "Where are your parents?" he asked as I closed myself into the backseat and leaned forward.

"It's just my mom and she cannot know where I am. I need you to trust me and not call her."

"I won't call your mom, but you need to explain what's going on." The officer turned around and focused on me through the grate that separated us.

"Okay." I hesitated. Where would I begin? "I live in Willow Grove and I'm going to a teacher's house to stay there until tomorrow morning. I have a lot going on in my house right now and I really can't go back. When tomorrow comes, there will be authorities involved and I'll get the help I need."

"Sounds like you have a plan in place, that's good." The officer smiled and looked out the window. "Well, I suppose you have a point. There's no need taking you down to the round house in Philly. You would have to spend practically the entire night just waiting around."

"The round house?"

"Yeah, it's where we take people to jail or bring them in for questioning. But, that's Philly and it's not your precinct. Plus, you don't wanna see what goes on down there."

"No, I don't want to go to a jail." I pressed my forehead against the window until I thought of what window it was. "So, do you know where the radio towers are?" I tried looking beyond all the row houses and through the trees.

"Yeah, is that where they live?"

"Well, Mrs. Shechtman said that she can see the towers from her place."

"You can see those things from everywhere, Roxboro and beyond." He glanced at me through the rearview mirror. "Tell you what, I'm going to call into dispatch and see if they can get a hold of these folks and have them meet me halfway."

"Really? Thank you." I grinned. "Wait, what time is it? I mean, is it really late?"

"What? You afraid of waking them? It's only eleven, don't worry about it."

I took a deep breath and spelled the Shechtman's name as the officer was on the phone with the dispatcher. I worried when they called out miscellaneous numbers back and forth. I wondered if Marge reported me as missing and he was going to change his mind or call her or something. It was very unnerving until all talking and beeping through his radio was over. "Okay, so Michael Shechtman is going to meet us in Chestnut Hill." The officer turned the corner slowly. "That's as far as I can take you and it ain't too far for them."

"Thank you so much." I exhaled.

"I can't believe you were gonna walk through this neighborhood like it was nothin'." He shook his head and chuckled.

I sat back and enjoyed the ride with great relief and just a tad of guilt. Mr. Shechtman had to drive to come and get me and he probably never even heard of me and Marge was probably worried. I hoped she wasn't bothering Emily.

"This must be him." The car slowed and pulled up next to a dark vehicle with just the orange lights on. It wasn't ZOT, but suddenly Mrs.

Shechtman jumped out from the passenger side and started looking for me and her husband got out of the car and shook the officer's hand.

The policeman opened my door. "You got her from here?"

"We'll take care of her. Thanks, officer." He grinned. Mrs. Shechtman held my shoulders and walked me to the back door of Mr. Shechtman's car.

"I'm so sorry to do this, but I didn't know where else to go." I sat forward a little in the back seat.

"It's fine." Mrs. Shechtman looked at me and then her husband.

"I'm Michael." Mr. Shechtman turned and smiled at me. "You're going to have to sleep in Alfie's bed." He turned the car around. Mrs. Shechtman gave him a slight shove. "Well, it's true. The spare room and bed in there is Alfie's."

"I would love to sleep there, as long as Alfie doesn't mind," I said. "Do you think he'll sleep with me?" I hadn't had a dog at the end of my bed since Blackie and I missed it.

"I'm sure he will." Michael leaned against his door as he drove.

I didn't mention how Mrs. Shechtman talked about Alfie smelling. I just knew I would love the dog, no matter what.

The Shechtmans showed me around the apartment and Alfie, a large German Shepard, followed. Everything was beautiful and rich in color. The place had just the right amount of masculine and feminine. Dark wood and white lace.

Mrs. Shechtman offered to make me something to eat, but my stomach was in knots and I couldn't. I talked to her about how things were a lot worse than what I wrote in my journals.

"I figured," she said

Michael found a new toothbrush and towels for me, along with an old shirt and some sweats that I could wear to bed. I was so tired that I prepared for bed immediately.

Soon, it was just me and Alfie, staring at each other. I patted the bed and he jumped up to lie beside me. I petted his head and stroked his fur while I tried to relax and not worry about what would happen next.

~ * ~

I woke to giggling the next morning. The Shechtmans were laughing because they found Alfie and me sleeping in spoons. I must have hugged that dog all night and Alfie was good enough to understand I needed it.

As Mrs. Shechtman drove toward school, she seemed nervous. "Unfortunately, I'm going to have to drop you off just outside Willow Grove town limits or I could get into a lot of trouble."

"But you were just protecting me."

"We know that, but the school district and the police might not understand that."

"But you've taken me to school before and I won't say anything." I thought about how I was going to get to school without Marge spotting me.

"I'm sorry, Julie. In this case, it's best."

If I could get into the school, then it would be a lot harder for Marge to get to me. "I know, just drop me off on the railroad tracks and I'll walk them right to the middle school."

Emily looked worried. "Are you sure the tracks go there?"

"Yes, I know they do. They go right into Hatboro. I would just need to exit near Byberry Road, run across the field and I'll be home free." It was a perfect idea.

"You can't go on the tracks, what about trains going back and forth?" Mrs. Shechtman stared at me and raised a brow.

"There is plenty of space. I swear, I'll be careful, it's the only way to keep everyone out of trouble."

I walked fast along the tracks. Sometimes, I ran. There were a few commuter trains that whizzed by, but I stayed well to the side. When I neared the Hatboro cemetery, I veered off into a neighborhood that would take me to Byberry Road. I was almost there and the whole trip had probably taken me only less than an hour. I could be there by second period.

I just had to go through the back parking lot of the Quik Stop, cross Byberry Road and then negotiate a field. Then, the doors to the school would be waiting.

As I came around the corner of the store, I saw a long boat of a car and an older black man standing close to it. "Here, Marge!" I thought he said. "Here she is."

His car was blocking my path to the street and as I turned to go around it, Marge came out from behind the building and grabbed my arm. "Where do you think you're going?" She had a long piece of rope in her hand.

"To school." I tried to pull away a little and her nails dug in.

"You better get in the car," the man said. "Your momma's been looking for ya. I saw ya as I was gitin' my coffee this morn. You was walking the tracks right past Burger King." He was talking and talking while Marge tied the rope around my wrists. Why was no one coming out of the store and seeing this rope? Why didn't I just run across Byberry and risk getting hit?

The man came around his car, opened the door, and tilted the seat forward so that I could get into the back. "My name's Chet," he said. "I'm a friend of your momma. You sho had her worried. Woo-wee!" He practically sang and then laughed nervously.

Marge pushed me toward the back seat and I got in. I could see my school through the trees and I wanted to wail.

As Chet drove us back to our apartment, Marge screamed at me about where I might have been and how worried she was.

"Where were you, huh?" Marge kneeled on the front seat and faced me. Her forearms hung over the seat and she looked very tired. "Where, Julianne, where?"

"I was just walking." I tried not to look at her.

"Just walking." She nodded and tightened her lips. "Just walking," she repeated slowly. I felt her glare and then she spit at me to get my attention. I looked at her hands that hung and waited for them to move in for a slap.

The spit was bad enough and I wasn't sure what was more degrading, being hit on my butt or her spit landing on my cheek.

None of it mattered. The bigger problem was whatever was going to happen once we got home. Could it be worse than a baseball bat? The thoughts made me shiver.

I wondered if I would ever see Emily or the Shechtmans again. We were going to move away, that was for certain.

"Chet and I looked all over for you! I was up all goddamned night and you were just walking around?" She turned forward in her seat and shook her head. "I was just walking around, too! I called all over the damned place, looking for your ass!" I pictured her pacing and dialing the closed offices of Aldersgate, over and over.

She turned around again to face me. "I even called your little friend, Emily." I tried very hard to not react. "That's right, little girl." She nodded. "I called her and she was right in the middle of screwing. She didn't care and she's not worried about you."

I made a face, showing my disgust. I didn't know how an educated woman could say such a thing, especially to her child. It made me angry and I wanted out of the car. "I should be at school."

"No way! No fucking way!" She slapped her hands on Chet's car seat. "You are never going back there, got me?"

I wanted to scream my head off at every stop light, but I knew it would only make things worse. Marge would like it and people would think I was crazy. I just had to be patient. When I didn't show up at school, Nancy would go to someone, Mrs. Shechtman would be worried, Emily would worry. There had to be help on the way.

When we got back to the apartment, Marge acted methodically. She got me out of the back seat by holding on to the rope. Chet smiled at me and nodded at Marge as he was pulling away. He was calm and I didn't want him to leave. "Get upstairs, use the bathroom or whatever you have to do and then you can stay in your room."

Once inside, she took off the ropes. "Hurry up."

I went into the bathroom and stared in the mirror at my worried reflection. I washed the remnants of Marge's spit off my face and wondered about school and what was happening there.

I could hear Marge waiting just outside the door. I wished there was a window in the bathroom, like in the movies. When I came out, Marge stood, blocking the way to everywhere but my bedroom. She moved quickly and escorted me there.

"Since you're a runaway, I'll be closing this door." She grabbed for the door handle and closed me into my room. I stood motionless and listened as she dragged furniture and placed it against my door. "There!" she yelled from the hallway. "See if you can get out now!"

I waited for a minute and then walked over to the windows. One window was painted shut and the other held a large air conditioner. There was a small grassy area in the back of our apartment and then a building, identical to ours, just beyond that. There wasn't any way to get out of my bedroom. I thought I heard someone outside, so I decided to write a little note and try to get help, call the police Apt 405 B.

I folded it into a small square and tried to put it through the side, between window and appliance. I couldn't get anything to budge. I tried to flatten the piece and slide it through the slats of the air conditioner itself, but it was so old the metal was pushed in, in all the wrong places. I sat on my bed and waited. Waited and worried. I could hear Marge talking on the phone and I wondered what she was planning. It had to be calls she placed because I never heard the phone ring. The attendance office at school wasn't even looking for me. When was Mrs. Shechtman going to realize the plan went awry?

I looked at my closet with its door wide open and the baseball bat, and at the rod that was torn down from months before. Then I stared at my stupid S.O.S. note.

Marge started moving the furniture away from the door. I stood quickly and shoved the note in my pocket. When she opened the door, she held out the same damned piece of rope. "Now let's put this on your wrists again so you can't run off." I held out my arms obediently. How long is this going to go on? It was completely horrifying, but I had to play along until I could bolt.

Marge led me to the living room. "Stay right there while I grab my files and purse." She walked about four feet from where I stood and gathered her things.

"We're going out in public?" I asked.

"Of course!" She opened the apartment door and tugged at my wrists. "We have to! We need to go to the bank so that you can sign some papers and I can get you out of this county." I wanted to just stop my whole body and not follow her. I wanted to just sit down in the stairwell and refuse to go any further, but I was terrified. I had no idea of what I needed to sign or what she was talking about.

Marge turned left when we exited the apartment. She wasn't going to her car.

"Are we walking?" I looked around to see if anyone was watching the bizarre scene.

"I can't control you if I'm driving the car, now can I?" Marge pulled on the rope. I was embarrassed, being led down the street like a dog. Maybe a police car would pass and notice. Someone would have to notice. Was she going to leave the ropes on in the bank?

Marge led me the half-mile or so into the business area of Willow Grove. As we approached an intersection, I shyly looked at the two lanes of cars that were stopped at the traffic light where we crossed. I saw Beth Kindt hanging out of the passenger window of a Subaru station wagon. She was about to yell something to me, I could see it, but then she stopped. She looked shocked. I wanted Beth to see what was happening, but I didn't want Marge to be aware of her.

I quickly raised my index finger to my lips, tugging the rope from Marge's hand. She pulled back on it and didn't seem to notice my friend. Beth slowly sat back in the car without a noise. She and the woman driving stared with lips parted. I had no idea why Beth wasn't in school, but I prayed she was headed there and could let someone know.

People stopped what they were doing when we stepped into the bank. Marge walked up to a man at a desk. "I need to speak with someone about transferring funds and I'll also need a notary."

"Uh, I can help you with that." The man moved slowly, like we might rob the place, as he studied my leash. "Have a seat." Marge sat down and pulled on the rope, signaling for me to do the same.

"I need the funds from this account in Michigan to go into my checking account with your bank." She looked for his response and seemed nervous. "I'll also need some cash."

"Ma'am, this appears to be a trust fund." He looked at me briefly and then back at the papers.

"I know what it is!" Marge snapped. "I have all the paperwork from my late husband's attorney." She pointed to the files that had been sitting on our kitchen table for the last month. "It's all legal!" The man examined each page and Marge watched him. "She'll get her money." Marge glanced at me. "Right now, I just need to concentrate on saving her ass."

The man looked at my wrists again and I shifted uncomfortably. He pushed away from his desk. "I'll be right back." Good, I thought. He's calling the cops. He went to another man's desk to talk. They both looked at us and then at the paperwork again. After more conversation, the man returned and started typing. "I'll have the papers ready for you in a minute. I'll need I.D. and I'll make a quick call to People's Bank in Grand Haven." I must be in a nightmare. I looked around the bank and no one seemed to notice what was happening.

Marge pulled out her wallet, handed him her driver's license, my birth certificate, and Social Security card. She sat back, pleased and content.

"Young lady, I'll need you to sign here and here." He pointed to sections of a wordy document. Marge let go of the ropes and I lifted my hand up and signed. I didn't read anything and I didn't care what it said.

"She's a runaway these days." Marge laughed nervously.

"Ah," was all he said.

My nostrils flared as I signed where he pointed on the second page.

Marge and I left the bank and instead of heading back to the apartment, she walked further into town. "I need something to eat." She walked fast, never letting go of my leash. I felt like she was trying to taunt me when she stopped at the Burger King that was only a few blocks away from Aldersgate.

Again, I looked for police. There weren't any. I thought of ways to escape. I finally had the nerve to speak up. "I have to use the bathroom."

"Okay. Let's go." Marge turned toward the bathroom and away from the counter. She walked briskly past a family that was dining and I regretted having said anything about the bathroom. Marge pulled open a stall and swung me in with her. "So, go." She stared at me.

"I can't go if you're in here with me." I thought about all the times she smacked me when I couldn't go on command.

"Julie, do you think I'm stupid?" She raised her voice. "I'm not leaving you alone for even one minute!"

"Then, I don't have to go."

"Oh, for christ's sake!" She unlocked the stall door. "Stop wasting my fucking time!"

Marge ordered us chicken sandwiches and decided we should eat lunch outside. Still no police. No help. I wondered if Emily would ever come to Burger King. I didn't think so, but she was right up the street or maybe she was at school. I wanted her in front of me.

I sat next to Marge with my tied wrists in my lap. I couldn't eat and it made her mad, but she quickly got quiet again. Her quiet was scarier than her spiraling lectures. What did she have planned? Even as we walked back to the apartment, she wasn't rambling or yelling about anything.

She had me sit at the kitchen table when we got back and she smoked a cigarette near the patio door. She looked pensive. She baffled me because we weren't frantically packing boxes.

We were only there for ten minutes when there was loud knocking at the door. "Mrs. Beekman?" The knocking continued. Marge looked panicked and my heart raced.

Marge cleared her throat. "Just a minute!"

"Mrs. Beekman? I need you to open the door now, I'm with the Willow Grove Police."

"Julie, hide the pot plants!" Marge quickly removed the rope and tucked it and her pipe in a drawer. "Hide the pot plants, flush them!" she whispered loudly. I stood frozen and couldn't move.

"Open the door, Mrs. Beekman!"

"Just a minute!" she called out. "Julie, the plants!" She glared at me and gritted her teeth.

I decided immediately that I wasn't going to help her one bit. "No." I almost laughed, I was so nervous.

"Then, get the fuck in your room and stay quiet!" She waved her arm and I pretended to follow the command by standing in the hallway, just out of sight.

When she finally opened the door, I listened to a pathetic hello and could actually hear her fake smile.

"Mrs. Beekman, I'm Sergeant Nelson and this is Officer McCormick. Ma'am, where is your daughter?"

"Well," Marge hesitated. "She's in her room. She stayed home from school today because she wasn't feeling well." I could hear her voice shake.

"Mrs. Beekman, may we talk with your daughter?"

"Uh..." Marge started. Before she could say anything else, I came out from the hallway. The men looked polished, square and shiny against the backdrop of our dingy apartment. I was so very happy to see them, though I didn't know what to say at first.

"I'm here," I spoke.

Beyond the pressed blue of their uniforms and heavy accessories, I saw something that took my breath away.

Chapter Sixteen

Emily was standing quietly behind them. I acknowledged her presence with just a smile. Marge disappeared into the kitchen and never even noticed that Emily was in our apartment.

"Julie, can we talk with you for a minute?" As the officer waved for me to come closer to him, Marge returned from the kitchen. "Mrs. Beekman, we would like to speak to your daughter alone."

"Oh, that's fine." Marge's eyebrows were raised. "Okay. Okay." She walked toward my bedroom while the officers led me to the kitchen. Emily followed.

"Hon, is your mom hurting you?" The officer spoke softly and his eyes sparkled. I could hear Marge coming back out to where we stood. One of the men spoke calmly to Marge and led her back out of the room.

I hesitated, not only because the officer might question me and just leave, but I also didn't want Marge to hear me.

"We heard from several sources today that your mom had you tied up walking through town." I nodded and opened the drawer that contained the rope and the pipe. "She used this?" The officer held the rope in the air.

"Uh huh." I looked at Emily who was shaking her head and looking like she might cry.

"Is it true that your mom hit you with a bat?" The police man tucked the rope over his wide belt.

I nodded and noticed a knife on the counter. "There is a really sharp knife on the counter." I pointed. "I would get rid of that if I were you. It wasn't there before."

The officer turned to see the knife. He picked it up and placed it under the sink. "There," he said. "She can't use it if she doesn't know where it is." He smiled. We all turned to hear Marge getting upset in the other room. She was starting to yell. I heard the words, my and daughter, but couldn't make out much else.

My mind was awhirl. Was this really happening? Was I correct in wanting to get away from her? Would I ever see her again? Would I get a beating tonight if I stayed? I had to take the risk. "She hits me, I'm afraid of her, and her pot plants are on the porch and a few in the bathroom," I said in a low voice.

"Hon." The officer touched my shoulder. "I want you to follow this lady down to the police car, okay? Everything is going to be fine."

Emily and I walked quickly toward the door. I could hear Marge getting louder as we headed downstairs. When we exited the building, I looked around to find police cars at every angle. A waiting policeman escorted Emily and me to the back of his car. We sat there for what seemed like forever. In some strange way, I hoped that Marge would completely lose it, so that they would believe me. What if they didn't believe me?

Emily touched the top of my hand, "you're going to be okay now. Just tell the police everything you've told me."

I sat nervously and looked up at our porch. I wanted to know what was going on and I wanted to just get out of there. I took the little note from my pocket that I was trying to get through the air conditioner and I stared at it.

Finally, when we started leaving, I worried aloud. "What do you think is going to happen?" I turned to look back at the apartment building, thinking I might see Marge running after the car.

"As far as Marge is concerned? I don't know. She just may dig her own grave," Emily responded.

"Oh, my God, there she is!" She wasn't looking back at me, she was talking to one of the men. I started to breathe heavily. "Do you think I'm going to have to go back there?"

"Honestly, Julie?" Emily was calm and spoke softly. "I don't know." She tapped my knee. "Right now, you're completely safe and you just need to tell the police everything, okay?"

"Okay." I knew Emily was repeated things, but I could only hold on to words for a few moments and fear just overcame logic. It all felt insane. I squeezed my hands above my knees as we pulled into the parking lot of the station. "Do you think they'll have her come here, too?" I instantly thought about Marge behind bars, pacing like a caged animal.

"I guess that will depend on her." Emily exhaled through her nose and grinned.

The policeman parked, opened our car doors and led us through the back area of the building. He stopped to talk with a lady sitting at a desk and then proceeded into a large room. "Ladies, if you could just wait here for a few minutes." He pointed to a few chairs near a long table.

"Sure." Emily moved to a chair and patted the seat next to her. I stood still and looked at equipment that lined the counters. "You okay, Jul?"

"Uh-huh." I crossed my feet, leaned forward and placed my hands on the side of my chair and gripped so hard that it hurt a little. It made everything that was happening more real. Now that we were just going to sit and wait, I felt sick. The previous half-hour had been exciting and scary and awful. "How did the police know?" I stared at marks on the floor that appeared to be from stomped-out cigarettes and grimy shoes.

"Well, I got a call from the mom of one of your friends," Emily said. "She said you were being led by a rope on Easton Road earlier. She wanted to call the police, but your friend, Beth, persuaded her to call me first." Emily took a deep breath. "Meanwhile, more than a few people called the police."

"Yeah, it was really embarrassing." I kicked my foot and continued to hold on to the sides of my chair.

"Julie." Emily paused like she was thinking of what to say next. "It's really sick behavior and Marge needs help."

"Hello there." A man, wearing slacks, a long-sleeved shirt and tie, walked into the room and shut the door behind him. He grabbed a chair and sat facing us. He had a clipboard and pen that he balanced on his lap while he rolled up his sleeves. "I'm Detective Green. I understand that today has been difficult for you." He looked straight at me and crossed his legs.

"Yeah." I chewed on the inside of my cheek. "Is my mom here?"

"No." He looked down at his clipboard. "Not that I'm aware of."

"Okay." I sighed. "Did they take her to the big house?" I asked jokingly.

A policeman who was at the apartment earlier came into the room with the rope in his hand. "She should be in the big house!" He chuckled and placed the rope on the table. He then took a seat near the detective.

"What's with the rope?" The detective looked at Emily and then at me.

"She thought I was going to run away because I ran away last night," I replied.

"So, she tied you?" He paused. "Why did you run away last night?"

"I was at my friend Nancy's house and I called my mom to tell her that I was going to be late. She said to get home and that she was going to beat my..." I stopped and looked at Em. "Can I swear if I'm just quoting her?"

"Since you're quoting her, yes." Emily smiled.

"Okay, so she said she was going to kick my ass and she meant it." I lifted my thumb to my mouth to bite at the nail. "I really didn't feel like being hit again, so I ran away."

"So, this happens a lot?" the detective asked.

"Well, not a lot a lot." I looked down. "But, sometimes, yes." I started to feel guilty. I felt I was betraying Marge again. I could handle most things she dished out. I could get through it. If her sons got through it, I could. Maybe I was just being a big baby. But she didn't hit them like she hit me. She didn't even speak to them the way she degraded me. I had every right to be sitting here, telling my story.

"Mrs. Beekman has used a baseball bat on Julie, as well as a metal rod." Emily stepped in. "I have worked with Julie for the past nine months. There is physical and emotional abuse going on in the home."

"And on the street!" the officer piped in and pointed at the piece of rope.

"When did the incident happen with the baseball bat?" Detective Green lifted a sheet from the clipboard. "And what kind of metal rod?"

"Um, the baseball bat was a few days back and the rod was from my closet. You know, where you hang your clothes," I answered calmly, but my stomach did flip flops and all I wanted at that moment was to know the future.

"Do you have any bruising or marks?" the detective asked. "Like where she hit you?"

I squirmed in my seat. "I don't know." I did not want to pull down my shorts in front of everyone to find out. "Probably not anymore." I felt the back of my butt and legs. Both were still tender.

"Miss Beekman, it would help a lot if we could get a photograph of the areas where she hit you." The detective uncrossed his legs and was not sitting forward. "It's no fun, I know, but this will help us."

I looked at Emily and down at my hands. I pulled nervously on my fingers one at a time. I felt the bones and their placement.

"Julie, they need to know and see what's going on." Emily nudged my arm with hers. "Right?"

"Yeah, I guess." I felt my heart through my chest. "I don't know if there is anything there, but I guess." I stood up. "I am not pulling down my shorts, though." I twisted to see if I could see anything when I lifted the bottom of my shorts. I could see a faint patch of yellow. I turned so that Emily could look. "Do you see anything?"

"Lift your shorts a little more. I'm so sorry, Julie." Emily sighed. "Okay, let's get this over with. Do you need to take the pictures or should I?"

"I'm sorry, ma'am, but we have to take the shots." The detective stood. "Do you want me to track down a female officer?"

"I don't want to wait anymore," I protested. "Let's just get it over with."

The detective asked me to step over to the counter to take the photos. I went ahead and lifted my shorts.

"Oh, Jul," Emily said.

"Yeah, hon, there is quite the bruise. This will only take a minute." He reached into a box on the table and pulled out a professional-looking camera. "Only a few shots, then I'll leave you alone."

Emily was patient as they finished with the photos and a few more notes. We left soon after and went directly to her office at Aldersgate. As Emily made phone calls, I watched the door.

"You must be starving," she said as she dialed another number. "Wanna share some Chinese?"

"I'm fine," I said. I was hungry, but I didn't want to eat in front of Emily. Plus, watching the door for Marge and where I was going to stay for the night were my main concerns. I barely heard anything Emily said during her calls, even though the office was quiet and I kept staring at her.

She was pretty and thin. I felt like a blob. A blob with a monster for a mother.

The chicken fried rice came and I liked the idea of Emily and I sharing something. It made me feel special. I never had fried rice. Even though I told her I wasn't hungry, Emily fixed two plates from the take-out bag. I took bites when I thought Emily wasn't looking. "Julie, you are going to be staying at the home of a lovely couple," Emily gushed as she put down the receiver. "The Barreres won the award for best foster parents in the area. They love children and they live in a big farm house." She poked at her dinner and took a bite. "There was an article in the Intellegencer about them."

I tried to imagine the farm house and for some reason, all I could think of was quilts. Quilts with strange patterns and a knitted rooster toaster cover. "Do they have animals?"

"I'm not sure." She continued eating and staring at a file. "We'll go there as soon as I get your paperwork done." She grunted. "Red tape!"

I wondered what the Barreres would think of me. I looked down at my dirty t-shirt that was far too big, but hid my fat nicely. "Do they have other kids there?"

"Not right now." Emily grinned.

"Will I be able to go to school for the last few days that we have?" I had to see Mrs. Shechtman and my friends again.

"I don't see why not," Emily said.

"Okay, good." I pushed my plate to the side of Emily's desk.

~ * ~

We drove to the Barreres which was in Warminster, a few towns north of Willow Grove. We pulled into a long driveway. It was dark by this time, but I could see a giant field and a tractor near their garage. The house was quite large and a side light was on. Emily parked her little Toyota Corona near the side of the place and we walked up to the house. The Barreres answered immediately. Mrs. Barreres spoke first, "Hi, I'm Gloria." She was bubbly and happy. "And this is Jim."

"Hey, kid," he said. "Are those all the clothes you have? I guess you can borrow some of mine, but I don't know if they'll fit." He laughed.

"Hi." I stuck my hands in my pockets and tried to laugh, too. Jim was at least a foot and a half taller than me and I instantly perceived that he was calling me fat. "I'm fine with my clothes," I replied.

"Suit yourself." He cracked a wide smile.

Emily touched my arm. "Julie, I'm going to see you tomorrow. Gloria is going to drop you off at school in the morning."

"We have our eighth-grade picnic tomorrow," I said to Gloria.

"Oh, good. That should be fun." She led me inside. We sat in the living room and I said very little, Jim mostly talked and made jokes. They did have a dog, a little white poodle named, Tippy. It was the first time that I didn't feel a bond with an animal. He didn't seem to care about me, either.

Gloria led me around the house, gave me some of her pajamas and a new toothbrush.

That night, I slept in my new bedroom. There were two twin beds and a dresser. I lay on the top of the comforter, since I didn't know the Barreres and I didn't know if I'd be back. I didn't want to mess anything up.

I lay awake for a while, wondering what Marge was doing and if she was going to show up at my school the next day. I wondered if I made the right decision in telling the story. I still felt guilt.

My brothers would feel that I made a big mistake. I couldn't have gone to them though, not even Dan. He had his own life and was trying to finish college. I was so exhausted, I needed sleep, but I could only worry and try not to move the bedding. I wished I had Alfie, or better yet, Blackie. At some point, I let it all go and I slept.

Gloria showed me all around the kitchen in the morning and gave me several options for breakfast. I chose a simple bowl of cereal. We chatted all the way to my school. Gloria told me about her accounting job and that Jim was almost retiring after twenty years in the Navy. She was easy because she didn't ask me questions about my situation. I worried as we pulled into the school lot. I looked everywhere for Marge and was relieved once I entered the building safely and saw Mrs. Shechtman's big grin.

The day at school was fun and calm and I decided that if I got to go back to the Barreres' that night, I would sleep under the covers.

Gloria took me to K-Mart to get me a couple more pair of shorts and some shirts so that I wouldn't have to wear the same thing over and over. I even smelled different, not like Marge's smoky apartment and cardboard from damp boxes that were never unpacked. Jim smoked, but he smelled good. He smelled like cologne, fresh country air, and the military.

Karen Bean invited me over for a swim at her pool once school was over and I was thrilled. Maybe I could tell her everything. In the past, I only gave hints that my home life was screwed.

Things were really getting better already. We didn't do any work on the last day of school. We played volleyball in the gym area and Mrs. Shechtman came in to watch. At some point, someone came up to where she and I were talking and took a Polaroid picture of us and then handed it to me. It was incredibly special. I hoped to someday have a picture with Emily, too.

Over the weekend, Gloria and Jim took me to the commissary grocery store on the same Naval base where the resident, Michael, tried to cash the phone bill. I didn't tell them about it, but I did laugh to myself. The commissary was huge. They sold groceries and clothing. Jim bought me a pair of aviator sunglasses. "Here, kid, put those on."

"I like them!" I looked in the small mirror atop the sunglass stand.

"Good, you can wear them to court on Thursday."

"Uh, Jimbo, I believe Emily was going to tell her." Gloria tightened her lips as she stared at him.

"Court?" I knew it was coming, but not this soon. "Where do I have court?"

"Montgomery County," Jim said. "You'll be just fine."

"Will she be there?" I wasn't sure how much they knew, but I'm sure they knew about Marge.

Gloria gathered shopping bags as we parked the shopping cart near the car. "Sweetheart, she can't hurt you anymore. Just be yourself, don't be afraid to talk to the judge and you'll be just fine." She loaded the last bag as I realized I should have helped. "Emily will be there and the police will be there. You'll have lots of support."

~ * ~

Emily picked me up that Thursday morning. I'd spent the past few days playing at Karen's pool and having fun. I hadn't let the nervousness set in until that morning. Emily drove and I asked a lot of questions. Mostly what-ifs. We arrived at the courthouse and Marge was standing outside the front door with a younger woman. They both had briefcases. I panicked. She has a lawyer!

"Let's go through the side door." Emily spoke before I could. We walked down a hallway and checked in at a desk where a few people were gathered. Emily recognized someone and then quickly headed toward them. I followed closely. "John Kimball, this is Julie Beekman."

"Hi, Julie, I'm your caseworker from Children and Youth Services." He reached out his hand.

"Hi." I shook his hand firmly, though I was confused. I looked down the hallway several times to see if I could spot Marge. I dreaded everything about this day.

"We need to get in there," John said. "Has anyone seen Vanessa?"

Emily and I just shrugged and then followed John into a large modern court room. John proceeded to a long table on the left, where a dark-haired lady in a suit was unpacking files from her bag. "Julie, this is your attorney, Vanessa Anthony Klein. You can sit right here." John motioned for me to sit. Emily sat behind me and a little to my right. John sat next to her.

"Don't worry," Vanessa said. "This is preliminary and you and I will get a chance to go over things."

"Okay." I looked at the doorway and Marge was staring back and pointing at me. I had to find my breath. I wanted to run. Her lawyer glanced my way and they sat at another large table on the other side of the aisle.

The security man announced the judge and everything went just like a court scene on television. The judge even slammed down his gavel.

Vanessa starting talking first and told the judge the state should be my guardian. When Marge's lawyer spoke, Marge interrupted her and yelled out, "This is a witch hunt!"

Vanessa looked at me with wide eyes and scribbled a note. IS SHE ALWAYS LIKE THIS?

Everyone in the courtroom was snickering at Marge's outburst. I was a little embarrassed, but I felt vindicated at the same time.

"Mrs. Beekman!" The judge spoke loudly through his microphone. "If you want to continue with these proceedings, you will not yell out randomly in my courtroom!"

"Yes, your Honor." Her lawyer answered for her. "My client is very distraught over the placement of her daughter."

"Well, her outburst is not going to help her case."

"We understand, your Honor." Her attorney bowed her head. Marge sat forward in her chair like she was ready to pounce. She could barely contain herself, I could tell. I looked around at others in the courtroom. There were a lot of people I didn't know, and then I saw Randy and Regina. They were looking back at me. Randy looked like he was disappointed and maybe put out, while Regina managed a smile and a little wave. They have no idea of what's been going on, I thought. They had been so wrapped up in each other that I hadn't even heard from Randy for most of the school year. I thought that if Regina witnessed any of Marge's wrath, I'd really feel sorry for her. She probably never had to deal with people like Marge in Brazil. I wondered though, if she thought I was wrong in telling on Marge. Randy obviously did, he continued to look dismayed.

The court proceedings only lasted for maybe a half hour. The judge said he would hear the case on a future date, next week. "Good." Vanessa clamped the small locks on her briefcase. "This will give me some time to get to know you." She grabbed the handle of her bag.

"In the meantime, do not have contact with her." Vanessa tilted her head slightly back, toward Marge.

"Oh, I won't." My eyes widened at the thought. I didn't look at Marge. I felt her, but I couldn't look in her direction. Instead, I watched Emily make her way to the table where Vanessa and I were now talking.

"That wasn't too bad, huh?" Emily's blue eyes danced and my fear subsided. "Let's go out the way we came in, shall we?"

Vanessa walked with us. "Julie, I'll probably be meeting with you tomorrow or Monday, your caseworker will let you know." She handed me her card. "You can call me at any time."

"Okay, thank you." I responded, but barely heard her. I was aware of the hustle of people around us in the hallway. I tried to find Randy and Regina, or even catch a long-distance glance at Marge, but they weren't there. I wanted to know where they were. Emily and I didn't need any surprises. Vanessa turned and walked down the hall to the front door while Em and I continued out the side doors. "Where are they?" I asked out loud.

"I'm sure her attorney is keeping her here for a few minutes."

"Yeah, but Randy is here too."

"Oh." Emily looked around like she wanted to catch a quick glimpse of him as we approached her car.

I still didn't see Marge as we drove out of the parking lot. Not until we got to the end of the drive where she, my brother, and Regina blocked the exit. Emily gasped and I locked my car door. "What are they doing?"

"I have no idea." Emily took a deep breath and inched her car forward and they moved. My heart was pounding, thinking they had a van waiting somewhere, ready to take me away. I was so afraid Marge would hurt Emily, too. Marge screamed something and slammed her hand on the roof of the driver's side as we passed.

"Oh, no!" I sat up, looking at the three of them as Emily drove faster. "Did she hurt your car?"

"I don't care about the car!" Emily exhaled her fright. "I care about us."

I looked back and could still see the three figures, still standing where we left them. "Well, they're not following us, so that's good."

"It's very good." She exhaled again.

Chapter Seventeen

The first real court hearing started with a bang. We all waited patiently in the courtroom for Marge, her attorney, and the judge to appear. Vanessa and I sat confidently, whispering to each other. Vanessa previously explained that there was a slight chance I could go back with Marge, but she would do everything she could to prevent it. I told her I would run far away if that happened.

I was a bundle of nerves right up to the point that Judge Albright came from his chambers, and Marge dramatically approached her table, slamming her baby blue briefcase down. "Good morning, mother fuckers!" Her attorney wasn't present.

The judge hadn't even announced anything yet, and was just getting his robe on when he heard her. Well, we all heard her. "Mrs. Beekman." He leaned over his desk and grabbed his microphone. "Please, I warned you before." He finally sat. "No outbursts in my courtroom!"

"But, your Honor!" Marge displayed a fake smile. "That is what these people are. They have fucked this mother over in their witch hunt!" She was outrageously dramatic. Thoughts of all the N.O.W. meetings that she attended in the 70's came to the forefront of my brain yet again. I pictured her holding rallies for Abusive Mothers' Rights.

The security guard guy seemed to ignore Marge. "All rise!" he bellowed. He introduced the judge and we all sat.

The judge read a few things and then looked to Marge. "Mrs. Beekman, where is your attorney?"

Marge stood up again. "Well..." She placed her hands on her suit skirt to neaten it. "It seems she's a little too naive to take on this case. I'll be representing myself."

"Thank God," I whispered to Vanessa. I looked for Randy and Regina, but they weren't there. I wondered if they weren't supporting her anymore.

The judge raised an eyebrow. "Ma'am, shall we take some time from this case so that you can find proper representation?"

"Oh, no!" Marge quickly replied. "I want my daughter back, now!" She pointed at me and my stomach jumped into my throat. "I don't want to prolong this any further! No, sir!" She shook her head.

Vanessa wrote on the piece of paper between us. You'll be just fine.

I drew a heart in response.

"Mrs. Beekman, please take your seat." The judge continued to look at Marge and she sat.

Judge Albright questioned Vanessa for a few minutes about what the intention of Children and Youth Services might be. "Your Honor, we would like to make Julie a ward of the state until Mrs. Beekman has been fully evaluated and can establish competency as Julie's guardian."

"I'm her mother!" Marge yelled. "You stupid prostitute!"

Prostitute? Where did that one come from? I wondered.

"Mrs. Beekman, I need you to step out of these proceedings until you can calm down!" The judge's nostrils flared and his lips tightened.

"Calm down?" Marge slammed her hand down. "That girl should never have been taken away from her mother!" She pointed toward me with the other hand. "Now I'm supposed to listen to a prostitute who is working for this county of mother fuckers, tell me I need an evaluation?" Her fist pounded the table. "You have got to be kidding me!" Oddly, she was preparing to leave, long before the security man came to her table. She wasn't quiet, she just kept ranting, but all he had to do was follow her out.

I blew out the breath I had been holding for what seemed like the last five minutes and realized I was shaking. She was a frightening presence and I couldn't help but feel embarrassed. Surely people might be judging me. Would I become her?

People spoke in hushed tones and I heard the occasional giggle. Once Marge calmed down, they brought her back in and the court session started again. I thought the proceedings would end there, but Marge still needed to be interviewed on the witness stand. The security guy, who followed her out during the preliminary, asked her to put her hand on the bible and would she swear to tell the truth.

"Goddamn right, I will!" Marge focused on me. "I want my daughter back!" The questioning went on and on because Marge talked incessantly. We were there almost the entire day with only a short break for lunch.

Once again, she discussed how difficult it had been to raise four of us, but especially me. "That girl has not been easy. She blames me for her dad's death and has hated me since we left Grand Haven. No, I have not been abusive! A bat? Yes, I took a bat and tapped her with it. I said, IF I was an abusive mother, I would use a bat, but I have not hit that child!" She surveyed the courtroom after every answer like she was waiting for someone to agree with her.

She refrained from cursing for the most part, but made herself out to be a victim. She said I had been manipulated into thinking I was abused. A few times, she pointed in Emily's direction. "Plus, if I had known that woman was in my home when those police showed up, things would have been a hell of a lot worse."

Thank God, she didn't recognize her! I thought. She must have thought she was a detective. She did have a lot on her mind that day.

I shuddered at the idea of Marge hurting Emily. None of this was Emily's fault and I didn't understand why Marge hated every woman in my life.

Somehow, I felt for my mother, and I knew by the middle of the afternoon I wouldn't be seeing her for a while. She was desperately trying to hold on to her last child. I put up with her craziness. I played along with being her adopted doll as well as her punching bag. I felt some guilt as I watched her struggle and it probably did seem like a gang-up from her perspective. But, the witch hunt part was just crazy nonsense.

The judge ended the day by announcing I would be testifying privately in his chambers in the morning. I was going to plead for my future to have a smidgen of normalcy. I would tell him everything.

~ * ~

The judge's chambers looked like a living room. Vanessa and I found the sofa while Judge Albright sat in an overstuffed chair. I stared at his family pictures that were placed sporadically on shelves, while Vanessa told him I should be a ward of the state. "Obviously, Mrs. Beekman needs a psychological evaluation and I think Julie's return should remain contingent upon that examination and recommendations of a court appointed psychiatrist." Vanessa seemed very confident as she watched the judge glancing at his file.

The judge placed his paperwork on a small table next to him, crossed his legs and looked at me. "What do you think? Do you think your mom is fit to be a parent?"

"Sometimes." I glanced down at my crusty sneakers and tucked them away. As the judge picked up his file again and started to go through the papers inside, I realized how crucial the moment was and that no one could hurt me or hear me from the courtroom. He would decide whether I was allowed to have a little normalcy in my life. "Actually?" I sat up and faced him. "No. No, I don't. I don't think it's right that she hits me and tells me that I killed my dad when he died of leukemia. I don't like wondering where we're going to live next or even what's going to happen next." I took a deep breath and hoped it all hadn't been for nothing. "I don't think she is fit and I don't feel safe. Did you see the pictures the police took?"

"I did and I'm glad you have expressed your feelings." Judge Albright smiled and stood. "I don't think I need much more." He walked purposefully away from us. "Shall we?" He opened the door that led back to the courtroom and motioned for Vanessa to lead.

The judge explained I would be a temporary ward of the state until Marge received clearance from a psychiatrist. She could find her own doctor or the court would appoint one.

"A ward of the state?" Marge opposed. "Un-fucking-believable! What's going to happen with her social security check?"

My jaw dropped a little. Un-fucking-believable is right, I thought.

After court, Emily took me to the Barreres' and we talked about what might happen for the next few months. "I think it's safe to say that you'll be with the Barreres for quite some time."

"That's good." I settled into the passenger seat. My mind was going a mile a minute. "Is there any way that she can find out where I am?"

"None whatsoever," Emily said.

"Will I get to stay at Upper Moreland for next year?"

"That's a good question, I'm not sure."

"Will I get to see you?" I sat up and turned toward her with the seat belt pulling hard against my shoulder.

"Sometimes, yes." Emily laughed. "We'll continue with counseling and the court is going to want you to see a psychiatrist at some point."

"Wait." I sat back. "I thought they wanted Marge to get evaluated and I already see you!"

"It's protocol, Julie." She drove, staring straight ahead. "You'll be fine."

"But, I'm not crazy!"

"Julie, the state just needs to have everything in order and documented and for you to have support. You've had a lot happen in your life."

The Barreres were excited when Emily and I got back to their house. "Well, kid," Jim rubbed the top of my head. "What are your plans for the summer?"

"You could teach me to mow with the tractor, I can work, and spend lots of time with Karen Bean at her pool." I stood awkwardly and wanted to cry about it, but decided a joke would be best. "And I'll be seeing a psychiatrist?"

They all laughed, so it worked.

I had dinner with the Barreres and called Karen Bean to let her know I was safe from going back to Marge. I settled into the sofa and watched Hart to Hart with Jim and Gloria. They sat in two reclining chairs. Jim had a two-liter bottle of Pepsi next to his chair and Gloria had Diet RC Cola. We didn't talk much, I just observed the comfort they both exuded. The dog was snuggled in with Gloria and I wished it was next to me, even if it was a poodle.

The next morning, Jim and Gloria left for work. It was just me and the dog, Tippy. Tippy let me pet her a few times, but she seemed wary of me and it just didn't make sense. I found out I had to go to a doctor appointment to get a basic physical. I remembered the last time I had been to a doctor was Dr. Pezzi for the stitches. I had to live with the Christian Science thing for the last year and before that, the case of chicken pox I got when I was eleven was the last time I was sick.

A van came that afternoon to take me to the doctor's office, and there were other girls on board. "What, is this the foster shuttle?" I joked after they all finished staring at me and I took a seat.

"Sho is!" I turned to look at a black girl and found a very pregnant white girl instead. She was rubbing her belly and she looked hungry. "I hate this shit!"

I looked at the other two girls. One had a few tattoos and the other girl had deep scratch marks all over her arms. She curled up to hide when she saw me staring. I felt horrible for having stared. I suddenly had the feeling I was going to be a breeze for the Barreres.

The doctor seemed to spend a lot of time with the other girls. He told me that I needed to lose weight. I was one hundred and forty pounds at the age of fourteen and I felt completely disgusted. We all got a tetanus shot and were sent on our way.

When I got back to the Barreres', I immediately made myself a peanut butter and jelly sandwich since I was fat anyway. Maybe I did need a psychiatrist, but I sure as heck wasn't going to bring it up.

The Barreres provided a great experience for me. I looked forward to running errands with them on Saturdays and wearing Jim's cowboy boots to the mailbox every day. Gloria taught me how to make chocolate chip cookies. We always made a special separate batch for Jim. Although we labeled his private cookie jar, JIMBO, I referred to them as cowboy cookies and they weren't really so private. I ate a ton of them. I felt that all that sugar in one house was too good to wait for. I made peanut butter and jelly sandwiches every day. I ate late at night too, when I couldn't sleep or when I was anxious. I was comforted by the sugary jam and sturdy peanut butter. I ate more when I received letters from Marge.

At some point, after the court hearing, Marge took a trip all over the country. She sent postcards and letters to CYS every day and they would mail out a large envelope weekly. Usually, she wrote about how I had been brainwashed and manipulated and she thought I was smarter than that. She wrote that God still loved me, even though I was dumb. Other times, she wrote the complete opposite. She felt I manipulated everyone and started a witch hunt. It was all confusing, but I was used to it. I tried to stop reading everything she sent, but I couldn't help it. I hoped one day, I would read something new.

Most days when Jim and Gloria were at work, I rode one of the bikes in their garage. I usually went to Karen Bean's house. She lived two towns away, so the six and a half miles felt like a huge athletic achievement. I loved riding. I rode to Aldersgate to see Emily a few times. I was careful to ride quick so that Marge wouldn't see me if she was back in town.

One afternoon, I had a real session with Emily, just like the times we shared at school. We met in a therapy room in the lower level of Aldersgate. She asked me to draw again and it made me happy. I penciled my tree and then another right beside it. I drew a fence that connected the two trees. Emily's eyes danced as she studied my artwork. "Look, Julie, you're not alone anymore, it's two trees!" She laughed.

"The trees represent you and me." I smiled.

"And the fence is our constant connection. I love it." Em understood.

I knew then that trees would always remind me of her and it could be our symbol. Emily and I talked for a few more minutes and then she had to go upstairs to take a phone call. When she left, I started to put the pencils away and roll up my drawing. I noticed she left some papers on the coffee table. I turned so that I could read some visible handwriting. All I could make out was, "Julie is highly intelligent, but has the emotional maturity of a seven-year old." I wanted to die. I felt instantly betrayed. When Emily returned to the room, I was waiting on the sofa with arms crossed.

"Julie, I'm so sorry, but I had to take that call." She sat next to me. "What's wrong?"

"Do you want me to answer as an intelligent fourteen-year old or as an immature seven- year old?" I barely looked at her.

"What?" Emily sighed and then leaped forward to grab the papers. "You weren't supposed to see that and I am so sorry you did." Her voice became soft. "It's not your fault." She lifted my chin. "You did not grow up under normal circumstances." Emily made quotation mark symbols with her hands. "You didn't get to be a kid, I think you kind of skipped that part and raised Marge a little." Emily looked sad. "Do you understand?"

"Yeah, I guess so." I nodded.

When I rode home, I thought about it and it made sense. "A seven-year old?" I said out loud. "A ten-year old, maybe, but not a seven-year old!"

Marge returned in the beginning of July and everyone knew it. Phone calls from the caseworker increased, I received copies of Marge's letters that had been sent to senators, congress, and even the president. People were getting threatening phone calls, too. I ate even more and got nightmares to boot.

Emily asked if she could pick me up one day. She needed to talk. I met her at the Beans since I had been hanging out there almost every day. She said she wanted to take me to a very special place that she thought was beautiful. I chatted about the Barreres and how they were a great temporary foster home. "I mean, I like them, but I hope the caseworker finds a place in our school district so I can stay with my friends." I looked at Em who had been awfully quiet. "I really wish I could just stay with the Beans, but they don't have a lot of room, plus, they have their family all set. I do love them though."

"Julie, that's really nice. They seem like wonderful people." Emily drove up a long narrow road and into the parking lot of a huge cathedral. "C'mon, I want you to see." Emily led me to an overlook from the cathedral grounds. The view was gorgeous. "This is Bryn Aythn Cathedral."

The building itself looked plucked out of a small town in England. The Cathedral was grey stone and stained glass.

"Lots of trees." I grinned.

"Exactly." Emily brushed the hair off her face. The wind was strong that day and we both took a lot of time trying to contain our hair. "Julie, I need to talk about something serious with you."

"Okay." I looked over the back landing and into a valley of green with multiple gardens. I pulled my hair into a would-be ponytail and held it there.

"I'm not going to be able to see you for a while." Her expression was serious and sad.

"Why?" I practically burst into tears, but held back, feeling pressure inside my face along with a trembling lower lip.

"Well, I'll be getting my master's degree, so I'll be busy with that and..."

"You're moving?" I interrupted.

"No, I'm not moving, it's just that..." Emily paused and searched for words. "My boss is looking out for my safety and Marge is so angry that it's just not safe for me to see you." She looked like she might cry.

"Okay," was all I could say. There were so many things in my head and I had to pretend this moment wasn't real. I didn't want to seem immature and I was also angry. None of it was real.

Neither of us said much on the way home. I knew Emily was so very sad, but I couldn't help her. I knew she was only getting away from Marge the way I had, but she was leaving me, and on that day, I didn't like Emily so much.

Emily pulled into the Bean's driveway and I immediately opened the passenger door. I had no idea of what to say to her. I was angry and I was sad, but I also wanted to protect her feelings.

"Julie, I am so sorry I can't see you, Really." Emily got out of her side of the car and walked around the front of the vehicle.

"I know." I dug my hands into my pockets and kicked at the edges of grass along the asphalt of the driveway. I wanted to look at her, but I couldn't. I thought about other things so I wouldn't feel or show the scream of sorrow that was stuck somewhere in my throat. Emily reached around me with her arms and held on tight. I left my hands in my pockets and kept my body stiff. "I have to go." I turned quickly and headed toward the Bean's front door.

Once inside, I went to the bathroom to wash off my face. I looked into the mirror, hated what I saw, and started to wail. I grabbed a towel and cried into it. Emily was leaving me and I just wanted to die because of it. When I looked into the mirror again, I heard myself whisper, "I hate you and you're ugly." Then I heard a knock.

"Jul, are you okay?"

"Yes, I'm fine." I quickly splashed more water on my face. "I'll be right out." I dried off, swallowed hard, and pushed all of my feelings down to settle where they always did, in the dump of my stomach.

Karen was waiting for me outside of the bathroom. "Guess what?"

"What?" I came out smiling.

"You get to go on vacation with us to the shore." Karen was grinning and had a look about her that said, I know my timing is perfect.

"Really?" I was so happy to be distracted by the good news. "I have to ask the Barreres if I can go, and I think I have to ask my caseworker if I can leave the state." I followed her downstairs where her mother, Lee, was reading a magazine.

"I told her," Karen said proudly.

Lee glanced over her reading glasses and smiled at me.

"Thank you." I looked directly into her eyes. "I'm really excited about going and I'll ask Jim and Gloria."

Karen and I spent the afternoon swimming while I tried to forget about Emily. When I did think of her, I felt incredible guilt. What if that was the last time I ever saw her and I treated her like that? It wasn't her fault. It was Marge's fault.

~ * ~

Later that night, I asked the Barreres if I could go to the beach with Karen's family.

"You can go if the caseworker is okay with that, but we would also like it if you spent a little more time with us." Gloria set a glass of Diet RC at her spot at the table. "You end up at the Beans and sometimes stay for days." She sat down next to Jim.

"I know, but I like being there." I pushed corn onto my fork.

"Karen's my best friend." I didn't say anymore for fear of hurting Gloria's feelings.

About this trip with the Beans," Jim looked over his glasses. "You're going to have to be here when Jay and Pinky get up here. They're here for almost a month." He looked so serious, but I knew I could get him to joke within a matter of seconds. Plus, they weren't coming until after I got back.

"The whole time?" I pretended to pout and then asked, "How old are they now?" I glanced at the wall where his kids' various school pictures hung.

"Jay is eleven and Pinky is going on eight."

"I'm going to have to refer to her as Laura, I can't call someone Pinky." I pushed my plate forward. "What is their mom like, your ex-wife?" I sat back and folded my arms.

Jim started laughing. "She's a fruitcake, but don't tell the kids I said so."

"Diana isn't so nice to Jim and blames him for a lot of things that have gone wrong in her life," Gloria disclosed. "But she re-married as well and seems to be doing just fine."

"That's good." I wondered how Jim could live so far from the kids. They were all the way in Maryland. Maybe it's why the Barreres were foster parents, I thought, so he wouldn't miss his kids so much.

~ * ~

When Jay and Laura arrived, things changed a little in the house, but not too much. I still had my own room and my own space. I still took off for Karen's house most days, but when I did stay home, the kids would look at me blankly like they were waiting for entertainment. I had no idea of what to do with them. Jay was an adorable kid with thick brown hair and perfect skin. Laura's lips just naturally frowned so that when she did smile, she looked like a completely different person. She had long red hair that I begged her to wash every day so I could braid it.

Cleanliness was a form of control for me. I didn't have anything better than these kids in the way of clothes or opportunity, but I made sure I showered daily and I thought they should do the same. I didn't realize, they were just kids.

Jim and Gloria informed me for the first weekend of the kids' stay, we would be going to Great Adventure, a theme park in New Jersey. I asked them not to tell Jay and Laura. I wanted to be the one to tell them. "We are going to the coolest place ever!" I toyed with them.

"Where? Where?" they pleaded.

"Well, I'll tell you that your friends back home would be so jealous!"

"Where are we going?" Laura tugged on my T-shirt sleeve.

"You'll see," I teased.

"Pete, where are we going?" Laura looked at Gloria, hoping she would respond.

"Gloria can't tell you," I interrupted.

"Her name is Pete!" Laura responded with a hiss and folded arms.

"Okay, whatever. The fact is, we are going to..." I looked at Jay and then Laura. "The cereal factory!" I raised my arms.

Jim grunted back a laugh while I stared at the two kids. "Why?" Laura asked. "Why would we go to a cereal factory?" She looked disgusted.

"Because it's really cool!" I acted excited. "You get to watch how they strip wheat stalks and add artificial flavoring and stuff."

The kids cringed.

They reacted the same way a few weeks later when I told them we were going to get new winter coats from the Burlington Coat Factory when we were really going to another amusement park.

The Barreres and Karen's family kept my mind off of looming court dates, missing Emily, and the fact a foster home still hadn't been located in my school district. I was assured the caseworker was trying. I wondered why I couldn't just ride my bike to Upper Moreland, but I was told I had to live in the district.

Plus, the Shechtmans stayed in touch and had me for occasional sleepovers. We dined out and went to the movies. I kept the ticket stubs since the occasions felt so special. I didn't think any other kids got to sleep over at their English teacher's house. When the summer was coming to an end, Michael gave me all of his old sweaters and Mrs. Shechtman gave me silver jewelry she didn't wear anymore, including a spoon ring I never took off. It was bittersweet loot. It wasn't that I felt like a charity case, because I didn't. I knew these people didn't expect me to have much. The problem was Michael's sweaters fit me and he was an adult man. They fit me perfectly, at least for what I needed. I had to have everything slightly baggy. There was no accentuating anything. Even when I felt so athletic while riding my bike, I still wore large t-shirts with baggy shorts. Large clothes were safe to hide behind.

~ * ~

My new caseworker, Nancy DeLeon, found me a foster home in Upper Moreland School District just two weeks before I was to start ninth grade. I was so excited, I called Karen to share the good news. "I get to stay at Upper Moreland!" I beamed through the phone.

"Yes! I knew it would work out. Where?" Karen asked.

"I'll be only a few miles away, in Hatboro." I turned to see that Gloria and Jim were looking at each other.

"What is the family like?" Karen was being prompted by Lee in the background.

"It's an older couple." I lowered my voice, afraid I might hurt the Barreres' feelings. "Their kids are already out of the house. I'm going there tonight because they invited me for dinner."

"You have to call me as soon as you get home!" Karen said.

"I will. I will." I promised.

Chapter Eighteen

The Kellers were very sweet. They lived in a beautiful two-story home with a perfectly manicured lawn and garden. Mr. Keller was grilling when I arrived, so Mrs. Keller took me for a tour of the house. "This was Diane's room." Mrs. Keller paused and waited for me to come all the way into Diane's room. "She's now at Clarion State on a scholarship." She looked around at all the trophies and awards that decorated the room.

I didn't even know what a scholarship was so I said, "Oh, wow!"

"And this is Stacey's room." Mrs. Keller moved to the next room that was also filled with school memorabilia. She mentioned Stacey's successes and then finished with a tour of David's room. David was the foster son they had before me. "This will be your room," Mrs. Keller smiled, "if you want to live here."

I felt relieved. David's room was fairly empty and didn't have all the stuffed animals and goofy awards. Mrs. Keller informed me that David became a successful doctor.

"That's good," I commented. "There's hope for me becoming an attorney and child advocate." I had no idea of where it came from, but felt it was expected.

"That's wonderful!" We headed back downstairs. "John, we have a future attorney in our midst." She practically sang.

She led me to the enclosed porch on the side where Mr. Keller was placing a plate of chicken smothered in barbecue sauce. "Have a seat, Julie."

I sat at the picnic table that Mrs. Keller slowly filled with colorful sides to accompany the chicken. "May I help you?" I asked.

"No." Mrs. Keller smiled. "You'll have chores when you get here. Don't worry about that now."

Chores sounded nice.

"Would you like some iced milk?" Mrs. Keller began pouring milk over ice before I could answer. "Our kids always drank iced milk."

"Sure." I could try it. When they both finally sat down, I started asking questions so I wouldn't have to answer any. I found out that Mr. Keller was a vice president at Reynolds' Wrap and that Mrs. Keller worked in a bank, part-time, "since the kids were gone."

"What kind of after school activities are you involved with?" Mrs. Keller spooned potato salad onto my plate.

"Well, I was in marching band." I cringed.

They both stopped eating and looked at me. "Well," Mrs. Keller said, "Diane was in science club and soccer, Stacey did well in track and basketball."

"So did David," Mr. Keller said before he bit into a cob of corn that somehow came across the table and splattered bits of kernel on my cheek.

"I'm sure I'll find something." I tried to wipe my face discretely.

"I'm sure you will." Mrs. Keller smiled.

I wondered what Karen would want to get involved with after school. I liked drama and art, but I didn't think she did. She liked watching MTV that just came out and her parents just bought games that we could play on the television, like Space Invaders and Atari tennis. Karen didn't even like school, so I didn't think I could get her to stay longer than the last bell. I was just going to have to figure out how to make all of this work.

~ * ~

Nancy DeLeon called me the next day and told me the Kellers were very interested in having me as a foster daughter and I could move in whenever I liked. Jay and Laura were staying for a few more days, so I waited until the Barreres drove them back down to Maryland so that I could go with them and spend a little more time. I left the Barreres the next week and promised I would stay in touch. "Thank you for everything and I wish you lived in my school district," I said without too much emotion.

"So do we, kid," Jim said sadly.

I kept my tough act. "I'll miss you, cowboy," I grinned. "and your boots."

~ * ~

School started and I was thrilled. I was at Upper Moreland with my friends, and now we were at the high school. I felt more confident wearing my Ralph Lauren sweaters from Michael, and my silver ring from Mrs. Shechtman made me feel special. The Kellers gave me a blow dryer and I looked nice and neat each day. I got an allowance too, so I bought Bonnie Bell lip gloss. I tried out for the school musical, but I was turned down. Mr. Hart told me that my voice was beautiful, but that I wasn't quite right for the part.

I thought about trying out for sports and mentioned it to the gym teacher. "We would love to have you in shot put and discus." Mrs. Meyer said. "You're a big girl and that would be perfect for you." I opted out.

There weren't any clubs for writing or art and I couldn't possibly fake another season of playing the clarinet. Especially since the high school marching band was a big deal. I knew the Kellers would be disappointed, so I didn't speak of it until they brought it up.

"What do you think you'll be doing after school?" Mrs. Keller set my iced milk down in front of me.

"I'm not sure. I think just homework for now." I sipped at the milk that I didn't even like.

"Okay." She looked at her husband and not me. "Well, until you find something, feel free to have a soft pretzel when you get home from school. David always liked soft pretzels, so we keep them in the freezer downstairs."

"Thank you." I sighed.

Mrs. Keller took her seat at the table. "You know, Katie from across the street is involved with a volleyball team that's part of parks and rec. You should talk with her on the bus tomorrow."

"Okay," I said.

~ * ~

It only took a week or so and I was exhausted by Stacey, Diane, David and Katie, too. They were all apparently perfect and I couldn't even properly use a fork, let alone get awards and trophies. The good news was, Karen could finally sleep over at my house instead of me always having to go to hers. But, the first time I had her sleep over was the last.

I'm not sure why, but we decided it would be fun to jump on my bed. I just bought a Rick Springfield forty-five and we were dancing around to, "Jesse's Girl."

Suddenly, Mr. Reynolds' Wrap-Corn-Spitter came flying into my room and was so angry I thought his head was going to spin right off of his neck. "Stop it!" he yelled. "Just stop it!" We immediately terminated our fun. I ran to David's record player and scratched the forty-five right into the garbage. We both stood silently, too afraid to move and then he left.

"I think they're too old for me," I whispered and Karen giggled from nervousness. After that night, I never had anyone over and tried to be as quiet as possible. I worked hard on my school work and joined Katie's volleyball team as the Kellers suggested. I missed the Barreres.

One afternoon, Mr. Keller came to pick me up at Karen's. When I wasn't waiting for him in front of her house when he pulled up, he displayed the same intense anger that he had when Karen stayed over and we were making too much noise. I'm not sure what came over me, but as he started yelling about how I should have been ready and I should get in the car, I swung my foot and kicked him in the shin. I stayed with the Kellers for a total of seven weeks.

~ * ~

Beth Kindt's family found out that I was getting moved from the Kellers into a group home out of the school district, and offered to be my foster parents. It turned out that they had been keeping a close eye on my situation, since the day that Mrs. Kindt and her daughter saw Marge leading me down the street with the rope.

I apologized to Mr. Keller for kicking him in the shin, but he didn't respond. It was a quiet two days of disapproval from the Kellers, right up until he drove me to the Kindt's house, took my bag of clothes out of the trunk of his car, mumbled something, and took off. Mrs. Keller wished me well back at their house. Clearly, I failed them.

Good riddance, you creep, I thought as I stared at the huge mansion where the Kindt's lived. The home even had a name, Stone's Throw. The sign for it was at the end of a very long drive. At least Mr. Keller drove me right up to the house.

Beth's mom greeted me near the garage and invited me through the back door. "Come on in." She laughed like the whole scene was just funny.

"Hi." I trudged with my trash bag.

"'Here, let me help you with that." She grabbed my bag and walked through what she called, 'a mudroom' that was lovelier than most homes I'd seen. I was careful and wiped my shoes before I entered.

"This is really nice," I said as we entered the kitchen. It was a large room that was painted white with navy accents. A black Labrador came rushing over to greet me while Beth and her sister Jennifer came in from the hallway.

"The dog's name is Pokey." Beth sat down at the table. "And this is my older sister, Jennifer."

"Hi." I looked up at Jennifer while I happily petted the dog. Jennifer was athletic and preppy. All three of the women looked like they just walked out of a Spiegel catalogue. They were thin and attractive. The clothes they wore were beautiful; sweaters rich in color. Mrs. Kindt's sweater was monogrammed near the neckline.

"Do you have any clothes that need to be washed?" Mrs. Kindt looked like she was ready to go through my things.

"Um." I immediately walked to my bag. "I'm not sure. I mean, I just kind of threw my things in there."

"Well, I'll let you give me anything that needs cleaning tomorrow when you come down for breakfast." She smiled.

"Thank you, Mrs. Kindt." I looked at the beautiful white washing machine and dryer. Next to the dryer was Pokey's bed. It was monogrammed too.

"Please, call me Liz and my husband is Chuck. He's at an appointment for work, but he should be home soon."

"Oh, okay." I continued to pet the dog because I didn't quite know where to go. Plus, I liked Pokey. She was like a giant-sized version of Blackie.

"Beth, why don't you show Julie her room and the rest of the house." Liz motioned with her head as she picked up my bag again.

"Yes!" Beth jumped up. "I would love to."

I followed Beth into a hallway that led to the stairs and other parts of the house. First, she showed me a room that was larger than the apartment where I lived with Marge. It contained beautiful leather furniture, a fireplace, a bar, and a ladder that went up to a loft that looked like a little bungalow. I was in awe and I wanted to climb the ladder. "This is the great room." Beth walked in and out like the room didn't mean much. She led me through a museum-like living room and then into a dining room. "We only use these rooms when my parents entertain." Beth seemed so nonchalant when she spoke. Like none of this was a big deal. I wondered if she knew that not all the other kids at school lived like this. All of the homes I'd been to were beautiful and my friends, like Karen, wanted for nothing, but this was beyond anything I'd seen. "Let's go to your room." Beth hurried up the stairs and turned left. "This is it." She jumped into place.

The room had a soft glow from a lamp that was turned on next to a large four-poster bed.

Comforting and rich, I thought. There was an antique desk and chair with another lamp and a pen holder. There were wonderful wooden ducks in a few places and pictures of ducks on the walls. I looked in the mirror that was hung over a beautiful dark wood dresser and couldn't believe I was where I was. The warm tones in the room made me look soft. "This was my brother Charlie's room. He's in the marines now."

"Yeah," Jennifer piped in as she stood in the doorway. "It's your room now, you can put your things anywhere you want." She now had my bag and placed it just inside the door.

I wanted to cry. It was a beautiful room.

"Hey, let's put your stuff away and then we'll go see my room!" Jennifer sat on the fluffy bed.

"Like she cares about your room," Beth teased.

I slowly took things from my bag, opened drawers and placed socks and underwear first. I then looked into my closet and saw that there were plenty of hangers. I took a sweater from the bag and placed it on a hanger. "Who puts sweaters on hangers?" Beth asked. I quickly took the sweater off.

"Oh, that isn't where they go?" I stood uncomfortably, sweater in hand, not knowing what to do next.

"No, sweaters get folded, especially when they're wool. You don't want hanger marks at the shoulders."

"Okay." I folded the garment, placed it in a drawer, and did the same with the rest of Michael's sweaters. "What about pants?" I held them folded over my arm, careful that the size wasn't exposed.

"If they are slacks, then they go on this type of hanger." Beth took a wooden hanger with two clips out and showed me. "If they're jeans or cords, they get folded."

"Thank you." I quickly put the rest away. I was a little embarrassed that I didn't know where things went, but Beth was good about it.

I was mortified, thinking that she and Jennifer would judge the brands, the size of my things, or the dinginess of my old bras and socks.

The girls showed me their rooms and the bathroom we would share. It was overwhelming. Their closets were loaded with nice things and Beth had a vanity table with make-up, including the lip gloss I remembered her wearing in eighth grade. Jennifer was a bit more sporty and since she was a few years older than Beth and me, probably a little more serious. She had an Air Supply poster hanging on her wall and it made me smile because I didn't think I would have to act cool around her.

After seeing the whole house, we went back to the kitchen where Liz was making a snack for everyone. She set some fruit and cheese on the table and then decided she should show me the alarm system for the house. "I'm showing you this now, so that you won't be startled if the alarm goes off in the middle of the night." She laughed. "It has been known to happen." As she was giving me the code, the garage door opened and car lights shone through the mudroom. "Chuck's home."

Chuck walked in, smiling. He grabbed Liz and kissed her. He might have been the happiest man I had ever seen. His cheeks were pink and his skin was swept with remnants of a tan. How could the whole family be so pretty? I wondered. He greeted me warmly and then kissed his children. We all followed him into the large room with the fireplace and we kids sat down. He fixed drinks at the bar for himself and Liz, while she set the cheese and fruit on a table in front of the sofa. I felt like I was in a movie. Beth and Jennifer shared a few things with their parents; Jennifer won her tennis match that day and Beth would be going to the stables on Saturday, but only if she got all of her homework done. They asked me about school, and then Liz asked me to make a list of the things that I might need. I couldn't think of anything.

Before dinner, I went to my new room and found an orange tabby cat lying on my bed. I was thrilled. Since Pokey obviously slept downstairs, I could at least have a cat to hug.

During a dinner of salad, chicken, and fresh vegetables, I learned there were two cats in the house, Pokey was named after Pocahontas and Jennifer was getting a new Cocker spaniel puppy and had already named him Christopher.

"This place is a dream come true!" I looked over at Pokey and gave a thumbs up.

"You can keep Andy with you." Beth said. "I hate that cat!"

"You like animals, huh?" Chuck's eyes smiled as he took a bite of broccoli.

"I do." I thought about Blackie, Ted, and Tiny. "I had a dog growing up, but she passed away when we were twelve." I looked at everyone when I spoke so they wouldn't think I was sad. "Blackie and I were the same age."

I guess I opened a door with talking about Blackie, because that night, the Kindt's started asking questions about my family. I trusted them, so anything they asked, I answered matter of factly. It was easy to talk about everything without feeling anything about it.

~ * ~

I liked the Kindt's. The house was run with structure, but it was a friendly home. We all had chores and there were very clear expectations and rules. There was a bed time, we took turns with loading the dishwasher, we did yard work, and school work. Some of the kids at school seemed to treat me differently. I didn't talk much about living at the Kindt's, but slowly, kids were finding out.

I was fascinated with Liz and all that she could accomplish in a day. Every morning, she put out a full breakfast of eggs, turkey bacon, toast, and fruit or homemade oatmeal. She even sectioned everyone's grapefruit. She kept the entire home clean and ironed everyone's clothes. I had to tell her that she didn't need to iron my shirts, because I just covered them with a sweater anyway.

Everything was pristine in the home and she managed to work at a veterinary hospital part time, too. She was amazing and she never once complained. One day, I came home and found that my dingy bras where bleached white and looked brand new.

On the weekends, the Kindt's had neighbors over for cocktails and sometimes Liz would have a dinner party. She set up the dining room so it looked like a restaurant. Intimate tables were set for five course meals. I loved the dinner parties because Beth, Jennifer, and I would help in the kitchen, where none of the guests would be. Liz came back and forth and laughed with us. She drank wine and made the presentation seem effortless. If she drank extra wine, she hugged us a lot and told us we were beautiful. I wanted to be Liz someday. I wanted to be able to do everything, so I could have everything.

Nancy DeLeon left a message on the Kindt's answering machine, apologizing for the huge mess that she left next to the garage. When Chuck and I went out to look, we found about twenty trash bags full of items that Marge originally left at CYS for me. "How did we not see all of this?" Chuck laughed. I was horrified.

Everyone came out to help with all the trash bags. Liz decided it would be best to place the bags inside of the garage and then haul one or two at a time to my room. Jennifer seemed most intrigued and helped me by carrying one while I dragged another. "What do you think is in them?"

"Who knows?" I muttered, as I followed her up the stairs.

Jennifer came into the room with me and then opened the bag she carried, to take a peek. "It looks like books and clothes."

I wanted to open the bags by myself. I wondered if a plume of cigarette smoke wafted into Jennifer's nostrils when she opened the bag. It didn't matter what we were going to find, I was going to be embarrassed. "Are you sure you want to see all this?" I grabbed an old t-shirt from inside the Hefty and tossed it on the floor.

"I do!" Jennifer insisted and sat on my bed.

"Okay." I took a deep breath. "Welcome to the white trash extravaganza!" I pulled out more shirts and some old shorts. "This is the garbage pile." I pointed to the clothes and threw the next item.

"You don't want any of this?" She watched as I threw item after item on to the heap.

"Nope." I smelled like our old apartment in the clothes. Smoke, hoagies, and possibly beer. "None of this belongs in my life now and some of it isn't even mine."

I got past the clothes and pulled out books that Marge held on to. Some were college textbooks and files. I carefully placed them in a neat stack on the dresser. There might be a message in one of them or maybe someday, I would want to try and figure out why Marge underlined and highlighted certain items and not others. Maybe.

The next bag contained some clothes, a locket of my hair, my Little Miss Coast Guard crown, some of my old school work, and a Snoopy Shrinky-Dink keychain with our old phone number on it. I made it for my dad during the divorce to make sure he didn't forget our number. I was happy to see these things. Other items just left me baffled. Why would Marge give her clothes to me? Why would I ever want them?

It took me several days to go through the bags. I kept family photos, my parents' wedding album, and all papers and books so I could sort through them at my leisure.

Pieces of our house in Grand Haven brought back bitter sweet memories. There was the mirror that Randy gave Marge in the 70's. It was small with dark wooden, decorative beads and mosaic little mirrors. I threw it away, even though I knew how happy Marge was when Randy gave it to her. Jennifer was watching and what if she thought it was ugly? There was my dad's bolo tie from his square dancing days, which I immediately threw into my sock drawer for keeping. A lot of the items, I tossed back into the bags without thinking. It just seemed that every time I sorted through, Beth would appear at the door, Jennifer would want to watch, or Chuck would ask if I needed trash taken down. They meant well, but it hurried the process. Maybe that was a good thing. Of all ten bags, I probably only saved the contents of one.

I wondered what Marge was up to. I hoped that she was giving up and moving away. But it wasn't like her to just give up. Only a few months ago, I heard she wrote to Congress to fight CYS and the state of Pennsylvania. Now she was giving me her things. It was strange, but I knew it wouldn't be the last of her and I was right.

~ * ~

About a month after Marge dumped all the bags, Liz got a call from Nancy DeLeon. This time, it was to inform us that Marge had been mugged and was in Hahnemann Hospital.

"Nancy thinks you should call her." Liz flitted about the kitchen, taking some soup off the stove.

"Oh." I scrunched my face. "Really?"

"I don't think she should have to." Chuck draped his napkin over his lap. "Unless you want to." He smiled at me and winked.

"I don't want to, but what if she's really hurt?"

"Hey, it's up to you." Liz placed bowls of hot vegetable soup on each of our navy place mats.

The conversation was serious and quite different from what had been going on at the dinner table for weeks. Usually, Chuck, Beth, and I giggled so much that we often got stern glances from Liz and Jennifer.

"Nancy said that I should?" I looked at Liz, hoping she would tell me what to do.

"She thought it would be appropriate."

Beth and I cleaned the dishes after dinner while I continued to worry.

"I'm going to call her," I finally announced.

"Do you want me with you when you call?" Liz asked.

"No, I'll be fine."

"Why don't you go up to our room to call then," Liz smiled. "We'll be downstairs if you need us."

"Thank you." I managed a grin.

I dialed Hahnemann and was connected to Marge's room.

"Hello?" Marge sounded groggy. I wanted to hang up. It was the first time I'd heard her voice since court.

"Hi," I said.

Her response was the usual, emotional and immediate. "I don't need no sympathy from you, little girl!"

I wondered why it was that she insisted on the usage of proper grammar when I was growing up, but whenever she was mad, she used double negatives. I waited to hear what she would say next. "You go back to your new mama and daddy, don't call and harass me!" I expected for her to hang up then, but she stayed on the line.

"I'm not trying to harass you."

"Oh, yes, you are!" she interrupted. "I bet your new family is getting a kick out of this!"

"No, no one is getting a kick out of anything." I held the receiver tightly against my head in case her voice carried. "Have Randy and Dan been there to see you?" I thought about how I hadn't talked to them, either. It made me sad, but I was afraid that if I did call them, they would be mad at me for leaving the family or try to persuade me to come back.

"What do you care if they've been here? You don't even care about your brothers!" Marge yelled for a while and talked over me each time I attempted to say anything. She told me she had been in center city Philadelphia and was jumped by a black man just outside of the Greyhound station. He stole her wedding ring, broke her collar bone, and took her wallet.

I wanted to ask why she was at a Greyhound station, but I couldn't have if I tried.

"This is your fault, you know. You and your friend, Emily."

"No, it's not," I whispered and felt the pressure of tears building.

"Well, it sure as hell is!" Marge raised her voice again and then I heard her yelling at someone in the background. "I will, for god's sake! Mind your own business!"

I stayed on the phone with her far longer than I planned. I stayed on while she berated me until I sobbed. I guess I had forgotten how that felt.

Finally, Liz appeared in the doorway and I had enough. I quietly put the handset back into its cradle. Liz sat down next to me, pulled me to her and held me tight. "That must have been very hard. I'm so sorry, Julie."

"I'm used to it." I wiped my eyes with my sleeve.

"Where was she mugged?"

"At the Greyhound station. Why would she be at the Greyhound station?" I started crying again.

"You would never just hang out at a bus depot."

Liz laughed. "Only if I was taking a bus." She let go and patted my knee. "I'll be downstairs. Come down when you're ready."

Looking around at Chuck's and Liz's room, I noticed that my school picture was on a table next to their daughters' photos. I was stunned that my picture was there with their kids. In the photo, I was wearing one of Michael Shechtman's sweaters while smiling shyly, a large gap in my teeth. Beth's and Jennifer's pictures were gorgeous. Their teeth were perfect and they looked so confident. Jennifer had blonde hair and looked a lot like Chuck. Beth looked like him too, but more like Liz. For a moment, I could see that I resembled Beth and I fantasized I found my biological family.

I thought about Emily and wondered if she knew where I was, in a beautiful home with nice people. She would be happy.

I joined the Kindt's downstairs where they were discussing Thanksgiving. I sat in a chair at the end of the table. Liz didn't miss a beat. She handed me a spoonful of sugary cookie dough as she described where we would be dining with Chuck's mom, "Gram."

"Oh, the scent is so lovely at the home." Liz laughed. "Julie, you're going to love it."

"Thanksgiving at the home and Easter, too." Beth sighed. "But, let's not get ahead of ourselves." She laughed.

"Anyway, next week is Thanksgiving and Gram would love to have us share dinner with her at Rydal Park." Liz kissed me on the top of my head.

"That's the home," Jennifer chimed in.

"Big duh." Beth made a face at her sister and then looked at me. "Wanna wheelchair race next week?"

I laughed, not knowing if she was serious.

~ * ~

Gram was resting when we got to her room, but she perked up when she saw us all standing in the hallway. Chuck introduced me to Gram and she greeted me warmly. "Welcome." She held out her hand.

We ate our Thanksgiving dinner in a dining facility which was more like a restaurant. There was wait staff and cocktails for the Kindts. Later, Beth and I raced wheelchairs down the halls while wearing our Thanksgiving plaid skirts and corduroy blazers. "Stop it," Jennifer whispered in a hushed voice. "You're going to get in trouble."

I stopped and immediately put the wheelchair back.

"Whaa, you're no fun!" Beth giggled and placed her chair next to mine.

Jennifer was sensible and Beth seemed bored by her. I loved them equally.

~ * ~

One afternoon, Beth and I got home from school and found a note from her parents. They were out of town and wouldn't be home until very late. Liz left dinner in the fridge for us and Jennifer was off somewhere with a friend. Beth studied the note, threw her books down on the table and took off for the big room with the fireplace. I followed. "Well," she said as she took glasses down from the bar. "It's time for you to learn how to bartend."

"What do you mean?" I stepped closer to the bar and took a seat.

"Sometimes my parents have us make drinks for their friends, so I know how to make just about anything." Beth grabbed bottles and placed them on the wood. "You should know too, and you should be familiar with how they taste."

"Okay." The idea thrilled me. I had only seen Marge drink beer with the boys. I was about to learn about manhattans, martinis, and old fashions. I figured Beth knew what she was doing and I had no thoughts about consequences.

"This is a tumbler." Beth scooped crushed ice into the glass. "Gotta love that clink!"

She poured bourbon into the glass and then added a bit of sweet vermouth. She reached into a small refrigerator and took out a jar of cherries. "This cherry," she plopped it into the drink, "is garnish. Now try it."

"Yuck!" I practically spat.

"It's an acquired taste." She sipped from the glass. "Try some more while I make the next drink."

Beth and I were drunk when Nancy Deleon knocked at the door. "Oh my god! I forgot that she was coming here today." I grabbed the bottles and put them back in the bar. We snickered while we fumbled to straighten everything and Nancy knocked again. "Coming!" I yelled and began to laugh uncontrollably.

I opened the door and invited Nancy to the big room where we could sit and talk. I suddenly wished that Nancy was one of the caseworkers I heard about on the news. The caseworker that never checked on the kids.

I felt that everything was going quite well until I saw Beth lying on the floor of the loft overhead, laughing at me. I laughed too, but quickly recovered. While answering Nancy's questions, my head started to bob backward. I couldn't hold it up. It nodded with a life of its own. I don't know what we talked about, but when our visit was over, I headed to the nearest bathroom to throw up. Nancy never mentioned that day, not to me or the Kindts. She was a caseworker from heaven.

Chuck's birthday was six days before mine and fifteen days before Christmas. Liz made a special birthday dinner for everyone when it was their birthday. Chuck requested pork and sauerkraut and the girls complained because the whole house smelled bad. I thought it was funny and I hoped he felt special.

The morning of my birthday, school was cancelled because it snowed all night. I walked to Karen's and spent the morning with her. I missed my best friend. We weren't spending nearly as much time together since I moved in with the Kindts. Karen gave me a card and a Rick James tape. We had a great time that morning and we made plans for the weekend.

Chuck picked me up in the afternoon and we went Christmas shopping together. Together, we picked out items for Liz and the girls. I felt so happy that he included me. Just before we left Wanamaker's Department Store, we stopped at the fancy candy counter and Chuck bought me my first dark chocolate-covered pretzel. It was the most decadent thing I ever tasted. He timed the shopping just right so that we would arrive an hour or so before dinner. I helped make a fire and we all sat in the now beautifully decorated great room. The tree was huge and almost touched the ceiling. There were already presents that were labeled for the neighbors and other friends.

I requested spaghetti for my birthday dinner. Partly because it was Beth's favorite, but also because I knew it would be easy. As we entered the kitchen, I noticed presents at my spot at the table. I felt uncomfortable when I saw them. I just watched Beth and Chuck open presents over the last month, but I never expected to be treated the same and I didn't know whether to run, cry, or laugh. I gracefully set the gifts on top of the dryer near Pokey's bed until we were finished with dinner.

I opened a polo shirt, a sweater, and rag socks. I was thrilled. Then Chuck handed me an envelope with a ribbon around it. "The best for last." He smiled.

Inside, I found what appeared to be train tickets. "TWA?" I questioned. "Are you sending me away?"

"No, silly!" Beth answered. "You get to see your old friends from when you lived in Norfolk."

"They're plane tickets to Virginia." Chuck took a bite of cake while grinning.

"Oh my God!" I tried to catch my breath. "I've never flown!" I quickly stood while gripping the boarding passes. I flipped them to make sure that I was coming back. "I get to see my old friend, Bonnie and I get to fly! Thank you! Thank you!"

"Was Bonnie your best friend when you lived there?" Jennifer asked.

"Yeah, I stayed with her a lot when my mom was on business trips with the state and stuff." I smiled, remembering. "She, Anthony Vitug, and Daniel Hubbard used to have parties and we played spin the bottle a few times."

"Geez!" Jennifer remarked. "You were kissing boys at a young age."

"You don't know the half of it." I regretted saying that immediately. "What I meant was, I was exposed to a lot at a young age."

Liz changed the subject. "In the next few days, you'll need to check with Bonnie's family and make sure those dates work for them." Liz cleared plates from the table. "Otherwise, we'll have to change them."

I looked down and saw that I would be going away over Christmas break. "I will, I'll call her tonight. I haven't talked to her in a long time." I stared at the tickets, gleaming. "This is going to be quite the surprise since we left Virginia in the middle of the night and I never got to say goodbye to her. This might be weird."

I could barely sleep that night. I was excited about flying, but would also see friends that I hadn't seen in two years. I would be going to Virginia in nice clothes, happier than ever, too. What an incredible present.

As I went to bed that night, I thought about Marge. Nancy DeLeon didn't call and say there was a letter or card from her, or one from my Grandma. I sat up. I never told Grandma where I was. I would have to send her a Christmas card.

~ * ~

Christmas came fast and it was quite a production. On Christmas Eve, we drove an hour or so, to Bethlehem, Pennsylvania, where Liz's parents lived. "We call them Mimi and Bob." Beth explained while we three girls sat in the back of the car.

"They're really nice and they have a lot of expensive things." Jennifer repositioned the silk ribbon around her collar. "We have to eat tea sandwiches and stuff before church, and I never feel like I can touch anything."

"It's very proper." Beth said with a British accent.

Mimi's and Bob's was exactly what the girls had described. Their home was in the historic part of downtown Bethlehem and reminded me of a museum. Mimi was attractive for her age and I understood why she didn't want to be referred to as Grandma or Grandmother. She had high cheekbones and piercing blue eyes. Bob, white-haired and stately, mostly talked with Chuck and although he greeted us with a big smile, he seemed all business.

After eating tiny sandwiches and cookies, we all walked to the Moravian church for a classical music service. The church was beautiful. Everyone in attendance held tiny beeswax Moravian candles trimmed with red paper lace holders. We lit them toward the end of the service. The beauty of it made me tear up a little and I felt grateful for the experience. It was like being in the middle of the Christmas hilltop Coke commercial where part of the world wanted to buy the rest of the world a coke.

After, we all walked back to the house and then the adventure seemed to just end abruptly. Bob placed some wrapped gifts in the back of Liz's car and we left. It wasn't like Marge's family's Christmas Eve, where everyone talked for hours and my aunts barely let us leave until they overwhelmed us with hugs and kisses.

When we returned home, Chuck read The Night Before Christmas aloud. All I could think of was the cover of a Burl Ives album I saw years before. Children were gathered at his feet, listening intently. Now, I saw Beth and Jennifer looking at their father, the same way. When he finished reading, we headed to our rooms. "The best part of being forced to go to that boring service is coming home and Dad reading to us. It's what I look forward to most." Beth smiled and walked down the hall.

I thought about what Beth said as I got ready for bed. I was happy that she seemed grateful for her dad. It made me wonder what my dad would have been like during my teen years.

The next day was mind-boggling. There were so many presents. We opened boxes from L.L. Bean and Santerian's department store. We all got sweaters and shoes. I got a bracelet and earrings, and we found cassette tapes in our stockings. I received The Best of Blondie, Jennifer got The Best of Air Supply, and Beth got ABACAB by Genesis.

That afternoon, Chuck picked up Gram so that she could come for Christmas dinner. After she arrived, she handed us all checks for one hundred dollars. "I've never had a hundred dollars!" My mouth hung open in shock.

Liz laughed. "We'll have to go to the bank and open a savings account for you." I suddenly remembered the account that my dad opened for me before he died. Marge was off somewhere with that money and I had no idea of how much it was. I knew I'd never see it.

The Christmas dinner on the table was larger than a wedding reception buffet I once saw in a church basement. Everything seemed to be in excess. It was nothing like any Christmas I ever witnessed. I kept thinking about how just last year, Marge said, "Christmas is Communist."

Even though it seemed like Liz and Chuck bought the entire inventory of L.L. Bean, the focus that day was on being together as a family. Beth and Jennifer were just as grateful as I was, and I believe they would have been just as happy to have spent the day together near the warm fire, without all the hoopla. It was all so lovely.

~ * ~

My trip over the break was fantastic, mostly because of the flights. Taking off and landing were extraordinary to me and it made me want to be a pilot. I had never felt such a sensation and I felt like an independent adult. Bonnie's family picked me up and Bonnie and I giggled the entire three days I was there. I felt a bit more sophisticated when I was there, because I finally had nice clothes and manners to match.

Two Trees

~ * ~

A week or so into January, Liz informed me that she and I would be going to Elaine Powers, the workout place for ladies. "You don't need Elaine Powers." I said to Liz. "Maybe you can just drop me off."

"No," she said. "I want to tone up a bit."

"Oh," I gulped. "When are we going?"

"Tonight." She touched my arms and turned me toward the hallway. "I think we should go at least three times a week. Now go get some gym clothes on."

I felt anxious and embarrassed before there was anything to get embarrassed about.

My only gym shorts were a pair that I got at K-mart when I was with Marge. I put those on, along with an oversized T-shirt to hopefully hide my rolls. I slinked back downstairs, hoping I wouldn't be noticed, but when I entered the kitchen, everyone was in there. "My God, you've got great legs!" Liz walked to me and grabbed my shoulders. "Look at her!" she said to Beth and Jennifer.

"You're athletic," Jennifer said.

"Thanks," I responded with tears streaming down my face. I just wanted to get out of there and get the aerobics over with. I didn't want my body to be the center of attention any longer. I felt like a fat turd and they were lying to try and make me feel better.

"Honey, please don't cry." Liz wiped the sides of my face with her thumbs. "What's wrong?"

"I'm scared." I sniffled. "What if they tell me I weigh two hundred pounds? Or, what if I can't do the exercises?"

"First of all, you don't weigh anywhere near two hundred pounds..." Liz held my shoulders at arm's length, "and you can do anything you set your mind to. Okay?"

"Mmm-hmm," I whimpered.

I figured that the worst I could feel about the evening, was at that moment the kitchen. But, then we got to Elaine Powers. The lady at the desk looked like she walked right out of the Jane Fonda workout ad. She wore a little pink and white leotard over white tights. Her tights matched her hair and I couldn't believe she might have perspired at any point that day since the rouge on her cheeks was thick and pink. "So, as new members, you'll need to have assessments."

"What's that?" I cringed.

"Well, you'll weigh in and then we'll measure you."

Oh no. I thought. Could this day be any more humiliating? I focused on an instructor in front of a mirrored wall. She was on a podium, stretching, while a dozen older women tried to emulate the moves. They were more like me, in baggy clothes and suffering.

"Okay, step on the scale." I heard a sweet, but stinging voice.

I slowly stepped up on the scale and watched the desk lady's fake fingernails slide the metal bar along the lever. Up and up. "I guess the person before me weighed a lot less." I laughed nervously.

"One hundred and thirty-three!" she announced so that all of Elaine Powers and people in the parking lot could hear. After that, all I heard was that my arms were thirteen inches around and that Liz only weighed a hundred and twenty pounds. Liz had to have been five foot eight, since she towered over me. The good news was I weighed seven pounds less than when I was weighed at the clinic.

That first night, I wandered around the machines and tried to remember what the Pinky- desk lady told me to do. Then I got on a machine with a big vibrating belt that wrapped around my hips. I hoped it would vibrate the fat right off of me. It didn't work.

~ * ~

Liz and I continued to go to Elaine Powers and, at some point my arms shrank to eleven inches and I dropped a whole three pounds. I actually started to look forward to going, since the winter months were so unbearably boring. I started to feel better, too.

The big excitement that winter was that B.B. King moved in next door to the Kindts'. All the neighbors talked about it when over for cocktails. It was neat to tell everyone, even though we never saw him. The not-so exciting thing was that a new judge that was assigned to my case, decided I needed to have hour-long visitations with Marge. I had to agree to see Marge in a public place, unsupervised. Nancy DeLeon arranged everything and I agreed to meet Marge at the Village Mall. It was a small shopping mall close to Marge's job, where the residents lived. I really hoped she would bring them because they would be a great distraction and I kind of missed them. I was incredibly nervous and I imagined her kidnapping me, throwing me in her trunk and driving across country. Instead of dropping me off to fend for myself, Chuck decided that he would go shopping in the mall or at least try to look like he was shopping. Marge had him figured out in a matter of minutes.

I approached her at the entrance of the drug store. She looked just as nervous as I was. She was doing her pacing thing.

"Hi." I stood in front of her while her eyes darted between me and various areas of the mall.

"Is that your daddy?" She quickly tilted her head to where Chuck was window-shopping.

"No." I replied. "My dad is deceased."

"And I bet you wish I was dead too, huh?" Her lips tightened and her nostrils flared, waiting.

"No." I looked down.

"Oh, yes, you do!" She stepped toward me like she wanted me to cower. "What is he, a detective?" She focused on Chuck again.

"What do you want?" I ignored her question.

"What do I want?" she yelled. "What do I want? What the fuck does that mean?"

"Why can't you go far away and just leave me alone?" I trembled and immediately regretted speaking to her like that.

"Never, Julie!" She poked my chest. "I will never leave you alone, you little brat!" I turned and walked away from her. "That's right, just go to your daddy!" Marge yelled. I walked out of the mall and waited for Chuck to get to the car. He was right behind me and thankfully, she wasn't.

"Well, so much for an hour visit." Chuck laughed while he opened his car door.

A few weeks went by and I was told that I needed to visit Marge again. We did the same thing, at the mall, only this time, she screamed and spit at me, so I left. This became the norm for 'visitations' that winter. Altogether, I saw her four times and my lawyer Vanessa got the decision turned so I wouldn't have to see her for a while.

Chapter Nineteen

I became obsessed with the television show, Dynasty. But even more so with Linda Evans and the lead character she played, Krystle Carrington. I loved Krystle because she was kindhearted, nurturing, feminine, and set up charities while other characters were trying to destroy everyone around them to gain power. I absolutely had to be home watching the show when it aired, even if it was a rerun.

I started collecting magazines with Linda Evans on the cover. Since my hair was dark, and I could never look as angelic as Krystle, I decided that I needed to have my hair cut like Fallon, the character that was Krystle's step-daughter. Her hair was shoulder length with gradual lengthening around the face. I felt a little guilty getting the cut because Fallon was always mean to Krystal and resented her very existence, even though Krystal was always nice to her.

Everyone loved the cut, but something became very apparent with my new do. "You really need to have your eyebrows plucked," Jennifer said when we were waiting for the show to start.

"What do you mean?" I had never heard of such a thing.

"Mom can do it, she does mine." Jennifer immediately went looking for Liz.

Liz came into the den with what looked like a little tool kit. "This is going to pinch, but you'll be shocked at how different you're going to look."

"Okay," I said excitedly. "What do I do?"

"Just come over here and lay your head on my lap." Liz sat on the loveseat and pulled a lamp closer. She started tweezing away while I winced. "Well," she laughed. "Now you have two eyebrows," she joked, "but I'm not finished." She continued pulling little hairs while Jennifer talked about how good it looked. "Now, go look in the mirror."

She was right. It was shocking. I looked like a completely different person. I looked like a girl. Krystle would talk to me, I thought.

I'm not sure why, but the more I did to improve myself, the more insecure I became. I felt I didn't deserve things. I was so used to drama and being dumped on, that sometimes I didn't feel alive. I wanted to be like Beth and take everything in, love life, but nothing made sense and I didn't know who I was. No one was treating me poorly anymore. No one was hitting me or touching me inappropriately. I was feeling more comfortable in the Kindt household, but I also felt like baggage. At night when I lie awake, just me and Andy the cat, everything was still and the dream I was living in came to an abrupt halt. I wouldn't be able to sleep.

One evening, when Jennifer and I were on dish duty, she started asking me questions about my brothers. "Don't you want to see them?"

"Sometimes, I want to see Dan." I looked away from her. "But, he's busy with college."

"What about your other brothers?" Jennifer pushed.

"Randy is nice, but he's married now and he lives in Brazil with his wife." I placed the silverware upside down in the machine like Liz taught me. "Scot did horrible things and I don't care if I see him again."

Jennifer stopped helping and stood motionless. "What kinds of things?"

"I don't want to get into it," I replied. Memories flooded my brain. We finished loading the dishwasher and I went off to my room. I wasn't sure why, but I wanted Jennifer to know just how bad it was. I had no one else to talk to and even if I did, I wouldn't have said anything about the icky parts of my background. I sat in my room, thinking about Scot, and the hate I felt for him resurfaced. I cringed when I thought about what he did to me and what he did to my dog. I went to the bathroom and slowly cut small lines across the tops of my hands with a razor and then I wrapped my bloody hands in toilet paper. I looked at myself in the mirror and saw the ugly girl, the garbage that Scot created, and I cut my cheek.

Jennifer was completely horrified when I came downstairs. "What happened?"

"It's what he did to me," I said calmly. Jennifer started to cry and I immediately regretted my actions and hated myself more. "But now I'm fine."

That night, I lay in my bed and prayed to be normal. Why had I done that? I wondered if I just wanted attention or had her questions pushed me that far. Now, not only was I fat and ugly, I was crazy.

~ * ~

The family seemed very confused by my actions and so was I. We didn't talk about it, we all seemed to pretend it never happened, but I felt I pushed everyone away. Liz wasn't giving me any reassuring pats on the head and Chuck wasn't making me laugh. After a few days, Liz sat down with me. She wasn't smiling. "Julie, we care so much about you, but you need more than we can give." She placed her hands on my knees. "I need more time with my children and I don't think I can take on one more."

"I'm sorry." I cried. "I didn't mean to take up so much time, I didn't." I wanted to say, I'll never do anything bad, I'll stay out of your way, I'll do anything you want. But I knew it was too late. "I understand," I said.

"Nancy DeLeon has a family in Souderton that would love to have you." Liz was now crying too.

"We would like you to have a party so that you can say goodbye to your friends here."

"I'm leaving the school district," I mumbled.

The party was a week later. I invited all of the popular kids, even though I wasn't that popular. Beth knew all of the kids and they seemed to have a great time. Liz took pictures of everyone so I could have keepsakes. I didn't cry anymore. I had to keep my chin up and go with the next family. It was, after all, better than being with Marge. I wanted to call Emily, but she couldn't save me either. I created this mess and I had to live with the consequences.

~ * ~

Nancy DeLeon took me to the new foster home in Souderton, about thirty-five minutes northwest of where I lived with the Kindts. Souderton was mostly farm area, but Nancy drove into the borough where there were a lot more homes. We pulled up to a two story yellow house and she helped me gather my things. I had luggage this time and a few totes, no garbage bags.

The entire family greeted us at the door. An attractive Latina woman offered her hand to me. "Hello, I'm Connie." She shook my hand and quickly turned to her family. "This is my husband, John and our kids, John Jr. and Rachel." John Jr. who was in his Underoos, grabbed his dad's leg and hid behind it while Rachel stood quietly, grinning at me.

Nancy spoke before I could. "This is Julie. I'm sure you'll like each other very much." She seemed rushed and took another step toward the inside of the house.

"Oh, yes." Connie laughed. "I'm sorry, come in." She scrunched her face at me and giggled like she knew I would understand her temporary loss of hospitality.

The living room was poorly lit with dark furniture and carpeting. Connie led us to the kitchen which was brighter, but not by much. The kitchen sink was overflowing with dishes and there were pans on the stove with bits of dried egg and bacon grease. I leaned against a counter while Nancy, Connie, and John talked for a few minutes. John Jr. stood behind his mother's chair, head barely visible and Rachel stood at the top of a stairwell across the kitchen, legs crossed like she had to pee.

I kept my bags close to me and waited for the next step in this process. I don't know what they talked about, it was all a blur, but Nancy stood up to leave after just a few minutes. "Julie, we'll talk next week."

Connie smiled. "Let's go see your room and get your things put away." She headed where Rachel had been standing. I don't want to put my things away, I thought. I followed Connie to the small upstairs. "This is Junior's room." She stood in the doorway for a moment, in case I might want to check out his Batman bedspread. "And this is Rachel's room that you will be sharing." I frowned at the pink princess layout and entered hesitantly. "I have to tell you, Rachel is so excited to have an older sister."

I looked at Rachel who seemed shy, yet excited to tell me something.

Connie had her hand on the top of her daughter's head like she was holding her in place. "Your bed is here and you can use this dresser." Connie started opening drawers. "John got this from one of the guys at the plant." I nodded like I knew what that meant. We stood silently until it became too awkward. "I'll let you get settled then." Connie left and Rachel sat down on her bed, across from mine. I dragged my luggage close to the dresser, but didn't open it.

Then it happened. The inevitable. "Do you wanna see all my dollies?"

Not really, I thought. "Sure."

Rachel displayed a parade of stuffed animals and dolls from her bed, her dresser, and the back of her closet. I hated every minute of it.

"Girls, come on down here!" I heard yelling from the bottom of the stairs. I got up immediately and Rachel followed.

John sat at the table, playing with the strings on a guitar while Connie stirred something on the counter. "I just thought we could get to know each other a bit before John and I head out."

"Where are you going?" I sat at their table while Rachel zoomed past and into the living room.

"We play in a band." John finally spoke. He ran his fingers through thinning blond hair.

"I'm the singer." Connie announced proudly.

"I guess I'm the babysitter," I replied.

"I hope you don't mind, we usually only have gigs on weekends." She turned and continued stirring. "Well, tonight, we're playing at a friend's club, but we rarely play on a school night."

"Oh." I couldn't think of anything to say. I sat miserably in the chair and studied the pattern on the table.

"Julie, I'm sure you'll like Indian Valley Junior High." Connie took a baking pan of what looked like chicken tenders out of the oven. "I know Rachel's looking forward to going in a few years."

"It's a junior high?" I scowled. "But I was in high school." I placed my elbows on the table and rubbed my temples.

"I'm sure it will be hard to start a new school, but after a while, you'll make tons of friends." Connie put a macaroni dish and the chicken nuggets on the table along with a bottle of ketchup and three plates.

"I'm used to it." I stood up. "Do you want help?"

"No. no." Connie motioned me to sit back down with an exaggerated wave. "Kids, come in and eat." She called into the living room. "Help yourself." She picked up a plate and handed it to me.

"Aren't you eating?" I took the plate and set it back on the pile.

"No. We'll get something at the pub." She tried to hand me the plate again.

"I'm not hungry," I said.

"Suit yourself." She shrugged and rushed out of the room. The kids were already seated and picking up the nuggets with unwashed hands.

John scooped a spoonful of macaroni and cheese on to each of their plates.

"So, you're just going to leave?" I laughed a little in disbelief.

"Nancy said that you're a good kid, so I trust you." Connie came back having pinned her hair back.

~ * ~

Connie took me to my new school the next morning so she could sign my paperwork. As we walked through the mayhem of hundreds of teens running around, I thought we made an odd pair. She was too young to be my mother and she dressed stylish and feminine with a long dress and boots. I wore bright red corduroys that I got for Christmas from the Kindts, a white oxford cloth shirt, and a kelly green sweater. I probably resembled a Christmas ornament. When we found the office, we were asked to sit for a few minutes. I didn't really want to talk about anything, but I knew I should be polite. "How was your band last night?"

Connie sat up a little straighter. "Oh, it was a good turnout."

"That's good." I stared at the large wood counter in front of me and tried to tune out all the sounds of clicking typewriters. "What kind of music do you play?"

"We play a lot of popular music and some CCM." She crossed her legs, exposing the knee length of her suede boots.

"What's CCM?" I folded my arms.

"It's Contemporary Christian." She pulled her long black hair back and looked at her watch. "We play other music, too."

"Wait." I looked at her face finally. "You play Christian music in a bar?"

"Yes. Why?" She grinned.

"I thought you played, like, Barracuda or something." I laughed.

"We play the music of Heart too, sometimes." She stared at me.

"What?"

"Nothing, it's just that I never heard of mixing booze with Jesus." I scooted up in my chair and hoped we would be greeted by someone in the office soon.

"Honey, this is Souderton." Connie leaned closer to me. "It's a Christian Community. Mennonites live out here."

"Great." I slumped in my chair.

I decided I would hate Indian Valley Junior High and wouldn't give it a chance. I was not comfortable and I just wanted to be at my old school. I kept thinking, no more walking home with Karen, no eating dinner in the white and navy kitchen at the Kindts. I wanted to cry all day, but I just went with the flow. I meandered from class to class, wondering if the teachers sipped wine during Bible study or if they lived on one of the nearby farms and had been up since four a.m., doing chores before work.

That night, I was on the phone with Nancy DeLeon. "I don't want to be here."

"Julie, I think you know by now, it takes a while to acclimate."

"This is different." I lowered my voice. Connie walked through the kitchen like she was busy, but I knew she was trying to listen. "I hate it here. I don't want to watch these little kids and I want my old school back."

"I have tried everything to keep you in your school district." Nancy sighed. "There's nothing I can do."

"I know you tried." I pulled on my eyebrow and stared at the floor. "I'm sorry."

"Just give it some time," Nancy pleaded.

"Sure." I exhaled loudly. "I have to go." I hung up the phone, feeling like the biggest brat in the world. None of this was Nancy's fault.

~ * ~

The following day, I took the bus to school and shuffled from one class to the next. I tried to be social, but all I could think of was my old school, teachers, and friends. I felt out of place and far away. I was even far away from Emily and I hadn't even seen her in months. I'd done this so many times and I always made new friends. This just felt unbearable and made my heart hurt.

I'm not staying here, I thought. By the end of my third class, I decided to leave. I placed all of my books in the locker I had been assigned and went out the side door. I walked back to the foster home, got a few of my things, and headed to route 309. Somehow, I thought I could make it to Upper Moreland before the school day ended. I trudged along as cars whizzed by. I wasn't quite sure what I would do when I got to Willow Grove, but anything was better than the singing Christians and Indian Valley Middle School.

I had only been out on the highway for a little less than an hour when a large truck slowed on the other side of the highway. Keep going, I thought. Soon the truck was in front of me and pulling over. I was going to run as soon as I got a break in the road. But then, I heard my name. When I looked at the driver I could see that it was John, my new foster father. Damn! Just leave me alone.

"What are you doing?" He jumped out of his truck.

"I'm going back home."

"Why don't you get in the truck? It's a really dangerous road and you shouldn't be out here." He reached for my bags.

"I don't want to live way out here." I held tight.

"I understand," he yelled over a semi's horn. "Just get in and we'll work this out."

I believed him. John talked about how hard all of this must be as we drove back to his house. He promised he would call Nancy DeLeon, but he had to get back to work. "Connie will be back in about an hour."

I decided not to wait for him to call Nancy and I dialed her myself. "I'm not staying and I'm sorry." I spoke calmly.

"Well, where are you going?" Nancy took a deep breath.

"Anywhere," I replied. "Isn't there somewhere?"

"Well, there's a group home in Pottstown, but…"

"I'll take it," I said, without realizing that Pottstown might be further away. I just didn't want to babysit little kids and live with a band.

"But, it's even further away from Willow Grove." She tried to reason with me.

"I'll wait there until something opens up."

"Okay." She paused. "I'll call Connie's work and then come and get you." Nancy hung up and I sat down at the kitchen table to wait.

Nancy was there within the hour. As she drove me to Pottstown, she talked about her own kids and how well they were doing in college. I pretended I was interested while I worried about what a group home might consist of.

We pulled up to a large house near the center of town. A few teenagers were hanging out on the front porch, smoking and rocking on a swing. Nancy politely knocked at the door while the kids stared at me.

A black man answered the door. "Well, come on in," he said.

Rodney was a tall man with gentle mannerisms. His soft voice and ready smile made me feel comfortable. He reminded me of Gordon from Sesame Street. "Have a seat, ladies." Rodney sat down in a chair, while Nancy and I sat on the sofa. " So we got your call and what brings Miss Julie to Generations?"

Nancy quickly answered. "I think we will use the group setting as a stepping stone for Julie, until a suitable foster home is available."

Rodney picked up a clipboard from the coffee table and began to write. One of the boys from the front porch entered the living room area and sat in a chair so that his legs dangled over the side. He no sooner got comfortable and Rodney told him to leave. "Get up from there, Joe. I'm sure you have something better to do." Joe slowly got up and shuffled away from us without speaking a word.

Rodney shook his head and reached across the table to give me the clipboard. "We have rules in the house and you must follow them." I took the paperwork and nodded. "First, wake up is at six a.m., you need to make your bed and get downstairs for breakfast." I read along as he cited the rules and regulations page. "Breakfast is only between six-fifteen and seven o'clock. You may take a shower at night or in the morning and you will have chores." He looked at me with questioning eyes as if expecting apprehension. "Everyone comes to a group meeting in the morning and everyone goes to school in the afternoon."

"Oh, good." I smiled.

"She likes school." Nancy shrugged.

"That's good, that's good." Rodney smiled. "If rules are broken, you will not be able to participate in group activities. If you become a problem, you will be sent to Juvie."

"What's Juvie?" I looked up from the paperwork.

"Juvenile Hall, you don't want to know." Rodney answered.

"You don't have to worry about this one." Nancy patted my knee.

I could only think of how drunk I was the day at the Kindt's when she came for a visit. She probably never said anything, because she didn't want me in Juvie.

Rodney had Nancy and me sign some papers and then he stood. "I'll show you your room and introduce you to everyone."

"I'm going to head out." Nancy smiled. "We'll talk tomorrow."

"I know the drill," I said.

I shared a room with one other female. She seemed a little rough and took no shame in examining my preppy attire. The rest of the house consisted of boys. Ten bad boys.

Shelly and I each had a twin bed with old Pottstown Memorial Hospital sheets and blankets. I placed my bags at the end of my bed.

"Aren't you going to unpack?" Shelly turned herself around on her bed so that her sweat socks rested on her pillow.

"I don't plan on staying." I looked toward the door and wondered where Rodney went.

"Are you gonna run?"

"No, I just know that I'll get a foster home." I sat on my bed and looked at the blank walls. "How long have you been here?"

"A few months." Shelly picked at her nails. "I'll be going back to my boyfriend, though."

"You live with your boyfriend?" I searched her face for dishonesty.

"When he's not in the slammer, I do." She laughed.

"Why is he in jail?" I tried to keep from looking disgusted, remembering how bad my family was, how I shouldn't judge.

"Theft." She left it at that. "C'mon, I'll show you the rest of the place, since Rod seems to have disappeared." Shelly walked me through the halls where we found Rodney, talking to a few boys. He looked up briefly and waved. The upstairs consisted of five bedrooms, a bathroom, and an office. "There is another bathroom on the third floor." Shelly pointed out. We then went down a back stairwell into a large kitchen. "You'll have chores in this kitchen." Shelly started opening and closing cabinets and drawers. She moved along so fast that I couldn't see what was in them.

"Sometimes you'll have to help put out breakfast or you'll have to do the dishes."

"Does everyone really get up at the same time?" I held the back of a chair tightly and stared at a table that could seat twenty.

"Six a.m." Shelly placed her hands on her hips. "You get used to it." She turned off the kitchen light and headed to the living area.

"There's a laundry room downstairs and it costs fifty cents for the washer and fifty cents for the dryer." Shelly plopped herself into a large chair.

"What if you don't have money?" I couldn't remember if I did. I thought about the hundred dollars that Gram gave me at Christmas time. It was safe in the bank.

"You earn quarters by having a clean room and doing what they ask," Shelly said. "It's not hard and most of us just save the quarters for ciggies and then share wash loads."

"Oh." I sat in another chair beside Shelly. For a minute, I wondered if I made the right decision. I figured that once Karen Bean found out where I was, she and her parents could help find me a foster home. "When do we go to school?"

Shelly looked up at a clock that read five-forty. "Actually, any time now."

"What do you mean?" I sat, mouth open. "We go to school at night?"

"Yep." Shelly looked at the clock again and wiggled in her chair. "Probably some bum teacher that needs some extra cash. You'll see."

After a few minutes, Rodney came down the stairs with keys jingling and a few boys following him. "Come on, people!" he yelled. "Let's go!" More kids came through the front door from the porch. Shelly jumped up from her chair and I followed her through the back door to a van. As all twelve or so took seats, I noticed no one had paper or pens or books. As we drove, some of the kids asked me why I was at the home and why I had been in foster homes, what I had done wrong. My story might have been very boring to them, so I answered with no more than a few words. What had I done wrong?

Rodney pulled up to the front doors of what appeared to be an elementary school and we kids went inside. As we entered the school, I couldn't help thinking of the residents, Betty, Grace, and Kathie. Monday through Friday, they all got on a bus and went with a group of others to a work facility where they would put little things together. I just rode in that same type of bus and, for all I knew, we were entering a child labor set-up. I followed everyone to a classroom.

A middle-aged man, with the beginnings of a beer gut, sat on the front desk, "Okay, take your seats. How's everybody doin'?" No one replied. "Great, great," he said. "I have handouts." He shuffled down the aisles and placed all kinds of worksheets in front of us. Geography, math and history. "How about you kids fill in the blanks and let me know if you have questions."

I found it strange that he didn't mention anything about me being new to the class. He seemed to treat the few hours that we were there much like the boys did, a joke. When the class ended, he asked for our sheets. I was happy that I was able to answer most of the varied questions without too much thought. I felt smart.

Once back at the group home, I asked if I could use the phone. I called Karen to let her know where I was. I heard her yell out to Lee, "Mom, where is Pottstown?" and then, "Julie, just hold on a minute, okay?" When Karen came back on the line, she sounded upset. "We have to get you back here. I can't believe how far away you are."

"I know," I responded.

"I asked my mom if you can live with us, but you know we don't have room."

"Karen, I would never expect that." I stood near the back stairwell, wanting to pound my forehead on the wall. "There has to be a place."

"I'll work on it on this end," Karen said. "So, what's it like?"

"What, the group home?" I smirked. "Its fine. Lots of rules, I suppose."

"You've got two minutes!" Rodney called from the living area. Perfect timing, I thought.

"See, they're yelling that I have two minutes. So it's prison-like, but not." I whispered and laughed nervously. "I have to go."

"Call me tomorrow, okay?"

"I will if I get privileges and the guards let me."

"Very funny. Goodnight."

"Bye."

~ * ~

The following morning, a woman woke us all by calling from the hallway. "Everyone up, up, up!"

I followed Shelly's lead and made my bed, tucking everything tightly. I was able to get into the bathroom right away and brush my teeth, but the woman who was now on duty informed me I would have to wait to take a shower. "Let's see how you made your bed." She followed me back into the room. "No, you're going to want to pull out the sheets, corner them and tuck hard."

She pulled and then allowed me to finish. "This quarter should bounce." She dropped a quarter and it simply landed on my blanket. "There's a quarter toward laundry." She smiled. "Good job."

I followed everyone downstairs to the kitchen. Shelly was already helping by putting out boxes of cereal and getting bowls from the cabinets. There was a loaf of bread on the table, along with a few gallons of milk, peanut butter and a bowl of fruit.

I took an apple and sat at the table with everyone. I was too embarrassed to get anything more. I didn't want the fat jokes to start.

After breakfast, I helped with the dishes and attended my first group meeting. As we sat all around the living room, I heard the worker lady ask, "Does everyone know Julie?"

Followed by a simultaneous groan of, "Yes."

"Well, my name is Kim." She glanced in my direction. "I have worked here for about four years and I love it. My goal today is to be supportive of all of you and learn from you." She smiled. "Now, everyone can go around the room and tell us what your goal is for the day."

Most of the goals had to do with getting permission to go to the store. Shelly, who was sitting directly to my left, said, "I want to be able to see Bobby today."

"We'll see what happens," Kim replied and looked at me. "Julie?"

"I'm Julie, I've been here for less than twenty-four hours and my goal is to find a foster home."

"Okay," Kim said. "That's probably going to take a while, so just allow yourself to be open and get to know folks here." She looked around the room and nodded. "You'll find that it's a nice place to be. It's not jail, so if you find you don't like it, you're free to leave, but then I guess you're homeless." I thought she was a little harsh, but I looked at everyone and they seemed completely unaffected. "So, today we're going on a field trip."

"Cool, where?" one of the boys, Brian, asked.

"We're going to Ringing Rocks State Park," Kim answered proudly.

"So, I'm not going to get to see Bobby!" Shelly crossed her arms.

"Do I have to go?" a boy with scruffy hair asked.

"Yes." Kim glared at him.

"It's so stupid, the rocks are supposed to make all these bell sounds, but they don't even work."

"You need to be patient, tap the hammer lightly, listen carefully, and find the live rocks, the ones that ring," Kim said. "Besides, it's a beautiful day to be outside and we all need exercise. And, Shelly, we'll talk about Bobby later."

When we arrived at the park, Kim announced that anyone who wanted to search for live rocks should come see her to obtain her help with hammering. Some kids just milled about, others sat down, and a few of us followed Kim.

"Why can't I just take the hammer?" Brian stood on a boulder like he was going to dive off of it.

"It doesn't work that way." Kim seemed annoyed.

"But..." Brian was jumping and laughing.

"But nothing." Kim gripped the hammer firmly.

"I would like to hear the rocks," I said.

"Okay, let's see what you can find." Kim gestured for me to go ahead of her.

"I think this spot is good." I crouched down in an area that was far removed from the other kids. Kim handed me the hammer while she sat down on a smooth rock surface. I began tapping the hammer against rock. It took about twenty tries on twenty different boulders before I heard a bell sound. "Got one." I smiled. "Hey, Brian!"

Brian climbed over to investigate. Hey tapped a few times until he heard it. "Whoa," he said. "It really does work."

Chapter Twenty

A few days later, I got a call from Nancy DeLeon. "Great news," Nancy said.

"Really?" I couldn't wait to hear. Maybe the Kindts changed their minds, I thought.

"The Barreres somehow found out that you were in a group home and they want you back."

"Really?" I repeated.

"Yes," Nancy answered. "I don't know why I didn't think of them before. Why did you stop living there anyway?"

"Well, Emily placed me with them when I first got taken away. I like them, but they weren't in my school district. I don't care now." I was thrilled. I thought about how I could ride Gloria's bicycle to Karen's again and I could make cowboy cookies for Jim. "I don't know why I didn't think of them either."

"Now, Julie, you need to stay put for a few days."

"I will, I will." I smiled.

"There is a lot of red tape I have to go through on this end," Nancy explained. "Also, I have some mail for you from your mom."

"Oh," I said.

"We can always read it together." Nancy offered.

"I'll be okay."

I continued for the next few days with a smile from ear to ear. Kim explained in the group I was very lucky to find a foster family. As I looked around the room, I felt a little guilty that I was lucky. I wasn't going to have to earn washing machine money. The Barreres had a washer and dryer right off the kitchen. I wasn't going to have the same chores and have group meetings. I would get to go to a regular school and watch Dynasty. I continued going to our night school and completed the handouts. I thought about my classmates at Upper Moreland and what kind of work they were doing. I longed for real classrooms and homework.

Nancy drove me to the Barreres, who were waiting at the Boston Sea Party restaurant in Willow Grove, just off of the turnpike. I hugged Jim and Gloria, but not too hard. I just wanted them to know that I liked them and I was grateful. We three sat down to dinner. The Barreres expressed some concerns after we ordered. "You can live with us and we want you to live with us, but you can't spend so much time at the Bean's." Gloria looked at me while Jim buttered his roll.

"Okay," I agreed reluctantly and noticed I couldn't control the squinting of my eyes.

"Really, we would like you to spend more time with us." Gloria nudged Jim.

"Yeah, what she said." Jim smiled and bit into his bread.

"Last summer when we had you, it just seemed like you were over there every day."

"Well, now I'll be in school and I'll be around."

"What about the summer?" Gloria took a sip of water.

"I just love to hang out with Karen. We laugh all the time and we swim in her pool and stuff, but I'll spend more time at your house." I smiled.

"It's not that we don't want you to spend time there, she's your best friend. It's just that we'd like to have some time with you, too."

"I completely get it." I replied. I didn't get it, but I would try.

~ * ~

The following Monday, I started school at Log College Junior High. The first day, we had an assembly with some guy that worked with reptiles and travelled to schools. He brought out a huge boa constrictor and asked for a volunteer. I immediately raised my hand. I figured I had nothing to lose. There were only three months of school left, so I might as well make the most of it.

After the snake crawled all over my neck and I just laughed about it, kids came to me and asked me questions. Between the snake charming and joining the chorus, I made friends in no time.

The farm near the Bean's house had a sign out front that read, "'Free Kittens'. My heart jumped at the thought of having a pet of my own. Since the Barreres' poodle was possessed and didn't take to me, I asked Jim and Gloria if I could get a cat. Jim took the time to explain to me how important it would be for me to take care of it and that it would be a big responsibility.

"I know, I can do it." I sat wide eyed and anxious, pressing on my knuckles.

After discussing it a few times, they agreed to let me have a cat.

~ * ~

The Barreres also reminded me a few times I had that psychiatrist appointment coming up, the one the judge recommended. Whenever they spoke of it, I dismissed it by changing the subject. I didn't get why I had to go. But, the day was inevitable.

"So, kid, I'm going to pick you up right when I get home from work." Jim grabbed the back of my head and pressed down lovingly.

"For what?"

"You've got to go see that shrink at Abington Hospital."

"Is that why you're squeezing my brains?" I looked up at him. "Is this just the start?"

Jim laughed. "It won't be so bad. They just want to make sure that you're on the right track."

"No, I bet Marge is convincing everyone that I'm crazy." I bit into my thumbnail and twitched my legs. "What if I end up in some place like, 'One Flew Over The Cuckoo's Nest'?"

"That's not going to happen." Jim grinned wider than the circumference of his coffee cup.

"What if I just say, no?"

"Kid, it's not going to be that bad and it's our responsibility to get you there." Jim rinsed his cup out in the sink and prepared to leave. "You don't have to tell him anything you don't want to."

"Really?" This made the idea more palatable. "Okay, I'll go." I wanted to kick myself for saying it. "You know," I followed Jim out the back door. "I might need some kind of candy or something from the hospital gift shop."

"Deal." Jim waved his hand but didn't look back.

Jim pulled up to the hospital's front doors and handed me a dollar for a candy bar. He was going to run errands. I waited nervously in Dr. Mandell's office. I looked at articles in Psychology Today so I could try to get an upper hand before our session. I was there alone in the waiting room, when finally a slight, curly haired scientist opened his door. "Julie?"

"Yes?" I stood.

"Come on in." He didn't smile and barely made eye contact. He held the door open and asked me to take a seat. There were only two chairs and his desk. The room had a wooden chest full of toys, a chalkboard, and a shelf full of paper, crayons, pencils, and markers.

Dr. Mandell took a seat at his desk and I sat in the chair next to him, facing him. "So, what brings you here, Julie?"

"I have to come."

"What do you mean?" he peered through fine rimmed glasses at my chest. "Is someone making you come here?"

"A judge!" I stretched my legs out and crossed them along with my arms. I stared at my shoes and tapped them against each other.

"Well, since a judge told you that you need to be here, how would you like to start?"

"I don't know."

"Why were you in front of a judge?"

"I was taken away from my mother, Marge." I looked at him and noticed he was reviewing my body. It was nerve wracking and I changed position.

"Why is that?" He found my face.

"Why is what?"

"Why were you taken away?"

"Abuse and stuff." I sat up. "Do you ever watch Dynasty?"

"I'm sorry?" His nostrils flared and he smirked, oddly.

"The show, Dynasty." I repeated.

"No, I can't say that I have. Does it have something to do with our meeting today?"

"Look," I faced him, "I have already had therapy and since I'm forced to be here, I may as well tell you all about Dynasty."

"Very well." He put his pen down and sat back in his chair. "But, do you mind telling me about your therapy?"

"Her name is Emily. Do you mind if I use the chalkboard?" I pointed.

"Not at all."

I jumped up from my chair and found the chalk. At the top of the board I wrote, DYNASTY.

"Okay, so first I'll write down the characters' names and how they're related." I wanted to put down Krystal first since she was my favorite, but I figured that Blake would be a better place to start since Dr. Mandell was a man.

"Okay, so Blake Carrington is a wealthy oil man, but he lives in Denver instead of Dallas and he's married to Krystal." I drew a line connecting the two names. "Krystal is the most beautiful woman ever. Not Natalie Wood beautiful, isn't it awful that she died? But, angelic beautiful"

Dr. Mandell wrote something down and nodded.

"Okay, so Blake just married Krystal but his daughter, Fallon doesn't approve even though Krystal is really nice to her. The son, Steven accepts her, but the weird part is that Alexis, the ex-wife lives on the estate!" I continued writing names and connecting the relationships. "I think she does that just to be a pest and she's like, evil."

I went on and on about the show right up until our appointment time ended. The sad part was, Dr. Mandell wanted to see me again the following week. The good thing was, I was going to get a cat soon.

~ * ~

The following week, I came in and started in about Dynasty again. I went directly to the white board and re-drew the diagram with all the characters. "Steven is gay and Blake beat up his boyfriend," I said. "Now Steven is going to marry Claudia, probably just to make his father happy." I thought for a minute and I wrote the name, Claudia, on the board. If I told Dr. Mandell that I find some women pretty and sometimes I wished that I was a boy, would he tell the courts that I was off my rocker?

Dr. Mandell asked some dumb question about Marge and if I ever did things to make her happy.

"I did." I turned to him and stared for a moment. "But, Emily already knows all of it.

Remember? I already had therapy." I turned back to look at my storyline on the whiteboard and then back at him. "Wait, is Marge going to her court appointed psychiatrist?"

Dr. Mandell wrote notes as he spoke. "I have no way of knowing that."

I guessed I would find out soon enough. We had another hearing coming up in the fall.

~ * ~

The following weekend, I spent with the Beans. Lee got me a litter box, some cat food and a few toys for my new kitten. On Sunday, she and Karen drove me back to the Barreres and on the way, we stopped at the farm. I picked out a calico and named her, Emily.

Emily wanted to play all the time. Especially at about five in the morning when she'd start attacking my feet through my sheets. It drove me crazy but, I really liked her and it was great to have her fall asleep on my lap. Her purr was louder than she was, big.

Toward the end of school, I found out that I was old enough to work. Bucks County was offering positions through a special program to kids that were wards of the state. I obtained my first job at a daycare center. I rode Gloria's bike the three miles to and from work, Monday through Friday. I spent all weekday evenings with the Barreres, and as many weekends as possible with the Beans, staying overnight and going to the mall. Sometimes I just spent the day so that Gloria and Jim would feel better. When Jim's kids came up from Maryland, I spent time with them, too.

~ * ~

In August, the Barreres took me out for dinner again. I guessed that they wanted to talk about how I was spending my weekends or how I needed to better tidy up after my little crazy cat, but that wasn't the plan.

"Julie, Jim has been transferred."

"What's that mean?" I played with the paper from my straw.

"His job in the Navy." Gloria looked sad. "We're moving to San Diego."

"When?" I sat up.

"Next month." Jim looked at me over his eyeglasses.

"Isn't that where you guys met?"

"It is." Gloria smiled weakly. "Julie, we tried to get custody of you, but Marge won't let that happen."

"Well, this sucks." I bowed my head and held back tears. I decided to think about biking and how fast I could go. Maybe I could be a racer someday.

Our food came and I could barely eat. I moved food around my plate and rested my head on fisted hand.

"So, there is a family here in Warminster and they have a daughter that is your age." Gloria kind of smiled. "They want you to go for a visitation to the zoo."

"The zoo?" I winced.

"Well, kid, the idea is that you and this girl can get to know each other and see if you're a fit."

Jim lowered his voice. "There's something else."

"What?" I sighed, "I can't have my cat?"

"No. They kind of changed your caseworker and kind of not." Jim took a bite of his food and swallowed. "Nancy will still be in the picture through CYS, but you'll be dealing mostly with a counselor from Aldersgate named Penny."

I sat forward quickly. "Is Emily still there?"

"I don't know," Jim answered.

"I hope she is." I realized that I needed to focus on the Barreres having to leave. "But I really hope that the Navy changes their plans."

Penny Freeman called me one night after work. She wanted to meet with me first and then go to the zoo with Tina, the girl who might possibly become my foster sister. Penny and I agreed that on the following Monday, I would take off from work and she would pick me up from the Barreres. She arrived smiling. I guessed she was in her late twenties. She was petite, fairly athletic and she wore a wedding band.

"Do you know Emily?" My heart was jumping as I asked.

"I'm sorry, I don't." Penny looked at me quizzically. "Should I?"

I was very disappointed that Emily was no longer at Aldersgate and a little baffled that Penny didn't even recognize the name. Penny could see my sadness and swore that she would find out where Emily went.

"So, enough about the past. Let's get to know each other a little, shall we?" Penny looked me over. "Do you have a handbag or anything?"

"I have a few dollars for the zoo." I patted my back pocket.

"Let's head out then." We drove to the Warminster Diner to sit and talk. "I think you'll really like this family." Penny stirred her coffee as she held the sugar container over her cup. "The mom is Greek and..."

"She's Greek?" I thought of Susan down on Taney Street and all of the wonderful things she taught me about my heritage. "I'm Greek, too."

Penny seemed surprised. "Well, that's really cool." She put the sugar container down. "See? This just might be perfect. Their daughter, Tina, is adopted."

The information completely sparked my interest. "Was she adopted when she was a baby?"

"Yep. They lived in Africa, too. I guess Tina spent the first five years of her life in Zimbabwe."

Penny scanned the pie menu. "They were in the Peace Corps or something."

"Do they have other kids?" I thought since these people had been in the Peace Corps, they might have a whole slew of adopted kids.

"They have a son, but he is much older and out of the house."

"So why do they want a foster kid?"

"Who knows?" Penny shrugged. "They had another girl, Angel, who is now off on her own with a baby." I flashed back to the first week that I was with the Barreres when I went for a Physical. There was a pregnant girl in the van and I wondered if that was the same girl. "Maybe they just like kids."

When Penny pulled into Tina's driveway, I got out and hopped into the back seat. Within a few minutes, a tall thin girl came walking toward the car. "Hi-eee, I'm Tee-na." She slipped into the front seat, closed the door, and turned to face me.

"I'm Julie." I sat slumped on my seat. I was in awe of Tina's beauty, and couldn't think of anything to say as Penny pulled out of the driveway.

"You can meet Tina's parents, the Eckenrodes, when we get back." Penny talked to me through her rearview mirror. "I mean, if you want."

"Okay." I felt my body getting heavier as we drove.

"So are you in pageants?" Tina focused on my polo shirt and tennis shorts. It was obvious that I wasn't in pageants.

"No. I mean, I was Little Miss Coast Guard, but I'm sure that doesn't count. You?"

"I just got Miss Hemisphere last year." Tina focused forward like she might have to give Penny directions. "I've been in tons of pageants, actually."

"Well, that's neat." I instantly felt like a dork. "I mean, wow."

"You should come with me."

I wanted to say, why in the hell would I want to do that? "Sure. That would be fun." I stared at the shine in Tina's black hair. "I heard that your mom is Greek. Are you Greek, too?"

"Naw. I'm not sure what I am."

"Julie is Greek." Penny glanced at Tina.

"Oh my gad, really?" Tina's inflection was drawn out with most words so she sounded like she was disgusted. "Have you been to Greece?"

"Not yet, but I know some Greek," I said proudly.

Suddenly, Tina started spurting off a dozen things in Greek that I couldn't possibly understand. I tilted my head into my hands and rubbed my temples. "I have no idea," I said.

"Oh." Tina looked out the side window. "We used to go every year, so I know Greek."

Penny chimed in again. "You know," she looked at Tina and then back at me, "you two could be sisters."

"Oh my gad, really?" Tina's upper lip shot closer to her nose. "Why do you say that?"

"You both have that olive skin."

"Thank you." I clasped my hands and stretched them in front of me. "That's a huge compliment." I wondered if Tina felt the same.

The day at the zoo was okay. I kept thinking that Tina and I were a little old for it, but we did talk a lot and that was the point. "Why don't you spend the night?" Tina said.

"I better not." I responded. "I probably should spend as much time as I can with the Barreres and I have a cat to get home to." I had left little Emily plenty of times when I spent the night at the Beans but, this just seemed awkward.

Penny pulled up to Tina's house and Mrs. Eckenrode was near the driveway, pulling weeds. She was wearing what I thought might be a house dress. "Well, hello!" Her voice was high pitched with the accent I remembered from Susan and her sister, Georgia. "I'm Helen."

"Ma, Julie's spending the night, 'kay?" Tina grabbed my arm.

"Oh, good!" Her tone reminded me of Miss Jane from The Beverly Hillbillies and didn't match her sturdy frame.

"Actually, I can't." I looked at Penny in disbelief and Penny responded with one of her shrugs that were now becoming routine.

"Sure you can." Tina pulled me closer. It was at that moment that I should have realized I would become Tina's possession and I was going to be living there.

~ * ~

When I did move there, Gloria dropped me and my crying cat off at the Eckenrode's, I stuffed all of my emotions during the ten-minute drive, and decided that I needed to dislike Gloria so that I wouldn't cry. My plan worked. When Gloria got out of the car to hug me, I held on to Emily and didn't hug back. I wanted to hate her for leaving me, even though I understood why.

Tina took over within the first hour of my arrival. While I set up my new bedroom which was next door to hers, she lay on my bed, watched me, and questioned me. "Where did you get that belt?"

"I don't remember." I looked at the belt as I hung it on a nail in the closet.

"Are you sure you're going to wear that?" Tina cringed.

"Wear what?"

"That shirt!" She pointed at a shirt I just finished re-folding.

"I like that shirt," I said.

"Eww." She laughed.

Tina questioned everything I did and then I did too.

~ * ~

I felt happy that when I started at William Tenant Senior High. I knew a lot of kids from the last few months at Log College. It made the transition much easier. Tina was in eleventh grade when I started tenth, so the separation was pleasant. Seeing Karen Bean on the weekends was also a reprieve that I cherished.

"I don't get why she has to know about everything you're doing," Karen said as Lee drove toward the mall.

"She's just inquisitive."

"I just think it's weird." Karen laughed. "I mean, she called our house to find out when you would be home."

"I think she gets bored very easily," I explained. I felt protective of Tina, and I liked her, despite her controlling nature. Plus, life was very entertaining at the Eckenrode's.

I woke one night to a sharp pain in my left earlobe. I jumped up to find Tina standing over me, laughing. "What are you doing?" I squinted.

"I just pierced your ear."

"My ears are already pierced!" I ran to the mirror.

"I know, but I thought you might like a second hole on the one side." She walked toward me and reached for my ear, as I tried to block her. "Wait, I need to finish before it gets infected."

"Are you kidding me?"

"It's going to look so good, you'll see." Her grin was pleading.

"Fine." I gave in.

I also gave in when Tina wanted to put make-up on my face or cut my hair. And I gave in when she wanted me to change what I was wearing to the Sunday night teen dances that we attended, because it was just easier that way. Slowly, I was losing all signs of my preppy past with the Kindts. Tina's choices for me were confusing. I looked like a mix from a corner page of The Preppy Handbook, tossed with a dash of Culture Club and Flock of Seagulls. My hair was choppy, some of my clothes were now torn and held together with safety pins. Tina loved the fashion from the New Romanticism punk scene with all the and glam rock styles and I could pull it off, where she was too feminine. I adored the music and treasured men wearing make-up. It just helped any crazy sexual confusion I was having, to seem normal. It freed me so I could put everything to the side and not worry that I found many women beautiful and only some boys, cute.

Mr. Eckenrode, started driving me to Dr. Mandell and it just wasn't the same. Jim bought me a Snickers bar and told me stories. Henry just played his classical music and we didn't say much. I tried sitting a few times with Dr. Mandell and maybe talking a little, but when his eyes went back to my very covered breasts, I had to get back up and start the Dynasty drills. I got him through the whole season. One time, he even asked what happened the Thursday before.

~ * ~

In the fall of 1982, I found out I could still get a county job placement during the school year. I applied for a clerical position at the

Warminster Police Department. I interviewed one afternoon with Julie Stockel. Mrs. Stockel had been working with the Police Department for more than thirty years and worked directly under the last five Police Chiefs who had come and gone. She was patient and kind. She gave me the job within ten minutes, even though I didn't know how to type and I had never answered business phones before.

"Be here after school tomorrow," she said. "Every afternoon, you'll work a few hours and then go home, okay?"

"Okay." I could barely stand still. "Thank you so much!"

"Great." She smiled and stood to walk me out. She wore light green polyester slacks with a matching button down short sleeve jacket shirt. Although she was probably in her late sixties, her arms looked strong and she moved with determination. "This is the code to get back to the offices from the waiting area." She signaled for me to watch her and then pressed a four digit number into a keypad. "Got it?"

"I've got it." I started repeating the numbers over and over in my head as I walked the few miles to the Eckenrode's. I was excited because I was getting two dollars and eighty five cents an hour, which was fifty cents more than I made at the daycare center.

I got home just in time for one of Helen's meat dinners. She served roasts of all sorts, and since I could never determine what anything was, I stuck to vegetables. "Maybe you should just eat at your friend, Karen's," Helen remarked.

"I'm just not a meat eater," I said.

Henry, Tina's father, who closely resembled an Amish man, often made large statements with only a few words. "Eat and be grateful." I wasn't sure if he meant that I should eat the unidentifiable meat or that Helen should leave me alone about it. So, I ate the vegetables and I was grateful.

"Everything is very good. Thank you." I watched Tina's bunny, her Siamese cat, and my cat, Emily, stare at each other on the living room floor. "Have your animals always been like that?"

"They were even better when I had my duck, Shoo shoo." Tina looked at them and took a bite of meat.

"I have never heard of cats and bunnies and ducks hanging out together." I shook my head. No one said anything. "Hey, I got a job today."

"That's wonderful!" Helen said. "Doing what?"

"Working at the Police Department," I replied proudly.

"Oh my gad!" Tina sneered. "Why?"

"Because I want to."

"Good," Henry said. "Good for you."

"I want a job." Tina whined.

"You don't need to worry about that, Tina," Helen snapped. "Just study."

"Are you working every day?" Tina pushed her plate away from her.

"Yep. Sometimes weekends, too," I answered, just to be smart.

"Well, what am I supposed to do?"

"I guess you can go through some of your own clothes and rip them for a change." I smiled at Tina and waited for a response, but she barely looked at me.

~ * ~

When I arrived at work the following day, I found that Mrs. Stockel had set up a small table and chair in her office where I would work. On the left side of the table was a small stack of papers and envelopes.

"Are you ready to get started?" Mrs. Stockel came out from behind her desk.

"Yes." I stared at the table.

"Okay. First, these are requests for incident and accident reports from different insurance companies." She flipped through the stack. "You will need to go into the main filing area of the Police Department to find the accident reports, make copies, and send them back." Mrs. Stockel suddenly tapped my shoulder. "Hey, I guess I should introduce you to everyone before I start sending you on errands, huh?"

I laughed nervously. "I guess that would be good."

First, we toured the administration area. I met the main detectives and the two lieutenants.

In the central area, were the clerk and the office manager. They were two older women with desks that faced each other. Mrs. Stockel explained that the clerk was a major multi-tasker that dealt with people in the lobby, handled all calls that came in to the department, and managed the officers, too. Next, we went to the file room where I would be spending much of my time, and then on to where the police met for each shift.

"There are thirty-three officers that work for the P.D." Mrs. Stockel walked quickly past three cells. "When you come through here, just keep moving fast." I took a glimpse and thankfully the cells were empty. Each held a stainless-steel cot, a sink, and a toilet that was right out in the open.

Finally, we went through another door using the same code and entered into the attached township building where I met the tax collector, the township manager, the Parks and Recreation staff, some secretaries, and other important people. "You'll need to come over here every day to mail off your reports and sometimes I'll send you over here for other things."

I felt important.

~ * ~

I worked every day through the school year and once my contract with the county was up, the Chief of Police went before the Board of Supervisors and asked that a job be created so I could stay on. So, for the summer before my junior year, I was making four dollars an hour and working full time. Mrs. Stockel trusted me enough to take her position while she went on vacation. The idea made me a little nervous because the Chief, Elmer Clawges, was somewhat intimidating. He rarely said much more than hello. He came and went so often that when calls came through, I had to look outside the window to see if his car was there.

I liked sitting at Mrs. Stockel's desk that week. She had drawers filled with little rubber thumb covers, colored paper clips, and lots of pens. After my reports were copied and put in envelopes for the insurance companies each day, I looked for other things to do. My little table in the corner was boring and had to be kept clean because there was no reason for me to have anything more than a typewriter.

One afternoon, about three days into Mrs. Stockel's absence, the Chief came into the office. He smiled and asked me how I liked the extra responsibilities.

"I like it." I shifted nervously in my seat.

"Good." The Chief opened a file drawer in front of the desk, pulled out a file, and rummaged through some papers.

"How old are you?" He took off his suit jacket and started toward his office. "What grade are you in?" he yelled from the other room.

I waited until he returned so I wouldn't have to yell out. "I'm going to be sixteen."

Elmer Clawges rolled up his sleeves like he was going to wash dishes. He pulled several more files and returned to his office. Just as I was going to head to the township building to mail the accident reports, he returned. "I want a Pepsi." He reached into his pocket. "Do you want something?"

"No thanks, I'm okay."

"I think I'm going to need change." He flipped through his money and walked toward the door that led into the hallway.

"Mrs. Stockel has a petty cash safe." I turned and opened the desk drawer, happy that I could assist.

Then, I heard the hallway door close.

The Chief walked toward the desk. "Why is the door closed?" My heart thumped.

"Because I can't help myself." He closed the curtains and the desk drawer was all that was between us.

"Well, I'll get your change." I continued to open the small lock box on the desk while he pushed the drawer closed with his knee.

"I don't care about the change." His hand was suddenly on my head, stroking my hair. "I care about you." He stood closer to me, over me. "I have since the day you started working here."

"Oh." I stared at the money and took deep breaths. I was terrified and felt stupid and small. He was the Chief of Police.

"Julie." He lifted my chin as he bent down. "I love you." I saw his eyes for a moment. Sincere and kind.

"Um, I don't know what to say." I stammered and looked at anything but him. Suddenly, pricks of whiskers pressed on my cheek.

"Kiss me." He slowly turned my head so that his lips were fully on mine. His tongue bobbed over my teeth and found a way into my mouth. He smelled nice. I gave in and kissed him back. He straightened and I could see his excitement as he adjusted his pants. "Wow," he said. "I have to go." He opened the curtains and the door as fast as he had closed them. "I'll see you tomorrow."

As he went to his car, I stared at his thick auburn hair and wondered what the hell just happened and why. He wasn't exactly attractive. Even if I was an adult, I don't think I would have ever considered him. The phone rang as he pulled away. I barely got the words out, "Chief's office."

"Uh, yeah, hi. Do you know where Elmer is?" the woman sounded almost frantic.

"He just left, may I take a message?"

"Who is this?" she demanded.

"My name is Julie. I work here." I cleared my throat.

"What do you do?" she asked.

"May I ask who this is?" I sat up, looked out the window in search of the Chief's car. Hoping he would reappear.

"This is Elmer's wife!" she said loudly.

"I'm so sorry ma'am." I started to shake. "I'm kind of Mrs. Stockel's assistant." I was surprised that she didn't know I existed. But, even more surprised that, for those moments of the kiss, I had forgotten he had a wife. Perhaps he did, too.

I biked home with crazy mixed emotions. While all of my friends were just starting to date, I was making out with the fricking Chief of Police. There was so much wrong with it.

He had a wife. I was only sixteen, he was probably forty, and I couldn't tell anyone even if I wanted to. Karen would think it was gross and no one else would ever believe me. Plus, I was back in the position of not wanting to get anyone in trouble. What if he really does love me? How could I do that when he's married? Why does he like me?

I couldn't talk to Tina or even call Karen when I got home. I went to my room, laid on the bed, and listened to Emily purr as she slept, rising up and down on my stomach.

I wanted to be somewhere else, but that was always the case.

Chapter Twenty-one

"What are you so happy about?" Tina looked disgusted.

"I don't know." I instantly felt deflated. "I just think it's going to be a good day."

"How?" She snarled. "I mean, why?" Tina looked at me as though it couldn't be possible that I could have any fun without her.

"I'm just being positive, geez." I ducked under her arm because she practically had me blocked me from leaving my room. "I have to get ready for work."

While showering, I kept thinking about the Chief's lips on mine. It made me shiver with excitement and yet I felt nauseous.

I took more than a few minutes to pick out my clothes. I thought about wearing a dress, but quickly dismissed the idea, since I needed to ride my bike. I was suddenly more concerned with my appearance and rolled on lip gloss.

The chief wasn't in all morning and I finished all the accident reports by noon. I answered a few phone calls and dusted. I looked out the window more than a few times, in search of his car. I couldn't grasp why I wanted him there. I guess I wanted to see what he would say about the day before, but I was also nervous that he wouldn't acknowledge me at all. Finally, close to the end of the work day, he arrived.

He smiled big as he entered Mrs. Stockel's office and shut the door behind him. He immediately closed the curtains and I panicked. I had no idea of what to do.

"Hi." I tried to look for something that would make it seem that I was busy. "Here are your messages from today." I held out a few slips of paper from the pink message pad and then sat behind Mrs. Stockel's desk.

"I don't care about the messages." He walked to the storage closet and pulled out a glass bottle.

"How was your day?" He placed the bottle on the filing cabinet and stepped closer to me.

"Um, it was fine." I felt his hands pull on mine and lift me from the chair. He led me to the filing cabinets and started to kiss me. Thick fingers ran over my shoulders and without warning, his hands were fully on my breasts. I heard him breathing hard and somewhere in my brain, something shut down. I could see what was happening, but I couldn't feel or muster any reaction.

He unbuttoned my shirt and reached to unclasp my bra like it was habit. The bottle read, Corn Husker's Lotion. I read the label as he smothered the oily stuff over my breasts. I had never heard of Corn Husker's Lotion and found it ridiculously funny. I pictured the Chief as an old farmer and it made me laugh out loud.

"Does that tickle?" He laughed with me.

"Huh?" He brought me back to what he was doing. I stood motionless. "Um, yeah." He grabbed my hand and placed it over the hardness in his pants. I pulled back and as I did, the office door opened. The evening dispatcher, Jean, glimpsed at my husker-coated breasts right before the Chief slammed the door in her face.

"She saw," I covered my chest then pulled my bra together. "Her eyes were like saucers!"

"I don't really care." He rushed to the window and opened the curtains. "She knows better than to say anything." He quickly opened the door that he had shut. "She doesn't know what she saw, anyway."

The Chief adjusted his pants and promptly left the building for the day. When I walked through the station to get to the Township Building, I felt Jean's eyes follow me from the dispatch desk.

The following day was the last day that I filled in for Mrs. Stockel. The Chief waited until it was almost five o'clock to close everything in the office. He stood at the desk and held out his hand for me to take. I stood with him while he kissed me and I could feel his hands fumbling with his belt and zipper. He pushed on the top of my head and directed me to the floor. "On your knees," he whispered. As I knelt, I could see a perfect line where freckles ended and white fatty skin began. He lifted me slightly and pressed his penis on my face. I felt stupid and ugly and weak.

"Put it in your mouth," he exhaled. I looked at his shirt tail hanging low, wrinkled from where it had been tucked. His slacks were around his ankles and I felt it pushing on my lips. It seemed I didn't have a choice. It didn't seem that I ever did.

I opened my mouth and he pushed further into me. He rocked back and forth and groaned. I gagged as salty wet streamed down my throat. Within moments, his pants were up, belt was buckled and jacket on. I remained on the floor like a piece of wadded-up paper that couldn't even make the trash. I slowly stood while he gathered things from his office. "Thank you," he said before he walked out.

Once Mrs. Stockel returned, the Chief went back to not saying much. I tried to make eye contact with him, but he rarely looked at me. Occasionally, when I delivered something to his desk, he would smile and wink.

After a few weeks, he called me into his office. "You live near Log College School, don't you?"

"Yes." I fidgeted with my hands, clumsily.

"I have a meeting there tonight. Can you meet me afterward?"

"Okay." I pulled my hair behind my ears. "What time? Where?"

"Seven will probably work. Behind the school at the soccer field." He looked back at something he was writing and continued like I wasn't there.

I went back to my desk and pondered why I couldn't say no to him. I didn't want to get on my knees again. I didn't want to feel like a stupid piece of garbage. Maybe when I got to the soccer field I could just tell him no.

"I'm going for a bike ride," I called out as I opened the front door to leave.

"At night?" I heard Helen ask.

"I'll be back soon." I shut the door and pedaled the few blocks to the school. The parking lot was full of cars. I leaned my Huffy that the Barreres' gave to me against the brick, and tried to peek in the windows. Everything seemed dark and I figured their meeting was in the auditorium. It was past seven.

Election signs littered the front lawn of the school. I took my bike back to the soccer field and waited. Once I heard talking and the closing of car doors, it seemed to take forever for the Chief to appear. He grabbed my arm and walked quickly, taking us further away from the school and into the darkness.

"I'm so glad you're here." He pulled me down onto the grass. "I've missed you." He kissed me hard and lay on top of me.

"You have?" My heart beat fast, wanting to believe.

I don't know much of how it felt. It was my first time and it may have hurt, but I could only hate myself. I didn't have to move or interact. He did everything on his own and like before, he said. "Thank you" and walked away. I lay on the grass with semen on my stomach. It wouldn't be the last time.

Over time, it became increasingly difficult to concentrate at school. I felt left out as I watched my friends holding hands with boys and girls in the hallway and going on dates. But, there was always Tina.

~ * ~

Tina decided one evening we were just, 'too mature' for the teen dances. "We need to get downtown where the real men are. The hotties."

She sat on her bed majestically, with a down comforter of hot pink and black. "I can't take this boredom." She flipped through the pages of Vogue and I skimmed her Glamour magazine. "Uh," she sighed, "I'm so bored!"

"Let's go to a movie or something." I suggested.

"Let's go out!"

"Where?" I leaned my head on the wall.

"Downtown." Tina sat up.

"Are you serious?" I looked at her in disbelief.

"Just start getting ready." Tina got up and went to her closet. "Slowly, so my parents have a chance to fall asleep."

"Why?" I started to worry. "What are we doing?"

"We're going to sneak out of my window and take the car."

"You want to steal the car." I looked over invisible reading glasses. "You're crazy!"

"Shhh. We have to."

I went to my room and started trying on different outfits. In the midst of getting ready, I ran back into her room. "Tina, Center City is at least forty-five minutes away! Besides, neither of us has a license and...we're not old enough!"

"Right, the clubs don't get going until eleven or twelve and I'll get us in." She brushed blush across her cheekbones as I stood there waiting for her to get some sense. "Trust me, I know how to drive."

No sooner did Helen and Henry go to bed, and Tina was tying sheets together to throw out of her second floor window like Rapunzel. We climbed down the sheets and I giggled so hard, I thought for sure we'd be caught.

Tina and I pushed Helen's little Ford Escort out of the driveway and then Tina jumped in and steered it into the street. She got out, held the door open and steered as we pushed with all of our might. I couldn't stop laughing, so I hardly had strength. Once the car was a few houses down, we got in and started it. Tina drove around the block and parked so that we were directly behind her house. "Do you see any lights on?"

"No, amazingly, I don't." I sighed a breath of relief.

Tina parked near South Street and we walked to the first bar we saw. Neon lights were flashing and Tina started to go in.

"Got I.D.?" A muscular man sitting on a barstool placed his arm out in front of Tina.

"Not with me." Tina flirted.

"Sorry." He smiled. "Bring it next time."

"See?" I said as we walked down the street. "This is a bad idea."

"Okay, let's try here." Tina turned into the opening of a building.

"Hi, ladies." Two older Italian-looking men in suits stood at the bottom of a darkened stairwell.

"Hey!" Tina beamed. "Is there a cover tonight?"

"Not for youse two ladies," one of the men said. "Welcome to Glitta."

"Perfect." Tina pranced up the stairs while I studiously followed her six-inch heels.

"Glitta? Really, Tina? He can't use the 'R'? The sign said, Glitter!" I talked the whole way up the stairs. At the top, the room opened up to a large bar and dance floor. Techno music was blasting.

"Let's get drinks!" Tina shouted and then yelled out to the bartender. "I'll have a Sex on the Beach!" She then turned to look at me. "What do you want?"

I shrugged. "Amaretto Sour?" One of the girls from the township building drank them and it was all I could come up with.

Tina shot me a discouraged look and then ordered it for me.

We stood awkwardly, staring at all the people. Tina found an open barstool and promptly sat on it while I stood next to her. For two hours, I watched several men approach Tina. She treated them like dirt and they seemed to like it. No one approached me, so I ordered a Sex on the Beach and nursed it, waiting.

Stealing the car and driving downtown to Glitter became a weekly event. It got to the point that we didn't even have to tie the sheets together and go out the window. We just quietly snuck out the front door and we were never caught. Often, Tina got drunk and I had to drive her home. Although the police at my job took me out for driving lessons a few times, Tina was the real reason I learned to drive.

I hated being at the club while she entertained the boys, but somehow I felt it was my duty. The night would always start out fun, but once Tina had too much to drink, I had to take care of her. Guys that fell for her wanted to take care of her, too. "Just leave her with me. I'll get her home."

"I can't, she needs to come home with me," I repeated so many nights. Tina objected, I grabbed her anyway and dragged her to the car. She would thank me later. Sometimes I thought to just leave her, it would have been easier. But, the thought of those guys maybe doing things like the Chief had, made me bring her home. She wasn't ready for that, especially when she couldn't think straight. I had to be the bad guy and risk Tina being angry with me.

When Tina was mad at me, she gave me the silent treatment and it lasted for weeks. I had to beg for her forgiveness, often not knowing why I was apologizing.

~ * ~

After work one day, I came home to an experience of her wrath. I don't know what I did to make her so angry, but she ripped down a collage of Linda Evans that I spent two years creating from People and US magazines. It covered my closet door and suddenly had claw marks through it. So, I immediately went into her room and tore down her Brook Shields shrine while Tina gasped. I returned to my room. "You'll never be a model!" I yelled to the wall.

I wanted to sob. All the hard work I had put into my collage was now just trash. She could not have hurt me more.

A few minutes later, Henry knocked at my bedroom door. I was scared. I knew he would never hurt me, but repercussions for my victimizing their Tina, might be rigid. They were probably very angry with me and I didn't quite know what to do. Henry knocked again and cleared his throat, "Julie?"

I walked close to the door then stood motionless. "What's going on with you two?" Henry began to open my door and I quickly shut it only to her a faint male whimper. I quickly reopened it and found Henry leaning against a wall, gripping his thumb.

"Oh my God," I said. "I hurt you." I moved closer and then backed away again. "I'm so sorry."

"What is going on?" Helen came running up the stairs. "Oh no, Henry." She glared at me and then at the hand that he had pressed against the other. "What happened?"

"I think my thumb is broken."

"I slammed the door on him." I stood helpless and felt awful. "I'm so sorry."

Then Tina came out of her room. "You broke my dad's thumb?" She didn't look at me, but walked toward Henry. "How could you do that?"

I looked at her with disgust. "Tina, you know damn well I didn't do that on purpose." I crossed my arms as we all stood on the landing, uncomfortably close.

"How dare you say damn in my house!" Helen yelled.

"What?" I backed up into my room. "Tina says damn, shit, fuck, you name it!"

"Henry, come on." Helen put her hand on Henry's arm. "We'll go to the hospital."

"I'm sorry, Henry." I closed my bedroom door and stayed in my room until they got back. Tina didn't try to talk and for once, I liked the silent treatment.

When Henry and Helen returned, Helen asked me to pack a bag.

"What do you mean?" I figured I was going on to the next foster home, but I wanted to hear her say it.

"You need to go away for a few days and think about what happened here."

"I do? Where am I going?"

"To a group home," she yelled back.

"Great!" I responded sarcastically and then quickly changed my tone. "How's Henry?"

"He's fine. Pack and we'll take care of your cat."

Helen drove me all the way to Pottstown. Right back to the group home I had been in before.

"I don't get it," I said as she drove. "I pretty much do my own thing unless Tina needs me. I work, I don't ask for anything, except maybe a ride to Karen's, and you get your money each month, so what is your problem with me? I'm going to a group home because of an accident?"

"That's not all!" Helen's hair shook as she turned to me. "You need to spend more time and act like you are a part of the family. You sit down for dinner and go to church."

I stared out the window. I couldn't wait to be old enough to leave. I was rarely home during dinner because of work and I didn't want to eat meat. I couldn't stand going to the Brethren church because it bored me and I didn't want to wash someone's feet.

"I need to be called out of work and school tomorrow and looked at Helen as she drove the car that I helped steal. "And, in a few days, it's my birthday."

"Well, I guess you will really need to think about things," she responded harshly and then seemed to soften. "It's true, you're a lot easier than the girl we had before." Helen gripped the wheel and stared ahead. "She ate everything. Of course, she was pregnant."

"Do you ever hear from her?" I asked.

"Sometimes she calls."

"Are you sure I couldn't just think about things at the Beans' house?" I pointed to the group house. "It's that one."

"Very funny," Helen answered as I opened the car door.

"Okay," I awkwardly exited the car. "Thanks?"

"We see you soon."

I shut the door and Helen drove away. Unreal, I thought as I felt the chill in the air.

Everyone who was there the year before, was gone, except for the counselor, Rodney. "Hey, preppy!" Rodney greeted me with a big smile. "I heard you were coming. What brings you back?"

"Linda Evans and Brooke Shields," I smirked.

I stayed at the group home for most of the weekend. I read magazines that were lying around and wrote in a makeshift journal. I called Karen Bean to let her know I was fine, and then I wondered if the Chief might feel strange about the idea of having sex with someone who still gets punished.

~ * ~

On Sunday I went back to the Eckenrodes. Helen made dinner and a small cake for my birthday. Tina sat at the table and acted like we all took her away from a very important appointment. She sighed occasionally so we all knew she was put out.

"Look, there are presents for you," Henry gave an envelope and a box a push in my direction.

I looked at the three of them and they at their plates. "Maybe another day," I responded.

"My parents got you presents." Tina crossed her arms. "Don't be rude."

"Right," I said and opened an envelope that had been placed in front of me. Inside was a card signed by Henry and Helen and sixteen dollars for my sixteenth birthday. They also bought new blinds for my bedroom. I figured I wasn't going to be there much longer so the blinds were and investment for them. I sure liked them though. I could pretend

I was in different places just by turning the blinds and bringing different light into the room.

~ * ~

After a few weeks, Tina and I finally started talking again. We went right back to her telling me what to wear and putting on my make-up. Even though we were having fun again, I constantly thought about leaving. I ordered California magazine and L.A. Magazine and dreamt of being there. Linda Evans starting appearing in ads for the Bonaventure Hotel. The ad was for the spa inside the hotel and Linda held a weight directly under her chin. If I ran away I could stay with the Barreres and even meet her. I was torn, because of the Beans and because of the Chief. I knew that what was happening with the Chief was so wrong, and running away might help me. But, I would miss him and I would definitely miss the Beans. Maybe if I told the Barreres about the Chief when I got to California, they could persuade Penny Freeman to let me stay out there. I plotted all the time and could think of nothing else. I figured I only needed about a hundred and fifty dollars. I called Greyhound and found out that a one-way bus ticket from Philadelphia to San Diego was only ninety-nine dollars, and the bus would stop in Los Angeles. I started to save.

~ * ~

The Chief had been playing a strange game for months. He approached me at times and asked me to stay until after Mrs. Stockel left. Then he would have sex with me on his office floor. After these times, he would ignore me, sometimes for a week and sometimes only a few days. Just when I would think he was just a jerk, he would smother me with attention and tell me how much he loved me. I spent a whole week once, just hating him, and then he left a cassette tape on my desk with a note that read, listen to the last song. It was Lionel Richie's "Hello." I played it over and over on my Walkman and wondered if he really felt that way about me. I sometimes see you walk outside my door, hello? Is it me you're looking for? He was screwing up my plans for California every time he drew me in.

If it wasn't for me trying to be such a big shot at school one morning, I don't know if I ever would have gone through with my plans.

While in health class, waiting for the instructor to come in and start, I informed a few classmates I would be moving to California.

"Yeah, right." Vicky, the girl next to me, said. "How are you going to do that?"

"I have money saved." I sat up straight and tried to keep a straight face.

"You're crazy!" Vicky laughed. "I mean someday after we graduate, sure, but…"

"You don't believe me." I folded my arms and held my mouth open.

"I don't," Vicky said.

I stood up. "Okay, I'll leave right now, I have nothing to lose." I gathered my books. "I'll send you a postcard." I winked and walked out.

I went to my locker, put my books inside and grabbed my coat and Walkman. I left the school with no one noticing. I walked across town to the bank, which was right down the street from the police department where I was expected to work that afternoon and took out everything but a dollar. When I left there to head to the bus station, I almost wished the Chief was driving by so he could stop me. But, I couldn't turn back now. I had to pray the Eckenrodes would take care of my cat until I could come get her. She had no business going on this adventure.

"What time does the next bus leave for San Diego?" I asked the woman at the Greyhound ticket counter.

"Twelve-twenty, honey."

I looked around and found a large clock that read, eleven-thirty two. "Okay, may I have a one-way ticket?" I dug through my pockets.

"Sure can." She typed onto a machine. "That'll be one hundred and three dollars and ninety-five cents." She didn't even look at me funny or ask how old I was. As I waited in the station, I watched homeless people walk in and check pay phones and vending machines for coins. A few police came through and still no one questioned why I was sitting alone in a bus station on a school day. I stared at my tickets and memorized the bus numbers. It would only take a few days to get there. When my bus was called to begin boarding, I jumped up and hurried to the doors. I got on and found people were already on the bus and had probably got on in New York. It seemed to take forever to leave the station. As we drove out of Philadelphia, I sat back in the cushioned seat and breathed in the scent of Pine Sol.

I tried not to worry about my cat, Emily. I felt so selfish, leaving her.

I played the Lionel Richie tape over and over until my Walkman died somewhere in Ohio. At the next stop, I loaded up on batteries, and pulled out a U2 tape and Duran Duran.

~ * ~

The next day we pulled into St. Louis and I had to wait a few hours to change buses. I walked a few blocks down to the Arch and remembered that I had heard it was considered The Gateway to the West. I was thrilled. I felt I was halfway there.

I boarded my next bus at one in the afternoon and was very excited to sit back, watch the scenery change and listen to my music, but there were a lot of people that wanted to chat. When we left St. Louis, I thought for a moment that maybe I boarded the wrong bus. The people were rowdy and talkative, like they all knew each other. Once I witnessed no signs of team jerseys or a field trip, I took a seat. A young guy, maybe nineteen or twenty years old, soon sat next to me and said, "Hi."

I had my headphones on, but volume turned down so that I could take in everything. I smiled shyly and then turned to stare out the window. I didn't want to talk, I just wanted to observe. I had been lucky until St. Louis, with two seats to myself. Now I had a presence right next to me. I could feel him shift in his seat and occasionally spotted pages turning from a small paperback.

We reached Oklahoma City around eleven-thirty at night. I had about forty minutes to transfer to the next bus to L.A., so I wandered around the bus terminal and got a pack of crackers and a Mountain Dew. I had twelve dollars and forty-four cents left. The guy that had been sitting next to me on the bus strolled around the terminal too and I caught him looking at me a few times. Although it felt good to be upright and walking around, I really wanted to get onto the next bus, so he wouldn't start talking to me. I hoped he wasn't going to L.A.. I didn't need a stranger asking questions.

I sat on the new bus at my usual window seat and stared through tinted windows. Dark shapes loaded the cargo area, and a fuzzy, but colorful movement danced inside the terminal. I thought about Marge and how she had been mugged at a bus terminal. She probably ranted so much that someone finally had enough. I knew not to talk to anyone. I could look and quietly observe, but never stare or speak. Within minutes, the guy was next to me again. "Where ya going?" he asked.

I turned in his direction for a moment. Los Angeles then San Diego." Uh, why did I answer?

"What's there?" I felt him staring at me.

"My family and stuff." I clicked the stop button on my Walkman and pulled my headphones down and around my neck. "What about you?" I pretended to care.

"L.A.," he stated confidently. "I have some business to take care of."

I laughed softly. From how he appeared, I doubted he knew anything about business. His sweatshirt was a bit dirty and frumpy. Plus, he was on a Greyhound. "Well, that's good." I tried hiding a yawn into my sleeve.

"Yeah, I guess that some rest would be a good idea since we're driving all night." He looked out my window like he knew where we were.

I leaned my elbow on the edge of the window and pushed my head into my hand to try and sleep. I could still hear chatter throughout the bus. We made a few more stops in Oklahoma, so sleep was fitful. I would have done anything to stretch out completely on my bed. My bed. My poor cat was probably sleeping alone on my bed, having nightmares about what a horrible person I was because I left her.

Mid-morning, we were in Albuquerque. I exited the bus fast to make sure I was away from the guy. The thought crossed my mind to wander away, hide, and take the next bus, but I really wanted to get to California. Besides, he wasn't exactly creepy.

Our stop was for an hour and I took full advantage of taking in everything. I could see craggy mountains between buildings as I walked. Something in the dry air made me feel that I belonged. I remembered the same feeling from our trip when I was a kid. I craved the feel of red dirt in my hands and bright sun on my skin.

Time passed quickly and I had about ten minutes left to get something to eat. Panic set in when I realized that I left a small brown bag with my money in it on the bus. I was in such a hurry to exit, that I failed to grab the bag and transfer the money back into my pocket.

I ran to the bus and when I got to my seat, I saw that the bag was gone. I thought maybe I had the wrong row, so I moved back one and forward another two. Nothing.

"Excuse me," I said to the driver who was standing outside. "Did you pick up any trash on the bus? Like a small paper bag?"

"I sure didn't." The driver smiled and took a puff of his cigarette.

My money was gone. Thankfully I still had my Walkman but, my money was gone.

I'm so stupid, I thought. I ran inside the terminal and found my seat buddy. When I asked him about the bag, he denied ever having seen it.

"Oh, I thought maybe you took it, thinking it was trash, " I sighed heavily.

"Sorry." He shrugged. "You missing something important?"

"Naw, it'll be fine." I turned to get back on the bus. I was hungry.

This time, he sat across from me. "Looks like a lot of people got off in Albuquerque." He leaned toward the aisle between us.

"I can understand why." I looked out at the big sky.

"So what was in the bag you lost?"

"My money." I squeezed my hands. "It wasn't much."

"Oh, that sucks," He shook his head. "Hey, if you need some help, I can buy you dinner later."

"No, I still have some money." I felt for a few coins and a couple wadded up bills that were in my pocket. "Thanks, though."

"Sure." He took out his little book. "Hey, my name's David."

"I'm Julie." I turned back to my window and started my Duran Duran tape and my daydreaming.

The bus broke down somewhere between Gallup and Phoenix. I loved it because I got to sun myself in the middle of the desert and now we wouldn't be arriving in L.A. at three in the morning. It took hours for help to come and another hour for the bus to be fixed. A lot of people complained, even when the driver handed out free water. I just enjoyed the beautiful day and people watching. The driver was nice too, he made us laugh.

When we reached Phoenix, I was famished. I broke down and spent the coins on a pack of crackers from a vending machine and took water from a drinking fountain near the restrooms.

I sat down outside and when David approached, I decided to just talk with him. He was nice enough and didn't seem to want anything more than to just converse. He told me that one of his favorite things to do in Los Angeles, was to see The Rocky Horror Picture Show at the

Tiffany Theatre on Sunset. "You should come see it tomorrow," he sat up excitedly. "It's really something else! If you're still in L.A., come to the Tiffany before midnight. I'll be out front."

"I'll think about it," I replied. I had no intention of meeting him or seeing some scary movie.

When we reached our destination, David reminded me about The Tiffany Theatre.

"Okay," I said as I hurried away.

~ * ~

L.A. was everything I hoped it would be. It was beautiful like I saw in the magazines. Union Station looked like it was constructed specifically to welcome starlets from the days of black and white films. Tall palms held sunshine and made me happy. I exited the bus and walked fast toward downtown. My first stop was going to be the Bonaventure Hotel. I could see the building from the station, rising like shiny cigars. I saw the Bonaventure plenty of times in movies, but more importantly, Linda Evans promoted their fitness center. I remembered the ad, "Bonaventure is truly the ultimate spa." -Linda Evans.

As I got closer, I thought about what I looked like. I had been wearing the same clothes for three days. I hoped the hotel would let me in, at least to look around.

I knew I wouldn't get to see Linda Evans because I read that celebrities worked out very early in the morning since they had to be on set all day.

The glimmering outside of the building took up at least a whole block. A doorman greeted me and held the door without even questioning me. I immediately saw space-age glass elevators whizzing up and down. The lobby was gorgeous with a large pool of water and fountains galore. I saw rich people sitting in big leather chairs. There were side tables that held dishes of nuts, and cocktail tumblers with the type of dark liquor that made me sick at the Kindt's . The Kindt's belong here, I thought. Then I thought about how great the mixed nuts looked. I continued walking a little so I seemed to have a purpose. Shops had beautiful garments and restaurant workers were setting up for dinner in another area. There was no sign of the spa. I approached the desk area to inquire. "Excuse me."

"Yes, ma'am." A guy, maybe in his twenties greeted me warmly.

"Where is the spa?" I tried to seem nonchalant.

"Oh, we have a few spas and workout rooms, as well as a rooftop pool and atrium pool."

"Whoa." I looked up and tried to figure out what an atrium was. I spotted more shops. "Are those all stores and more restaurants?" I asked.

"Sure are." He smiled. "There are nineteen restaurants. Even one that revolves on the thirty-fourth floor," he answered proudly.

"This place is amazing!" I backed up from the desk. "Thank you." I said. "Oh, do you know how far it is to Century City?"

"I would take the bus." He seemed to know my predicament. "The 728 goes right to Century City and Beverly Hills." He pointed, smiled again, only now with compassion in his eyes.

"Thanks again." I looked back at the bowls of nuts and decided against taking them for fear of being arrested. I left the Bonaventure through the door where the desk man pointed.

I found the bus stop for the 728. I couldn't imagine that the bus would cost too much, so I waited at the stop with a few other people and then asked the driver when he pulled up.

"Sixty cents!" he yelled. "Less you needs a transfa."

I was a little disappointed when the bus got on the freeway. I thought maybe I would get more of a feel for the city if we took the streets. I got off in front of CBS studios and still had seventy cents. The sun was low and the CBS logo was lit up. I walked around on Beverly Boulevard and saw the shops on Rodeo Drive. The palm tree-lined streets even smelled expensive. So many things that I had only seen in photos were right in front of me. My Walkman batteries had long given out, yet I felt like I was dancing as I walked. I didn't need music, I was in Beverly Hills.

Homes got bigger as I strolled toward the Beverly Hills Hotel. The sign was so gorgeous that I sat down on the curb, just to stare at it. The hotel was pink, well lit, and engulfed in palm trees, probably for the privacy of all the stars that were there. I grinned as I read the lettering over and over, The Beverly Hills Hotel and Bungalows.

It was getting dark out and I laughed at the thought of my being there. No one would believe me. What am I going to do? I thought. I'm so hungry!

I sat for a while longer until a limousine slowed, and started to back up. I quickly stood and began walking toward the brightest area of the sky, directly down Sunset Boulevard.

Within a minute, the limo pulled up along the curb where I walked and the back window went down. "Do you need some help?" A well-dressed man hung out the back window.

"No thanks!" I called back and continued my plight to nowhere.

"You sure?" the man continued. "I can help."

I stopped and looked at him. I walked toward the car and looked closer. My hunger pulled me, even though every other part of my mind told me to just keep walking.

"Really, if you need a ride somewhere." He looked into my eyes with fatherly concern. "It's up to you, but you probably shouldn't be walking around by yourself."

"It's not late, I'm fine." I stalled. "Um, actually, I don't know what I'm doing." I threw the words out like vomit and I was relieved to be waving a white flag of vulnerability.

"Here." He opened the door. "Let's just go to my house and get everything figured out. You can call someone or whatever."

I hopped into the back of the limo and said hello to the driver. I placed myself close to the window, but still looked at the man next to me. "Do you live in Beverly Hills?" I asked.

"I do."

"Do you live in Coldwater Canyon?" I tried to contain my excitement.

"Not too far." He turned to face me. "Do you know someone in Coldwater Canyon?"

I tried to stay calm. "Linda Evans lives in Coldwater Canyon." I blurted it out.

"I know Linda." He smiled and picked a piece of lint from his trousers.

"You do?" My eyes widened.

"Sure, I was her realtor." He pulled on his necktie. "Maybe she'll be at this party I'm going to tonight. Do you want to go?"

The idea of a party made me think of food and then, appearance. "I don't have anything to wear." I looked down at my clothes. "This is it."

"We'll figure out something." He paused. "Maybe you can work the party."

"Work the party?" I felt the driver looking at me through the rearview mirror. I smiled at him and looked for any reaction. He just squinted and then I did too.

The driver pulled into a gated community and dropped us off in front of the man's house.

"That's it for tonight." The man clasped the driver's hand, walked around and then tapped on the hood.

"What about going to the party?" I asked.

"I have a car." He laughed and showed me inside.

As we entered the house, I started worrying and I thought maybe nothing bad could happen because the driver knew the guy and could testify. I hoped we were going to the party.

"Have a seat." He took off his tie and held it. "Do you want a drink?"

I sat down on a sofa closest to the door. "Uh, maybe a Coke?" I took a few deep breaths and moved my hands across the front of the cushion.

"You don't want anything stronger?" He tilted his head and grinned.

"No, thank you." I clasped my hands between my knees and squeezed my legs together.

"What time is the party?" I called into his kitchen while taking inventory of his expensive things.

"It's later tonight." A few seconds later, he returned with two tumbler glasses that had shaved ice in them. He handed me my Coke. "If you work the party, you'll need to wear a special outfit."

"Like a uniform?" I sipped my Coke and felt the tingle down my throat. The sugar tasted amazing. My stomach growled loud and he responded.

"Wow, we need to get you something to eat." He stood and started toward the kitchen. Thank God, I thought.

"I really am hungry. Thank you." I said.

As he reached the entrance to the kitchen, he stopped and turned around. "First, show me your tits."

I placed both hands around the tumbler and held the glass against my chest. "What?"

"I don't know if you can work the party unless you show me your tits."

"What do they have to do with the party?" I wanted to cry.

"Look, do you want to meet Linda Evans or not?" He raised his voice.

"She won't want to see them." My lower lip quivered.

"No, but I do and you have to be able to fit into the outfit." He sat on the arm of his sofa like he was trying to reason with me. I didn't respond, so he yelled, "Do it!"

"No." I put the glass on a table and stood. "I want to leave."

"Oh, what the fuck, you want to leave?"

"Yes." I grabbed my Walkman and tapes and headed for the door.

"Just wait." His voice lowered. "I'll drive you."

"No." I turned the knob and tried to leave.

"Jesus Christ! Hold on a minute!" He ran into his kitchen and I heard him grab his keys. "Look, you have to go this way to get to my car." He pointed to another door. I stood still, not believing him until he opened a door to his garage. "See?"

I followed him to his car and he continued to berate me. He said he didn't want his neighbors to see someone like me walking around his neighborhood and repeated how stupid I was, that I was giving up good money to go walk the streets. He pulled over almost exactly where he first called out of his limo. "Get the fuck out!" He reached across me to open the door, but I was almost all the way out. I closed his car door nicely and walked away, thanking God.

~ * ~

The Tiffany Theatre was in Hollywood on Sunset, right where David said it would be. He was standing in line by himself and clearly stood out. It seemed the show started outside. People were dressed in all types of costumes. There were men dressed as women and characters of all sorts. David just wore his jeans and a T-shirt. He stood frumpy as before, with his hands in his pockets. He seemed so short next to all the men in heels. I surprised him when I walked up to him in the line. "Can you pay for my ticket?" I smiled.

"Of course." He reached out with his arms and laughed. "You came, You're going to love this."

Anything was better than what happened only a half hour before. I stood in line and talked about a whole lot of stuff that didn't matter. I wasn't going to tell David or anyone else what happened. I didn't want anyone to know that I was stupid.

Before the movie, there was a play. Some of the dressed-up people stood on the stage and belted out lines from the movie. Once the movie started, the audience called back to the screen and threw food. At some point, a piece of toast landed on the seat next to me. When David wasn't looking, I ripped away a portion and shoved it in my mouth. I couldn't think about where the bread came from.

David was right, The Rocky Horror Show was like nothing I ever experienced, but unlike most of the crowd, I didn't care if I saw it ever again. I didn't like toast flying and creepy characters.

We stood and talked outside the Tiffany. He laughed about how it was always the same people at the theater and how cool it all was and he had cancer and would I please stay with him so he could have sex before he died.

I was beginning to hate Los Angeles. I thanked him for the movie and continued my walk on Sunset Boulevard.

I was so freaked out that all I wanted to do was find a pay phone. I did eventually find one and, instead of calling the Barreres first, I made a collect call to Karen Bean. It was still only eleven or so in Pennsylvania.

"Where are you?" Lee questioned when I finally got through.

"I'm in Hollywood."

"Where? What?" I couldn't tell if she was mad or worried.

"I'm on Sunset Boulevard in Hollywood." I looked up to see a man with a jheri curl and pretty eyes, staring at me, smiling. I put my finger in my ear and turned away from the man so I could hear Lee.

"Julie, you need to get to the police right now." I heard Lee repeating to someone where I was.

"There's a warrant out for your arrest in five states. You have to go to the police and get back here!"

"But why? I'm not a criminal," I whispered.

"I guess because you're a ward of the state. Just get to the police, do you hear me?"

"Okay." I turned back and noticed the jheri curl man still smiling at me.

"You promise, you'll go right to the nearest station?"

"Yes, I'll go now. I promise." I hung up and felt relieved. The only problems were that now I wasn't going to see the Barreres and I was just going to get further from Linda Evans. I looked at the smiling man that I thought was waiting to use the phone. "Do you know where the police station is? Turns out I need to get back to Pennsylvania and fast."

He spoke quietly. "I'll show you where the police is, but if you ever want to get back to L.A., call me." He handed me a business card.

The card simply read, Dante and had a phone number on it. "Thank you," I said.

As we walked the few blocks to the police department, Dante told me that he helped young women get a start in Hollywood. "It's not always easy work but, it'll help you get on your feet." He stopped on the sidewalk out front. "This is as far as I'll go."

"Well, thanks for showing me." I looked down at the card that was now wrinkled in my hand from squeezing so hard. "And, thanks for your card."

"You're welcome. Call me anytime." Dante turned and left and I headed into the station.

The tanned police officer behind the glass wall typed slowly. I waited patiently and looked around for other action in the station. This place had to be more active than Warminster P.D.. I half-expected to see Officers Reed and Malloy from the show, Adam 12, since Hollywood was their beat. The police officer didn't seem surprised when he finally looked up. He got up from his desk and came to the window. "What can I do you for?" I could hear him perfectly, even though he wasn't speaking directly through the hole in the glass.

"I ran away and I want to go back home," I said.

"Okay." He grinned. "Come on back." He walked to a side door and let me in. "Have a seat." He pointed to a chair next to his desk. "You shouldn't be out here in the middle of the night, so it's good that you came into the station."

"I know." I looked down and felt ashamed. "I don't know what I've done." I found myself staring at his uniform. His chest looked square and hard, like I could knock on it. I hadn't seen a shape like that on the Warminster cops. They all seemed to have a pooch or be a little stringy. This guy was still young enough to lift weights and this was L.A., so I figured he worked out.

"Okay, so what's your name and where you from?" He shuffled a few sheets and began writing as I told him.

"Julie. Pennsylvania."

"Julie, Pennsylvania," he repeated as he wrote. "That's a long way! Got a last name?" He glanced at me.

"Beekman."

"Okay, age?"

"Sixteen."

"So why did you run away?"

"Curiosity." I pressed my lips together and blew out a cheek like a giant bubble. I wanted to lie down. It had been so long since I just lay out flat. I was so tired that I wasn't even hungry anymore. I yawned and placed my elbow on his desk.

"Tell you what. I'm going to get you into a home for the night and they'll help process your return home." He wrote some more and then placed the paperwork into a file. "I'll call in an officer to drive you."

"Okay, thank you." I yawned again while covering my face with both hands. I immediately thought of a new foster family and how cool it would be to stay in California. I came all this way and hadn't experienced anything but the crazy Sunset Boulevard night life. Maybe I could get to go the beach and see the Pacific Ocean. I listened as the officer made several calls on his walkie talkie and then a phone call where he informed someone I would be spending the night.

"Do you need to call anyone?" He held out the receiver to me.

"No, they know I'm safe."

~ * ~

As I rode in the back seat of the police car, I spotted the Hollywood sign lit up in the hills. It was so beautiful and amazing and surreal. I smiled, knowing that someday, I would see it again under better circumstances. I listened to all the calls coming in over the walkie talkie with codes that I didn't understand. Once in a while, the older officer would answer and explain that he was en route to wherever he was taking me. Occasionally, we talked.

"Why don't you have a partner?" I sat forward and looked through the plastic windows that he opened before we left the station.

"Some of the guys on the force do. I just prefer riding alone." He glanced back at me as he spoke.

"I just thought that all L.A. police would have a partner. I mean, Cagney has Lacey, or were they in New York? Ponch has Jon on C.H.I.P's." I couldn't stop talking. "I think even Columbo has someone, right?"

"You must watch a lot of television." He laughed.

"I used to." I sat back "It was a good escape."

The officer pulled up in front of a large house that was dark with the exception of a few lights on the ground floor. We walked up to the porch and the porch light popped on. A young blonde guy with massive curls answered and immediately shook the officer's hand. "How's it go'n, man? Come on in."

I followed them both and watched the curly guy drag flip flops across the floor. He also wore faded Levis and an Ocean Pacific T-shirt.

"Do you surf?" I asked.

"Sure do." He took some papers from the officer and signed his name.

"How far is the beach?"

"It's about a twenty-minute drive." He returned the officer's clipboard and slid his hands into his pockets. "Come on, let's get you settled."

I turned to the policeman, thanked him and then followed the surfer.

"How about you?" he asked, "are you a water girl?"

"I'd like to be." I looked at all the doors as we went down a hallway and up a set of stairs. "I grew up on Lake Michigan and then the Chesapeake, but I never surfed."

"Well, if you're here for a while, maybe we can getcha out there." He stopped at a door and held out his arm. "This is actually a staff room, but we're filled right now."

"How many people live here?" I looked to find a twin bed, a desk, and a shelf filled with books that appeared to be all about mental health. Books that I might have seen in Emily's office, I thought.

"I think fifteen girls." He ran his fingers through his locks. "I usually work at the boys' place." He grunted a laugh.

"Fer Sher," I nodded.

"Oh, you'll probably need to know where the bathroom is." He quickly turned and scanned all the doors in the hallway. "Uh, right there." He pointed. "I'll find you some supplies, too."

I sat down at the desk and waited for him to return with towels, a robe, a little kit that included a razor, toothpaste, and a toothbrush. Heaven.

"Do you think I could take a quick shower now? I mean, if I'm really quiet?"

"Sure." He grinned.

"Great." I practically ran to the bathroom. I took a hot shower and shaved. I used one of the many shampoo bottles that were in the tub and hoped no one would notice. After the shower, I put on the robe and went back to the staff bedroom and locked the door. I got right into bed with my clean robe and let out a deep sigh.

Chapter Twenty-two

I heard knocks on the door, pounding, really. And girls' voices. "Anyone in there?"

I was so groggy, I couldn't figure out what was going on or where I was. I pried my eyes open and looked out the window to find the most spectacular view of mountains. The sky was warm and it made me smile. I quickly got up and opened the door to find three girls staring at me with wide eyes. "I knew it!" one of them screamed. "There's a girl in here!"

"Who are you?" a Latina girl asked.

"My name is Julie and I really need to brush my teeth. My mouth tastes like I ate a poop sandwich." I covered my mouth and found my toothbrush.

"When did you get here?" She followed me into the bathroom.

"Last night."

"Nuh-uh." She shook her head.

"No, really," I said with a mouth full of toothpaste, then spit. "Some surfer guy signed me in and gave me that room."

The other girls stood in the doorway watching us, but not saying anything. Then, a black woman with coffee and cream colored skin arrived with a clipboard. "Hey, girl, when did you get here?"

"Last night. May I shut the door so I can use the bathroom real quick?"

"Sure." She looked confused.

When I reopened the door, everyone was still standing where I left them. "I've got nothing on you for last night." She shook her head and flipped through the pages on the clipboard. The three girls peered over her shoulder. "What you say about a surfer?" Other girls began appearing in the hallway. "Last night, Juanita worked, she didn't say one thing about you and she sure in heck ain't no surfer. There's nothin' in the notes, either." She looked like she might laugh out loud, like I was an alien. She turned to glare at all the young women gathered around. "Now what are ya'll doin?" She seemed serious for a moment and waved her hand. "Go make this poor girl something to eat!" The girls giggled and scurried down the stairs. The Latina girl ignored the command and stayed. "You need some clothes?"

"I don't know if you have anything I can wear, but I was wearing those clothes," I pointed to a small folded pile on the floor. "For the last three days."

"We have plenty of clothes and Rosa can help you with that." She began to leave, still flipping through the clipboard. "My name is Ronelle and if you need anything, let me know. Rosa will show you down to the kitchen." She looked at both of us. "I need to make a phone call and clear this mess up."

"I'll be right back." Rosa left the hallway and I went back to the room to make the bed. When she returned, she was dragging two large trash bags. "In here, you'll find a whole lot of clothes to choose from." She tossed her long hair and opened the first bag.

As I bent down to start sorting, I remembered all the trash bags I dug through in the past.

"You look like that Brooke Shields girl." The Latina girl smiled. "I mean, you have those eyebrows."

"Um, thanks?" I remembered that I probably hadn't plucked my eyebrows since I lived with the Kindts, almost two years ago.

I found a few pairs of shorts and some T-shirts. There was also a pair of flip flops that looked reasonably new. I thought about where they might have come from and Rosa must have read my mind. "Everything's been washed. Just left behind over the years."

"Okay." I sighed. "That's good."

"After you're dressed, just come down the stairs and you'll find us."

"I can already smell something incredible." I smiled.

When I came into the kitchen, I could smell eggs and pancakes and bacon. The girls seemed excited. "Here, sit down," someone said and pulled out a chair. Another girl brought a huge plate of food and placed it in front of me.

"You were sleeping for two days!" A blonde, about my age, said.

"What?" I looked up at everyone as I cut through fluffy pancakes.

"Lord knows!" Ronelle walked in and sat across from me. "Girl, what day is it?"

I thought for a moment and remembered that Rocky Horror with David was last night on a Friday. "It's Saturday," I answered. All the girls laughed.

"Mmm, mmm, mmm, Lord Jesus, help me." Ronelle shook her head some more. "Now this boy, Matthew?" She set down her papers. "He's your surfer and he never wrote bout you getting checked in. Girl, it's Sunday afternoon and if Rosa didn't keep knockin', you mighta slept all day and into tomorrow."

We all laughed. "Where am I anyway?" This caused even more laughter.

"Pasadena," Rosa blurted out. "Welcome to Pasadena!"

I ate all the food that the girls served me, except I gave Rosa my bacon. Everyone seemed fun and happy and no one tried to change my hair or wanted to tell me what to do. We told stories of how we got there. Many of the stories were similar to mine. Some had come from abusive families, some were runaways, but all of them seemed to live well together. They told me about the school they attended that was located in the building behind the house.

"Do other kids from the neighborhood attend the school?"

"Na, it's just us and a teacher. She's nice though and we cover all the subjects." Rosa clasped her hands in front of her as we sat at the table.

"Do you graduate like other kids?"

"We can take our GED and some girls even go to the community college."

I thought about the idea of staying there, but something bothered me about the idea of not graduating normally and what if boys needed to be a part of a girl's high school experience. I wasn't so sure that Children and Youth Services would let me stay anyway and I was sure that I would have more court dates with Marge.

I started helping a few of the girls in the kitchen, including Rosa. I had such a late breakfast that we were already cleaning up from that and starting dinner. One girl, Terry, seemed to be in charge of the menus and where everything was kept. She was patient and kind. "Okay, we're going to need two cans of black beans." I raced to the pantry to find the beans. Everything was jumbo-sized. There were huge packages of sugary powered drink mixes, that Marge would never approve of. I hoped we would have some with dinner.

Rosa put on a vat of water to boil for rice and then began shredding meat off of a few chickens. It was gross and I felt helpless and clueless in the kitchen. I just waited for instructions from Terry and then I set the table. I set everything the way Liz Kindt would, even folded the paper napkins to look like cloth.

I wandered around the house a little, too. I found two girls playing Scrabble and some other girls watching a movie. When I returned to the kitchen, I asked Rosa if anyone ever went outside or to the beach.

"Lots of girls feel safer just staying in, but occasionally, we all go to a park, the zoo and even the beach." Rosa picked all the meat off the bones.

I had to look away and find a window. "Oh, that's good. It just seems so beautiful here and I would want to be out all the time."

When everything was set, Terry had me place large serving spoons in all the dishes. Rosa set out a container of warmed tortillas and covered it with a towel, then poured Kool Aid into all the glasses I placed at each setting. Then Terry called everyone in.

"Now this is real Mexican," Rosa said. "This ain't no Chi Chi's." We all laughed.

After dinner, five girls cleaned the kitchen and then we all watched a movie. Juanita, the night worker, was on and informed me that she left a message with CYS in Pennsylvania and we would probably be hearing from them in the morning.

~ * ~

Monday's breakfast wasn't nearly as eventful as it had been on Sunday. The girls were moving about with purpose. Terry had to be at a part-time job at Albertson's grocery store, Samantha worked at an office nearby, and other girls like Rosa and me, needed to go to school.

Rosa and I ate some of the pancakes Terry left in a warm oven. After taking care of our dishes, we went outside and waited for the mobile home school to open. "I hope you stay here forever." Rosa sat on the back steps while I swung side to side on the handrail.

"Oh God, I don't." I laughed.

"You know what I mean." Rosa made a funny face. "I don't want you to go back to Pennsylvania, unless you want to go."

I stopped playing on the handrail and sat next to her. "I don't know what I want." I sighed. I was torn. I started thinking about Karen Bean and how much I missed her. Then I thought about the Chief and how screwed up all of that was. I wondered if I still had a job and if Tina was taking care of my cat.

"You got a boyfriend?" Rosa stood and started to walk to the school.

"Um, no," I answered, not sure if I was lying.

"I had a relationship, once." Rosa stepped up into the mobile home. "If you can call it that."

The inside of the classroom was modern and the teacher welcomed us with a big, "Hello!" and "Welcome, new student!"

"Hi, I'm Julie." I stood at her desk and waited for some sort of instruction.

"Oh, you can take a seat," she said. "I hope you like Tom Selleck." It was then that I noticed that every wall had a least one Tom Selleck poster on it. "I love Tom Selleck."

"I can tell." I sat down at an empty desk near the front.

"I'm Patty and this is our little school." She opened a notebook and wrote, looking up as other girls came in. Then the phone rang. Patty answered and looked at me immediately. "Okay." She paused. "Okay, I'll let her know." She nodded and hung up. "Well, it was nice to meet you." She exhibited an expression of fake worry while she pushed her short hair behind her ears. "I wish we could have gotten to know you, but, it looks like you're heading to the airport."

"I am?" I was startled at how quickly it was all ending. I turned to a pouting Rosa. "Bye, Rosa." I got up and hugged her. "Bye, everyone, and thank you." I gave a quick wave and walked slowly out of the mobile home school.

~ * ~

As I rode in the back of a van to the airport, I looked for the Hollywood sign, but never spotted it. It was still sunny and the palm trees were everywhere I looked. There was a huge part of me that was really disappointed to be leaving. I liked the girls and I kind of fit in.

What an experience, I thought. I laughed to myself that no one would ever believe me and then I wondered if I would somehow have to pay for my plane ticket when I got back.

When the driver dropped me off at LAX, he handed me a note and said, "Just go in there, straight to the counter." I got the feeling that he was supposed to park and go to the counter with me, but I could handle it.

"Thanks for the ride."

The note had the name of the Airline and flight number along with the name, Nancy DeLeon. Nancy DeLeon the caseworker from the days of the Kindts. Now that was a blast from the past, I thought.

The American Airlines ticket counter did have my reservation and the woman behind the counter promptly issued my ticket along with some directions for the gate.

At the gate, The flight attendant informed me that I would have to sit in first class since my reservation was last minute and there were no other seats available. As I sat in the big leather seat, I read my ticket stub. Los Angeles to Philadelphia-nonstop-four hundred and seventy-three dollars. I thought about everything. With the price of the ticket and the warrant for my arrest, I might be in a whole lot of trouble. For a moment, I considered getting off the plane. I couldn't settle my thoughts. What if they send me to Juvenile Hall, or worse, back to Marge? I decided not to worry until I got back and I needed to focus on the moment. The plane ride is going to be so cool. The flight was exhilarating and I would have loved if we just took off and landed the entire way across America. The flight was great. I drank Cokes and read all the nice magazines from the front cabin.

When we arrived in Philadelphia, I thanked the flight attendants and the pilot. Nancy DeLeon was waiting just inside the terminal. She didn't look mad and that was a good sign.

"What were you doing in L.A.?" She gently placed her hand around the back of my neck and ushered me toward the exit.

"I don't know," I answered. "I wanted to see the Barreres and other stuff." I walked with her toward the parking garage. "Why are you here? I thought Penny was my caseworker."

"She is at Aldersgate. I'm still your caseworker out of Children and

Youth Services."

"So, I'm in big trouble?"

"I'm not sure." Nancy opened her car and unlocked the passenger lock.

"Does Marge know?"

"Yes, she does. She is planning on suing us and believes that we are at fault and should have kept a better eye on you."

"Sorry." I sunk into the passenger seat and cringed as Nancy paid the Airport parking fee. "Do you think I'll still have my job?"

"I don't know, Julie. You're going to have to go in and straighten all of that out."

"Is anyone mad at me?"

Nancy drove and only looked forward. "I couldn't tell you. I know that I'm not mad, but I was worried."

"Am I going to get arrested?"

"I wouldn't worry about that. You are going to have to answer to some people, but you're not going to get arrested."

When Nancy took me to the Eckenrode's door, she said, "Julie, please don't ever think of doing this again."

"I won't," I lied. "Are the Eckenrodes going to be mad?"

"You'll need to find out." Nancy brushed bangs from my forehead. "You have to deal with how people react to what you've done."

I took a deep breath. "Will you go in with me?"

"For a minute, sure." Nancy looked back at her car while I opened the front door.

Helen didn't seem too thrilled to see me when I walked in and Tina didn't even come out of her room. "So, are you finished with your adventure?" Her accent seemed to be missing as she nervously laughed.

Nancy DeLeon spoke before I could respond. "I'm sure she is. I'm sure she's spent some time thinking about how she worried everyone." She touched my shoulder.

I nodded, but I couldn't answer. I really hadn't thought about how anyone might have worried. Except for the Beans, and some people at work, I doubted that anyone had been very concerned. I'm sure my cat, Emily wondered where in the heck I was and I hoped she hadn't gotten too close to Tina. She was, after all, my cat. I had been negligent in asking anyone to take care of her and that made me sad. I started looking around for her as we all stood in the doorway. "I'm sorry that I just left without saying anything."

"You make no sense to me." Helen quickly responded.

"I don't make sense to me either." I cautiously moved further into the room and looked downstairs into the family room. Henry sat, reclined in a double wide chair, watching television.

I waved and looked hard to see if Emily was on his lap. She wasn't. Henry waved back as I began to look away. I heard him place the chair in an upright position to sluggishly come and greet us.

"Glad you're back." Henry managed a smile and I believed him. He was likable and his white goatee and bald head begged for a wide-brimmed Amish hat, which to me, meant he couldn't lie.

I felt uncomfortable standing there with the three adults. Tina wasn't appearing and Helen seemed to radiate condemnation. "May I go to my room?"

"Sure." Henry waved at the stairs.

"Go," Helen responded curtly.

"Thank you, Nancy." I turned and bolted up the stairs to see my cat. When I turned on the light in my room, there was no sign of Emily, and everything was exactly how I had left it a week before. I turned and knocked on Tina's door.

"What?" Tina responded.

"Hi," I spoke through the closed door. I waited and she didn't respond. "Is Emily in there?"

"Nope."

"Thanks." I responded with a little extra cheer in my voice. I headed back downstairs and stood on the landing that continued down into the Eckenrodes family room. Nancy was gone. Henry was back on the extra-wide recliner and Helen was next to him. She took her eyes away from the television for a moment and focused on me.

"Hi, um, I'm looking for Emily."

"She's not here anymore." Helen quickly looked back to the T.V.

"What do you mean?" I started breathing hard.

"You weren't here, I didn't know if you were coming back, so I took it to the pound." She was so agitated that her hair rattled.

I was completely taken off guard. I felt like running down the stairs and punching her. I wanted to scream and noticed my mouth hanging open. Once connected with the rest of my body, I managed to move away from her and go back to my room. At that moment, I officially hated Helen. I flew across my bed and cried hard into my pillow. I prayed that Tina couldn't hear me because I thought she might get pleasure from my crying. When I finally turned over, I looked up at the underside of my bookshelf and stared at a small photo of Chief Clawges that I cut out of the newspaper and strategically taped so that no one could see it unless they lay in my bed. The picture no longer mattered. It didn't comfort me, it made me feel weak and trapped. I sat up and went back down to the landing. Helen and Henry looked up again.

"Would one of you take me to the pound tomorrow?" I started to cry in front of them. "Or, wherever you took her?"

They both answered at the same time. I barely made out Henry's, "Sure," under the harshness of Helen saying that she doubted that Emily was still alive or gone because someone adopted her and that I should go to school instead of looking for a cat. I retreated upstairs again. I brushed my teeth and went straight to my room. I changed, turned off my light and bawled. I sobbed for my Dad and whimpered over my entire predicament until I couldn't stay awake to feel sorry for myself any longer.

~ * ~

In the morning, Helen begrudgingly drove me to The Bucks County SPCA, while Tina got on the bus for school. Helen waited in the car while I went into the lobby to get my Emily. When I gave the woman the information on my cat, she sighed and said, "I'm sorry, but she's not here."

"Was she adopted?" I mouthed the top of my hand and bit down on skin.

"Honey, generally, we put down older cats." She paused. "Older than a kitten, I mean, if they're here for more than five days."

"Why?" I blurted out. "Why would you not wait for the owner or an adoption or whatever?"

"I'm sorry, Miss, with dogs, we wait longer, with cats...we would be over-run with cats if we didn't euthanize."

"Can I look?" I was hoping she was wrong, that Emily hadn't been factored in to their stupid rules and why would Helen have taken her here so soon after I left?

"Sure." She looked disappointed in me. "The cats are on the back left, through the doors," she pointed.

There weren't many cages, but there were some kittens and a few older cats, just not Emily. I was relieved to see that the cages were lined with fluffy blankets and toys. I couldn't look any of the cats in the eyes because as I heard barking from the next room, I just wanted them all.

Getting another cat wouldn't be fair, since I didn't know where I was going next.

My cat wasn't there. Not in the cages, not wandering around, and I prayed that she was adopted by a loving family.

I gathered myself before going outside to Helen, waiting in the car. I was so sad and so angry. I would not cry in front of Helen and if I lost my temper, I might be put away somewhere. My fist balled as I sat in the passenger seat and I wanted to scream at her, but I resorted to thinking about what a horrible pet owner I was. How my cat's last days may have been in a cage because I had to run off to California.

I said nothing the whole way to school, even when Helen apologized and even when she pulled up to the curb and told me to have a nice day. As far as I was concerned, she now had joined the ranks of Scot.

I saw Tina in the lunch room. She left her table to approach me. "Hey, did you get your cat?"

"No. It was too late." I stared at the floor.

"Sorry," Tina said. "Eat lunch at my table."

"I don't feel like eating and aren't you having lunch with your friends?"

"Yeah, but you can sit with us," Tina grinned. "At least, today."

I sat with her and she grilled me about my trip west. I wanted her to know only so much. She had been so bossy to me for the last year and now I had yet another item I could keep from her. She didn't know about the Chief and she didn't know everything about my trip.

~ * ~

After school, I had to go and face Mrs. Stockel and the Chief. I was nervous that I was fired and kind of afraid that I would walk in and find another girl sitting at my desk.

I stood just inside Mrs. Stockel's doorway and waited for her to look up. When she did, she jumped a little, but then she grinned. "Where have you been?" and then she called out to the Chief, "Look who's here."

The Chief entered from his office and he was grinning, too.

"I'm really sorry," I said. "I took off for a while and I didn't even call you."

"So you needed a vacation?" Mrs. Stockel winked at the Chief.

"Kind of." I squinted. "I'm really sorry."

"Well, you better get to work, that pile is huge on your desk." The Chief wasn't grinning anymore.

"Thank you." I ran across the hall to clock in and started typing envelopes for the insurance companies.

Chapter Twenty-three

After pedaling home from work one evening, I parked my bike, bent down to secure the lock, and found myself looking at hairy gray hooves. "Baaaaah." A goat stared at me and moved closer.

"Oh my God!" I stood and put my hand out like I was meeting a dog. "What are you doing here?" The goat pushed my hand like I was hiding food. "You scared the heck out me." I petted its head and scratched behind its ears. The goat looked back at me like it was waiting for me to pull food from my pockets. After surveying how the goat was attached by rope to the clothes line and assuring myself that it had plenty of space to walk around, I ran into the house to find out why it was here and whether I could feed it.

"There's a goat out there." I drove my forefinger in the direction of the backyard.

"I know." Helen chopped an onion on a large cutting board, careful to keep her floral house dress clean behind an apron.

"Okay, so, why is there a goat in the back yard?" I looked out the window over the kitchen sink.

"I like-ah the goat," Helen replied in a heavier than usual accent.

"I like him, too." I waved out the window. "Is it a him?"

"Yes, it's a boy goat."

"What's his name?" I opened the fridge and searched the overflowing produce drawer. "Can I feed him?"

"Call him what you want." Helen moved quickly in her pantry. She

339

seemed distracted, as usual.

"Am I allowed to feed him?" I repeated.

"You can feed him some apples or carrots until I put his meal together." Helen scurried to the stove and turned on a burner.

I grabbed an apple and went out back. I bit off pieces of the apple that I thought were a good size for him. He stared at me as he gnawed. I felt a kinship with him. "We're both strangers in this family, so let's just rely on each other, okay?" I swung my arm around his neck and he didn't seem to mind. I talked with him for a while. I told him about my job and how I liked the bands U2 and Duran Duran, how Michael Jackson was the best dancer ever and I really wanted to be able to buy Guess jeans, and how there was a really cool ad for Calvin Klein underwear and the guy was super good looking but I didn't think I would want to have sex with him. "It's so overrated. Penises are gross. Especially scrotums. Hey, I know, Calvin. Calvin would be a great name for you. I mean, you don't want some stupid name like Goatee, right?" The goat didn't seem to care either way.

Calvin became a great distraction for me. I wasn't so focused on the Chief situation. Although, when the Chief did pay attention to me, I responded with a vacillation between feelings of love and dread. An influential man desired me and told me he cared for me, so I was confused and felt like garbage every time he discarded me, better than average garbage. Every time I got a little sick of how it all made me feel and decided he should just leave me alone, he talked me into hanging around the office a little late. Now, with the goat, I was often able to decline gracefully, which helped shave off a few layers of shame.

~ * ~

On the days I took the bus with Tina, kids teased us with goat sounds. Tina usually just sighed, but once I yelled, "Calvin is cool."

Tina shot a look of disgust my way. "You named the goat?" She sat

Julie Beekman

with arms folded, obviously horrified.

Of course, I named him, I thought.

~ * ~

When school ended, I started working at the Police Department full time almost right away. It was surprising I wasn't placed in summer school since I failed Algebra last year and barely passed it this year. The football coach was my teacher the second time around, and I believed he only passed me because I asked a lot of questions.

I was going to be a senior and Tina graduated. Her birthday was in July so Helen was planning a big party for her. Tina quit her job at the auto parts store and started working at the women's clothing store, The Limited. I was really happy for her. She was working in fashion and would start college for Fashion Marketing in the fall. We continued to take Helen's car late at night sometimes and go to the clubs, and I resumed my caretaker role, making sure Tina didn't drink too much or go off with the wrong guy.

I worked Monday through Friday, came home to visit with Calvin after work, and spent my weekends with Karen Bean and her family. It didn't seem that Calvin missed me too much when I was gone. He never seemed overly excited to see me. The problem was, I didn't realize I was going to have to miss him. I came home one day after work and found Helen standing at the dining room table. She was whistling and had quite a production going on with phyllo dough. It was everywhere, along with bowls of chopped spinach and cheese mixtures. "Hello, hello" she practically sang.

"Hi. You seem very happy." I walked past her to the refrigerator to grab a snack for Calvin.

"I am. I'm getting ready for Tina's party." She continued to whistle and make the cheese triangles dance in her chubby hands. "I have everything almost ready."

"What can I do?" I bit into an apple, readying it for Calvin.

"Maybe tomorrow, you can help with decorations, okay?" Helen peeled a wet cloth off the layers of rolled-out dough.

"Okay." I turned and walked toward the back door.

"Where are you going?" Helen called out.

"To feed the goat," I replied as I opened the door. Duh, I thought.

"The goat is at the butcher!"

"What?" I stopped and looked out into the yard. I gasped, "What do you mean?" I hurried to the table where Helen prepped her hors d'oeuvres.

"I mean what I say. The goat is at the butcher." Her tone seemed indignant.

"Why?" I stammered. "Why would you do that?"

"Goat is delicious!" She pounded on the table causing a bowl full of spanikopita filling to spin off to one side and fall to the floor. "Now look. Look at poor Tina's appetizers."

"Oh my God!" I grabbed my hair with both hands in a grand dramatic tug while I raced back to my room. "I will never eat here again!" I screamed.

"Fine!" she yelled and followed that up with a load of Greek words I didn't understand.

I cried in my room and wished I could transport myself somewhere west. I kept thinking about the colors that made me feel happy in Albuquerque. Terra cotta and big sky blue. I listened to my music, but kept the sound low in case Helen went on about the appetizers or decided to send me off to the group home again.

When Tina got home, she knocked on my door. "Can I come in?" she asked as she walked right in.

"Sure." I sat up and turned off my tape player.

"My parents want you to come downstairs and eat dinner with us." She stood, waiting like I was just going to jump up and follow her.

"I'm not eating in this house," I stated firmly.

"It's not like we're having goat tonight." Tina folded her arms.

"How do I know that? How do I know that we're not eating some squirrel she caught in the front yard with her bare hands? Or a pigeon she shot off the roof, or my cat for that matter? I lay back down and fidgeted with my tape player.

"Just come down." Tina continued standing and waiting.

"No, thank you." I put my headphones on and then quickly pulled them back off. "Why didn't you tell me that she was going to kill him?"

"I thought you knew."

I sat up. "You thought I knew?" I huffed in protest.

"Well, you're Greek, aren't you?" Tina turned to leave.

"What's that supposed to mean? Do you think all Greeks just innately keep live animals in their back yard, make friends with them and then slaughter them?

"You made friends with it?" Tina shook her head and snorted as she was leaving. "Unbelievable."

I got up and threw on a pair of sneakers. I decided to go out walking and maybe get a look at the Chief's wife. She worked at Elaine Powers which was only a half mile away and at this point I had nothing to lose. I really didn't care about anything.

"I'll be back." I said as I went out the front door. I walked and listened to music. I tried not to think of how Calvin might have died. When I reached the strip mall where Elaine Powers was, I strode slowly, trying to catch a glimpse of Nancy Clawges. She would have to be older, but probably in great shape. There were so many colors jumping and lunging, I couldn't get a good look so I kept walking. What good would it do anyway?

~ * ~

Once again, I buried myself in work and spent even more time with the Beans. In July, I went off with the Beans on their summer vacation to the Jersey shore. This was my third time with them and I felt lucky to be asked to go again. Plus, the trip was conveniently scheduled during Tina's party. I wouldn't have to see Calvin spinning over an open fire and served up on a Gyro.

I loved the beach and Karen's mom, Lee, wanted to be there all day. At night, we went to the boardwalk, and this year, Karen and I were old enough to walk around by ourselves. We met some cute boys, but I didn't know what boys our age expected from us, since I had only been with the Chief and none of the boys in school were attracted to me. They just wanted to be friends. We talked to the boys on the boardwalk, but I would have rather been hanging around with just Karen and her mom. Lee had a Sophia Loren quality about her and I was struggling internally with some sort of attraction to her. Yet another secret I had to keep.

During the third night of the trip, I started having awful itching and a little bit of pain in my private area. It got so bad that I told Karen.

"You have to tell my mom." Karen stopped in the middle of brushing her hair.

"I can't" I tugged at my pajamas.

"Seriously," Karen grinned. "You can't keep scratching and obviously, something's wrong."

I finally agreed and Karen took Lee away from cocktails on the porch for our private discussion. Karen's little sister, Sherry, followed Lee in, and was promptly escorted out. It was incredibly embarrassing, but Lee made it all easy for me to talk about.

"Sounds like you have a yeast infection." Lee sipped on a gin and tonic. "I've had them before and they're just awful." Lee stood and patted me on the head. "I'll call my gynecologist and get some Monistat prescribed and sent to a drugstore down here. You'll start feeling better after the first night.

"Well, what is it?" I looked at Karen and then at Lee. "I mean, what is a yeast infection, is it V.D.?

Karen and Lee laughed and looked at me like I had two heads.

"How would you have V.D.?" Karen asked.

"Oh, I wouldn't" My eyes widened with pretend innocence.

Lee seemed unfazed. "You can get a yeast infection from intercourse, yes. But, you can also get it if your diet isn't very good or from being in a wet bathing suit." She stood at the door a moment longer. "I'll call in for the script," she smiled "don't worry."

"Thank you." I felt heat on my cheeks and wondered what she thought of me.

When Lee shut the door, I looked at Karen. "I have something to tell you."

"What?" Karen laughed uneasily. "We've been eating too much boardwalk pizza while sitting around in our wet bathing suits?"

"No," I pulled at my crotch and winced. "I've had sex,"

"What?" Karen practically yelled. "When, who with?"

"You can't tell anyone or my life will be ruined." I sat up and crossed my legs.

"I won't," she promised.

"I don't know how to explain this and you're going to think I'm disgusting." I bit on my bottom lip. I regretted ever saying anything and considered just shutting up.

"No, I won't, just tell me."

It was too late. "Okay. I had sex with my boss."

Karen's mouth hung open. With that old lady, Mrs. Stockel?"

"No!" I laughed so hard that my vagina hurt.

"I'm confused." Karen glared in disbelief.

"The chief," I whispered.

"Okay." Karen's lip twinges. "That's really screwed up."

"I know." I placed my hands on my knees and squeezed. "He approached me a while ago and I didn't know what to do."

"You should have told me,"

"What could you do?" I got up and started looking for a hair band. Anything to fidget and get through the conversation. "What could I do, he's the Chief of Police," I explained, "and he's my boss."

"That doesn't mean he can just do whatever he wants."

"I know." I felt stupid and weak, realizing how I must have sounded. "You weren't there, and you don't understand." I pulled my hair back into a ponytail and sat next to her on her bed.

"I think I do understand," Karen said. "I understand perfectly, he's a dirty old man."

"He's forty-three," I responded.

"That's like my parents' age."

"I know, so he's not old and... he loves me and stuff." I looked at the floor. Tan rugs hid beach sand well, until I stared hard enough to find it.

"Julie, he doesn't love you!" Karen was riled up and sounded like a counselor. "Is this why you ran away to California?"

"It's part of it." I shrugged. "He's married and I have a tremendous amount of guilt."

"I can't believe you didn't tell me any of this before." Karen placed her fingers at her temples like I gave her a headache.

"I'm sorry," I said.

Karen waited a few minutes. She appeared deep in thought. "So, now you have V.D. from the Chief of Police." She laughed. "My mom and dad would kill him if they knew."

"No one can know," I said. "I'm serious."

~ * ~

I came back from our trip, tanned and yeast infection free. I went back to work and became anxious any time I saw the chief. At home, I figured out ways to eat without sitting at the Eckenrode's dinner table. I went to the store, bought my own things, labeled them, and placed them in the fridge. This worked until Helen spotted my cache and had a cow. "I would never label our things."

"I wish you would." I laughed.

"You are ungrateful. We bring you into our home, I cook and share everything, now you go and mark all your things like you cannot share."

She was right. "I'm sorry, Helen. I think you're a wonderful cook, I just can't eat some things because I'm afraid it's goat."

"I show you the goat, okay?" Helen rushed to open the freezer door.

"No!" I backed up.

She took small square packages from the fully stocked freezer. "This?" She shook the package from her fully extended arm. "The brains."

"I don't want to know." I walked out of the kitchen.

"This?" I heard her calling out. "The eyes!"

"Aghhhh!" I covered my ears and ran up the stairs to my room. I could still hear Helen. She was saying something about how they brought me into their home so Tina could have a friend and I didn't even have the decency to come to Tina's party. She blabbered about how ungrateful I was and then went into a full-out Greek spoken lecture with herself.

I decided to leave the house for a while. I went out to the backyard and into the shed. I remembered the absence of Calvin and moved quickly. I found Tina's tennis racquet and a few limp balls to stuff into my pockets. I hopped on my bike and pedaled to Log College school to hit against the brick wall. I slammed the balls as hard as I could and called out as I did. "This is for Helen and her brains and eyeballs!" Whack! "This is for Marge and having to go back to court next week!" Whack! "This is for the Chief and empty promises!" Whack! I ran back and forth, hitting the ball like I was in a match. "This is for me getting the hell out of here!" Whack! I ran around until it was dark and I was exhausted. When I got home, I looked in my nightstand and pulled out Dante the pimp's 'business' card and stared at it. I laughed when I thought momentarily of becoming a prostitute. I could never do it.

Two Trees

~ * ~

Court was early on a Thursday in August. Instead of going to the small court in Montgomery County, Henry took me to the big county courthouse in Norristown where I met up with my attorney, Vanessa. It was great to see her again and I was grateful she didn't run away from my case.

As Vanessa and I climbed the courthouse steps, she whispered, "Is that your mother?"

"Where?" I looked up, alarmed. I saw Marge sitting on top of one of the cement landings that lined the courthouse steps. She was dressed in a black cape. "Oh my god, she looks like a witch!" I gasped. My heart pounded and I prayed that she didn't see me. Vanessa and I hastened to enter the building. We took our seats in the court room and, a few minutes later, I heard snickering and whispers from behind us. People were laughing as Marge walked to her table next to us. I felt her glare, but I couldn't return the favor. I looked down and doodled on the notepad Vanessa placed in front of me. That notepad always helped. She was good to me.

"All rise!" someone called from the front of the court. Judge Albright, the same judge who met with us on several occasions, including our first hearing, walked calmly to his seat and motioned for us to sit. It all reminded me of the times I attended Catholic church with Lee and Karen Bean. We were constantly sitting, then standing.

Judge Albright read from a file and looked at all of us. He spent a longer amount of time eyeing up Marge, surely wondering about her attire. Vanessa spoke for a moment and then it was Marge's turn. She rose, smiled, turned to address everyone in the court and said, "Good morning, motherfuckers, I'd like my daughter back."

Many in the courtroom nervously laughed, except for the bailiff who perked up at the sound of the swear word and the stenographer who

348

stopped typing to look at Marge over lavender reading glasses.

Marge had been doing the same thing for almost three years and the result never changed. The Judge usually ended the proceedings with a large smack of his gavel and instructions to meet in another six months. This day was a little different.

"Mrs. Beekman, do you really want to have custody of your daughter?"

"Of course, I do!" Marge raised her arms at her sides. "I have worked tirelessly to do so, I have written to all of our legislators, congressmen, and our President, for fuck's sake!"

Judge Albright crossed his arms and sat back. "Using profanity in the courtroom isn't the way to make that happen." He seemed somehow amused. I couldn't believe he was entertaining her for even a second.

"But you aren't the one who's hunted in this witch case, now are you?" Marge sounded sarcastic, but maybe a little unsure of what to do next. She stood at her table, palms open, looking persecuted and crucified. I thought for a few seconds about the bizarre intermingling of Jesus and witch.

Vanessa and I sat at our table calmly. Still, I wondered why the Judge was taking any time with Marge. Vanessa sat upright and attentive like a smart student. Marge was describing all she had been through with Montgomery County when Judge Albright called out, "Mrs. Beekman!" Marge stopped talking. "Mrs. Beekman, I'm going to recommend you have weekly visitations with Julie."

I stopped drawing and looked at Vanessa. I wanted to be sure she heard what I heard. "No," I whispered. "I can't do all of that again." I immediately considered the fact that this time, I didn't have Chuck Kindt to spy on the visitations.

"Ms. Klein, may I speak with you?" the Judge asked Vanessa.

As Vanessa approached the bench, I felt Marge staring at me, smirking. My stomach was in knots and I couldn't believe this was happening.

When court was over, Vanessa and I walked across the street to the Children and Youth offices. I surveyed the area before we entered the building, to see if the witch was lurking, but she was nowhere to be found.

"The judge just wants to try this for a few months." Vanessa put her files and bag down in her office.

"I can't do it." I slouched into a chair across from her desk.

"I'm sure it's really scary." Vanessa pulled the receiver from her phone and dialed a few digits. "I just need to check messages and then we can get some lunch." She listened, took a few notes, and then placed the phone back into its cradle. "So, where would you like to go?"

"I can't go." I stood "I'm getting braces today and I have to go and meet Mr. Eckenrode downstairs."

"Well, that's wonderful." Vanessa rose and walked to the door where I was lingering. She looked at my mouth. "But I like your gap."

"So does Marge." I faked a pout. "Seriously, Vanessa. I can't do the visitations."

"We'll talk," she said.

My braces made me feel rich. I was probably the only kid going into twelfth grade who had them, but at least I finally did. I finagled them by asking Penny, my caseworker from Aldersgate, if Marge was still getting social security checks for me.

"I'm not sure," she said.

"Well, she's complained about it a few times in court and I wonder, if she's not getting the checks from my dad's death, then who is?"

"I suppose the state, since you're a ward of the state."

I shook my head, not understanding. "The checks are more than what the Eckenrodes get for me, so wouldn't there be something left over?"

Chapter Twenty-four

I ran away about a week after the court hearing. Once I found out the visitations were going to be unsupervised, I called Dante, the pimp. I didn't know what I was going to do about the prostitution part, but I needed to get back to L.A. and I didn't have enough money.

Dante wired me a hundred dollars and I took out fifty-four of the fifty-five that I had in the bank. He didn't even ask me any questions and I wondered how he remembered me.

I had to have Dante help me. I felt if I called the Barreres', they wouldn't just let me come out there. They would go through the proper channels like they did when they tried to adopt me and the state denied them. I just couldn't risk having good citizens getting involved.

The bus ride took the same route as my previous excursion, just different times, so my favorite places, I missed, due to passing through at night. I kept to myself, played my music, and spoke to no one. My biggest problem was trying to sleep while sitting up. It was torture.

Dante met my bus in the Los Angeles depot late at night. When I saw him, I knew I would have to get out of a mess.

"Hey, how was the ride?" Dante took my backpack and slung it over his shoulder.

"It was fine. It went a lot quicker than the last time I came out here."

"Yeah, sorry I couldn't get you a flight. I got some things going on right now." Dante walked to where the driver was unloading luggage.

I wondered what 'things' he was talking about. "It's fine, I get to see the country when I take the bus." I realized that Dante was waiting for my luggage. "That bag is all that I have." I pointed to my backpack.

"Shit. Really?"

I felt bad for disappointing him. Tina would have been better equipped. I didn't even own a dress or any make-up.

"So, you're ready to live out here, huh?" Dante walked out of the station and I followed.

"Yep. Where are we going right now, anyway?"

"Yeah, I got this hotel apartment set up for you till you get settled." Dante pointed down the street where we walked.

"Settled?" I looked at him.

"You know." He laughed "L.A. is crazy and I got some nice girls you can live with, they know what's up."

Suddenly, I felt whiter than my first days in Norfolk. I was not hip and I didn't know what was up. I made a huge mistake.

"So, I don't remember you hav'n braces." Dante's eyes narrowed and he seemed less friendly.

"I just got them last week." I followed Dante into the lobby of an old building.

"You think you can get them off?" He jabbed the elevator button.

"I guess." I hesitated, wondering how on earth I would do that. "I can try." I ran my fingers over the metal on my front teeth. I wanted my gap closed and having braces was a dream come true. Would I have to do this now, to survive?

As we got to the room, my hopes of lying down and going to sleep quickly fizzled. Dante came into the room with me and his plan was to stay.

The room was small and dark. I wasn't sure if it was a hotel or apartment since there wasn't a lobby when we came in.

Thankfully, Dante turned on the television to keep himself busy.

I went into the bathroom with my backpack and locked the door. I

Julie Beekman

started a weak shower and glanced in the mirror. My reflection was lit by dingy yellow bulb above the sink. "You cannot do this," I said to the mirror.

I found a bar of soap and hopped into the shower. I kept thinking about being with ten different chiefs every day and how horrible that would be. At least Chief Clawges had some kind of love for me. I wasn't cut out for this and I wasn't supposed to be here. I could have worked out the Marge visitation issue somehow and not run off scared. I would have to tell Dante that I used him and I couldn't be a whore or live with a bunch of other prostitutes. I would have to somehow get back home and face everything.

When I emerged from the bathroom, I wore a polo shirt and khaki shorts. Surely not prostitute material. Dante looked me up and down and shook his head. He was lying on the bed like he was waiting for me and I wanted to say, "Ta Da, I love the boy band, Menudo!" just to turn him off. Instead, I awkwardly sat in a chair and pretended to watch the television. I was so tired.

"Did you get those braces off?"

"Um, no." I retreated to the bathroom and tried to pull at the wire. I took the bottom of my toothbrush and jammed it under the wire. My mouth still hurt from just having gotten them put on. I tugged and pulled until I had a rounded piece of wire band sticking out. I had to do this between each tooth until I finally freed the connection on the back teeth. I then had to pull the wire through the metal. The metal pieces were not coming off and the whole process was a waste of time. It was awful and I wasn't sure how I was going to explain this to the orthodontist. "I'm sorry, I took the wiring off, but my pimp didn't like the braces."

When I emerged from my attempt, I said, "I got the wiring off, but not the metal pieces on my teeth."

"Alright, I'll get some pliers in the morning. Get some sleep." Dante patted the bed next to him.

Holy Shit, I thought. He really wants them off.

I walked slowly to the bed and lay on the edge.

"I was going to test you out, but you don't seem ready." He clucked his tongue on the roof of his mouth. "Tomorrow." He got up and turned the television off.

I lay awake, thinking about where I was and what I was going to do. "I made a huge mistake," I blurted out. "I shouldn't have called you and I shouldn't have taken the wiring out of my braces. I thought maybe I could do this, but I can't. Please don't be angry"

"I know." Dante said. "You ain't got it and you can stay here tonight, but in the morning, you need to boogie on outta here and stop wasting my time."

"Oh my God, thank you."

~ * ~

I woke to find grease marks from Dante's jheri curl all over his pillow case. He was gone. I got up, brushed my teeth and quickly gathered my things. I was out in the fresh smog within ten minutes. I walked at least a mile from the building before stopping at a pay phone. I called the operator and asked for a collect call to the Barreres in San Diego. Gloria was on after a few minutes, her voice shaky. "Where are you exactly?"

"I'm at the corner of Olympic and Flower" I looked around for someplace that would serve food.

"Are you safe? I mean, can you stay there?"

"Yes," I answered.

"Okay, my brother Charlie is going to come and get you and then we'll be up there to meet with you. Charlie is safe and a good guy, okay?"

"Okay." I described what I was wearing and told Gloria I would wait patiently.

I got some juice and a muffin from a market down the street and then went right back to the corner, so to speak.

Charlie picked me up within a half hour and drove me to his ranch house just outside of L.A.. He was nice and just made small talk. I read magazines while I waited for Jim and Gloria. I was really excited to see them.

When they pulled up, I ran into the front yard to great them. I hugged each of them tight and thanked them for driving from San Diego to get me. "You'll take me back with you, right?"

"Of course," Gloria smiled.

We didn't stay long at Charlie's and I was happy to get into their van and get on the road. It was the same van they had when they left Pennsylvania two years before. It had big comfortable chairs and drink holders.

As we drove, I told them all about life with Tina, my job, Karen Bean and her family, and how I came to L.A. by bus. I left out a few minor details, like how I was having an affair with my boss who was married and how I almost became a prostitute just yesterday.

"I understand this wasn't your first bus trip out here." Gloria turned to look at me.

"Yeah, I came out here before, but I got scared and ended up going to the police."

"Well, why didn't you just take the bus all the way to San Diego?"

"I don't know. I just wanted to see L.A., I guess." I sat back in my seat and stared out at the freeway. I thought about what they would think if I told them I wanted to meet Linda Evans and a pimp paid for my second ticket. "How do you know that I was out here before?"

"Nancy the caseworker, told me." Gloria sat sideways in her overstuffed van chair. "She called and said you were missing again and that we might be hearing from you."

"Oh." I brushed my eyebrows with my fingers. "Did she tell you that they were going to make me see Marge unsupervised?"

"Yes, she told us, and that you were probably really scared."

"Well, I am."

"We know, Jul, but you scare the heck out of everyone when you just take off." Gloria used her hand and made a fluttery motion. "I mean, it's understandable, but there are other ways you can handle this. Plus, aren't you going to be eighteen next December?"

"Yeah, but I'll still be in twelfth grade."

"Well, you can do anything you want at that point. You could even come live with us and graduate from Mira Mesa high school."

It was all overwhelming, but sounded great. I stayed with the Barreres for a few days. Jim showed me the beaches and where he worked in Point Loma. Gloria showed me downtown San Diego and we toured the Balboa Park area and Horton Plaza. The city was gorgeous. We took a ferry ride to Coronado and ate at a fancy restaurant on the water's edge called, Pheohe's. It was Hawaiian themed and I ate shrimp. The trip was amazing and the best part was that the Barreres' had a pool. I didn't want to go back to Pennsylvania, but I had to.

I took a red-eye home and was once again picked up by a caseworker. Penny Freeman told me to just, 'grow some' and deal with Marge. "She's not that bad," she said.

"Seriously?" I felt my nostrils flare. "Unreal."

~ * ~

The Eckenrodes didn't say much and I called Karen Bean as soon as I got the chance. Karen got a car while I was away and she was going to take me to see this really cool movie she just saw the night before, Purple Rain.

The movie was crazy good and we drove around, listening to the soundtrack in her car tape player. She was proud of her 1972 Mustang and was loving her job at Bloomingdale's. I told her about the Barreres' house and how fabulous San Diego was. "It's probably the prettiest place I've ever seen."

"Yeah, but you can't live there, because I live here."

"There's the chief, too. I would miss him." I watched the red light above us turn green.

"Fuck the chief!" Karen accelerated so fast, the tires squealed

Senior year didn't get off to such a great start. It only took three weeks for the geometry teacher to kick me out of his class. The class was first hour and if I wasn't asking a million questions because I didn't understand, I was falling asleep because I didn't understand. It already took me two years to pass algebra and now I had to go to the guidance counselor and explain that I was kicked out of the next phase.

"Tell you what." Mr. Acker flipped through a schedule. "Let's get you into tech math and then you'll be able to graduate."

I was horrified. "Otherwise I can't graduate?"

"No, you need a certain amount of math to be able to get that diploma and you're way behind."

"But I'm doing fine in other classes. Doesn't that count?"

"It counts, but you'll probably have to start at a community college or junior college. First, let's get you to graduate, okay?"

I felt like he must have been talking about someone else. I had other plans since I was little. I thought I was smart. Even through all the times Marge made fun of me and told me I was dumb or Randy told me to buckle down and concentrate on my school work, I really thought I would do well in life, even if I did make some poor choices along the way. Now, I had Mr. Acker getting creative so I could actually graduate.

Tech math was simply the basics, adding, subtracting, multiplication, and long division. It was called 'tech math' because the kids that were in technical school for most of the day had to fulfill basic math requirements before heading off to culinary school or beauty school. Suddenly, math was the easiest 'A' in my workload.

~ * ~

Chief Clawges was a member of Rotary International. The Rotary

Club of Warminster decided to host an exchange student from Bolivia. Millie Zorilla was my age and the chief turned her over to me when I walked into work one afternoon. I was a little jealous at first because the two of them were laughing and chatting it up in his office. After he called me in, he asked that I show her around school the next day and keep an eye on her. Millie had an endless grin and I couldn't help but like her right away. Plus, she laughed at everything I said, especially my attempts at speaking Spanish. I had taken two years of it and could barely remember a thing.

Millie lived just a block from the police station so she often stopped in to see us. Except for her sitting with me and my friends during lunch, I didn't have much time for her. Besides, she smelled like burlap and wet wool.

A few times, she came into the station, crying. I could hear her trying to explain things to the chief through sobs. I figured she was homesick, but it was something quite different. Mrs. Stockel would look over and make faces at me when Millie arrived. "Here we go," she would say.

~ * ~

After a week or so of Millie showing up, Mrs. Stockel informed me that Millie's host family was being mean to her and that the chief's family took her in. Hearing this, I thought I would vomit. Not only was I worried about Millie and her innocence, but I was jealous. She would get to eat dinner with him, go places with his family.

I didn't even know where he lived, not until he asked me to come over and babysit his kids with Millie. He and his wife, Nancy were going out for dinner and they wanted help for Millie. I got the directions and biked to his house.

His daughter, Kim, was about thirteen and Eric was just in the sixth grade. I had never seen a cuter kid than Eric. Nancy Clawges was petite and just how I remembered her from peeking in the windows at Elaine Powers where she worked. A long thin nose, short dirty-blonde hair and an inability to focus on my eyes for long, she was what I referred to as a forehead communicator. She looked at everyone's forehead when she spoke to them. She didn't smile at me, she just seemed hurried and kept repeating. "El, let's go!" I wouldn't want to call him Elmer either, I thought.

Their home was large and had a huge family den. We kids all watched a movie and when the Clawges came home, the chief insisted on putting my bike in the trunk of his car and taking me home.

"Why is Millie staying with you?" I sat close to the passenger door. "I mean, were things that bad at her host home?"

"She's only here for a few months and the Rotary Club thought the woman she was staying with would be a great option." He rested his hand on my thigh. "She was mean to Millie and we just couldn't have that."

"So, you had to take her in?"

The chief looked at me with a sly grin. "Nothing to worry about."

I stopped pouting. "Your kids are cute." I leaned into his touch. I didn't feel so mad at him anymore.

"We could have cute kids," he said as he drove the car down an old road behind the Navy base.

"Yeah, they would be super cute," I lied. I was worried that if he was being honest and really wanted to be with me someday, our kids would be fat freckled red-heads.

He pulled the car over on the side of the road. There wasn't a house or car to be seen. "Want to get in the back?" His glance was devilish.

"Okay. Isn't your wife going to wonder what took you so long?" I moved slowly to open my door.

"She won't know the difference and it won't take long."

He was right. Within a few minutes, I was getting back into the passenger seat, zipping up my pants. It was degrading, really. What would I say next? "Thanks for the ride?"

Somehow, it was all exciting too. I didn't feel anything sexually, but my heart beat fast and I thought I felt love.

It felt a little shitty however, when we arrived at the Eckenrode's and he slipped me a twenty before removing my bike from the trunk. "For watching the kids."

~ * ~

With Millie being at the Clawges, I was invited over more often. I figured they didn't know what to do with her. It was weird, spending time with his family. I liked Nancy a little, but she was far too inquisitive. She asked questions about my background, foster homes and school. I answered in summary, "My dad died, I was taken away from my mother, foster homes are fine, I like school." And then the inevitable.

"Do you have a boyfriend?"

The chief was standing behind her, nodding strongly. I glanced at him quizzically for a second.

Millie sat next to me at the kitchen table and I thought she had to know what we were talking about. She knew enough English. I wondered if she knew why he was nodding.

"Yes. Yes, I do."

"Oh, good. What's his name?" She was obviously relieved as she stared at my hairline.

"Allan." I thought of a guy from school who asked me out once. I thought he was cute until he started talking.

"How long have you been dating him?" Her tone seemed suspicious.

I thought about how long things had been going on with me and her husband. "Oh, on and off for like a couple years."

"Doesn't sound serious." Nancy stared at me and then at Millie. I caught the chief's eyebrow raise.

Millie piped in and looked at me like I had two heads. "Donde? Where?"

"He doesn't have the same lunch period as us," I quickly responded "You know, comida el different hora." I put my hand to my mouth, pretending to shove food in.

Millie laughed. "You crazy."

"Si, loco." I smirked. "Millie has a boyfriend, right Millie?"

"Yes." She grinned, probably knowing I wanted the direction of the questioning to change. "He nice."

"Her family has a dry-cleaning business in La Paz and her boyfriend works there. They're going to get married." I folded my hands on the table in front of me.

"Lemonade, anyone?" The chief opened the refrigerator.

"I'll take lemonade!" Eric came running in from the family room. Seeing his eager face made me want to curl up and die of guilt. I felt horrible and I wondered how the chief could live with himself.

~ * ~

Every time I left the police station to take the mail to the township building side, I stopped and chatted with everyone. I especially liked to stop in at Parks and Rec and talk with Whitney and Kathleen. Whitney was in charge of all kinds of activities in Warminster and Kathleen was a receptionist or something. I got to know them fairly well because they started asking me to go out for dinner with them on Fridays, when we got paid. I could barely afford to join them, but I did. I liked hanging out with these girls that were in their twenties. I told them stories about the Eckenrodes and having to visit Marge.

"I just show up and then after a few minutes, I leave." I dipped a nacho into sour cream.

"Wait, so the Eckenrodes drop you off and then what, you just stare at Marge for a minute and take off?" Whitney laughed.

"Pretty much." I swirled my straw in my coke glass. "It just sucks, cause it's always a long walk home and whatever Marge's last words were stick in my head the entire way home."

"She doesn't follow you or anything?" Kathleen leaned into the table.

"Are you kidding? I take off so fast, I hide, and then take different routes back to Warminster."

Whitney cut into her wedge salad. "Why don't you call the Eckenrodes to come and get you?"

"I'm not about to waste the quarter and I'm afraid they would just take me right back there since it's court mandated."

"Couldn't you get into trouble for taking off and not trying?" Kathleen asked.

"I'm going to be eighteen in like two months. I'm making a statement to the judge. I'm afraid of Marge. I'm not going to be inside her apartment or whatever and risk her hitting me."

The discussions weren't always about me. Kathleen would talk about a guy she really liked and how he flirted with her. How she worked out at the YMCA every day so he'd flirt with her more.

Whitney talked about her family and her boyfriend, Howard. We discussed upcoming events. She even invited me to go skiing with the Parks and Recreation bus trip to Jack Frost Mountain in the Poconos.

I had never skied before, but I was sure willing to try. Plus, Whitney let me make installment payments for the trip. It was something to look forward to in the winter.

~ * ~

Marge called the judge after complaining to Children and Youth Services that I wasn't holding up my end of the bargain. Penny Freeman and Nancy DeLeon both called me and implored me to follow the rules.

"Fine, but I'm not staying for long." I agreed to visit Marge at her workplace. For some reason, she wasn't working with Betty, Grace, and Kathie anymore. She was now working upstairs with the men at the Residence. Michael, Gerald and Ernie were still there.

I sat on a footstool close to the stairwell exit. "Can we see the ladies?" I asked.

"No, you aren't here to visit with the ladies, you are here to visit with me." She sat across from me with her elbows on her knees, glaring at me. Behind her, Gerald was racing down the hall. He jumped over the breakfast bar and ended in a tumble, only to run back down the hall and start all over. "He does this shit all day long."

We both laughed and he was a wonderful distraction.

"So, what's going on little girl?" She leaned forward. "Look at me when I'm talking to you."

"What?" I caught her eye for a second and then watched Gerald's performance again.

"Jesus Christ!" She got up and placed a chair in front of the breakfast bar so when Gerald approached it for his jump, he stopped in his tracks, completely confused and did a jumping jack pose which he held without moving further.

"Now can you pay attention to me?' she asked.

"Sure." I folded my arms. I watched Gerald march off in a huff, grunting.

"Are you still seeing that manipulator, Emily?"

"Nope." I stood and then sat again.

"Oh, I'm sure you are. You two get together and just go on and on about what a horrible mother I am.

I stood to leave and she quickly got up to block me. "Oh, no, you don't."

My heart was pounding, but I pushed past her with my shoulder and she fell back. I was certain she would get up and hit me.

"Abuse!" she yelled. "I'm telling the judge you abused me."

"What?" I turned and sneered at her in disbelief.

"You just pushed me."

"Tell him whatever you want." I skipped down the stairs and ran out.

I heard her yell out the upstairs window, "I'm calling the police, you abuser."

The entire way home, I worried I was going to get picked up by the Horsham Police. I hated her.

~ * ~

The next month, on Thanksgiving Day, I had to see Marge again. This time, I had to go to her apartment. I was also invited to the Clawges for dinner, so I was going to make the visit quick. Marge answered the door, came out into the apartment hallway and shut the door behind her. She looked panicked.

"Scot's in there," she said.

"What?" I hadn't seen Scot in almost four years. "I thought he lived in South Carolina. Is he visiting for Thanksgiving?"

"Well, not exactly." Marge spoke in hushed tones. "Let's go outside." We walked out to the front of the building. "Julie, Scot's very sick."

"I know." I thought about his screwed up behavior with me. "He killed my dog, remember?" I didn't want to bring up the sexual stuff because when I reported it, Marge denied it to the caseworkers, said she would have known about something like that.

"No, I mean he's really bad. He tried to rape me last night." Her eyes were wide. "He had me pinned against the door and he's strong."

"What the...? Why didn't you call the police?"

"He never went through with it and he took off." Marge looked around like she was completely paranoid. "I'll call the police today if I have to. I just wanted to warn you because he's acting nuts."

"So...you expect me to go in there?" My mouth hung open

slightly.

"Well, yeah. I made Thanksgiving shit. Besides, I'll protect you."

First, I tried to remember the last time that Marge cooked and then I wondered what cosmic joke I was a part of that she was going to protect me. "I can't stay long." I couldn't believe I was going to do this, but I was a bit curious about Scot.

When we walked into the apartment, Scot was standing in the kitchen, trying to shove a peeled banana into the top of an empty 2-liter soda bottle. He was whispering something about Lucifer and didn't even notice me.

I walked past him and took a seat at her kitchen table. The place smelled just like our old apartment, smoke and cardboard. Books, magazines, and files were everywhere. Scot retreated to a back room and I could still hear him whispering. Memories came flooding into my head and my body got sweaty. I thought about bolting, but I felt paralyzed. "I have to go."

"Oh, no, you don't. We are not playing this game!" Marge walked from her stove to where I sat and stood in front of me. "You're going to eat this fucking dinner and be fucking grateful like your fucking forefathers."

I still couldn't move. The sights and smells made me feel like I was twelve again. I was trapped by memories. Scot came out of the back room and seemed surprised by my presence. "Blackie is Lucifer!" he shouted.

That was my cue. "Fuck you!" I yelled and got up to leave, Marge went to block the door but I already opened it, just not quick enough. Something sharp scraped against my cheek as I left. Blood trickled down my face as I opened the apartment building door to outside freedom. I'm never coming back here, I thought.

~ * ~

I briefly told the Clawges about the mark on my cheek. Nancy kept shaking her head. "El, why would the judge make her go there? I don't get it."

"The goal of the state is to get the child back with his or her family." He spoke deliberately. "Now that this has happened, I'm sure he'll retract the order."

A few weeks later, the chief asked me about Scot. "His name is Marvin Scot?"

"Yeah, why?" I walked slowly to his desk.

"He's in Norristown State Hospital. Apparently, he was at the Village Mall in Horsham, putting on quite a show." The Chief looked over his reading glasses. "He had a knife and was carving into his own chest and legs."

"What?" I looked on his desk to see if there was a report or something.

"He was at Village Mall in Horsham, standing on the podium. You know, like where Santa or the Easter bunny would be? He was naked and carving letters into his body."

"Oh my God." I stared at the chief for a moment. "I'm going to go work now and keep in mind, I don't share that guy's blood." I quickly went to my desk.

The chief didn't know anything about my family except that I had been taken away. I occasionally asked him questions about how I could find my biological parents.

He would say I had to wait until I was eighteen to see if there was a way to view my records or maybe my parents were looking for me.

I stayed after work several nights in the past, writing letters to the adoption agency. Mrs. Miller, the caseworker, always took the time to write back and tell me that I had to wait. This day, I would write and remind her that I was turning eighteen soon and I would like my information.

~ * ~

The closer I got to my birthday, the more I thought about how to get out of the Eckenrodes. I discussed it all the time with the girls from Parks and Rec. Finally, one day, Whitney approached me. "My roommate is moving out. Do you think the state would let you live with me?"

"Really?" I was beyond excited. "I don't know. I can ask my caseworker, because she has said that I can become emancipated, but that the money the state would give me wouldn't be enough for my own place." My eyes darted around the floor thinking of possibilities. "Maybe it would be enough for half a place."

"Yeah, ask her." Whitney smiled warmly and then I wondered why she was offering. I wondered if I talked so much about everything that I made her feel guilty or something.

"Are you sure?"

"I'm positive. Let's just see what they say."

~ * ~

My emancipation wasn't exactly freedom, but it was close. My hopes of being out on my own were put to bed once I found out that Whitney wouldn't just be my roommate, she would also be my guardian. Even though I was eighteen, I was still in high school and still a ward of the state. I wouldn't have to see Marge, but I could still get government aid. By moving in with her, she would technically be my foster mother. She had to take some parenting classes at Aldersgate and I found it amazing that she was so easy going about it.

"This is just so weird that you're going to be my foster mother." I stood inside the doorway of Parks and Rec., shuffling Mrs. Stockel's mail.

"I know," Whitney got up from her desk and walked to the front of it. "Just a few more days." She exhaled as she sat on her desk.

"Are you absolutely positive that you want to do this?" I squinted at her like I was searching for a lie.

"I'm positive, Julie." She sat up straight and folded her hands. "It's going to be great. It will be your birthday and Christmas is just around the corner. Really, it'll be great."

"Well, I have my bike, so I don't expect you to cart me around and I can pretty much take care of myself."

"I know." Whitney walked to the door and tousled the top of my head. "You better get back to Mrs. Stockel, she's going to be calling over here in no time."

Tina stood in my bedroom with her arms folded. "I don't understand what the rush is." She watched as I piled my belongings into boxes that I took from work. "Like, why do you have to move today? Can't you just wait until the weekend? I mean, are my parents that horrible?"

"No, of course not." I stopped packing for a minute. "It's just a little crowded around here with Walt's family living downstairs now and you have your boyfriend, Lou, and you're busy with college." I resumed my packing. "Things are just different." I looked up at her. "I still love you and we're still gonna hang out."

"I hope so." Tina pouted as she sat on my bed. "We've had a lot of fun."

"Yes, we have." I laughed, thinking about her drilling a hole through my wall, piercing my ear and us stealing the car all the time.

~ * ~

I unpacked everything quickly at Whitney's. She already had a bed and a dresser from her parents' house set up in my room. She made a pasta dinner for my birthday, along with a little cake. It was really sweet. I felt relaxed, even with the gnawing part of my brain that asked, where are you going next?

The following week, Whitney took me to her parents' home for dinner. They were a lovely couple and I especially liked her mom. She seemed very self-sufficient and artsy. When I pointed things out in her house I liked, she replied with, "Oh, I made that."

Then, what started as a search for a single button for my coat, turned into me making a character out of all the buttons, once I dumped them on the floor. I felt like a little kid, but the buttons were too fascinating not to play with. Whitney's mom seemed to enjoy my character as much as I did.

On Christmas Eve, we went to Whitney's parents' again. Her mother gave me a beautifully wrapped gift. I brought them store bought cookies and felt like a schmuck when she handed me such a pretty box. After dinner, I sat down and opened my present. Inside were a slew of colored tissue wrapped items. They were ornaments she hand-made for me. There were eighteen of them and most were made from wood. There was a goose, a little house, a knitted ball, and my favorite was a little white crib with a wooden baby inside. The outside of the crib had my birthdate painted on it. I was completely amazed at not only her talent, but that she did this for me. I couldn't stop looking at every detail and she sat across from me, watching. "You can get a lot done when you're retired." She giggled.

"I guess so!" I lifted one of the ornaments to show her.

Whitney was very much like her mother. She was creative and patient. She taught me how to make apple pie and lasagna. She knew how to make just about anything and she was a kind teacher.

She also listened when I told her all about the chief. In fact, she didn't say a word for a long time.

When she finally did speak, she said, "You need to get away from him."

"I know. I tried to avoid him at times, but then he just draws me back in." I sat, slumped and defeated. "He gives me cards and music." I sighed. "He told me he loves me."

"Julie, this isn't love." Whitney sat across from me and used her hands to emphasize every word. "He's using you and this is wrong." We sat quietly for a moment. "You need to get a different job." She said it with finality.

She was twenty-four years old and smart. I knew she was right, but I couldn't imagine not going to work at the Police Department. I would miss Mrs. Stockel and the dispatchers. I would miss the witty detectives and the cops that were teaching me how to drive. I couldn't imagine not walking over to the township building and socializing. I would miss him. Then I wondered if he would hire some pretty, thin girl to take my place.

~ * ~

For the next few days, I looked at his cards and newspaper clippings that I cut out over the past few years. I tried to imagine telling him that I quit, but none of it seemed right. I imagined myself going to work at Burger King after school, knowing the police department was less than a mile away and the thought made me sick. I started thinking about California.

Millie went back to Bolivia in the beginning of February. I rode with the chief to take her to the airport. As she sat in the front seat, chattering away in English, I realized she no longer smelled odd. She wore American clothes and I watched her earrings shimmer as she talked. She was quite beautiful. I wondered if her parents would be receiving a rebellious, funny smelling girl on their end.

We said our goodbyes and then the chief drove me straight to my apartment instead of going back to work.

"What are you doing?" I asked as he turned down Grape Street.

"I want to see your place, and Whitney isn't there." He winked.

"Oh." I placed my hands between my knees. I wondered if he wanted to do it on my bed.

We had only done it in his car, or in a field, or the office. My heart raced and yet I felt angry he didn't ask me. I didn't feel like I had a choice. Maybe I never did. Whitney was right. I need to stop this and get away from him. I remembered the Barreres offered San Diego and finishing up at Mira Mesa High. I would have to be really strong to do that.

The following day, it snowed, so I couldn't ride my bike to school. I stood at the bus stop with a bunch of kids I didn't know. As I stood there, feeling cold and empty, I switched on my Don Henley cassette tape. The Boys Of Summer blasted into my ears and I made the decision to move away. Now that I was eighteen, no one could tell me what to do.

That evening, I phoned the Barreres. They were thrilled and said they would pay for my ticket to San Diego. How would I tell Whitney after everything she had done for me?

~ * ~

I had a hundred reasons to move to San Diego and only a few reasons to stay. I thought about how I would tell Karen and her family. They had been so good to me and I was going to miss them something awful.

First, I had to tell Whitney since I wouldn't be living with her anymore. I walked into the living room and Whitney was hanging out with her boyfriend, Howard. Luckily, I never saw them kissing or anything. They just seemed to laugh all the time and he never even stayed over. I found it odd and I felt a little guilty because I had sex in the apartment that one afternoon, but she would never know.

"Hey, Jules," Howard grinned. "Join us."

"Yeah, um. I have something I need to tell you anyway." I sat down and rubbed my knees.

"Oh no." Whitney's eyes widened. "Not..."

"Huh?" I stared at her for a second and thought of what she might be thinking, that maybe I was pregnant. "No!" I laughed. "God no!"

Howard looked at Whitney and then back at me. He may or may

not have known what we were talking about. I was hoping for the latter. I started again. "I, um, well?"

"Get it out girl!" Whitney said.

"I really appreciate everything you've done for me, but I'm going to move to California."

I looked up at Whitney's face. Her expression was caught somewhere in the middle of laughter and anger. I didn't know whether she was going to burst into a giant stream of cackles or she was going to tell me to fuck off. And, the moment of silence was awful. "Oh, and I made a long-distance call that I'll pay you for."

Suddenly, Whitney sat up straight. "Look, I can't tell you what to do, but I wonder if you've really thought about this."

"I have." I lied. The truth was, I thought about it all the time, but I hadn't really thought about it. I just knew I felt like I needed to get out of there. "It would be a great way to get away from stuff, you know." I gave a dramatic nod.

"Oh, I know," she said. "You could still get away by just looking for another job." She placed her elbows on her knees. "Jul, your friends are here, people who care about you."

"The Barreres care about me." I quickly responded. "Plus, I don't know that changing my job is going to change anything."

"You have a point." Whitney sighed while Howard went to the kitchen. "What about school?"

"I'll finish high school out there," I smiled broadly. "Mira Mesa High School, class of nineteen-eighty-five."

"So, you have this all figured out." Whitney blew out a big breath.

"I do." I felt relieved. I was heading to warmth and sunshine and maybe I could start acting again in a school play or something. I could go to the beach all year round like Ralph Macchio did in the movie, Karate Kid, and the Barreres had a pool. I was set.

~ * ~

Karen had so much going on and I wanted to be supportive, but I wasn't sure how. She was going through stuff like probably a normal eighteen year old and I wasn't sure how to handle that. She had a major crush on her hairdresser in the mall and she got a job at Bloomingdales in the baby department. I didn't even know what half the shit was for in the baby department. She was finishing high school with all of our friends and although I had friends at William Tennent High School, it just wasn't the same. The kids at Upper Moreland had been there when everything went down with Marge and I felt like they knew me. Lee was probably the greatest mom I ever met and Karen was living I life that I wish I had. What would she want with me once she had Richard, the hairdresser? It was kind of easy to tell her about San Diego and I explained that it had to do with the chief situation and getting out of here. She understood and I was grateful.

When I told the chief and Mrs. Stockel, she seemed more upset than he. He was a hard one to figure out. I was going away forever and he acted like it was just fine, at first. He later told me he would miss me so much and that he might just join me in San Diego once Eric graduated.

"Great," I said. "So, you want me to wait around for five years?"

"You can always come visit," he said. "Then, you won't have to wait." He hugged me long and hard. "Or...you can just get this out of your system and come back to me."

I felt my stomach drop and my body got tingly. Why did he have to say that?

~ * ~

Whitney drove me to the airport. I had three large boxes and an old suitcase that Whitney's parents gave me. Whitney had tears in her eyes as she helped unload my stuff. For some reason, I wasn't feeling anything. I told some kids at school that I was leaving without any emotion and I felt cold. I had one thing on my mind and it was getting to

California. I thanked Whitney for everything and entered the terminal. As I stood in line, I looked around half expecting to see Marge. I knew the caseworker already told her about my leaving. She probably just didn't tell her how or when. In a way, I was free.

Flying into San Diego was thrilling. The flight path seemed to almost touch the downtown skyscrapers. Jim and Gloria were waiting with huge smiles. "Welcome home, darling." Gloria squeezed me and then we walked to the luggage area where my boxes were in perfect shape.

"Come on kid," Jim said. "Let's get outside so you can see that you're overdressed." Jim pushed a cart with all of my things. Palm trees lined the lanes of the airport and the parking lot. It was gorgeous.

"I think all of your transcripts have been sent to Mira Mesa already." Gloria faced me from the front seat. "You can start tomorrow."

I thought about it as I stared out the window. I had changed schools a million times, but something about a California high school scared me. These kids were going to be cool and sunshiny and blonde. "Is there any way I could go to the beach tomorrow, instead?"

Jim and Gloria looked at each other. Jim was smiling while Gloria looked concerned.

"Just tomorrow. It doesn't seem right that I'll start school as white as I am, I mean these kids are going to be tan and fit." I followed them into the parking lot.

"Julie, the kids are going to love you, just the way you are."

"I'm not comfortable, not yet."

There was were a few moments of silence as we loaded up the car.

"I don't see the harm in one day." Jim grinned at me through the rearview mirror. Gloria playfully socked him in the arm. "What?"

~ * ~

The next morning, Jim loaded one of their bikes into the back of his

El Camino. I was ready with my bathing suit on under my T-shirt and shorts. I had a towel and suntan oil ready to go.

He dropped me off in Mission Bay and headed off to work in Point Loma. I rode along the beach and found a perfect spot. I watched runners and surfers and wondered if one day I would be doing the same. I spent the whole day on the beach soaking up the rays. I met Jim at our pick up point and he commented on my tan. "Sure doesn't take you long, does it?"

"Nope," I smiled "I had color fifteen minutes after you dropped me off."

"Well, then I should have just brought you down here, let you out of the car for a few minutes and then taken you to school." He teased.

"Very funny."

I tried to find something special to wear on the first day, but I only had a mixture of preppy stuff from the Kindts and punk clothing from the influence of Tina. I walked to the high school, certain I looked like a mix of Alex Keaton from Family Ties and Adam Ant. At least I was tan.

The school was really neat because it was all one level and I had to walk outside to get to each class. I didn't really bother to talk to anyone. For the most part, I day dreamed. I thought about the Beans and the chief. I thought about how I probably hurt Whitney's feelings. I wondered if Mrs. Stockel was stuck doing all of my insurance paperwork or if they had hired someone. I couldn't stop thinking about what the chief said and I began wondering if I had made a mistake.

~ * ~

Over the weekend, the Barreres had friends over for a pool party. I stayed off to the side and watched the activities. I felt too insecure to wear a bathing suit in such close quarters and it was fun to just observe. I played with the Barreres' new dog and sat at the table outside. Everyone seemed to be having a great time, but something caught my eye and made me feel instantly nauseous. Jim was in the pool with one of the wives of a guest. They were flirting and then he kissed her. No one seemed to care. I got up and hurried inside. Gloria was in the kitchen preparing side dishes. "Hey, how's it going?" She tightened the lid on a pickle jar.

"Uh, not so great." I was feeling like a hypocrite. "There is a woman who is all over Jim and I'm sorry to tell you that, but, I think it's really disrespectful."

Gloria calmly turned on the sink to wash her hands. "I forgot something at the store." She walked to the back patio door and yelled out, "I'll be back in a few, will someone light the grill?"

It seemed that everyone called back to her with cheery tones. "Come with me." She grabbed the keys to her MG. Gloria and I rode in silence for a few blocks and then she pulled over and turned off the ignition. I stared at her and waited. "Jul, this might be very hard to understand, but, it's okay that someone is flirting with Jim."

"Huh?" I scrunched my face. "Cause they're just flirting and it doesn't mean anything?"

"Kind of," Gloria paused. "Jim and I have friends that we are open with."

"Open with?" I nervously pulled at my bottom lip and stared ahead. I wasn't so sure I wanted to know anymore. "If you're telling me that Jim can be with the woman and you don't care then I don't understand at all. Jim should be with you and you only." I felt guilt flush through my body.

"It's not a big deal, really." Gloria faced me. "Jim and I love each other."

"Well, it's weird." I couldn't look at her. I felt awful because I had my secret and why should I be judging anyone? "I just need to digest this whole thing."

"I understand." Gloria started the car and drove toward the store.

When she parked, I spoke before she had a chance to open her door.

"Look, I don't get whatever it is that you and Jim do, but I have no room to think poorly about it." I let out a deep breath.

"I've been having an affair with my boss for a few years now."

Gloria looked completely confused and shocked. "What boss, exactly?"

"The chief of police." I glanced down.

"Julie, I wouldn't call that an affair, it's called statutory rape."

"No, you don't understand, I love him and he loves me." I pleaded with my eyes for understanding.

Now, Gloria was the one facing forward with nothing to say. "Huh," she said at one point and got quiet again. Finally, after what seemed like ten minutes, she squeezed my knee. "Let's get burger buns before Jim calls in the national guard."

As we walked around the store, I knew I was going to start planning my move back East.

~ * ~

I was back at Philadelphia Airport within four days. This time, one of my boxes fell apart and my personal things came down the conveyor belt, little by little. Nancy Clawges shook her head in embarrassment as she and the chief watched me gather my things. While Nancy went off to use the restroom, the chief touched my hand and said, "If all goes well in your conversation with Nancy, you'll be living with us."

"What?" I shot him a look of disbelief. "Why? Why would...oh never mind." I really didn't know what was going to happen. I didn't think I should ask Whitney to go back with her, I did not intend to go to the Eckenrodes with all those people living there, maybe I could go to the group home until I could get on my feet. Why would Nancy want me living with them?

As we drove, Nancy asked me a myriad of questions. What were my plans? Where was I going to work? What was I going to do with my future? Then she told me what she thought. "You should not be living in an apartment with some twenty-four-year-old, you need structure." and "You cannot go back to working at the police department, you need to find another job. A young woman should not be working with all those men." and finally, "You can stay in our basement, but you'll have rules."

There I was, in the back seat of yet another car of another couple with the husband looking at me through the rearview mirror. This time, I got a wink. I didn't know what to think of any of it. The freedom I felt for six days was now out the door and gone. "Thank you." I responded and put my head back.

The chief carried my stuff down into the basement where there was a cot, a nightstand, a dresser and an area rug. It was all set up for me. The following morning, I woke to him getting on top of me. "What are you doing?" I covered my mouth to hide my breath.

"You have to go to school, young lady." He smiled and brushed my hair with his fingertips.

"I know, but aren't you afraid of getting caught?" I squirmed and felt like I was betraying a woman who might just have my best interest in her heart. "This isn't right."

He slid my underwear down and I crossed my legs to prevent them from coming off. He had his penis out and I realized that if I didn't let him inside, he might put it in my mouth. It hurt, but I knew it wouldn't be long.

A small pool of sperm was on my stomach and he wiped it off with a T-shirt from a laundry basket across the room. "Thank you." He pulled his robe together and tied it closed.

I sat there wondering if this is what I should expect. If this is what I am now, a basement girl. I got up, showered, and went to school. Everyone was just coming back from spring break, so most of the kids just thought my tan was from a vacation.

~ * ~

That afternoon, I called Karen Bean to let her know I was back. She was thrilled and I was wrong, she had plenty of time for me. I told her all about Nancy and the new rules, I did not tell her about what happened that morning.

"Don't you think it's a little effed up that you're living there?"

"I absolutely do, but it's kind of my only option right now."

"What if he tries anything?"

"He did, but he won't. Not again."

"So, why don't you apply at Bloomingdales and then we can work together."

"Okay. I'll try, but I don't want to work in the baby department. Do they have a sporting goods area or something?"

Karen laughed. "No. But, I'm sure you'll find your niche. They'll put you somewhere good. Your personality will force them to place you in a great department."

~ * ~

Within a week, I was working in hosiery. I hated it.

I couldn't believe how important panty hose and tights were for so many women. Plus, I couldn't understand how there was an entire department devoted to just hosiery. Mostly, I people watched because my department was located under the escalators and I could see everyone coming and going.

"Excuse me?" I looked up to find a woman in a full-length fur. "Do you carry Evan Piccone petite Lace?"

I wanted to say, lady, I have no fucking idea and...stop wearing poor little animals. Instead, I smiled. "I'd be happy to look for you."

At least I had the same schedule as Karen. We both worked on Wednesdays and the weekend. I often took a lunch break with Karen if I could coordinate it with someone in Accessories.

~ * ~

It was tiring for the Clawges to keep running me back and forth to Bloomingdales. Luckily, the Chief was good friends with a mechanic. He worked on all the police cars and had access to some used vehicles. After only a month of working, I was able to pick up a white, 1972 Datsun B210 for two-hundred and fifty dollars. The car was previously owned by an old lady and it had tropical seat covers she had sewn herself. I loved that car and as soon as I bought it, I put my bike away. The car was a stick shift and I only knew how to drive an automatic. The chief solved that issue in about twenty minutes. He took an old township car and drove me to the bottom of a hill at a busy intersection. He explained how I should work the clutch and gas and then told me to drive. It was beyond nerve wracking. Horns sounded and people whizzed by while flipping me off. The chief just sat calmly and let me work it out. I guess he figured we could pull this off since he was the head of everything, police wise.

The car conked out on me over and over and my heart raced. I had no choice but to keep trying and get this car up the hill and out the way. When I finally got it, I never had a problem again. Between the cops taking me out for driving lessons in the police cars and now this, surely, I would pass my exam and be able to drive my new car.

The whole Clawges family took me for the test. The two kids sat in the back, while the Chief and Nancy sat in the front with me. It wasn't any fun because Nancy had me drive there in the Chief's police car and she continuously corrected my driving. "You're too close to the line." She crawled her petite frame into the backseat to eye my viewpoint. "El, tell her she's too close to the middle of the road."

"It's a big car," I said.

"She's fine." He sat comfortably in the front since now the rest of the family was in the back seat.

I passed my test and knew that I did a good job, even though I felt like maybe we cheated by using an important car.

All the way home, Nancy kept talking about how I needed to pay for my own insurance and she would use the money from the state for my housing and food. "What are you eating at school, anyway?"

"I don't know." I stared at the road. "Sometimes salad or a sandwich."

"Well, I've noticed that you don't eat a lot and you have lost a little weight. There's nothing wrong with that, but I don't want you to have some eating disorder."

"Trust me." I glanced at her with a wrinkled brow. "I don't have an eating disorder."

~ * ~

Things at school were going well, for the most part. I was driving to school like most of the other kids, I had a discount at Bloomingdales, so I bought a pair of Guess jeans, my braces were off and some crew from the school yearbook came and pulled me out of Government class one day to take pictures of me. They told me I was nominated for two categories for seniors. I could not imagine what they were and I was hoping I wouldn't be humiliated by getting least likely to succeed or something.

The chief came down to the basement at least once a week and I dreaded it. I started keeping a journal and when my English teacher asked us to write a paper about our future, I wrote about the chief. I wrote about how all of it made me feel and that maybe I didn't have a way out because I was emotionally torn and I didn't know what I was going to do in my life. I felt that all of my dreams were a joke and I wasn't going to amount to much. The more I wrote, the worse I felt and I guess it started to show.

Mr. Tyler asked me to stay after class one day. "Julie, you have written some very good papers in my class. The essay about your father's death was poignant and exquisite." He sat on the edge of his desk, rolling my paper in his hands. "This paper, however," he sighed "this paper scares me. It's good, really good, but you need to get out of this situation."

I stood in front of him grasping my backpack. "I know." I felt pressure in my face. Tears were on the way.

"Is all of this true?" He let out another large breath and crossed his arms. My paper was tucked in there somewhere. I just wanted my grade.

"It is." I wiped my cheek.

"Good God." He unraveled my paper and tried to flatten it out.

"You can't tell anyone, please, Mr. Tyler."

"But it's my job to…"

"No, please." I stepped toward him. "You said that our papers are confidential."

"I know, but this is wrong."

"I'll take care of it. I promise. Please," I pleaded.

"Okay, I need to think about all of this." Mr. Tyler shook his head and walked around his desk.

"You got an, A, of course. Careful with your comma placement."

"Thank you." I took my paper and stuffed it in the bottom of my bag.

~ * ~

At home, Nancy harped on me and told me I was depressed. It was interesting she never asked me if I was, she just told me. "I called Aldersgate and you're going to see a counselor there." If only Emily was still there, I thought.

"But I have a caseworker already and I already went through seeing a psychiatrist a long time ago and he said that I was normal."

"Julie, something is wrong and you need a counselor." She stared at my forehead longer than usual.

~ * ~

At Bloomingdales, some older lady employee in handbags wanted to switch to hosiery and I was grateful for the change. Women were even nuttier about purses than they were about stockings. They had to caress the bags and go through the pockets and stand in front of the mirrors. I had to bullshit my way through that as well. During slow times, I looked closely at the tags and found that Carlos Falchi used water buffalo for leather and Gucci not only made bags, wallets, and key rings, but there was also a Gucci T.V. guide cover for only one-hundred and twenty-five dollars. I wondered why these ladies were buying Louis Vuitton bags for four hundred dollars when you could get one in downtown Philly off a cart, for only twenty bucks. It made me mad that so many people could just come in and get these items when my entire paycheck was now going to gas and that damn car insurance.

When summer came and I was going to work full time, maybe I would have enough to get out on my own. I would never buy a Gucci T.V. guide cover, even if I did have lots of money, but at least maybe I could fend for myself. The state said I could apply for help with college, but that would be even more money for gas and books. Things were not turning out how I planned.

I started seeing the head honcho at Aldergate, Moises Paz. At first, it was awkward. I didn't say much except that I didn't know why I was there. He was kind and helped me with planning as far as college went. He gave me some hope. "Community college only has to be for two years and then you can finish up at a four-year college."

"I don't know what I'm doing. I don't even know what classes to take." I felt helpless.

"You don't need to know right now. Just get the basics out of the way and maybe take a few side classes that spark your interest." His eyes were warm and smiley.

~ * ~

I continued to see Moises every week and I finally started to open up to him.

Nancy questioned my therapy if she wasn't asking me about boys or what I ate. "You're going to your prom, right?"

"Absolutely not," I answered.

"You have to go to prom, you'll always regret it if you don't."

"I don't want to go. I don't have anyone to go with and I don't want to wear some frilly stupid dress." I looked at her like she was crazy.

"What happened to that boy you liked at school?" She sat down at the kitchen table and shoved a grilled cheese in my direction.

"It didn't work out." I pushed the plate away. The more she wanted me to eat, the less I complied. She was getting out of hand.

"I know. Bob Berns!" She jumped up.

"You want me to take the man who sold me my car?"

"No, his son, Paul."

"Oh no, I will not go with Paul. He's a dork and he used to draw cats getting tortured and pass them back to me in homeroom."

"Boys are stupid sometimes. He doesn't do that anymore, right?"

"No." I put my elbows on the table and pressed my head into my palms. She was going to win. She was going to push this issue until she won.

When the chief got home from work, she went through the usual list of questions about where he had been and why he was late and now I was beginning to wonder, too. After the interrogation, she said, "Wouldn't it be great if Paul Bern took Julie to the prom?"

He placed his keys on the counter and looked at me. "If that's what she wants."

"I don't," I responded.

"She has to go to her prom."

~ * ~

I was dress shopping the next week. It seemed that every dress in 1985 was pastel. It made no sense to me, because it was a time of punk and edgy fashion. I didn't want to look like Madonna for this prom, but I also refused to look like a cracked Easter egg. I found a royal blue fitted gown in a boutique and put fifty dollars down on it. The dress was far more expensive than the average prom gown, but if I had to do this, I was going to do it right. Every week, I drove to the boutique and put more money down. With the shoes, my outfit was almost four hundred dollars and luckily, I needed no alterations.

Paul pulled up at the Clawges with his dad's 300z. Nancy promptly took out the camera and took pictures of all of us. Her mom even came for the event. Eric stood close to me and grabbed onto my dress like he didn't want me to leave the house. I wore make-up that evening and walked cautiously in heels down the front walkway. Maybe this wasn't going to be so bad.

Twelve Caesars was so fancy with beautiful pillars and chandeliers. I attended a wedding or two in the past and went to a township dinner once, but this was by far the most upscale place I had ever been. Girls in my class approached me and commented on my dress. "I didn't know it was you, I did a double take," one girl said.

I wasn't sure if that was a compliment, but I surely took it as one.

"Everyone looks so beautiful," I responded. The air smelled like Aqua Net and just as I imagined, I thought the Easter Bunny might pop out in the crowd due to all the pastels. I felt like my dress was even better than Dynasty and Nolan Miller's designs.

Paul and I got in line to get our pictures taken, but only because he wanted to. I wasn't too thrilled about the idea, because although I accepted the whole evening and really felt good, I didn't want a foo foo souvenir of the event. Plus, even in my heels, Paul was about a foot taller than me.

As we stood in line, a girl that I barely even knew approached me. "Did you know that you got class wittiest?

"I did?" I felt my heart speed up. It was the best compliment of all.

"Yeah, and you got nominated for best smile, but you came in like, fourth."

"Wow, thanks for telling me."

We all sat down at a table with Paul's friends. I didn't care where we sat because I could always get up and visit with whomever. We ate a salad, a chicken dish, and then cheesecake. During dinner, the DJ played, "Follow You, Follow Me." by Genesis. At some point, our class decided that would be our song. The song was magical. I forgot about Paul sitting next to me, I forgot about everyone in the ballroom, and I forgot about the chief, too. I took a few minutes and felt overwhelming joy. I felt hope for the future and I felt strong. Maybe I could become a comedian.

I barely ate dinner and I definitely didn't eat dessert. No one on Dynasty ever ate sweets. I got up from the table a few times to go visit with friends. When I returned to my seat, Paul nudged me. "I don't feel good."

"What?" I glared at him and then noticed he was pale and a little sweaty.

"We need to go. I think I'm sick from the cheesecake."

I didn't know if I was relieved or pissed.

Paul tipped the valet when his father's 300z was brought to the entrance. For some reason, Paul drove into Philly and went up Broad Street. This way was going to add an extra half hour to our drive. He swerved every so often and I had to push his shoulder or call his name. He seemed to be falling asleep. I wondered if he drank something. He went off with his friends a few times, but he swore it was the cheesecake. It seemed to take forever to get back to the Clawges, but when we got there, I opened my door, said, "Thanks," and rushed inside.

Kim and Eric were in the family room, watching Saturday Night

Live. "What are you doing here?" Kim asked.

"Paul got sick." I pulled my shoes off and hurried toward the basement so that I could get out of the dress. When I returned, I asked where their parents were. "They're with Paul's parents." Kim laughed. "My mom was saying she hoped you guys would head down to the shore afterward."

"What? Why would we do that?" I sat down and Eric moved close to me.

"I don't know." Kim shrugged. "To do the nasty, like everyone else on prom night."

I shuddered. "Eww."

"I'm glad you're home." Eric said.

"Me too." I winked.

When the Clawges returned, Nancy came in, shaking her head. She was giddy, but kept saying, "I can't believe it. I can't believe you're home already."

"Yeah, what a waste of money and time, huh?" I responded.

~ * ~

When I graduated, the Clawges came to the ceremony. I really didn't want them to. It all seemed fake. I didn't want a party or anything, I just wanted to take a drive and get away. I took a few friends to northern Bucks County and we scouted around, looking for a Llama farm I heard about. One of my friends said, "Julie, when you write a book someday, you have to call it, In Search Of The New Hope Llama. We never found the farm.

~ * ~

Since working at Bloomingdales didn't pay enough for me to cover my car insurance, gas, and college classes that I would be starting, I got a job at a sheet metal company. I wore a uniform just like the guys that worked in the tiny factory. We all looked and smelled like we worked at Jiffy Lube. At first, I worked a metal stamp press. I absolutely hated the stamp press and it bored me. I couldn't imagine being content just sitting on a stool and pulling a lever down on metal. Of course, the guys seemed to have much more detailed machines and some were welding intricate pieces.

The supervisor, John, shuffled from one station to another checking on jobs. If the job was finished, it went straight to the packing area and usually, Yuri would leave his station to drive the parts to a client. First, the pieces were boxed and then John would fill the box with foam peanuts from a large overhead chute. I liked watching him. He looked like an old man happily tinkering in his garage.

Lunch time was awkward, I couldn't sit around with all the guys, so I usually went outside and sat against the building. Once, I made the mistake of walking around and found myself in an alley where I spotted a Warminster Police car. I was excited to see an old coworker, so I headed to greet him. As I approached the vehicle from behind, I realized the officer was staring at a magazine and masturbating. I quickly escaped, hopefully without being seen. They really are just a bunch of pigs, I thought.

Within a week, I got Yuri's job of driving parts. I was sure it had to do with poor workmanship on my part. I was probably slower than most and my shoulder was killing me from pulling the lever.

John allowed me to work the peanut chute and many times I accidentally over-filled the boxes. "That's alright, no harm done," He always came quickly to my aid before I could even apologize.

I usually drove the company station wagon to places that were not more than a half hour away. Occasionally, I drove a truck that was the size of an average U-Haul. The entire trip, I would keep the windows shut in the heat, thinking I could sweat my excess weight off.

I wasn't eating much either. The more Nancy nagged me about

food, the more I wanted to give it up. I got salads sometimes for lunch and would occasionally meet Karen in the mall for a bite.

Things had to line up to spend time with Karen. It had to be a day that we got breaks at the same time and when she wasn't with Richard, which was, practically all the time. I missed her. I sometimes went to the baby department to visit her. Each week, she seemed to be thinner. She had never had a problem with weight, but she was looking like a matchstick.

"I've practically moved in with Richard," Karen said.

"Really?" I pulled a baby dress off the rack and tugged on the ribbon. I felt self-conscious and couldn't make much eye contact. "How are your parents doing with that?"

"I think they're getting over the fact that Richard is older than me. Plus, my mom is now getting free haircuts." She laughed.

"Well, that's good." I thought about her mom's beauty and her laugh as I unfolded a baby Bloomies sweatshirt and held it up. "How is your mom?"

"She's good."

"Good. So, any change of heart regarding college?"

Karen grabbed the sweatshirt from me and folded it perfectly. "You know I hate school."

"Well, you could have changed your mind." I crossed my arms. "Tina is going for fashion marketing. I don't know what I'm going to go for, I'm just going."

"That's great." Karen smiled. "I'm not. I want to work here and I want to someday be a Mom."

The wonderful thing about Karen was we never really argued. She was just so easy going. But, now we were growing apart because of our plans.

My plan didn't amount to much, but it was a step in the right direction. I needed to get back to California, away from the chief, away from his wife. I wasn't about to ask the Barreres to assist in that, not after what happened last time. I could get past their indiscretions, but I didn't think they would be willing to get over my indecision. I would have to make it happen on my own.

I worked at the sheet metal company through the second semester of summer classes at Bucks County Community College and then quit. It wasn't worth forty hours a week to me. Bloomingdales wasn't much better, but if I worked there full time, at least I wouldn't have to dress like a dude. I moved into accessories and worked with three really great girls. Michelle worked across the aisle in fine jewelry and Terry and Mary worked with me. We laughed all the time and work wasn't so bad. After a few months, someone in HR offered me a position in the boy's department with a slight raise and I took it.

The boy's department was right down the hall from babies, so I would see Karen more often. My manager was female, but I was back to working with mostly boys. They were all very cute, but Jonathan was beautiful. He had beautiful brown eyes and thick black hair. He referred to himself as a 'Jamaican Jew'. He looked Italian, but with fine features. His estranged father was a movie director, his mother a realtor, and he was expected to do great things. Like me, he didn't know exactly what he was going to do, but whatever it was, it would be big.

Jonathan and I started spending time together. He wanted to take breaks with me and go to movies and we laughed all the time. I started spending a lot more money. I needed gas and books for school and nice clothes to be with Jonathan. Thankfully, I was getting a few grants for still being considered a ward of the state, because I was spending everything so that I could keep up with him. He seemed to do everything in a big way. He talked about opening drive-thru video stores and he and his friend, Stuart, were going to open a slew of these places. He talked about Stuart a lot. Stuart was a comedian and Jonathan really wanted me to meet him.

On my nineteenth birthday, Jonathan invited me to his house. "We'll have a nice evening in." he said. We had made out a few times, but I think we were both willing to go farther. His neighborhood was filled with mansions. The homes were beautiful and tastefully adorned with Christmas lights.

We had sex within a half hour of my arrival and it was extremely painful, but I didn't care. He was just so gorgeous and I couldn't believe he would ever want me. Afterward, we went to get take-out Chinese. The entire way there, he talked about how maybe we shouldn't have done that and he really liked me, He did hurt me, and just, maybe we shouldn't have done it.

"Well, we did it and that's that." I responded.

"Did you like it?"

"It was okay." I answered. "Maybe I can learn to like it."

~ * ~

Thankfully, there was nothing too awkward between us. We continued to hang out and Jonathan started driving to Warminster to pick me up. I watched the Chief's reaction to see my beautiful boyfriend and looked like he might get sick. Nancy flirted and giggled in his presence.

We did so much together that sometimes I would miss class, just to be with him. I took him to a Christmas party at the Kindts and I felt so proud to be with him. Of course, I spent quite a bit of money on my outfit and we had to bring a house gift to the party, so I used my Bloomingdales discount. I bought everyone gifts that year.

When the holidays were over, Jonathan came to pick me up one night so that I could meet Stuart.

Like us, Stuart was only nineteen years old, yet he had a beautiful apartment that overlooked the Philadelphia skyline and the art museum. Jonathan and Stuart were playful with each other and I suddenly became Jon's shadow. "Let's go to Atlantic City," Stuart opened a bottle of champagne and poured us all a glass.

"Will those people let you go and then just stay down here tonight?" Jonathan asked me.

"I'll go. I don't care what they say." I looked for a phone.

"You can call them, but dial star six-nine first, this guy is a cop or something, right?" Stuart laughed and clicked Jonathan's glass again.

I dialed and Nancy answered. "Hi, Um, I'm staying with Jonathan tonight."

"Where?" Nancy sounded so rude.

"Downtown. I'll be back tomorrow."

"I don't think that's a good idea."

"You wanted me to go to the beach with Paul, right?" I looked at Jonathan and rolled my eyes. He and Stuart got very quiet so they could listen in.

"That's different, we know him."

"Well, I know Jonathan and I'll be back tomorrow." I hung up on her.

"Well done!" Stuart ran to me and hugged me.

I sat in the back of Stuart's Porsche while Jonathan rode up front. The two chatted when Stuart wasn't blasting music. I was definitely the third wheel and beginning to regret my decision. We were in Atlantic City within an hour.

Stuart somehow got us into a casino even after I was carded and initially denied access. I spent a total of five dollars and inadvertently pulled Jonathan away from a game of Black Jack when I yelled, "I won!" after getting ten dollars from a five-dollar slot machine. I kept my winnings and watched Stuart and Jonathan laugh and lose.

Once back in Philly, Stuart set Jonathan and I up in a gorgeous master bedroom. We started to have sex and Stuart came back into the room, naked. I sat up quickly.

"Stuart, go to bed." Jonathan laughed. He seemed so nonchalant and I couldn't understand why Jonathan wasn't as freaked out as I was.

"What did he expect?" I slouched the covers back down so that I could feel Jonathan's skin.

"He may have wanted you or he may have wanted me." Jon stared kissing my neck.

"Is that normal?" I pulled his face so that I could see his eyes.

~ * ~

Jonathan drove me back to the Clawges the next morning. The whole way, I tried not to ask too many questions, but the idea of Jonathan being with Stuart was very much on my mind and it freaked me out. At the same time, I thought about some of the women I thought were gorgeous and how I had even wondered about what it would be like to kiss them. That was my secret though, and there was nothing I could do about it, nothing I would do about it, anyway.

"Jonathan, are you just using me as like a front?"

"No, Julie, I really like you. I just don't know what's going on. I just want to live and be free."

"But, others' feelings are involved and I can't be with you if you have some weird thing going on with Stuart. I've been the other person and it sucks."

As we pulled into the Clawges' driveway, the Chief came out and started yelling at both of us. I never saw him angry before. When I got out of the car, Jonathan rolled down his window and yelled, "Let me know if you need me to come back and save you," as he pulled away.

The Chief called me a slut and wanted to know who I thought I was. I walked past him, got my keys, and went back out to my car. He followed me. "Your car is dead," he said. "It's not going to start."

I suddenly felt like I would completely lose control, an anger that was similar to when Marge hit me and I was supposed to just take it. I unlocked my car door, got in and tried to start the ignition. Nothing.

"What the fuck? This is my car!" I screamed. I tried to start it again, in vain. "I hate you." I looked at his eyes as he stood next to my car.

"You don't hate me," he said quietly. "You love me and I love you." He reached out his hand to touch my shoulder.

"Get off of me!" I leaned further into my car. I sat in the driver's seat for what seemed like forever, just staring ahead and trying not to cause a tantrum. My jaws clenched and I could only feel hatred. He just lingered around the car for a while and then finally went inside the house.

When I felt somewhat calm, I went into the house to find him. Instead, I found Nancy sitting at the kitchen table. She looked exhausted.

"Do you know how worried we were?" She looked at some spot on the refrigerator instead of me.

"I was just with Jonathan, I was fine." I started for the basement steps.

"How do we know that?" she squealed with a tired voice.

"Because I'm nineteen, you're not my parents, and you can trust me." I pounded down the steps.

"I need to go to work today. I need my car!" I yelled.

"Well, guess what?" she yelled back. "Your insurance is due and that car is in our names."

I ran back up to the kitchen. "I paid for that car, it's mine. You're just some kind of control freak" I wanted to cry, but I was not going to give her that.

"Your insurance is due." Nancy got up and walked away from the table. "Pay it by tomorrow."

By the time I needed to go to work, the chief had my car started. He must have pulled some wire or something. Maybe he just unhooked the battery that morning. I drove to work and thought about how I was going to come up with the insurance money. I had been spending like crazy, either doing things with Jonathan, or trying to look good for him. I worried the entire shift and started thinking about the unthinkable, stealing.

I looked around the boy's department after a woman bought some polo shirts with cash. I slipped the money into my pocket instead of the drawer. I was a nervous wreck leaving the store that night. The employees all had to walk past security guards and out through a narrow hallway. The guards could check bags if they felt it necessary, but I wasn't sure if they could check pockets.

There were a group of little black and white screens from all the cameras in the store and I didn't know if one had been on me that night. I tried to act confident as I walked through.

I gave the money to Nancy that night and lay awake, wondering what I had become. I was a cheating thief who wanted to kiss a girl, with a gay boyfriend and no future.

~ * ~

Every day felt aimless and I could barely get myself to class. Jonathan and I weren't spending much time together and Karen was always busy. I went out with another guy, Alan, from the store, but he probably thought I was a little weird after I convinced him to take me to see this really cool movie I heard about. It was playing at an artsy theater. I knew Desert Hearts was a film about lesbians. I read about it. I acted shocked and disgusted as we left the theater.

I continued to steal money from Bloomingdales. Sometimes it was five dollars, sometimes forty. I even continued to do it after I saw the maintenance crew up in the ceiling and I wondered if they were installing cameras. My stealing went on for a little over three weeks. It came to an end on a Saturday, as I was passing the security area. A female police officer pulled me into a small room where other security was waiting. I was taken to the Abington Police Department and arrested. Within an hour, the chief had the charges dropped and I was to pay one hundred and seventy-five dollars in restitution, plus I was obviously fired and told never to enter Bloomingdales again.

I was embarrassed, but only because I didn't want the Beans or Jonathan to think poorly of me.

They were all I had left. Other than that, I felt numb and I really didn't care about anything. I got another retail job at the first place that would take me, a small boutique in the same mall as Bloomingdales. I hated it, but a job was a job and I needed to make money for the restitution.

The boutique was filled with frilly pastels and everything I wasn't. I put on a great show and convinced the manager that I could sell every pink and mint green ensemble that the little store carried.

~ * ~

I paid my restitution early so I wouldn't have to appear in court. I went to work, sometimes showed up for class, and tried not to talk to the Clawges. Nancy pried more than ever and sometimes followed me to the basement. "You need help. I think you should talk to someone."

"I do talk to someone. I talk to Moses, at Aldersgate, remember? I need to get out of here, is what I need."

"Where are you gonna go?" she asked. "You have nowhere."

"Sure I do," I responded.

"Oh yeah?" She crossed her arms like a child and stood at the bottom of the stairs, not crossing into 'my' space. "Where?"

"I'll figure it out," I said.

"I think you're headed for trouble and you know what?"

I looked at her. "What?"

"I think you're going to try to kill yourself."

I stopped pretending to fold clothes and looked at her in disbelief. "What?"

"I think you're going to commit suicide and my kids will be devastated. They love you. Please call Moses." Nancy turned and went back up the stairs.

I sat on my bed and pulled out my journal from beneath the covers. There were no entries regarding the idea of suicide, but there were plenty about an unnamed guy that was using me and how he was becoming more disgusting and how I had no idea what love was or if there was love to be had. The entries were pathetic and I was certain Nancy saw them. It didn't matter. What did matter was that her idea was brilliant. The idea of just leaving the planet seemed calming to me. I felt an odd sense of relief.

~ * ~

I started thinking about different suicides the detectives at my old job told me about. I didn't want to leave a mess for anyone and most of what they told me was horrific. Especially the guy who left his car running in his garage during the summer. His body was found about six days after his death and he was full of maggots. Then I remembered the dryer hose death. Someone tied a dryer hose to their exhaust pipe and died that way.

A few days later, I started packing my stuff and slowly took it out to my car. I packed everything I owned into the trunk so there would be no remnants of me in their house. Luckily, no one was home when I left.

I drove to a hardware store, bought a rubber hose and some wire. I had no idea of where I was going to go, but I knew it had to be somewhere away from the general population, yet somewhere where I wouldn't be dead for days.

I remembered a small church on a riverbank. It was just outside of Warminster and quite remote. I picked the sixth parking spot because six was my favorite number. I systematically set up my demise without much thought at all.

I restarted the car. I had my Purple Rain tape in, but I didn't really hear it. I stared ahead at the church and I begged through the silence and smelly air that I be freed from all of my sins and I would be forgiven for having been a bad person.

Chapter Twenty-five

I woke to bright lights and a humorless nurse.

I had a pounding headache and the nurse seemed to take pleasure in moving me around, almost forcefully. "Are you mad at me or something?" I squinted.

"Oh, does that matter?" She moved a tray in front of me with a large Styrofoam cup and straw. "A few hours ago, you wanted to be dead, right?"

I didn't respond. I remembered stumbling around the church parking lot. My car died and then I decided I wanted to live. I got out to get fresh air and now I was obviously in the hospital. I didn't want to regret not starting the car again

"Drink some water. A psych doc will be by to talk with you."

"I don't need a psychiatrist, I decided that I want to live."

"Right." She abruptly left, yanking the curtain shut.

I lay there thinking about the stupidity of my actions that day. How am I going to explain this away to some shrink, I wondered. And, why did my car die? I wasn't sure what to feel or think, because if I died, I wouldn't have to explain anything to anyone. Now, I was just going to somehow get out of there without anyone finding out.

Just as I was able to sit up a little and drink some water, the chief peeked in and my ideas of secrecy were squashed.

He slowly walked toward me and then reached out to touch my head. I turned away from him and he quickly retreated, "I'm sorry. I'm sorry if I had anything to do with this."

I focused on a certain speck on the ceiling and kept my eyes there. "Yeah, well, you didn't. Feel better?"

"I realize I'm probably not the person you want to see right now and Nancy is kind of feeling the same way." He stood a few feet from my bed like he was afraid. "Nancy called the Beans and had them call Jonathan so you can have a support system."

There went the idea of keeping this semi-private, I thought.

"She also called the people out in California and I guess your old foster mom is on her way here."

"What?" I sat up further. "Is she crazy?" Just then, the psychiatrist walked in and chuckled.

"I think we are all a little nuts, don't you?" He looked at me and then at the chief.

"Yeah," the chief sighed. "I'm going to go now. Call if you need anything." He began to leave but then stopped and turned. "Oh, your car is in the hospital parking lot and your keys are at the nurses station. I had an officer bring it over."

"The car works?" I asked.

"Of course it works, and that hose has been disposed of."

The chief left and I was there alone with the psychiatrist. Now, I just had to convince him I was fine and could leave.

"How are you feeling?" The doctor casually sat back in a chair near my bed.

"With the exception of a headache, I feel fine." I smiled. "I made a very poor decision this morning and I realize I'm meant to be here, I mean, here on Earth."

"Uh, huh." He stared at me. "So, what led you make such a decision?"

"I don't know, things were getting rough and I didn't want to deal."

"There are other options, you know."

"Yes, I know. I'll be sure to utilize other options if things get tough again. When can I leave?"

"You're going to need to stay at least a few days for observation."

"Why?" I grabbed the sheet under me and tugged at it. What he was saying was not what I expected and I wanted out.

"Look, it's not so bad down there. You'll probably have your own room and there are activities."

"Down there?"

"Yes," the doctor stood. "The psyche unit is downstairs and it's lovely, don't worry."

I was transferred downstairs and slept most of the first day. The whole experience was a blur.

Karen and Jonathan visited and I apologized to them while feeling like a freak. I played gin rummy with some of the other hostages and made the most of it.

Gloria came into town and visited a few times. She asked me to return with her to San Diego. She even threatened that she would go to the authorities and tell on the chief if I didn't agree to go back with her. I somehow convinced her not to do that and I should have just gone with her right then and there.

~ * ~

When I left the mental facility at Warminster General, I did not return to the Clawges. I went to stay with the Beans for a while. Karen was living with Richard, so I just stayed in her room. It was great to have her little sister, Sherry, around and Lee helped me in planning my future.

I had a part time job with Wilburger's Ski Shop, selling ski apparel, which I knew almost nothing about, and Bill Bean got me a job at his workplace, National Label Company. At night, I attended school and worked some more. I just wanted to get my own apartment and not have to rely on everyone.

At school, I excelled in psychology and acting. I was the only teenager in my psychology class, so I felt really honored when the adults in my study group accepted my offer to write a play for our presentation. I figured I would have no problem covering many of the diagnoses for mental illness. I would use my family members to build the characters. Our group walked away with an 'A'.

I usually pulled an 'A' in acting, too. Once, I performed a monologue playing Marge. I knew her so well. I could easily repeat a tantrum or one of her lectures, verbatim. Sometimes I may have a gone a little too far. I guessed people weren't used to that type of behavior. So, when I jumped off the stage after my presentation, I found my classmates to be wide-eyed and shaken.

"I'm not like that." I explained while I returned to my seat.

~ * ~

Bill was an executive at the label company and he worked upstairs. I worked on the factory floor. I was part of a team that inspected Vaseline and Jergen's labels as they whizzed by our eyes on waxy coated sheets. Often there were bad prints that went through my machine. I would have to stop everything, find the next good label and splice everything together. It was so boring and many of my coworkers had been doing it for years.

A few months in, when the receptionist upstairs needed to go on maternity leave, I was asked to fill in for her and possibly take her job full time. I was nervous because she was beautiful and her professional voice could be heard throughout the plant all day long as she called for the bigwigs over the loud speaker. She even called for the owner sometimes and the thought of doing that made me a little nervous, "Jim Shacklett, call the operator, please. Jim Shacklett, call the operator."

I took the offer and hoped my factory coworkers wouldn't judge me. Suddenly, when I was wearing dress clothes and clopping along the factory aisles in my heels to get upstairs, I always made sure I stopped and said hello to everyone. They were still my associates and I respected them. Plus, I was really hoping they weren't laughing at me.

~ * ~

Within six months, I was living in an apartment with a roommate and I had a new car. I also had some weird pain in my stomach that seemed to get worse every day after lunch. I tried changing what I ate and nothing seemed to help.

Since I had insurance, I decided to visit my doctor and after a few tests and a lower G.I., a lab technician called to tell me I had a volvulus my intestines had turned around. Since I had the procedure, my volvulus had, "Most likely flipped back."

"I still have pain," I told the woman on the phone.

"Oh, well, that's probably just the barium chalk. That'll pass and you'll feel better by tomorrow."

The pain continued and I started to feel clammy. I passed out at my desk just around four-thirty in the afternoon. Mrs. Shacklett was the one to take me to the emergency room. X-rays were taken and then a surgeon, Dr. Pezzi, came to speak with me.

"I recognize your name," I said.

"My wife is a doctor," he smiled. "Maybe you have seen her."

I remembered my mishap in eighth grade when I fell off my chair and accidentally stabbed myself with scissors. "I did see her, yes," I thought about how Marge refused to take me back to Dr. Pezzi to get my stitches out and instead took them out herself.

"So, Miss Beekman, I have to ask you some questions and I want you to be honest, okay? No need to be shy."

"Okay," I answered quietly.

"How often do you go to the bathroom?"

I looked at him, with an eyebrow raised.

"Number two," he clarified.

"Once a week, I guess." I shrugged. "Like a normal person does?" Inside, I was second guessing my assumptions about other's habits.

Dr. Pezzi pulled up a chair and sat close to the gurney where I was sitting. He spoke slowly and now softer. "Normal people don't go once a week," he said. "They go once a day, sometimes more than that."

I stared at him in disbelief.

"Let me ask you." He paused to glance down at my chart. "Is there some reason that you didn't know this? Can you think of anything?"

I didn't know how to answer him.

"Anything traumatic or maybe some family habits that you may have grown up with that led you to believe this was normal?"

"Yes," was all I answered, even though I knew what he was getting at.

"Okay." He grinned weakly. "So, you are nineteen." He sifted through my paperwork. "The problem is, you are nineteen and you have intestines of an eighty-year old."

"What do you mean?" I sat up and pulled the hospital sheets up to my neck.

"Your colon is far too long and it's winding around your stomach. If you were to do some of those Jane Fonda aerobics today, you could have died, because your stomach could burst."

"Really?"

"Really." He stood. "So, you need surgery and I'm going to admit you. You can't have much to eat for a while, maybe some clear Jell-O or apple juice, okay?"

"Well, there go my big dinner plans," I joked.

In the following days, any modesty I had was diminished by biopsies and procedures. I wouldn't even wish any of it on Marge. Thankfully, the Beans came to the hospital a lot, which kept things light.

My surgery was a sigmoid colectomy. The intestine was cut at two ends, part of the colon was removed, and then the ends were reattached.

If for some reason the reattachment didn't work, I would have had a colostomy bag. The idea was great fodder for discussion with visitors.

Lee Bean was there almost every day and the Kindts came to visit often. My boss, Jimmy Shacklett, came and brought me a paycheck and told me not to worry about anything.

~ * ~

One afternoon, a nurse came in and handed me a carnation. "A gentleman just came by to drop this off for you."

I hated carnations, they smelled like my dad's funeral. Attached to the flower was a note from the chief. He hoped I was feeling better and sent his love. I threw it in the trash and promptly called Mrs. Stockel. He wasn't going to reel me in again.

"Mrs. Stockel, it's Julie. I'm so sorry to swear, but when you see the chief, could you tell I said he can fuck off?"

"I would be happy to," she snickered.

Being in the hospital for almost a month gave me plenty of time to think. I needed to know more about my family history and stop depending on the Beans and the Kindts. I had been adapting to how others lived and tried to emulate all these families that weren't even mine. I wanted my own way of living and my own history.

I went back to work and started taking more trips to Michigan. Any long weekend or days I could get, I made the drive. I stayed with Uncle Lou and Aunt Dolores. They seemed to enjoy my comings and goings as I discovered little tidbits of information.

~ * ~

I was getting ready to embark on another journey to find my biological family. As soon as the semester was over and I got some time off of work, I drove to see Mrs. Miller, the caseworker at the adoption agency in Michigan, where I was born. It had been nineteen years of wondering, but only a few years of searching, usually letters and phone calls. Maybe in person, I could get more.

I had been given a folder when I was younger that stated my nationality and how my parents appeared physically, but not much else. At first, the caseworker wouldn't tell me any more than I already knew, which I expected, but I wouldn't accept. A few times she slipped and referred to me as Shirley. "Shirley," I repeated. "Is that my mother's name?"

"Now, Julie," Mrs. Miller said, "You can register to find your parents." She closed my file and tapped it on the desk like she was straightening it. "If they're looking for you, they will have registered too."

I exhausted Mrs. Miller and I knew it. After a series of prying questions, she stood up and excused herself from the room, closing the door behind her. She left me with the answers to my past on her desk. My heart thumped as I fumbled through the pages, memorizing what I could, stealing my heritage. I wanted to just take the whole file and run. As I sifted through the papers, the room got smaller. Shirley might have signed the papers in that very room. "Bill." I whispered. "Bill Pappas. Owned restaurants" I kept repeating their names and information. "Shirley Kesteloot, Bill Pappas"

"Is there anything else, Miss Julie?" I flung around to see Mrs. Miller. I need more time.

"No, but thank you very much." I wanted to cry. "I won't hurt anyone." I headed for the door. "I mean, I won't ruin any lives or anything."

I ran out of the building and down the street to the Muskegon Mall and found a pay phone. I called information for Shirley Kesteloot. "One moment" was all I heard and then the number.

I dialed and a man answered.

"Um, hi. May I speak with Shirley please?" I didn't even know what

I was going to say.

"Who's calling?" The man questioned gruffly.

"Uh, my name is Julie." I exhaled. "I'm looking for …"

"Don't know of any Shirley!" The line went dead.

Since the whereabouts of my biological mother came to a dead end, I decided to focus on finding my father. My concern was his last name, Pappas. I learned that having the last name Pappas is like having the name Smith. It's a very common Greek-American name and is usually shortened from a much longer name like, Papadopoulos or Pappatonis. This wasn't going to be easy.

Chapter Twenty-six

Aunt Dolores warmed some frozen blueberry muffins she made the previous summer and poured herself a cup of coffee and me, a glass of orange juice. We chatted about Philadelphia and she asked about Marge.

It was weird to talk with the Tripps about Marge. I knew they didn't really care for her, but when my dad was alive, they all went square dancing together and played cards and stuff. I never wanted to divulge too much. Luckily, I had no information since I really hadn't seen or heard from Marge in over a year. Aunt Dolores switched the topic to methods of facial hair removal and pondered aloud whether bleach or waxing was better.

"I'm sure electrolysis will make its way to Michigan." I finished my juice and hoped I didn't seem pretentious. "Speaking of facial hair and female mustaches, I think I should go try to find my Greek side of the family." I took my dishes to the sink and thanked her for the great breakfast.

"Well, where will you start?" She laughed a little as she walked me to the door.

"Any restaurant," I smiled.

I drove the twenty minutes from Grand Haven and took the first Muskegon exit where I knew there was a small pizza place. It was only ten in the morning, but the parking lot seemed busy, so I ventured in. There was a counter directly across from the entrance and a large dining room to the right. There were probably twelve to fifteen men sitting around a large table, talking and drinking coffee. As I approached the counter, some spied me from across the room and stared. It became obvious that the place wasn't quite open for business. I smiled at them and then spoke to a young guy behind the register. "Hi, um, I'm not sure if you can help me, but I'm looking for a gentleman by the name of Bill Pappas." The chatter in the dining room ceased as I impulsively said the words, "He's my father." The men got up from the table like they were a hundred roaches and I just turned the lights on. My heart sank and I thought for certain that he was one of them.

"I don't know a Bill Pappas, but I do know a Gus, a George, and a Nick Pappas." He grinned.

"Well, that's a start," I said. "Do they own restaurants or maybe one of them used to go by the name of Bill? I mean, are any of them old enough to be my father?"

The guy stayed relaxed despite my frenzy of questions. "Do you want to sit and talk?"

"I would." I peeked around the corner at the table where the men had been sitting. All of them were gone, even their coffee cups were gone. "Why did those men all leave so suddenly?"

"Well, maybe you frightened them off." He smiled wryly. "Maybe they don't want to be a father."

"They were all Greek, weren't they?"

"Yes, and I'm Greek, too. My name is Yanni or John."

"Hi, Yanni. I'm Julie." I rubbed my hands on my thighs in case he might want to go through the whole shaking gesture.

We talked for a while and I explained my situation. "I just want to meet him, and maybe he can tell me where my biological mother is too. Maybe they're still together."

Yanni looked at me sadly and said, "Maybe, but you must not count on it." He stood and told me he would be right back, he had to make a phone call. He was gone for maybe ten minutes, but it seemed like an hour. Workers shuffled in to get the restaurant started for the day. I watched as they turned on ovens and placed aprons over their heads and I felt anxious. I wondered if Yanni was being honest with me.

He returned to the table with a broad grin. "Okay," he said. "I want you to go see this priest, Father Lambrakis, he may be able to help you and he knows what you've told me."

"Okay, great," I said.

Yanni wrote down the address and gave me directions to the priest's home. We then exchanged numbers and I explained that I was from out of town and would only be in the area for a few days. I gave him my home phone number.

"I'll ask around. If I hear anything, I let you know." He handed me the sheet of paper.

"Thanks for all of your time, Yanni."

I got back in my car and suddenly felt like I was being watched, like all the men that were at that table were part of the Greek mob, and now Yanni was sending me to see the Godfather.

Despite having some fear about going to see Father Lambrakis, I drove straight to his house. It was only a ten-minute drive from Yianni's pizza place. I parked in front of his house and he met me at the door before I had a chance to knock.

"Hello," he said, with a hearty, thick accent. He was probably seventy years old and was handsome with wavy gray hair and deep set eyes.

"Hi." I sounded shy compared to his energetic greeting.

"Come in, Youlea," he said. "That is your name in Greek, You-lee-a."

"I love it." I stepped inside and wondered what my name was on my original birth certificate.

The godfather lightly touched my arm and led me to a chair in his living room. It was dimly lit in his home and not what I expected. I thought there would be large furniture with puffy pillows and clear plastic mats on the floor, like I remembered from Susan's Greek palace.

I thought he would be living like a king. Instead, he had a comfortable setting with patterned furniture. There was also artwork, like pictures of saints with tall bishop's hats and the Madonna with child. The pictures were beautiful with intricately designed frames. There were statues, huge lamps and vases. All were gold and gaudy.

"I think I might know about your father, uh?" he said as he sat next to me. "What about your mother?"

"I just know that her name is Shirley Kesteloot," I answered anxiously.

"Oh." He frowned and shook his head slowly.

"What is it?" I wondered if he knew something about her or maybe he was disappointed that she wasn't Greek. "What do you know about my father?"

He stared at me for a long time and answered with a question. "Did you go to Greek school?"

"No." I started feeling inferior. "I wasn't raised by Greeks."

The godfather slowly stood and I stayed put. Now what, I thought. Was he going to ask me to leave?

"I get some paper," he said.

"Okay." I exhaled in relief and put my hands through my hair as I watched him.

He walked to a small desk that was rather bare compared to the rest of surfaces that were covered in chachka. He took out a small notepad and pencil and returned to sit next to me. He handed me the items and said, "Write down your mother's name and write down your address."

I did so and as I wrote, he said, "You know, your father's name is not Bill." I stopped writing. "His name is Vaslilios," he said.

"How do you know?" My heart was beating fast

"Because Vasilios means Bill in English," he smiled.

I felt a little let down, like I was being teased. I handed him the notepad and pencil. He took them and stood again. This time, I stood, too. "I go get you something," he said as he walked back to his desk. He placed the notepad back in the drawer without tearing the sheet off. He then disappeared into the hallway and returned a few moments later with what appeared to be a wooden box. "This? For you, Youlea." He handed me the gift and placed his palm on my head. "You must always hang this over you bed, uh?"

"Thank you, sir." I looked down to see what I was holding and was both amazed and amused. It was Mother Mary and Jesus punched out in silver tin. There were three layers of tin that were beautifully patterned. All were held inside a box frame with a leather backing.

Father Limberakis seemed so pleased to have given me the gift and I felt honored to get it. I knew that when I got home, I would indeed hang it over my bed without ever knowing the meaning of doing so.

He walked me to the door and assured me that my father would be found. I hugged him goodbye and then went to sit in my car for a few minutes and stare at Mother Mary. My heart was still beating hard. I was getting closer, but once found, would my parents accept me?

~ * ~

It was close to one o'clock in the afternoon and although all I could think of was pizza, I drove to the nearest sandwich shop. I asked for a phone book along with my grilled cheese and sat at an empty plastic booth. This was probably the twentieth time I looked in a phone book since I first found out my parents' names. I even called most of the numbers and even wrote letters, but no one seemed to know anything when it came to Bill and Shirley.

I went directly to the listings for Pappas. The same names I called before, but no Bill and no Vasilios. For the heck of it, I went to the listings for Kesteloot and knew exactly what to expect, an Edward Kesteloot and an R. Kesteloot, the jerk that once hung up on me and that would be it. I was wrong. This time, there was an S.M. Kesteloot. "Holy shit," I whispered.

I quietly ripped out the page and took the phonebook to the woman behind the counter. "Do you know where Grove Street is?"

"Sure do, whatcha looking for?"

"2714 Grove," I answered.

The woman seemed disappointed. "Well, I can tell ya how to get to Grove, but I'm not sure about the address."

"That's okay." I stood up on my toes, stretched my calves, and wiggled nervously while she wrote down directions.

It took me about a half hour of driving back and forth, but I finally found the house of S.M. Kesteloot, 2714 Grove. I parked down the street and walked to the house. It made me feel sneaky. I took a deep breath and walked right up to the side door of the house, where there were potted plants and a few cement steps. It seemed common to have a side door in southwestern Michigan and use that as the main door. To me, it made a home more personal.

I knocked and heard footsteps almost instantly. A woman, who was maybe twenty years older than myself, came to the door and opened it wide, like she was going to invite the whole world in. "Hello?" She looked at me, waiting for my sales pitch.

"Hi, this is going to sound strange," I said, "but I am looking for Shirley Kesteloot." I stopped when it came to the part about her having given birth to me.

"Oh, I'm Shirley's daughter," she replied. "Let me go get her. Do you want to come in?"

"Sure." I smiled. "Thank you."

She let me in and hurried up some more stairs into their kitchen. I stood on the landing between the kitchen and the basement. I stared down at the linoleum flooring and thought I might puke all over it. My mother is in this house, oh my God, oh my God, I thought. That is my sister, holy God, oh my God. It's happening, please don't turn me away.

Within a very short time, I heard, "Hello?" I looked up to find a very old woman looking at me standing on her landing. She would have been far too old to take care of me when she gave birth. I instantly thanked God that I wasn't born with Down Syndrome.

"Are you Shirley?" I straightened my shirt.

"Yes, dear," she answered.

"Well, did you give birth to a girl in 1966?" I felt my arms cross as I asked. I knew this old lady was just as capable of lying as anyone else and my sister, her daughter, whoever she was, hadn't come back yet.

"No, honey, I would have been far too old for that!" she laughed. "Perhaps you're looking for the other Shirley Kesteloot."

"Well, who is the other Shirley Kesteloot?" I questioned. "Is she around here?"

"Now, I don't know," She put her forefinger on her chin. "I haven't had a problem with the bank in a long time." She chuckled.

"I'm sorry, ma'am?"

"Well," she started, "I used to have problems with my checking account because the bank would get me confused with the other Shirley Marie Kesteloot. Can you believe it?" She looked down at me on the landing. "Come up here for a minute." She waved her hand. "Same middle name and everything. Of course, Kesteloot is my married name." She was now leaning against her kitchen cabinets. "I'm quite sure her uncle lives down on North Shore Drive near the paper factory. His name is Richard and his wife is Emma."

"Oh." I shook my head. "I called Richard one time and he claimed that he didn't know of a Shirley."

"Oh yes, he does," she corrected me. "He knows me and he knows his niece."

I believed her. I was disappointed and yet relieved to know she was not my mother; she might not live long enough for me to get to know her. I also felt really dumb that I assumed so much and just walked right up to her house. I promised Mrs. Miller at the adoption agency I wouldn't disrupt anyone's life and I would take the process easy, yet I was running all over Muskegon, knocking on doors. I gave Shirley my information and explained I lived in Pennsylvania, but if she heard anything, maybe she would call me.

After leaving, I drove directly toward the paper factory and Richard Kesteloot's house. One more time, I thought. I'll just knock at one more house and make sure this Richard doesn't know Shirley. There were only a few houses on North Shore Drive. It ran parallel to a river, so Richard's couldn't be hard to find. I was on that road before. It was an odd way to get to the Muskegon beach. You ran smack into industry before you got to the beautiful lakeside. Sappi Fine Paper Company sat right on the edge of Lake Michigan and was the cause of a putrid odor since the early 1900's.

R & E Kesteloot was painted on the mailbox at the road. At first, I couldn't see the house, but then I looked up a hill and saw faint hints of what was once a sidewalk, blocked by weeds and overgrowth. With another glance, I could make out a very small house, a shack, really. I thought the place was abandoned until I saw the back of a vehicle that was parked at the top of a dirt driveway. Scary as it was, I came so far, so I headed up that hill.

It was a shack. The closer I got to it, the more garage-like it became. The place had an enclosed front porch of sorts. This area had boxes, coats, boots, and various yard tools in it. I knocked on the outside door. I wasn't sure if the porch was part of the living area or what was going on. I knocked several times until a slight older woman, about five feet tall, answered the door in a little pink house dress.

Before she could get the door open all the way, I asked, "Are you Emma?"

"Uh. huh." She nodded and then she immediately looked behind her.

"Who is there?" It was the voice I heard on the telephone, hard to forget.

"My name is Julie!" I yelled past Emma.

Richard came forward and his wife scurried back into the musty darkness of their little home. Richard's belly was all I could focus on at first. I felt like I was in a movie or on television. I envisioned Hee Haw meets an After School Special where a kid is taken away in a white van by some old crusty stranger. He was a little frightening and his dirty overalls didn't help.

"My name is Julie," I repeated.

"I know who you are," he said as he sought a breath.

"You do?"

"Yep," he answered. "You're the one who called looking for Shirley awhile back." He motioned for me to follow him into his creepy little abode. "Too bad about what happened," he softened his tone.

"What do you mean?" I looked around inside. There was more junk everywhere.

"Well, I take it you're the girl she adopted out." He started looking around.

"I am, yes." My palms opened at my sides. "Too bad, what?"

"Well, I didn't want to tell ya on the phone," he paused, "your mom is dead." He stopped and looked in my eyes. "Car accident, her and her three boys. I think it was one of them VW Beetles." He looked down and shook his head. "I'm sorry."

I stood there with my mouth open. I couldn't believe that he was telling me this and he was just so matter of fact. What in the hell is happening? I couldn't speak.

"Bout nine or ten years ago," he continued, rubbing the edge of his nose. "Terrible accident."

Shut up, I thought. Just shut up. I stood there, with him looking at me sheepishly and frequently averting his eyes. "Who are you to Shirley?" I asked calmly.

"I'm her uncle," he said. I was grateful he didn't say anything about the fact he was related to me.

"So, she had three sons?" I asked.

"Yep, three boys after you were born." He took a deep breath and looked out the window like he was avoiding me or just tired of talking about any of it. "I don't know what else to tell ya, young lady. I'm sorry."

I was in complete shock. "Do you have any pictures of them?"

He immediately looked around like he might. I figured if he did, he would have turned them over to hide them from me. "Got an address?"

"Yes," I said as I looked for a sign of paper in the heaps of junk. Richard found something to write on and I took a pen off of a table and wrote down my address. I was writing down my address an awful lot this trip.

I looked for little Emma. She was in the corner, smiling and waving. I sighed and waved back with tears building quickly.

These were my relatives and, for a minute, I was grateful for having been raised by Marge.

I got back to Aunt Dolores and Uncle Lou's house and my head hurt. Aunt Dolores asked me about my search and I could barely talk. I sank into one of her living room chairs. "If I told you all that happened in this day, you wouldn't even believe it."

I drove back to Pennsylvania, feeling defeated and confused. I thought about Richard's attitude on the phone and how he hung up on me. I reviewed everything that was said during my visit and his strange demeanor. My gut told me he was lying. My mother and brothers weren't dead and it was doubtful they were even in an accident.

~ * ~

I went back to work and school and constantly considered what to do next. I already paid vital statistics for birth records, only to receive a copy of my adoption certificate, again. I would have to pay to get Shirley's death certificate, too, if there actually was one.

Three months into my being back in my routine, a woman called to tell me she knew of my search. "Hi, Julie, I really can't tell you my name, but your mom is in Phoenix and her last name is now Dibble."

"Are you sure?" I found myself shaking. "Is this Emma, Richard's wife? Hello?" The response was a dial tone. I'm not sure why, but I believed her. It would kind of explain why I couldn't find her in Michigan. My mind reeled.

Phoenix was closer to San Diego than it was to Philly. I had to take Gloria Barreres up on her offer to live in San Diego. My mother wasn't dead and suddenly it felt like my life might change.

I took what money I had, packed some belongings. I left the label company, my roommate and my car. I couldn't think and just selfishly left. I felt desperate and boarded a plane to San Diego.

The Barreres welcomed me, just as they always did. They hugged me, made plans with me and gave me my own room. They loved me, unconditionally. I was now safe and secure. But, I felt completely disconnected and unsure about everything. I knew I had it made with the Barreres, but I just couldn't calm my brain enough to take it in. Seemed I just kept running in life, trying to find answers and something that felt better than before.

I spent the first few days applying for jobs and hanging at their house with no purpose. I realized how absolutely stupid it was to have left my car. I was only three hundred and fifty miles from meeting Shirley. I talked myself out of it and talked myself into writing myself a check for fifty dollars from the Barreres' checkbook and walked over to their bank to cash it. While I stood in front of the bank teller I felt incredibly nervous. I was either going to jail or boarding a bus. She handed me the fifty bucks and I was outta there. I don't know what came over me, but all that mattered was meeting Shirley. It was selfish and a poor decision, but I didn't care. I got back to the house, packed a change of clothes, got on a Greyhound and went to Phoenix. The whole ride felt freeing and shitty, all at the same time. I was running. I was running from god knows what exactly, into the unknown. It was like life with

Marge, repeated. Criminal.

When I got off the bus, I wandered. I looked for a phone booth with white pages. Finally, I saw some activity in the back of a church and I entered to find a food bank. A few women were working in the kitchen and I approached them with my story. They fed me and gathered around as I looked through the phone book. There she was. Shirley Dibble on Vineyard Road. The church ladies discussed where they thought Vineyard was and I felt my heart race. "Use the phone," one of them said.

I dialed and there was no answer. I looked up at the clock and it was four forty-five in the afternoon. "She's probably at work." I exhaled.

Two of the ladies offered to stay until I could reach her. They chatted and I sat, anxiety ridden. I just pulled a bunch of stunts because finding Shirley was the most important thing in the world. I hadn't considered anyone and now I was using these women and their hospitality.

I dialed again at five thirty. No expectations, no expectations, I repeated in my head.

"Hi, is this Shirley Dibble? Please don't hang up. My name is Julie and I have wondered about you for the last twenty years and I wonder if maybe..." I heard a giant sigh. "Maybe you don't want to even meet, but I'm in Phoenix and every time my birthday comes around, I wonder if you think of me." I didn't know if I was making sense, I didn't know what to say. I clenched my eyes and pressed fingers into my eyebrow. There was silence on the line for what seemed like forever.

"Meet me at the Waffle House at fifty-fourth and VanBuren, tomorrow at five," she finally said.

~ * ~

I stayed at the home of one of the church women, Nita Dennison. She and her husband were older, they had grandchildren already. They

418

were very kind people. After I called the Barreres to tell them that I was safe and I stole from them, I felt a ton better. Gloria of course was loving when I told her. "Sweetheart, do you know how many dumb things I've done in my life? I'm just so glad you're safe and finally meeting Shirley. Just be very careful, Jul."

The Dennisons and I sat in their living room. They watched a show while I thought about what tomorrow would look like and what the hell was I going to do with the morning? I couldn't sleep. I just kept thinking about how I'd grasp onto that missing piece and never let go. Everything would fit into place, I just knew it. I'd know myself, my true self. Things would make sense. She was going to be so nice and loving. I was going to take it in and relish the cellular memory. I was going to be strong and if she asked about my life, I was going to tell her I learned a lot and leave it at that. I wouldn't hurt her with what I'd experienced. I wouldn't tell her about the mistakes I'd made, the shame I felt.

She'd be everything Marge wasn't, but no expectations.

The Dennisons drove me to the Waffle House the next afternoon, after Nita and I finished working at the church.

Chapter Twenty-seven

The restaurant was empty when I arrived. I hoped she would be there waiting, but I was half an hour early, so I was the one who had to wait. Wait and watch people pull into the parking lot, wondering if one of them was my mother. Waitresses in bright yellow and brown sat huddled together, making small talk and filling condiments. The place smelled of maple syrup and old coffee.

After a few people came in, I felt more at ease. I'd found myself worrying the servers would hear our conversation. I wanted it to be private, personal. Still, a part of me felt like screaming out, "Hey, everybody, I'm meeting my biological mother for the first time!" I'd been searching for her for so long.

I sat and thought about all the phone calls, the letter writing, and traveling to find her. What it might be like, would she embrace me, would we have things in common, would we look similar, all of it went through my mind. I had been in Phoenix less than twenty-four hours and it was finally going to happen.

Around five-thirty, an older model white Volare pulled into the Waffle House parking lot. The driver, a woman, parked the car and sat there. I watched from the window and nervously picked at my cuticles. She sat there for quite some time, sat and smoked. She adjusted her rearview mirror and put her fingers through short hair. I watched every move because I knew it was her. My heart pounded hard. When she finally opened the car door, she got out and flicked her cigarette to the side. As she walked toward the restaurant, she pulled at the hem of her black stretchy dress that nicely hugged her tall, thin frame. Once inside, Shirley stood at the door, motionless. I scooted toward the edge of the booth and she finally walked toward me. I didn't stand up to hug her, like I imagined I would. Her sunglasses were still on and I sensed no enthusiasm in her stride. She approached the booth and slid in across from me.

"Hi." I smiled and took a deep breath.

"Hi." She focused on placing her handbag just right. Her hands were shaking. "Do you want something to eat?" Her wall seemed a mile thick.

"No thanks," I placed my water glass in front of me. "I'm okay." I started to think I made a huge mistake in tracking her down. I waited so long for this moment and she didn't appear to want any part of it.

The server came to the table with a small pad of paper ready. She took a pen from her uniform pocket. "What can I get you girls today?" The tip of her pen waited against the paper.

Shirley looked up at the waitress and finally removed her sunglasses. "I'll just have coffee right now." The waitress managed a low huff of disappointment, shoved her pen back in her pocket and turned away. Shirley looked at me. "Did anyone tell you that you were born in the back of a police car?"

I bit down on my bottom lip and grinned. "No, I didn't know that." I studied her brown eyes as they began to tear. "I was told I was born breech," I said. "But nothing about a police car."

Shirley picked up her napkin, blotted her eyes, and wiped her cheeks. "I understand. I mean, whatever happened, I understand and I don't blame you." I wanted to cry too, but I couldn't. If I did cry, I might have to identify what the tears were about and I wasn't so sure.

"I thought you would hate me." Shirley reached into her purse for her cigarettes. "It was a very difficult decision." She lit her smoke and inhaled deeply. Her tongue trembled between her teeth and then smoke billowed from her mouth. "My parents, well, your grandparents, were Catholic and very much against the idea of keeping you."

"Are your parents still alive?" I jumped in.

"Oh, yes." Shirley smiled. "They live in New Mexico. They're just not Catholic anymore." We both smiled.

Shirley finally looked at me. I mean, really looked at me and I inspected her. We looked nothing alike. I searched for a familiar feature, but nothing. It was a bit disappointing for me. I wondered if it was for her too. "You look like some people in my family," she said.

"I do?" I straightened my torso.

"Your skin is darker like two of my sons." She hesitated like she was waiting for my reaction. "My third son is lighter, like me."

"What are their names?" I sipped from my water. I already knew about her sons, but I still felt a twinge of hurt because she kept them.

"Michael." Shirley cleared her throat. "He was born about eleven months after you." She put out her cigarette and exhaled. "Brian. He's the middle son, and Joe is the youngest."

First, I thought about what she said. Michael was born only eleven months after me. Ouch. "I'm confused." I leaned back. "Is my father Michael's father?"

"Oh, gosh, no!" She laughed and I wiggled uncomfortably. "With your father, it was just once."

"Oh." I nodded like I completely understood and tried desperately not to show emotion.

"What happened?"

Shirley took a deep breath and placed her almost empty coffee cup at the edge of the table. "I was working in Grand Rapids where Bill owned a restaurant."

The waitress stopped to fill Shirley's cup. "Thank you." Shirley watched the coffee flow into the mug.

"I was a waitress and worked for him." She paused to pour sugar. "On my birthday, Bill, your father, bought me a nice dress and took me out for dinner." She stirred her coffee slowly and stared into it. "He was a charmer." She reached for another cigarette. "You have his eyes."

"So, you went out for dinner?" I waited for the rest of the story as she took a drag.

"Dinner and a night's stay in a motel room." Shirley grabbed on to her wrist and held it like she was taking her pulse. "It was only once."

"He only took you out once?" I was confused. This story was not part of my fantasy.

"He took me out once, and we slept together once." She stared out the window toward the mountains that looked craggy and uninviting. She appeared as distant as the view of Bluffs.

I decided to change my line of questioning. "So, why was I born in a police car?"

Shirley laughed. "Well, my parents decided to let me come home when it got closer to my having you. I woke them up really early one morning when I went into labor with you. I told them that I was having contractions and they told me to go back to bed."

"They did?" I squinted and shook my head a little.

"Yes, they did." She stared at her cup. "I woke up my sister, Laurie, and she called a cab. It was snowing like crazy that morning." She snickered. "The taxi dispatcher must have called the police when Laurie told them that I was about to deliver. You were born right in the driveway."

"What did Bill do?" I asked. "I mean, did he know about me?"

Shirley exhaled a small snort. "Oh, he knew. He fired me."

"Whoa. He fired you, why?" She could not have been talking about my father.

"When I told him that I was pregnant, he fired me." She smiled weakly.

"That's awful." I crossed my arms. "I'm so sorry."

"Yeah, it was a bit rough. My parents kicked me out, I got fired, and when I tried to abort you, that didn't work." She sipped from her coffee with nonchalant ease.

At first, I didn't know how to respond and I may have stopped breathing. "You aren't joking, are you?"

"Nope. I guess you were determined to be here."

"Is that what this hanger mark on my side is from?" I pretended to examine my torso. "I always wondered what that was."

She laughed and I felt slightly better. Perhaps she wasn't taught any manners and just didn't know any better, otherwise why would she have told me that she tried to abort? I'd have to tuck it all away, try to forget she said it.

We talked for four hours. We compared feet and hands, the only things we seemed to have in common. Our second toe wasn't longer than the big toe, like most people have. Instead, we had downward slants.

She ended up driving me back to the Dennisons and we ended our conversation with the idea that she would go home and tell her sons about me. I'd spend time with her and the boys the following day. She hugged me goodbye.

As I tried to fall asleep, I thought about Emily and when I finally felt close enough, safe enough to draw those two trees. Maybe with Shirley and her sons, my little brothers, I could finally pencil a forest.

About the Author

Julie Beekman is an avid runner, hiker and skier and lives in Boulder, Colorado with her dog, Francesca.